Direct Legislation

Direct Legislation

Voting on Ballot Propositions in the United States

David B. Magleby

The Johns Hopkins University Press
Baltimore and London

© 1984 by THE JOHNS HOPKINS UNIVERSITY PRESS
All rights reserved
Printed in the United States of America

The Johns Hopkins University Press, Baltimore, Maryland 21218
The Johns Hopkins Press Ltd., London

LIBRARY OF CONGRESS CATALOGING IN PUBLICATION DATA

Magleby, David B.
  Direct legislation.
  Bibliography: p. 239
  Includes index.
  1. Referendum — United States. I. Title.
KF4881.M33   1984   328'.2   83–22265
ISBN 0–8018–2844–9

To Linda Waters Magleby

Contents

Preface

In most American states laws are made not only by the state legislature but also by the voters as they decide ballot propositions. With increasing frequency, voters in several states are directly deciding important questions of public policy, such as how much a government should tax its citizens, whether nuclear power should be developed, how to structure labor-management relations, and whether through school busing racial balance in the public schools should be achieved. The controversy surrounding these and other propositions appearing on recent statewide ballots has drawn increasing interest from scholars, journalists, and citizens. Because of the wide effects of many propositions, direct legislation has been the subject of considerable discussion as well. This book is about that process.

The issue of whether voters should initiate and vote on specific policy proposals has a long history. In the recent past direct legislation has enjoyed considerable popularity, as well as a resurgence in use. Several jurisdictions have considered adopting the process. Even a constitutional amendment to create a national initiative has been seriously considered. In jurisdictions that already have the process the 1980s may well be a record-breaking decade for initiative and popular referendum activity. Despite the widespread popularity of "letting the people rule," widespread popular involvement in the legislative process is not uniformly accepted.

The debate over the initiative and referendum — or, more broadly, direct legislation — is a debate between advocates of direct democracy and advocates of representative democracy. Advocates of direct democracy value widespread voter participation both in choosing candidates (primary elections) and in drafting and deciding legislation (the initiative and referendum). They seek to enlarge the role of the electorate while at the same time minimizing the power of intermediary organizations such as legislatures, elected executives, and political parties. Advocates of representative democracy, on the other hand, stress the need for knowledge and deliberation in drafting legislation, in selecting candidates, and in the daily business of governing. While advocates of representative democracy often are accused of being "undemocratic" and lacking faith in the people, they assert that the most important democratic act is the selection of representatives.

In recent elections the populace has voted on several controversial issues that have generated increased interest in the process of direct legislation. Most of the attention given to direct legislation, however, has focused on single issues or particular campaigns rather than on the mechanics of the process. Because legal provisions affect how many and what types of issues qualify for the ballot, the extent of confusion resulting from ballot titles and proposition wording, and whether voters receive materials from the state explaining what the ballot measures are all about, a study of direct legislation requires an understanding of the legal provisions, how they vary, and what effect they have on the functioning of the process.

It is important to understand the history of direct legislation, as well as the motivations of those who established it as a policy-making process. The initiative and popular referendum are part of a much larger reform effort whose ideology includes broad popular participation and hostility towards parties, legislatures, and elected officials.

The central focus of this book is citizen participation in direct legislation. Because the initiative and popular referendum require citizens to sign petitions to qualify a measure for the ballot, part of the focus is on forms of participation other than voting. Primarily, however, attention is directed to measuring the rates of voting on ballot measures and to explaining the voting choice of those who vote. Because so much of what we know about voting behavior is limited to voting in the partisan/candidate context, this book generates some new theories about voting in a context where candidate appeal and party cue are absent. From the literature on voting choice in referendum elections three specific explanations of proposition voting are examined to determine the extent to which they predict voting behavior: campaign spending, alienation and negativism, and elite and media endorsements. While these explanatory variables have been applied to specific election contests or, occasionally, to a series of votes in a single issue area, this book is the first effort to examine voting on ballot propositions across issue areas and over time.

The potential extension of direct legislation into new states and perhaps even the establishment of a national initiative make examination of voting behavior of interest both to policymakers and to citizens generally. The scope of issues confronting voters includes vital matters of public policy, yet few studies exist concerning who participates, how decisions are reached, and the effects of campaigns and expenditures on election outcomes.

One reason why so little has been written about direct legislation is that data on these questions are not easily gathered. In 1977–78 and again in 1981–82 I conducted a nationwide search to assemble as much survey and aggregate data on statewide propositions as possible. I consulted with editors of major daily newspapers in twenty of the states that have the initiative and referendum to find out whether they knew of any survey data on propositions in their states; I likewise inquired of political scientists who study elections, voting behavior, parties, and state government whether they knew of statewide survey data on referendums. Overall, more than 73 percent responded. Survey data at the national level came from the Inter-university Consortium for Political and Social Research at the University of Michigan in Ann Arbor; the Roper Center at the University of Connecticut in Storrs; the Gallup Poll; and Cambridge Survey Research in Cambridge, Massachusetts. Survey data at the state level were provided by the State Data Program at the University of California at Berkeley; the *Boston Globe* and Research Analysis, in Boston, Massachusetts; the *Boston Herald American* and Becker Research Corporation, also in Boston; the Rand Corporation, of Santa Monica, California; Florida State University; The Eagleton Institute of Politics at Rutgers University; the *Denver Post* and Research Services, in Denver, Colorado; and the *Los Angeles Times*. I am especially fortunate in having had access to the California Poll, which has been archived by the Field Institute at the University of California and constitutes the single most important data source on the question of direct legislation. In addition to survey data, I have also compiled and analyzed aggregate election data, campaign expenditures data, and data on elite and media endorsements of propositions. The original collectors of these survey and aggregate data are not responsible for the analysis or interpretations presented here.

Eugene C. Lee and the Institute of Governmental Studies, University of California at Berkeley, provided important early support for this research. The readability analysis of voter pamphlets was funded by a grant from the University Research Policy Council of the University of Virginia. Support for the acquisition of data and computer analysis for this version of the book was given by the Faculty Research Committee of the College of Family, Home and Social Sciences, Brigham Young University.

I am indebted to professors and colleagues who have read and commented on this book. Raymond E. Wolfinger, Austin Ranney, and Allan P. Sindler constituted the committee for whom the initial version of this book was written. Their careful reading and critical comments helped to refine my thinking and clarify my writing. Others who read and commented on the manuscript either in whole or in part were Elizabeth Wilkinson, Mark Westlye, Don Norton, and Joanne Allen. Computing assistance was provided by David Swan, Earl Marshall, Harlan Hatfield, and George Monsivais. The staff of the Faculty Support Center, Brigham Young University, typed and retyped the manuscript with skill and patience. Henry Tom and Jane Warth at Johns Hopkins University Press were helpful editors. Finally, I am most grateful to my wife and children, who provided continual encouragement and support.

Direct Legislation

The Initiative and Direct Democracy

Direct legislation is the process by which voters directly decide issues of public policy by voting on ballot propositions. Voters may act as legislators in states that have the initiative and popular referendum. In an initiative a specified number of voters petition to propose statutes or constitutional amendments to be adopted or rejected by the voters at the polls. In a popular referendum a specified number of voters can petition to refer a legislative action to the voters at the polls. While there are other forms of referendums, the popular referendum in generally considered in conjunction with the initiative. In virtually all states voters may vote on propositions placed on the ballot by the state legislature. These ballot propositions usually involve legislative actions requiring popular approval, bond issues, or changes in the state constitution. Some states provide for advisory referendums as well.

There are four reasons why an examination of direct legislation is necessary. First, direct legislation is an important manifestation of the direct democracy reform movement in the United States; as such it raises broad, theoretical questions about direct democracy as opposed to representative democracy.

Second, voting on ballot propositions raises important questions in the area of empirical theory and voting behavior. Social scientists have learned most of what they know about voting patterns and voter decision making from partisan/candidate elections, particularly presidential elections. In this book voting behavior is examined in a context where political parties and candidates typically have provided voters with no cues on how to vote. This study should shed new light on important aspects of voter rationality and voter understanding.

Third, the process itself has once again become an issue in American politics. During 1981 alone, twenty state legislatures considered legislation that would have either established some form of initiative or referendum or significantly expanded its scope. At the national level, in the 1970s, efforts to expand the initiative process led to congressional hearings on a proposed constitutional amendment establishing a national initiative. At the same time, however, in some states that already have the initiative and referendum the process has come under fire because of the large sums expended in campaigns, the dramatic increase in numbers of initiatives filed, and the expansion of an initiative industry.

Finally, the dramatic growth in interest in direct legislation is an indication of broader trends in American politics, notably the decline of the political parties and the ascendancy of single-issue politics. Moreover, the increased importance of direct legislation has had important consequences for elected state executives, state legislatures, and the courts.

Direct versus Representative Democracy

Granting voters the option to propose legislation and decide issues themselves through either the initiative or the popular referendum is one important manifestation of the theory of direct democracy. Other manifestations include direct primary elections to nominate candidates for public office, direct election of U.S. senators, and the proposal to eliminate the electoral college in favor of direct election of the President. Advocates of direct democracy value more widespread voter participation both in choosing public officials (candidates through primaries, senators and presidents through direct election) and in drafting and enacting legislation (the initiative and referendum). They seek to enlarge the role of the electorate and at the same time to minimize the power of intermediary organizations such as legislatures, executives, or political parties. In a system of direct democracy the voter is not limited to choosing his representative but may also petition to place statutes or amendments on the ballot and later vote on those laws and amendments.

In a system of representative democracy voters choose their elected representatives and delegate to them the principal responsibility for governing. Advocates of representative democracy stress the need for knowledge and deliberation in drafting legislation, in selecting candidates, and in the daily business of governing. In their view, voters have neither the desire nor the means to obtain the relevant knowledge or to participate effectively in these deliberations. While they may be accused of being "undemocratic" and lacking faith in the people, advocates of representative democracy argue that the most important democratic act is the selection of public officials, which is still performed by the voters.

Proponents of both direct democracy and representative democracy share an important common ground: they agree that most of the business of governing cannot be done directly by the people but must be delegated to elected representatives. The initiative and referendum process, even at best, is a complement to the legislative process.

Recurrent Issues in the Debate over Direct Legislation

The most intense period of debate over whether to adopt direct legislation was during the Progressive Era, the first two decades of this century. Although more than fifty years separate the end of the Progressive Era from the late 1970s, there is a striking similarity between the issues raised in 1900–1912 in California, Oregon, Washington, and other western states and those raised in 1978–82 in New York, Texas, Minnesota, and Virginia. Moreover, in the 1977 U.S. Senate hearings on the proposed national initiative and in the debate in Great Britain over whether to permit a national referendum on entry into the European Economic Community, essentially the same issues about the process of direct legislation recurred.

Proponents of the initiative and referendum frequently cite as examples of the successful operation of this process the Greek city-states, Swiss cantons, and New England town meetings. More recently they have drawn upon the experiences of several American states, most notably California. Opponents of direct legislation challenge the utility of the historical cases for large-scale polities, caution against generalizations on the basis of so few cases, and argue that the U.S. Constitution demonstrates a preference for representative democracy.[1]

The most important questions raised in debates over direct legislation are these: Will there be majority tyranny? What effect will direct legislation have on representative institutions, fundamental rights and liberties, and the capacity to govern? Will better laws be enacted because of the process? Will people participate intelligently in deciding propositions? Will issues be over-dramatized or oversimplified? Will direct legislation educate the public and lead to heightened political consciousness? Will direct legislation decrease public apathy and alienation? Will direct legislation cure such ills of representative democracy as the political party machines and powerful special interests?

Participants in the debates disagree on the answers to these questions. Rarely, however, are these disagreements resolved with evidence from actual experience with the process. Even though the United States has more than seventy years' experience with direct legislation, the proponents and opponents of direct legislation seldom do more than speculate about its effects. The academic literature on direct legislation focuses principally on single elections or referendums in one issue area and typically avoids any overall assessment of the process. The research reported in this book is an effort to resolve to the fullest extent possible these important questions.

The central issue in the debate over direct democracy versus representative democracy is how large a role voters should play in governing. The case for direct legislation rests on the claim that initiative and referendum elections provide a greater degree of democracy than do candidate elections, that referendums provide a workable policy-making process, that results of the process of direct legislation are superior to those of the legislative process, and that direct legislation at the least corrects legislative inaction or error. These arguments in turn rest on the assumptions that (1) citizens will participate in direct legislation; (2) referendums provide greater representation than, or at least as much representation as, candidate elections; (3) voters will understand the issues thoroughly enough to make knowledgeable decisions; (4) the ballot will effectively translate voting preferences on referendum issues; and (5) power of special interests and party machines will be minimized in referendum elections.

A major purpose of this book is to determine the extent to which direct legislation meets these claims and assumptions. What arguments in the debates over direct legislation has experience proven correct? Despite the importance of these questions, very little scholarly attention had been given to them. This is the first study to examine these questions and assumptions across several states and over time.

VOTER DECISION MAKING WITHOUT POLITICAL PARTIES AND CANDIDATES

This book also explores differences between voting on propositions and voting for candidates. The almost universal focus of voting studies to date has been on candidate elections. Discussions of direct legislation have almost always been issue-specific, and the single-issue elections studied usually are not typical of the general process of direct legislation. In contrast to our increased understanding of how voters function in partisan/candidate races, we know very little about the dynamics of voter decision making on ballot propositions. Voting on propositions is distinct from most other kinds of voting because it requires decision making without the simplifying devices of party label and candidate appeal. This book explores the extent to which party identification, candidate appeal, ideology, and social class help us understand voting on direct legislation. Because voting on propositions is in some important ways different from voting in candidate contests, a study of voting on propositions provides an unusual opportunity to learn how voters make decisions.

In addition, four hypotheses from the referendum-voting literature are tested. In brief, the hypotheses assert that people vote for the side that spends the most money; that alienated citizens turn out to vote on propositions; that alienated voters vote no on propositions; and that voters are aware of elite opinion on propositions and follow elite and media endorsements when voting on statewide ballot measures. (These hypotheses are described in greater detail in chapter 8.) This study attempts to advance our general knowledge of voter decision making by examining voting behavior on several ballot propositions.

Renewed Interest in the Initiative and Referendum

Until the late 1970s, the process of direct legislation was not seen as a political phenomenon of major significance.[2] Only a few western states had demonstrated a willingness to use the process extensively; and although many cities and counties routinely vote on ballot propositions, these elections have rarely generated much interest elsewhere.[3] Except in Switzerland, direct legislation at the national level is rare.[4] Consistent with James Madison's views on the subject, the U.S. Constitution does not provide for national referendums.[5]

In the 1970s, however, direct legislation began to expand. Two states adopted direct legislation in the 1970s: Illinois in 1970 and Florida in 1978. What is more, interest in direct legislation grew and moved eastward from its traditional western base into virtually every state and the the U.S. Congress. Not since the Progressive reform movement during the first two decades of this century had there been such intensive efforts to adopt direct legislation and expand its use.

What accounts for this increased interest in direct legislation? The nature of the issues is certainly a partial explanation. Reducing taxes, restricting cigarette smoking to certain areas, prohibiting the advocacy of homosexuality in public schools, and imposing a freeze on nuclear weapons are only a few examples of issues that apparently interest voters and the mass media in ways quite different from conventional candidate elections. These ballot propositions have important consequences for public policy. California's Proposition 13, for instance, started twenty-seven tax- or spending-limit movements in nineteen states.[6] But Proposition 13 was not unique: during the 1970s, voters in several states voted directly on regulation of nuclear power, fees for nonreturnable containers, and the death penalty.

Equally important to our understanding of the rising importance of direct legislation is the fact that the news media interpret some state-level propositions as having important national political significance. Proposition 13 made news not only in the United States but abroad as well. Reporting on the California campaign, the *Economist,* a British news weekly, titled its editorial on Proposition 13 "Taxes Overboard" and concluded that "California's vote, like most things Californian, was just bolder, better, more innovative — in short, a harbinger of things to come."[7] This same theme was echoed in cover stories in both *Time* and *Newsweek.* The *Newsweek* article, titled "The Big Tax Revolt," characterized the California tax revolt as "the new gut issue in

American politics."[8] Even though political commentators did not uniformly agree on the causes and consequences of Proposition 13, all of them agreed that it was a major political event.[9]

Such widespread media attention is generally reserved for presidential elections. Yet the vote on a single ballot proposition in a single state became the principal focus of the 1978 midterm election. *Time*'s review article on the 1978 general election began as follows: "Taxes, taxes, taxes! Ever since the resounding triumph of California's Proposition 13 last June, the nation has been shuddering with a kind of tax-cutting fever."[10]

Thus, not only did the California tax-cutting vote overshadow the candidate races and other propositions of the 1978 primary election season but its importance also grew as it received national attention. Political commentators frequently expanded their observations on the passage of the proposition to argue that its passage signified a new move to conservatism, a resurgent middle class, a tax-cutting tendency, and a message to government. Indeed, one of the most important consequences of Proposition 13 was the new conventional wisdom that the public had become more conservative and desired less government.[11] One commentator even argued that Proposition 13 was a catalyst for electoral realignment.[12]

The mandate-setting nature of ballot propositions is best exemplified by Proposition 13, but the outcomes of several other state and local initiatives have assumed national significance as well. California's rejection of the 1976 nuclear power initiative, in effect a vote *for* nuclear power, was widely interpreted as a plebiscite on the nuclear development issue and may have played a role in the outcome of nuclear referendums in six other states. The Dade County, Florida, "gay rights" referendum, the Missouri right-to-work initiative, and California's anti-smoking proposition are also examples of ballot propositions that came to have national political significance.

Because ballot propositions directly affect special interest groups, the campaigns are well financed and intensively contested. Spending on propositions frequently exceeds spending in contests for governor or U.S. senator. The personality of issue activists has also amplified interest in the process. Relatively obscure figures such as Anita Bryant, Howard Jarvis, and Paul Gann, when successful in campaigning for or against an issue, can surface on the cover of *Time* or *Newsweek* or as the nominee for the U.S. Senate from the nation's most populous state. Media attention itself must be credited with a substantial part of the growth in interest in direct legislation. Newspapers and electronic media alike love political conflict, especially when it involves subjects as controversial as homosexual rights, abortion, the equal rights amendment, and oil company profits. All of these issues were voted on in the 1970s and 1980s, and these campaigns and their outcomes were usually reported nationally.

An additional reason for the increased interest in direct legislation is that citizens and groups of varying political persuasions see the process as a means to achieve their political goals. Proponents of direct legislation do not occupy a single ideological position; both liberals and conservatives are found among those who advocate its wider use.[13]

An important manifestation of the increased interest in direct legislation is the attention given to the 1977 proposal for a constitutional amendment providing a national initiative process. Proposals for national referendums on specific issues, most typically foreign policy questions, have surfaced periodically in U.S. history. The best-known of these proposals was the Ludlow amendment, a constitutional amendment proposed in the 1930s that would have required a popular referendum before war could be declared.[14] The Ludlow amendment and others like it were defeated. In the case of the proposed national initiative, however, the scope of direct legislation would not be limited to declarations of war but rather would function in much the same way as within several states.[15] Perhaps because the scope of the national initiative is difficult to anticipate, persons from quite different persuasions have united in support of the concept.[16]

One recent convert to the national initiative idea is Congressman Jack Kemp (R–N.Y.), who argues in a book titled *An American Renaissance* that "the time is right . . . for the United States to take the lead in a fresh global wave of democratization that demonstrates the efficiency of government forms that rest on the wisdom of ordinary citizens. The most fundamental change we could make . . . is to provide for a national initiative, through an amendment to the Constitution." Kemp's advocacy of direct legislation as one means of democratization raises another theme consistently voiced by advocates of the process: that more democracy will reduce the high levels of alienation and distrust found in many citizens. Kemp argues, "I feel as strongly as I do about this reform because I believe it goes to the heart of our national malaise."[17] In short, the national initiative is seen by some reformers as a remedy for much of what ails democracy and is therefore likely to remain a political issue at all levels of government in the foreseeable future.

Understanding the Initiative's Popularity

Advocates of direct legislation frequently claim overwhelming public opinion in favor of the voters' deciding issues via the initiative and referendum. However, an in-depth look at the available evidence shows that these claims are rarely substantiated by surveys and polls. A New Jersey study is an example.

As was the case in so many states in the late 1970s, the state legislature in New Jersey considered adopting the initiative and referendum. Responding to the growing interest in direct legislation, the Eagleton Institute of Politics at Rutgers University in New Jersey conducted an insightful survey among residents of New Jersey on the initiative and referendum process. Over half of those surveyed (53 percent) had heard about the possibility of changing the state's constitution to allow for the initiative and referendum. After briefly defining the initiative process, the interviewer asked respondents what they thought about it. Perhaps because voters in New Jersey have had such limited experience with the initiative, 57 percent indicated that they did not know whether the initiative was a good idea. Of those having an opinion, 88 percent thought that on the whole, the initiative was a good idea.

The extent to which an individual has an opinion on the initiative process is related to the individual's level of education. Less educated respondents are far less likely to have an opinion about the initiative. Over 70 percent of those with less than a high school education either didn't know whether the initiative process was a good idea or had not given it much thought. In contrast, only 42 percent of the persons with more than a high school education gave the same response. More educated individuals not only may have learned about the process in school but are more knowledgeable about politics and government generally. For all categories of education, the proportion of persons who believed that the initiative and referendum process was a good idea was much larger than the proportion who believed that it was a bad idea. Among those who have completed schooling beyond high school, there is also a greater tendency to believe that the initiative may be a bad idea.

The Eagleton Poll data provide an insight into how people view the pros and cons of the initiative process. Respondents were asked a series of questions covering many of the issues that arise whenever the initiative and referendum are considered for adoption or expansion. Most people appeared to agree with the central contentions of both the proponents and the opponents of the initiative and referendum. On the one hand they overwhelmingly agreed that citizens should be able to make laws directly, and more than three-quarters of those surveyed agreed that citizens ought to be able to vote directly on issues; that when representatives are afraid of offending some groups, the public should be allowed to decide; and that if people voted on issues, they would be more likely to participate in government and politics. On the other hand they also agreed that the public is ill-suited to cast an informed ballot; that the special interests will gain power by spending money to promote their side of an issue; and that the job of making laws should be left to elected representatives.

But the New Jersey data also indicate public agreement with four of the claims frequently made by those opposing adoption or expansion of the process. Roughly two-thirds or more of the same respondents felt that the job of making laws should be left to elected representatives, that many people would not be able to cast an informed vote, that many issues were too complicated to be decided by a simple yes or no vote, and that special interests would gain power through the initiative process by spending more money. A cross-tabulation of these conflicting viewpoints makes it clear that generally more than half of those polled — 58 percent — agreed that citizens ought to vote on issues but that issues were too complicated to be decided by voters, that interest groups would gain power, and that people could not cast an informed vote.

Citizens have mixed feelings towards direct legislation. There is a generalized support for the idea of letting the people rule, but when more specific elements of the process are presented, most agree that, at best, the people can play a very limited legislative role. The New Jersey data allow us to examine the nature of public support for direct legislation among residents of a state with limited experience with ballot propositions. But what are the public perceptions about direct legislation in a state where voters are likely to be very familiar with the initiative process?

California, perhaps more than any other state, is known for placing many propositions on each ballot. Thus, the California electorate is an experienced population to ask whether more issues should be decided by the voters. In October 1982, Mervin Field asked Californians to compare law making by elected representatives in the state legislature with citizens' voting on laws directly through proposition measures on election day.[18] The results of the Field survey are consistent with the New Jersey data. Two-thirds of the California voters felt that elected representatives were better suited to decide upon highly technical or legal policy matters. Only 27 percent saw the voting public as better suited to this task. Most California voters also indicated that elected representatives gave a more thorough review to each particular aspect of a proposed law and enacted more coherent and well-thought-out government policies than the voting public.

A majority, 51 percent of these same California voters, however, indicated that the voting public was better suited to decide upon large-scale government programs or projects. Even larger proportions trusted the voting public to do what was right on important government issues. On the question of special-interest-group influence, California voters indicated that they perceived that influence to be greater on elected representatives (64 percent) than on the voting public (29 percent). As with the New Jersey data, education was correlated with preference for the indirect process of elected legislators.

In earlier surveys, which asked more general questions, Mervin Field found high proportions of Californians — 85 percent — indicating that proposition elections were a good idea.[19] More than three-quarters of voters in all categories of party, ideology, occupation, race, and education felt that having propositions on the ballot was good. Even 71 percent of those who never voted in statewide elections felt that direct legislation was a good thing for Californians. More Californians felt that ballot propositions made little difference, and 11 percent felt that they were a bad idea.

The same California sample was asked which type of election — candidate or proposition — was more effective in influencing government. More than three-to-one said that propositions elections were more effective. Similarly, far more Californians felt that they were more affected by the outcome of proposition elections. Voting for or against ballot propositions is consistently perceived as a more effective way to influence government than is voting in candidate elections. Here again, virtually all groups viewed propositions as the more effective mechanism by about a three-to-one ratio. Indeed, voters most likely to see propositions as more effective were those who reported that they never voted in statewide elections: over 80 percent of these citizens perceived propositions to be more effective.

Roughly three-quarters of all of those surveyed viewed the outcomes of proposition elections as more important than the outcomes of candidate elections. These data are consistent with a 1976 survey following the California vote on the future of nuclear energy development. Shortly after voting on the nuclear power initiative, Proposition 15, California voters were asked, "Do you think having a question like the Nuclear Power Plants Initiative on the ballot is a good idea or a bad idea?" [20] Only 6 percent of those who voted in the June 1976 primary election felt that ballot propositions were a bad idea. In sharp contrast, 70 percent felt that the process was a good idea, and 24 percent either didn't know or felt that the process was both good and bad. Support for the process of direct legislation on issues such as nuclear power was especially high among self-identified liberals, Democrats, independents, those under thirty-five years of age, women, and low-income voters. Even those who paid little or no attention to the news about the nuclear initiative overwhelmingly felt that having voters decide issues via ballot propositions was a good idea.

Californians are not unique in expressing this opinion: a very high percentage of the U.S. electorate consistently favors the idea of direct legislation. National data on the question of citizen attitudes towards more widespread use of direct legislation were gathered by the Center for Political Studies in its American National Election Studies for 1970, 1972, and 1974. In all three years, when respondents were asked whether more issues should be decided by voters at the polls, 77 percent or more answered yes. Two-thirds or more of the respondents in all categories of education, income, occupation, subjective social class, race, sex, party identification, and region favored having more issues decided by voters. The categories with somewhat lower levels of support for more direct legislation were consistently those of higher socioeconomic status. Respondents with a college education, those earning over twenty-five thousand dollars a year, and those who saw themselves as in the professional or upper middle class were somewhat less inclined to favor having more issues decided by the voters at the polls.

Clearly, most citizens view wider use of direct legislation positively. However, favoring the idea of more propositions and actually voting on them are two different things. Little relationship can be found between favoring additional propositions and voting on those already on the ballot.

Respondents who voted on all, most, some, or none of the issues already on their state and local ballots stated that they desired additonal issues on the ballot, and this was indicated to the same degree — about 75–80 percent — in all categories in all three elections. Such widespread support for the idea of having more issues decided by voters at the polls, even among those who reported not voting on any current ballot propositions, can be seen as evidence that the extension of direct legislation is a widely held value, and not necessarily as an indication that those who favor more widespread use will actually participate in the process. Clearly, some respondents were giving what they considered to be socially desirable answers to the question. After all, who can be against allowing the people to decide more issues of public policy? [21] Nevertheless, these data show that the widespread support for the placement of more issues on ballots is not necessarily an indication that voters will actually demonstrate their interest in additional propositions by voting on them. [22]

Another way to determine the degree of public support for more widespread use of direct legislation is to ask what issues, if any, citizens would like to be able to vote on. Presumably, if commitment to the idea of additional referendums is more than simple adherence to a general political value, respondents should at the very least be able to mention one or more issues that they would like decided at the polls.

While 77 percent of those surveyed in 1970 favored additional issues on the ballot, only 38 percent of that group could mention one issue that they would like decided by the voters. Even fewer voters — only 12 percent — were able to mention more than one issue that they would like to see placed before the voters. Apparently, most citizens support the general idea of direct legislation but do not have specific issues in mind that they would like to see placed on the ballot. Other studies have found that when voters are asked direct questions about issues concerning taxes, government waste, and health care, to name but a few, they frequently express discontent with the government's lack of responsiveness. [23] Yet in a situation in which they can suggest any of these concerns as issues to vote on directly, very few are inclined to mention them. The issues that voters named in 1970 as ones they would like on the ballot tended to be in the areas of revenue and taxation (10 percent), health, education, and welfare (8 percent), and government organization (7 percent). In contrast, 62 percent said that they did not know what issues should be decided by voters at the polls.

Much of the debate over the initiative and referendum assumes that the voters know the meaning of the terms. However, in two 1980 surveys commissioned by the *Denver Post* and conducted by Research Services, it was found that the vast majority of Colorado voters did not know what was meant by the phrase "the initiative and referendum process." In the August survey only 20 percent indicated that they knew what the initiative and referendum process was, and in the late October survey, 30 percent. It is important to note that unlike New Jersey, Colorado has had many initiatives on the ballot. Despite their extensive experience with the initiative, however, Colorado voters are apparently unsure of this term. As in New Jersey, level of education was highly correlated with self-expressed knowledge of the initiative process. Only 6 percent of Colorado respondents with less than a high school education indicated that they knew what the initiative process was. At the other end of the educational ladder, 56 percent of respondents with advanced degrees knew of the process. Others who appeared to be uninformed about the process were low-income, blue-collar, nonwhite, and female respondents. The findings from these surveys serve as an important reminder that voters are rarely as interested in politics as political activists assume and that when describing public opinion in the area of direct legislation, political scientists and pollsters must be especially careful about how the questions are phrased.

To summarize, voters favor direct legislation if the question is worded in general terms. More precise questioning reveals that most voters have mixed feelings about direct legislation. Even in California, large majorities of voters preferred elected representatives over ballot propositions in some respects. While the idea of placing additional issues on the ballot is prevalent, it does not reflect either widespread interest in the process or a willingness to vote on propositions. Respondents who report having little interest in politics or campaigns and respondents who presently vote on only some or none of the propositions are nevertheless supportive of having more issues decided by voters. In addition, most respondents think that having more issues on the ballot is a good idea but are not able to suggest specific issues; over 70 percent of those with less than a high school education have no issue to suggest. Those who have specific issues to suggest tend to be better educated. An analysis of those issues actually suggested shows a wide array of topics and generally little clustering in any single issue area. The most notable exceptions to this generalization are the somewhat greater tendency for those with a high school and/or a college education to suggest revenue and taxation issues, while the least educated disproportionately favor referendums on government organization. These findings raise important caveats for those who cite public support for direct legislation as one important justification for its establishment or expansion.

Public Support for the Proposed National Initiative

As discussed previously, national attention has recently focused on the politics of direct legislation in states having the initiative, and political pressure has been mounted to establish the process in other states. This heightened interest has also led to a campaign for direct legislation at the national level.

In January 1978 and again in April 1981, pollster George Gallup asked national samples of Americans whether they favored a national initiative process. Gallup concluded that "the voters of the nation like the idea of being able to pass judgment on proposed national legislation."[24] While age, party, and region did not appear to make much difference in whether respondents favored establishing a national initiative, it is clear that amount of education was strongly associated with having an opinion on this question. Of respondents with a grade school education or less, 42 percent did not have an opinion on the proposed amendment. In sharp contrast, only 11 percent of the respondents who had attended college reported having no opinion. Despite the clear differences in the likelihood of having an opinion on this proposal, most respondents in all categories of education favored the proposed national initiative. The data from the Gallup poll are strikingly similar to those gathered in November 1977 by Cambridge Survey Research for the U.S. Senate Judiciary Committee.

In the Gallup and Cambridge Survey Research surveys more than half of those questioned responded that they would favor a national initiative process. Support for a national initiative has consistently been twice as strong as opposition to it. Gallup sees the public's disillusionment in the post-Watergate era as the cause of the "broad support" for the proposed national initiative.[25] But if the events of Watergate fostered a greater sense of disillusionment, then support for direct legislation in 1974 presumably would have been greater than in the years prior to the Watergate scandal. The cross-sectional data from the University of Michigan lead to a very different conclusion: voters in 1970 and in 1972 were equally desirous of a greater use of direct legislation. Overall, 77 percent of the national sample in 1970 favored more propositions, 78 percent in 1972, and 79 percent in 1974. The evidence from the American National Elections Studies for 1970, 1972, and 1974 provides further support for the conclusion that most citizens have supported wider use of the direct legislation process at least since 1970, well before the Watergate scandal.[26]

It is important to observe that the first Gallup Poll on the proposed national initiative took place prior to the passage of California's Proposition 13, the Jarvis-Gann property-tax initiative. Levels of support for the idea of a national initiative might have been even higher if the poll had been conducted after the June 1978 election. By 1981, however, support for the idea of a national initiative had declined from its early 1978 levels; the overall percentage favoring the idea had dropped from 58 to 52. Support for the process among some groups dropped by as much as 12 percent. Groups less favorable towards the idea of a national initiative in 1981 were college graduates, semiskilled workers, whites, and Democrats. These national-level data nevertheless indicate that most people remain initially supportive of the direct legislation idea. The data analyzed here further corroborate the New Jersey and

California data analyzed earlier. While Gallup didn't ask whether issues were too complicated to be decided by ballot proposition or whether people believed that most voters could cast an informed vote on a ballot measure, it seems likely that more than half of those favoring a national initiative believed that the process has serious shortcomings.

In sum, citizens readily express support for the concept of direct legislation. Fewer respondents favor a national initiative than favor use of the initiative at state and local levels, however. In both cases, many more respondents favor the idea than oppose it. When voters are asked questions that call for more than levels of general support for direct legislation, we learn that most citizens are not prepared to suggest issues that they would like to see on the ballot. In fact, many do not even vote on those already on the ballot. When those who report having voted on only some or none of the propositions on the ballot are asked if they favor the idea of having more issues on the ballot, they are even more likely to say yes than are the respondents who voted on most or all of the referendums. Moreover, according to the New Jersey and California data, citizens feel that there are problems with the process itself and that most voters are ill-equipped to decide ballot questions. It is a mistake, therefore, to assume that the high rates of popularity afforded to direct legislation will necessarily lead to widespread participation on actual propositions or even that the public will necessarily vote to adopt the initiative process.[27]

The Initiative and Broader Trends in American Politics

The data just analyzed indicate that direct legislation had substantial popularity even before Watergate. But Gallup's more general point may well be on target: that the disillusionment with government, politics, and political parties is part of the reason why direct legislation was more widely used in the 1970s and why voters appear to support the idea of taking matters into their own hands. These broader themes are introduced here, but they will be discussed in subsequent chapters as well.

DRAMATIC GROWTH IN DISTRUST OF GOVERNMENT

The public presently views government with substantial distrust; this was not the case in the late 1950s and early 1960s. The best measure of this declining confidence in government is found in responses to five questions asked since 1958 by the Survey Research Center of the Center for Political Studies at the University of Michigan. In the late 1960s and early 1970s citizens were more likely to feel that government wasted a lot of tax money and could be trusted only some of the time. They were also more inclined to believe that government was run for the few big interests by crooked people who did not know what they were doing. Between 1964 and 1968, for instance, the number of people who believed that government was run for the benefit of a few big interests rose by 13 percent, and the number who believed that government could be trusted to do what was right only some of the time increased by 15 percent. The Watergate scandals appear to have accentuated these trends. It is more than coincidence that the percentage who believed that government was run by a few big interests rose by 20 percent between 1972 and 1974. Also, apparently in response to Watergate, significant numbers of citizens came to feel that quite a few of those running the government were crooked. An analysis of the responses to these questions in the 1976 and 1980 surveys reveals that the increasing citizen distrust of government has leveled off but remains high — it is typically twice as high as in the 1950s and early 1960s.[28]

Direct legislation is seen by some as a cure for the low level of confidence in government. This asserted remedy for the ills of government is not new to the 1970s, however. Progressive era reformers, as we shall see, also ran against government, in particular against the boss-controlled state legislatures. One additional factor linking direct legislation to the disillusionment many feel towards government is the fact that the most publicized recent propositions — the anti-tax propositions — have been distinctly anti-government in nature. Many of the campaigns have focused on waste and corruption in government, not only to justify cutting taxes but also to appeal to these popular sentiments. The vast majority of Americans believe that the government wastes a lot of tax money. Much of the recent interest in direct legislation may be related to a more deeply rooted distrust in government.

Single-Issues Politics, the Initiative, and the Decline of Political Parties

The recent interest in direct legislation is also related to the declining influence of political parties and the ascendancy of single-issue politics. Not only are parties increasingly unable to influence candidate choice and discipline party members but elected representatives are increasingly judged by their stand on single highly charged issues or issue dimensions, such as abortion, the Panama Canal Treaty, or the environment. Single-issue groups establish hit lists of the ten congressmen they would most like to see defeated. When such groups work within political parties, their primary goal is issue advocacy. Rather than compromise on their issue, they would prefer to leave the party, and victory in the general election is less important than being "right" on the issues. Other arenas to which issue advocates frequently turn are the state legislatures or the ballot via the initiative process. The single-issue groups of the 1970s are not exclusively conservative or liberal but come from both ends of the political continuum. Thus, on issues such as gun control or abortion, candidates and parties may be confronted with groups of people expressing very different positions, none of whom are willing to compromise.

Single-issue groups are not new to American politics, of course, but their importance has increased because of several changes that occurred in the 1970s. These changes include legislation permitting the establishment of Political Action Committees (PACs), which command substantial resources and perform many of the functions traditionally performed by political parties; the mass marketing of candidates by the electronic media, especially television, so that groups with sufficient funds can challenge representatives directly and circumvent the parties; and new campaign technology, especially the use of computers and directed mailings to reach targeted audiences motivated by the appeal of the issue group.[29] Political parties — which once performed the important functions of selecting the nominee, integrating issue constituencies, and arriving at compromises — are now severely limited in their impact. As a result, candidates can no longer depend upon their party to buffer them from the demands of such single-issue groups. Among the most notable of the single-issue groups in the last few elections have been taxpayers, consumers, environmentalists, gun-control and anti-gun-control advocates, proponents and opponents of the equal rights amendment, and pro- and anti-abortion groups.

Not only are single-issue groups a significant factor in many candidate contests, but in initiative and referendum campaigns their influence is more direct and the mandate often more precise. The recent anti-nuclear, anti-tax, and anti-homosexual votes are but a few examples of ballot propositions in states or localities which magnified the increased attention given to single-issue groups. Many of the same factors that have helped these groups gain influence in candidate contests — direct mail, election technology, money — are also part of the increased attention given to the initiative process. As I will discuss in subsequent chapters, an initiative industry has developed which circulates petitions to place questions on the ballot and then organizes the campaigns for the propositions that qualify for the ballot. This initiative industry is also involved in single-issue politics within the parties and in candidate elections.

The initiative and referendum process is important not only as a policy-making device, a means of voter decision making, and a public issue in its own right but also as part of broader trends in American politics. Distrust of parties and legislatures makes direct legislation an attractive alternative. The initiative process means that single-issue groups do not have to worry about unseating politicians; instead they can go directly to the people with their appeals. The politics of direct legislation is only one part of the fragmentation of American political life; but as this book demonstrates, it is becoming an increasingly important part.

A BRIEF OUTLINE OF THE BOOK

Using survey and aggregate data from California, Florida, Massachusetts, and Washington, as well as national surveys, this book examines direct legislation and the ways voters function in this electoral context. Rather than focusing on a single proposition or campaign, the book attempts to discover the regularities of electoral behavior in direct legislation. Who participates? Why? To what extent do voters understand the propositions they are deciding? How do voters learn about the propositions? What factors are important in their voting choice? Direct legislation challenges many of the assumptions of representative democracy by arguing that voters should play a much more direct role in the policy-making process. Discovering the regularities of political behavior in this form of direct democracy will allow us to assess voter rationality and competence and improve our understanding about the way this form of government actually works.

Even though interest in direct legislation has grown recently, it is important to understand its history and the motivations of those who established it as a policy-making process. The initiative and referendum are part of a much larger reform effort whose ideology includes broader popular participation and hostility towards intermediary organizations. In chapter 2 direct legislation is examined in historical and comparative perspective. This cross-national review shows that a variety of approaches have been taken in implementing direct legislation. Chapter 2 also contains a brief examination of the growth of direct legislation in America.

The ideology of the Progressive reformers persists today. While the agenda of issues and institutional power are clearly different, the underlying assumptions about politics and government of early and contemporary advocates of direct legislation are quite similar. Efforts to extend presidential primaries further, to reduce the importance of state conventions as a means of candidate or delegate selection, to abolish the electoral college, to mandate citizen participation in federally funded programs, and to establish a national initiative are present-day manifestations of the same perspective on politics as that held by the Progressive reformers in the early years of this century.

In recent elections the populace has voted on several controversial issues, and these issues have generated increased interest in the process of direct legislation. Most of the attention given to direct legislation, however, has focused on single issues or particular campaigns rather than on the mechanics of the process. But the necessary foundation from which to study direct legislation must be an understanding of the legal provisions, how they vary, and what effect they have on the functioning of the process. The legal provisions establish the signature requirements, which in turn affect how many and what types of issues qualify for the ballot. The process by which propositions are titled and summarized varies from state to state — a large factor in the extent of voter confusion. The margin needed for an initiative to be successfully adopted also varies. In the case of the Minnesota initiative amendment, a majority of those voting on the measure favored it, but the law required a majority from among all those who turned out to vote. Because some people did not vote on the proposition, it fell short of the number of votes needed.

The political mechanics of direct legislation are examined in chapter 3. The legal regulations on the process in the twenty-six states using some form of initiative or referendum are reviewed. The courts have played an important role both in determining the electoral procedures and in deciding whether successful propositions will be implemented. The involvement of state and federal courts, from the original constitutional challenges in the early years of this century to more current legal disputes, is reviewed in chapter 3. Methods of validating signatures and the role of elected officials in giving a title, number, and ballot description to each proposition are also examined.

The types of issues that voters have faced in statewide propositions, their overall success and failure rates, and the extent of usage over time are summarized in chapter 4. The initiative industry which has grown in recent years is also examined. For a price, initiative and referendum professionals will qualify a measure for the ballot and then manage the subsequent campaign. Chapter 4 focuses attention on the means by which propositions are placed on the ballot and the ways that signatures are gathered.

Chapter 5 presents an examination of citizen participation in statewide proposition elections. Many voters tend not to vote on all propositions. In fact, on many propositions the rates of nonvoting, or drop-off, are substantial. Which candidate contests or types of propositions have low rates of participation, as well as the extent to which participation in voting on candidates and propositions varies, are revealed in chapter 5. The chapter concludes by exploring variations within these rates of participation.

The representativeness of voters on propositions is ascertained in chapter 6. An analysis of surveys in California, Florida, and Massachusetts determines the extent to which the voters who decide propositions are representative of the total adult population or even of just those who turn out. These same surveys compare the representativeness of candidate voters with that of proposition voters. The effects of over- or underrepresentation on election outcomes are also explored in chapter 6. Finally, the chapter contains an explanation of why a significant number of citizens who go to the polls do not vote on some statewide propositions.

The central focus of chapter 7 is how informed and knowledgeable voters are about statewide propositions. What kinds of voters are attentive? Are the voters who are attentive to candidate politics attentive to direct legislation issues? When do voters decide how to vote on propositions? What sources of information are used? Is there evidence of voter confusion in casting ballots on statewide propositions? Are voters able to comprehend the state-provided voter's pamphlet? In short, chapters 5, 6, and 7 provide an analysis of which voters participate and how informed they are about the propositions.

Why some propositions win and others lose is the focus of chapter 8. One feature of many proposition campaigns is widespread change in voter intentions. Such opinion change during direct legislation campaigns is considerably more widespread than in candidate campaigns. Records of campaign expenditures from 1958 to 1982 are used to determine when and to what extent campaign spending makes a difference in election outcomes. The extent of elite endorsements in initiative campaigns and the extent to which the mass electorate is aware of the endorsements are documented in chapter 8.

Studies of single-proposition elections frequently assert the importance of alienated voters to the outcome of these elections. These alienated voters, unable to vent their frustrations in candidate elections, supposedly do so by turning out and voting no on propositions that are seen as reflecting the interests and desires of the politically powerful. The evidence for alienated voters' having an impact on statewide propositions is reviewed in chapter 8. Chapter 9 explores the extent to which party identification, ideology, and social class influence election outcomes for statewide propositions.

Chapter 10, the final chapter, answers the question most frequently asked about direct legislation: Who is benefited by the process? The recurrent questions in the debate over direct legislation are reconsidered and the evidence relating to those questions is summarized. Areas for further research are described, and speculation is provided about future developments in direct legislation politics. Finally, chapter 10 returns to the central issue of direct versus representative democracy by attempting to answer the question; Does direct legislation enhance the democratic process or detract from it?

The Idea of Direct Participation
in Government

T o what extent should the people rule? Should government be run by citizens directly, or should political decision making be entrusted to elected representatives? The debate between advocates of widespread citizen participation and those who prefer a system of periodic elections to choose representatives is not new. As was discussed in chapter 1, when confronted with the choice between greater or lesser citizen involvement, the founding fathers preferred to limit direct participation in national politics. They made the House of Representatives the only directly elected body and through a variety of institutional and constitutional devices established checks against rash decisions by momentary majorities. Over the course of U.S. history, constitutional amendments, court decisions, and actions taken by the state governments have significantly expanded the scope of direct participation.

The most far-reaching period of democratic reform in the United States occurred in the first two decades of this century. The Progressives, working at both the state and the national level, not only encouraged more widespread citizen participation but institutionalized it whenever possible. They significantly broadened the scope of citizen decision making through direct legislation, established popular control over nominees for public office through the direct primary election, expanded popular suffrage, and sought the withdrawal of government-sanctioned economic privileges, as well as the withdrawal of economic exploitation. Especially significant in its impact on American politics has been the Progressive doctrine of trust in the individual citizen and distrust of politicians, political parties, and legislatures.

The Progressive movement drew strength from the Populist movement's inroads but differed from previous reform movements in the scope of its agenda and in its success in achieving so much of it. The direct primary election alone constitutes one of the most important political reforms of our history, but direct primaries were only a small part of the Progressive program. The dramatic expansion of citizen participation in politics and government achieved by the Progressives leveled off in about 1920, and few states adopted the initiative or the referendum after that date. By then, however, senators were directly elected, and the franchise had been extended to women. Further significant expansion of direct participation would not come until the 1960s and 1970s.

During the 1960s and 1970s American politics again were changed significantly by reformers who, like the Progressives, assumed that the amount of direct citizen participation should be increased and that intermediary organizations were not to be trusted. They concentrated on expanding the levels and types of citizen participation in politics and government. Efforts to increase the number of presidential primaries, to adopt a national presidential primary, to institute a national initiative, to change the Democratic party's delegate selection procedures, to abolish the electoral college, and to mandate citizen participation in federally funded anti-poverty programs all reflect many of the attitudes about politics held by the Progressives.

THE PROGRESSIVE REFORM IDEOLOGY

"Give the government back to the people!" "Let the voters decide!" "Take politics out of the smoke-filled rooms!" These demands, characteristic of those made by the early Progressives, demonstrate faith in the capacity of citizens to govern themselves. Equally important to an understanding of this perspective on politics is the reformers' distrust of organizations, especially political organizations.[1] In the early 1900s, among the most despised organizations were the political machines. Reformers likewise saw economic trusts, monopolies, and cartels as the results of organizations that perverted the rationality and incorruptibility of individuals. Richard Hofstadter observed that "if big business was the ultimate enemy of the Progressive, his proximate enemy was the political machine."[2]

A central tenet of the Progressive ideology was that the vigor of democracy and democratic institutions could be restored only with the overthrow of bosses and machines, and that reforms should ensure that public officials remained accountable to the voters. The reformers were not revolutionaries seeking to destroy the major public institutions but rather individuals convinced that democracy, individual liberty, and the rule of law could best be achieved through the enactment of their reform agenda. Stated in the extreme, the Progressives believed that "bad people had pressure groups; the Man of Good Will had only his civic organizations."[3]

At the core of the Progressive ideology was the belief that direct democracy is preferable to government by politicians and legislatures. The reformers' profound distrust of legislatures was reflected in their writings:

> If the Initiative and Referendum are given to the people of this state
> [California], the fraudulent claims bills that slide through our legislature will be
> vetoed by the people, and legislative extravagance will be checked.[4]

The citizens of every state have seen legislature after legislature enact laws for the special advantage of a few and refuse to enact laws for the welfare of the many.[5]

The constant, unremitting application of corrupt influence to control the action of legislative bodies comes to be expected, almost tolerated . . . That politics should be a school of corruption is enough to make the angels weep. What can be more deadly to democracy than this? What plague can equal this plague of political leprosy?[6]

The Progressive reform agenda assumed that the citizenry was educated and informed and that citizen involvement in government decision making was good for both the individual and the government. The ideal of participatory democracy as practiced in New England town meetings and in direct legislation in Switzerland helped structure Progressive thinking. J. Allen Smith, a noted Progressive scholar, has argued that the initiative and referendum are "merely an attempt to get back to the basic idea of the old town meeting, where local measures are directly proposed and adopted or rejected by the people."[7]

The town-meeting model is still frequently evoked in discussions of direct legislation. These meetings, characterized by political equality, popular sovereignty, and open and frank discussion, allowed the citizens to govern themselves in matters of local affairs. The experience with town meetings teaches that the practice will only work in small cities where the population is homogeneous and not yet divided into contending special-interest groups. Direct legislation via the initiative and referendum typically occurs in much larger units, and contending special-interest groups are a part of the process. Moreover, in initiative and referendum campaigns there is rarely the kind of community interaction and discussion so characteristic of town meetings. For these reasons the town-meeting analogy has little relevance.[8]

To the Progressives, it was important to elevate to positions of political power the enlightened, dispassionate, independent citizen. Even more important, however, were the institutional and procedural reforms that would excise or severely limit the power of special interests, political parties, and corporations.[9] A related Progressive belief was the notion that much of the business of government, especially at the local level, was administrative rather than political. Thus, the Progressives supported efforts to insulate administration from political forces.[10] Many functions of government were seen as purely administrative; the remaining policy choices could be made directly by the people and not by party officials or corrupt political machines. One exponent of this view was John Rogers Commons. Writing in 1902, he argued that "the initiative and referendum, used in city government, would settle questions of policy and leave the municipal officers free to work out the business end of the administration without being disturbed by political influence."[11]

Most Progressives, however, did not assume that all political or policy questions could be decided via direct legislation. Rather, their intent was that direct legislation should complement a more open process for choosing representatives. In 1915 Benjamin Parke DeWitt, a young professor of government, provided an accurate summary of the components of the Progressive ideology:

> The first of these tendencies is found in the insistence by the best men in all political parties that special, minority, and corrupt influence in government — national, state, and city — be removed; the second tendency is found in the demand that the structure or machinery of government, which has hitherto been admirably adapted to control by the few, be so changed and modified that it will be more difficult for the few, and easier for the many, to control; and finally, the third tendency is found in the rapidly growing conviction that the functions of government are too restricted and that they must be increased and extended to relieve social and economic distress.[12]

The Progressive reform agenda represented a theory on politics, each part of the agenda complementing the others.[13] Among the most important reforms implemented or expanded by the Progressives were these: home rule, nonpartisan elections, the commission plan for local government, merit systems, initiative, popular referendum, recall, direct primary, direct election of U.S. senators, women's suffrage, and independent regulatory commissions. From the perspective of the 1980s it would be difficult to choose the single most important reform of the Progressive era. At the time, however, most scholars agreed that the advent of the initiative and referendum constituted one of the most important changes in twentieth-century U.S. political institutions. Writing in 1912, W. B. Munro concluded, "There has been no more striking phenomenon in the development of American political institutions during the last ten years than the rise to prominence in public discussion and consequently to recognition upon the statute book, of those so-termed newer weapons of democracy — the initiative, referendum, and recall."[14]

These new instruments of democracy were seen by some reformers as providing a dramatic opportunity for a new type of popular consultation. One of the most far-reaching proposals for direct legislation was contained in a 1921 proposed Labor party platform. In part, the platform called for a national plebiscite on a wide variety of issues.

> Plebiscites shall be held at regular intervals, and on special occasions, in order to make valid the following governmental acts:
>
> (a) *Any increase in the public debt. . . .*
>
> (b) *Any increase in departmental budgets above 1 percent annually. . . .*
>
> (c) *All treaties with foreign countries. . . .*
>
> (d) *Any declaration of war, or conscription of men or of wealth for military purposes, except in case of actual invasion of our territory. . . .*

(e) *Decisions of the Supreme Court* (except unanimous decisions) declaring legislation unconstitutional.

(f) *Changes in form or rate of taxation.*[15]

This proposal was more extreme than most in the scope of proposed direct legislation, but such proposals were not uncommon in this period. Less radical schemes have surfaced periodically in the succeeding decades. Prior to World War II, support grew for the Ludlow amendment, a national referendum on the declaration of war. Recently, a group calling itself Initiative America has advocated a national initiative process. By the late 1970s, citizens of Columbus, Ohio, and in Hawaii could telephone in their reactions to a policy question after hearing a discussion of the question on television. Qube and Televote, as the systems are sometimes called, provide an immediate plebiscite on a question or candidate by having viewers record their opinion through an electronic device connected to their television. The Columbus, Ohio, Qube, the first viewer-response television system, generated national notoriety in an electronic poll of viewer reaction to President Carter's "crisis of confidence" speech. During the 1980 presidential election, candidate George Bush appeared on the Columbus Qube channel and obtained instantaneous viewer reaction to his candidacy.[16] The pros and cons of these systems are discussed later; but the fact that reformers have proposed a government by plebiscite reflects an underlying distrust of the "representative" governmental structure and an assumption that voters can and will participate daily.

While the single most important motivation for the advent of direct legislation was the widely perceived corruption of legislators and other public officials, other factors may also have been at play. Is it possible that the accusations of bossism and corruption were really smoke screens hiding other political motivations? Conceivably, the real motivation may have been that some classes or interests were unable to prevail under the status quo; to improve their chances, they sought to change the political rules. For example, suppose the city council had already decided which municipal railroad to license. Interests favoring a competing railroad, unable to win the contract, could then accuse the incumbents of corruption and "machine politics" and seek a vote of the people, or referendum, on the proposed contract. Having already lost with the municipal government, the proponents of the referendum would have nothing to lose and everything to gain. While the campaign would almost certainly be waged on the issue of municipal support of "special interests" and corrupt bargains, this might not be the real issue.

Thus, the banner of political reform allows a diverse group of special interests to assert that they represent the public interest. To what extent, then, did the Progressive movement represent persons or groups whose real motive was good government? Did the Progressive movement draw from diverse segments of society, or was it the tool of the upper class? Some historians argue that many Progressives were middle-class, urban, and well educated and that they often were self-employed businessmen. Historians such as Alfred D. Chandler, Jr., Richard Hofstadter, and George E. Mowry link the zeal of many reformers to a concern about their inability to influence public policy. Hofstadter has characterized this concern about the power of labor unions, corporations, and increasingly powerful organizations as "status anxiety." [17]

"PROGRESSIVISM" OF THE 1960s AND 1970s:
DIRECT CITIZEN PARTICIPATION EXTENDED

The Progressives' efforts to enhance popular control of government via direct primaries, the initiative and referendum, direct election of senators, nonpartisan municipal elections, and the recall have left a lasting effect on American politics. Their perspective on politics and government was based on two reinforcing beliefs: (1) that political organizations were corrupt and that many of the ills of American democracy were directly attributable to political parties, party officials, state legislatures, mayors, and city governments; and (2) that individual citizens desired to exercise greater control over government and were capable of determining for themselves the public good.

More recent reformers have also sought to "democratize" American politics by requiring that a larger proportion of presidential convention delegates be chosen through direct primaries. In 1968, 38 percent of the delegates to the Republican convention and 40 percent of those to the Democratic convention were chosen in direct primary elections; in 1980 over 77 percent from each party were chosen in direct primaries. As a result of the reforms of the Democratic party, elected officials were conspicuously absent from the 1972 and 1976 national party conventions. Both of these changes — more delegates selected via primaries and a decline in the number of elected officials at the convention — result from the belief that voters' decisions are preferable to those of party officials acting in caucuses or conventions and that elected officials have no greater stake in the outcome of a candidate selection process than does any other registered party voter.

The idea of direct citizen participation has become pervasive in U.S. politics. In addition to the dramatic expansion in the number and importance of direct primaries and the party reforms of delegate selection for national conventions, advocates of direct citizen participation pressed for a national initiative process, abolition of the electoral college, federal funding of elections, expanded suffrage for blacks and eighteen- to twenty-one-year-olds, and legislatively mandated citizen participation in federally funded projects. Samuel H. Beer, writing about the requirement of "citizen participation" in federal anti-poverty and other programs, concluded that "in qualified form the formula requiring participation was incorporated in many Great Society programs and has become a normal ingredient of program structure. It would be difficult today to find a program involving regulation or delivery of services in such fields as health, education, welfare, and the environment that does not provide for 'community input.' In a more diffuse, but more important way, the participatory idea has affected the whole process of representative government." [18]

The expansion of citizen participation in politics is thus one of the similarities between the two periods, but there are also some important differences. The more recent reformers encountered a political system already made substantially more participatory by the earlier Progressive reforms. In some areas, the more recent reformers have simply picked up where the Progressives left off. After 1920 there were few movements to adopt direct primaries or the initiative and referendum, but the more recent reformers have stimulated renewed interest in these reforms and have substantially expanded them. As noted above, the number of states using direct primaries in presidential delegate selection has risen dramatically since the late 1960s, and more than twenty states have considered adopting the initiative since the mid-1970s.

Another important difference between the two periods is the nature of the party system and the extent to which the political system was permeable. The Progressives encountered strong, well-organized political parties and a relatively closed political system. As a result of the Progressive reforms, the parties were substantially weakened and the political system made more open and permeable. Thus, the more recent reformers encounter little opposition from the weakened political parties and do not face the institutional hurdles encountered by the Progressives. In addition, politics are now more nationally focused, and the scope of government activity has been substantially enlarged.

Reformers in both periods attacked bossism. The Progressives focused their principal attack upon the state legislatures for favoritism, abuses in the enactment of legislation, and corruption in the election of U.S. senators. The participationists of the 1960s and 1970s also fought against bossism — one of the more important targets was the presidential nominating conventions — and advocated more open delegate selection procedures and, indirectly, the adoption of the direct primary as the preferred means of delegate selection. In the more recent reform period, participationists have capitalized on political corruption, especially as uncovered in the Watergate affair, to enact a series of election finance and disclosure reforms that attempt to correct the abuses of big money in politics and make citizen participation less susceptible to the influences of campaign spending. In both the early and the more recent reform periods, interest groups were strong and politically active. Just as the Progressives were not the first group to see expansion of direct citizen participation as the cure for the ills of democracy, the participationists of the last two decades will not be the last advocates of more widespread direct democracy.

There are important differences between the two reform periods, however, and the comparison could be overdrawn. The essential point is that during the recent period the idea of direct participation in politics has been substantially advanced and institutionalized. Direct democratic reforms have come in two surges which appear to be related in their approach and ideology. This book does not focus principally on the entire agenda of the Progressives and participationists. Others have already studied much of that agenda, and its scope is too broad for a single volume. Instead, this discussion examines the extent to which the people rule via the initiative, referendum, and ballot propositions more generally. Understanding the scope and consequences of direct legislation will help us determine the extent to which efforts at democratization may prove successful. Because the individual voter is so essential to both the theory and the implementation of direct legislation and most of the other Progressive reforms as well, the individual voter is the central referent. While this is not a study of the other Progressive Era reforms or their modern descendants, it will probe the extent to which, in one central area, the voters meet the reformers' hopes.

DISPUTES OVER DIRECT LEGISLATION

Even though the early Progressives and more recent proponents of direct legislation are separated by almost fifty years, the arguments that arise when the initiative and referendum are debated are the same today as they were in the early 1900s. As with almost any public policy debate, the participants tend to overstate their case to highlight their points. Here in brief detail are the main contentions over direct legislation. Proponents generally make the following arguments:

1. *Direct legislation will reduce the power of political parties and party bosses.* Representative political systems tend to become party-dominated, and that generally leads to party bossism. Party machines, when in power, generally establish and maintain a spoils system. This may mean that public policy is the result of greedy self-interest rather than an open and impartial determination of the popular will.[19] Direct legislation and, even more important, direct primaries appear to have weakened political parties and contributed to their decline.

2. *Direct legislation will reduce the power of special interests.* Because access and resources are centered in special interests, these groups tend to dominate the elected representatives and can usually obtain what they want from government. All of this could be changed by allowing the people to

decide major issues of public policy. Direct legislation is a better expression of popular opinion than is voting for representatives. Without direct legislation, the people will not be consulted, and the party boss or special interest, rather than the people, is therefore likely to be sovereign.[20]

3. *Direct legislation is a political safety valve.* The initiative and referendum allow the voters to force action on issues that would otherwise result in legislative stalemate and deadlock. On other issues, direct legislation, by going directly to a popular vote, allows a "final" decision on an issue of some controversy. In short, it can be argued that the people have spoken, and the issue decided.

4. *Direct legislation will educate the people and allow them to develop civic virtue.* In political systems where direct legislation is not provided, the voter's decision is framed by the parties, and his options are generally restricted. Because voters have so few choices, they do not bother to educate themselves about politics. Instead, they vote out of political inclination, respond to an attractive personality, or, more typically, withdraw from politics altogether. Direct legislation is a means to restore citizens to interested, active, and involved roles, because when voters have a chance really to express an opinion, they will become educated on issues and participate in elections.[21]

5. *Citizens are better suited to decide public policy questions than are elected representatives.* Presumably, elected representatives are in large measure concerned with representing their constituents. Often, however, they neither know nor care what their constituents want.[22] Citizens, moreover, can focus on the handful of ballot propositions, while legislators must decide many more issues in a shorter period of time.[23]

6. *Citizens want to decide issues directly, and permitting them to have full participation will decrease public apathy and popular dissatisfaction with government.* Direct legislation has widespread popular support; only party machines, special interests, and the political elite are opposed to the concept. Decisions reached by ballot proposition will be seen as more legitimate than those reached in the state legislature or by the national government because the people decide. The public's alienation and dissatisfaction in government will decrease because the public will recognize that they have only themselves to blame for mistakes in policy decisions.[24]

7. *Direct legislation will strengthen democratic government.* Direct legislation is the most accurate way to determine public opinion on political issues. Votes on propositions more accurately reflect public sentiments than do votes in candidate races. Furthermore, the power of the few, represented by the arbitrary and corrupt policies of representatives, will be directly checked by the will of the many. While some critics assume that the people are not capable of such extensive political participation, the advocates of democratic government argue that they should be given the chance to show their interest

and capacity for good judgment. In short, advocates of direct legislation argue that opponents of the process have little faith in the people.[25]

The arguments against direct legislation also tend to arise again and again. Opponents generally make the following arguments or rebuttals:

1. *The true beneficiaries of direct legislation will be not the people but the special interests.* Those special interests that so concern proponents of direct legislation will simply adopt the initiative and referendum as the political means to their desired ends. Groups with money will set the agenda of direct legislation by placing measures they desire on the ballot and then financing the campaigns for passage. In the event that a proposition runs counter to their political desires, they will dominate the ensuing campaign and defeat the issue. Thus, under direct legislation, it is not the people who rule but the special interests.[26]

2. *Direct legislation will result in an unreasonably complex ballot and "frivolous" legislation.* Because most citizens will not be interested in direct legislation, only groups or interests with issues to push will use the process. Often these groups will be at the extremes of the political spectrum, proposing ideas unacceptable to most voters. When the legislative agenda of the issue extremists is combined with that of the special interests, the result will be an unreasonably long ballot. If voters fail to endure their long ballot and do not vote on these measures, they will facilitate the passage of unwanted legislation — or, even more important, through inaction, they may assist in amending the state constitution.[27]

3. *Voters are ill-equipped to understand complicated proposals and unprepared to grapple with the confusing campaigns and appeals that are a part of the initiative process.* Because voters may not have the education or expertise to understand complicated ballot propositions, many will not participate on this part of the ballot, and their sense of efficacy will be diminished. For those voters who choose to vote on the proposition, many will not understand what they are deciding but rather will vote on the basis of advertising or whim. Citizens may favor the concept of direct legislation, but when it is put into practice, the result is nonparticipation on the propositions and greater alienation in the electorate.[28]

4. *The legislative process is a much better way to make public policy.* The legislative process provides for debate over alternatives, compromise, and consensus or agreement. Direct legislation provides none of these important features; instead, it presents to the voters a proposition that may not be amended or compromised. Voters must either accept or reject the proposal, and all votes are counted equally. Citizens whose interests may be directly affected have no more input in the decision than voters who are only marginally interested in the issue. Representatives, in contrast, can assess the inten-

sity of concern among groups and are more knowledgeable about the substance of the issues and the proposal's administrative workability.[29]

5. *Direct legislation will not educate the voters, nor will it increase interest in government.* When confronted with the complexities of direct legislation proposals, most voters simplify the task by voting for the side that advertises more or by voting the way the newspapers advise. Voters will not be sufficiently involved or interested in direct legislation to study the proposition and vote accordingly. Direct legislation will not result in increased civic virtue and widespread interest in government.[30]

6. *Direct legislation will endanger democracy and undermine representative government.* Democratic government is more than popular elections: it also involves the retention of fundamental rights and liberties. Once established, these rights also become a part of the democratic process. Unpopular minorities or interests could become the object of direct legislation that would restrict their rights. Thus, popular elections on fundamental rights may run counter to democratic principles. Further, the practice of direct legislation runs counter to the representative government envisioned by the founding fathers, who sought to minimize the impact of momentary or transitory majorities. Direct legislation seeks just the opposite; it elevates a momentary majority to a preeminent position and exacerbates the problem of faction. Few would argue that all issues should be decided by plebiscite; but the mere threat of initiative and referendum will result in legislatures that are skilled in deferring to the people decisions on controversial questions.[31]

These themes in the cases for and against direct legislation are more thoroughly developed in subsequent chapters. In some instances, other arguments also arise, but the issues discussed above are most common in debates over adoption of direct legislation. Present-day proponents of direct legislation consistently communicate their case with the same religious fervor that was evident in 1912. Opponents of the process often have a liability: they must defend a status quo that has actual problems against a reform that has only potential problems. Opponents also face the formidable obstacle of seeming undemocratic and elitist when voicing reservations about the people and their potential behavior. Two of the assumptions underlying opposition to the referendum are that parties serve useful purposes in focusing political debate and that representative democracy is in fact representative.

DIRECT LEGISLATION IN COMPARATIVE PERSPECTIVE

A cross-national comparison of direct legislation is important for at least two reasons. First, the experiences of other nations have been widely used as evidence of the merit of direct legislation. Second, important differences exist in the way the Progressives structured direct legislation in this country and in the way other nation-states have employed referendums.

While many American Progressives traced the concept of direct legislation to ancient Athens, the more important precedent was nineteenth-century Switzerland. But even Switzerland was preceded by France in using a national referendum. In 1793, the French submitted a new constitution to a direct popular vote, and it was overwhelmingly adopted. This became an important precedent, but referendums were infrequently used by the French until the mid-1900s. More important was the adoption between 1831 and 1890 by several Swiss cantons of the initiative and referendum for both ordinary legislative measures and constitutional proposals.

American advocates of direct legislation assert that the Swiss experience with direct legislation has been so positive that many of the frequently posited arguments against the initiative and referendum cannot be borne out by actual experience. In fact, based upon results of the Swiss experience, proponents of direct legislation argue that government could become efficient, honest, and nonpartisan as a result of direct legislation. In 1899 John Rogers Commons described the effect of direct legislation on the Swiss system as follows: "The Swiss people are free from the corrupting extremes of wealth, largely because the referendum headed off the encroachments of boodlers, bribers, and monopolists, together with all kinds of special legislation by which so many American fortunes have been created. . . . No longer could the lawmakers sell out the people; they could no longer 'deliver the goods.' The people themselves must ratify the sale. The referendum was the people's veto." [32]

While Commons's attribution of so many positive accomplishments to direct legislation is clearly overdramatized, the extent to which American reformers pointed to the Swiss example is impressive. [33] In many writings the pre–direct legislation politics in Switzerland are likened to "machine-ridden" America, and then the author argues that the initiative and referendum changed all of that. [34] The Swiss reputation for successful experience with the initiative and referendum persists. Writing recently, Congressman Jack Kemp (R–N.Y.) concluded: "One country of the world that has more democracy than the United States is also, I believe not coincidently, more peaceful and prosperous than the United States. In Switzerland, the citizens can initiate legislation at the national level and also nullify legislation through the referendum." [35]

Not all national experiences with direct legislation have been as positive as that in Switzerland. While direct legislation is often considered a vehicle of democratic government, several examples of profoundly anti-democratic national referendums exist. Governments in totalitarian countries can appear democratic by holding a plebiscite; but by limiting the voting options, they reduce the election to a meaningless facade. In October 1933, for instance,

Hitler announced the German withdrawal from the League of Nations. At the same time, he announced that he would submit his decision to a national referendum. Hitler thus invoked "the sanctions of democracy against the democratic nations." [36]

Based upon observations of elections like this, Carl Friedrich has argued that referendums on foreign affairs are problematic. [37] The exploitation of referendums by undemocratic leaders did not stop with Hitler. Recently such leaders of nation-states as the Ayatollah Khomeini and Idi Amin have used national referendums to legitimize their regimes. One observation that applies to referendums of this type — indeed to all referendums — is that the person or group who frames the question also structures the campaign and thereby may affect the outcome significantly.

Some national referendums do provide real choices to the voters. The 1975 British vote on entry into the European Economic Community is one notable example. This referendum constituted Britain's first national experience with the referendum. Unlike in American referendums, the question was straightforward and understandable: "Do you think that the United Kingdom should stay in the European Community (the Common Market)?" [38] The debate about the advantages and disadvantages of the referendum was similar in many ways to the debate over direct legislation in the 1911 California election. Whether the proponents of the referendum were committed to the process or to political expediency is debatable, but the British electorate overwhelmingly supported joining the Common Market.

The particular form that direct legislation may take varies by nation-state. A breakdown by subject matter of the number of referendums for European democracies since 1900 is provided in table 2.1.

In most European democracies a national referendum is a rare event. The overall average number of referendums for each country in this century is five. Even the heaviest users, Denmark and France, average less than two national referendums each decade. In sharp contrast, the Swiss voters have decided 249 national referendums. [39] Thus, at the national level the only frequent user has been Switzerland. Most national referendums in Europe are not held as a matter of right when people sign referendum petitions. With the exception of Switzerland and Italy, national referendums in European democracies are legislative referendums; the government or legislature decides when the referendum will be held and how the ballot question will be worded. The legislative referendum is thus distinct from the popular referendum, which is initiated by citizen petitions and in which the wording of the question is determined by the proponents.

While in most European countries national referendums have been few in number, some have been historically significant. In France, de Gaulle used the national referendum as a vote of confidence. It was argued that the referendum would "reveal the existence of a national consensus which was disguised and often perversely hidden by the political parties which had every

Table 2.1

REFERENDUMS IN EUROPEAN DEMOCRACIES SINCE 1900

Issue	Belgium	Denmark	Finland	France	Greece	Iceland	Ireland	Italy	Luxembourg	Norway	Spain	Sweden	Turkey	United Kingdom	Total
Constitutional															
Approve new constitution	0	1	0	3	0	0	1	0	0	0	1	0	1	0	7
Approve or end monarch(y)	1	0	0	0	4	1	1	1	1	1	0	0	0	0	10
Change in constitutional machinery	0	1	0	4	0	0	0	0	0	0	1	0	0	0	6
Change in voting age	0	5	0	0	0	0	1	0	0	0	0	0	0	0	6
Change in electoral system	0	0	0	0	0	0	3	0	0	0	0	0	0	0	3
Ban on extreme parties	0	0	0	0	0	0	0	0	1	0	0	0	0	0	1
State financing of parties	0	0	0	0	0	0	0	1	0	0	0	0	0	0	1
Antiterrorist legislation	0	0	0	0	0	0	0	2	0	0	0	0	0	0	2
Possession of arms	0	0	0	0	0	0	0	1	0	0	0	0	0	0	1
Subtotal	1	7	0	7	4	1	6	5	2	1	2	0	1	0	37
Environmental															
Nuclear energy	0	0	0	0	0	0	0	0	0	0	0	2	0	0	2
Moral															
Divorce	0	0	0	0	0	0	0	1	0	0	0	0	0	0	1
Prohibition of alcoholic beverages	0	0	1	0	0	1	0	0	0	2	0	1	0	0	5
Position of church	0	0	0	0	0	0	1	0	0	0	0	0	0	0	1
Abortion	0	0	0	0	0	0	0	2	0	0	0	0	0	0	2
Subtotal	0	0	1	0	0	1	1	3	0	2	0	1	0	0	9
Pragmatic															
Land, law, pension, rule of road	0	4	0	0	0	0	0	0	0	0	0	2	0	0	6
Territorial															
European Community membership	0	1	0	1	0	0	1	0	0	1	0	0	0	1	5
Other territorial	0	2	0	2	0	2	0	0	1	0	1	0	0	2	10
Subtotal	0	3	0	3	0	2	1	0	1	2	0	0	0	3	15
Total	1	14	1	10	4	4	8	8	3	5	2	5	1	3	69

Source: Data through 1978 are from Butler and Ranney, *Referendums,* 14, 227–37. Data for 1979–81 were collected from Keesing's Contemporary Archives for 1979, 1980, and 1981.

Note: Switzerland is not included because it alone has had nearly 250 national referendums since 1900, making it a unique case; Estonia and the German Weimar Republic are omitted as special interwar cases; and 4 of the 8 Greek referendums are omitted as undemocratic.

interest in emphasizing the divisions in French Society."[40] The French referendums on Algeria, constitutional revision, and European Community membership were tools used by the president to assure and expand his power. De Gaulle skillfully campaigned on the issues and achieved a form of political leverage by so doing; had he been less successful, the tool most likely would have been used less frequently.

Conclusions

The initiative and referendum are electoral institutions that reflect certain assumptions about political organizations and individual citizen preferences. The Progressive reformers who instituted these reforms believed that government would be better and citizens more involved and interested as a result of their use.

From the earliest debates over the initiative and referendum, proponents and opponents have argued that the experiences of other countries substantiate their argument. The national experience that has most profoundly affected the debate over direct legislation in the United States has been that of Switzerland. As the United States considers the adoption of a national initiative, the experiences of Switzerland and other nations that have used national initiatives will receive even closer attention. Aside from being of historical interest, the cross-national experience has been useful as a reminder of the variety of ways in which direct legislation may be structured.

The same reform ideology has motivated reformers seeking the initiative and the referendum, even though they may be seeking adoption at very different times and in different places. Moreover, advocates of direct legislation in other countries use many of the same arguments and have many of the same assumptions as the advocates of the process in California, Oregon, Texas, and Virginia. Critical and unanswered questions raised time and again in debates over direct legislation are: Do all voters participate in deciding ballot propositions? What factors influence their decision to vote? What factors influence the decision on how to vote? Does direct legislation educate the voters and reduce alienation, or does it confuse voters, thereby adding to their frustration and alienation? What effects does direct legislation have on other political institutions and processes such as legislatures, parties, and candidate elections? After a description of the basic legal and structural dynamics of the process of direct legislation in the United States, the remainder of this discussion seeks to answer these questions.

□□□□□□□□□□□□□□□□□□□□□□□□□□□□□

Legal Provisions for Direct Legislation and Judicial Review of the Initiative Process

P roponents of direct legislation have defined the initiative as the means by which voters can correct legislative sins of omission and the popular referendum as the means of correcting legislative sins of commission.[1] While the ideology behind these reforms transcends state boundaries, the procedures for direct legislation clearly are not uniform. How states structure direct legislation influences the extent to which the process is used and how it is used.

The current legal mechanics of direct legislation at the state level in the United States are reviewed in this chapter. First, the various types of direct legislation are defined, and the ways in which different states have chosen to structure the process are detailed. Because state and federal courts have continually been involved in adjudicating disputes about the process of direct legislation, the most important legal cases are also reviewed, and current constitutional status of direct legislation is summarized. In addition, this chapter covers the responsibilities of state and local election officials in administering direct legislation.

TYPES OF DIRECT LEGISLATION

In general terms, all statewide propositions seek a popular mandate from the people on a specific policy issue, but there are significant differences among the four types of propositions:

Direct initiative. Constitutional amendments (or statutes) are proposed by petition and submitted directly to the voters for approval or rejection without any action by the legislature. Upon adoption, they have the force and effect of constitutional amendments (or statutes).

Indirect initiative. Statutes are proposed by petition but are submitted prior to a set date to a regular session of the legislature. If, after a specified time, the statute has not been approved by the legislature or if the legislature has amended the original initiative in a way unacceptable to the original proponents, the proponents may then gather the remaining required signatures and submit the original initiative to the voters for approval or rejection. Some states provide that if the legislature does not approve the indirectly initiated proposal, it may offer a substitute proposal on the same subject to accompany the original one on the next general election ballot.[2]

Popular referendum. The voters are empowered to accept or reject specific laws enacted by the legislature when these laws are referred to them by popular petition. Within a specified time after adjournment of a legislative session, petitioners wishing to have a referendum on an act must submit a required number of signatures. In such a case the law does not go into effect until it has been referred to the voters and approved by them.

Propositions submitted by the legislature. Either because of constitutional mandate or by voluntary action, the state legislature submits to the voters proposed constitutional amendments, bond issues, or amendments to statutes originally adopted by initiative and requiring voter approval. In these instances, no petition from the voters is required.

Twenty-six states currently provide for some form of initiative or popular referendum; of that number, twenty-one provide both, three provide referendum only, and two provide only the initiative. Of states having initiative, twenty-one permit the statutory initiative and seventeen permit the constitutional initiative. Five states have both the direct initiative and the indirect initiative, while fifteen have only the direct initiative and three have only the indirect initiative. Popular referendums are permitted in twenty-five states and are generally limited to statutes, but every state except Delaware submits all legislatively derived constitutional amendments to a vote of the people. The following analysis, drawn from state election codes and state constitutions, details the similarities and differences in the various state provisions for direct legislation.

State Provisions for Direct Legislation

Consistent with American federalism, each state's provisions for the initiative and popular referendum may contain some distinctive requirements. At the same time, there are substantial areas where initiative and referendum law is quite consistent across states. Thirty of the most important constitutional and statutory provisions for the twenty-six states with the initiative or popular referendum are presented in table 3.1.

Signature Requirements

In the provisions for initiative and referendum the twenty-six states listed in table 3.1 have varying signature requirements. For every state, the essential

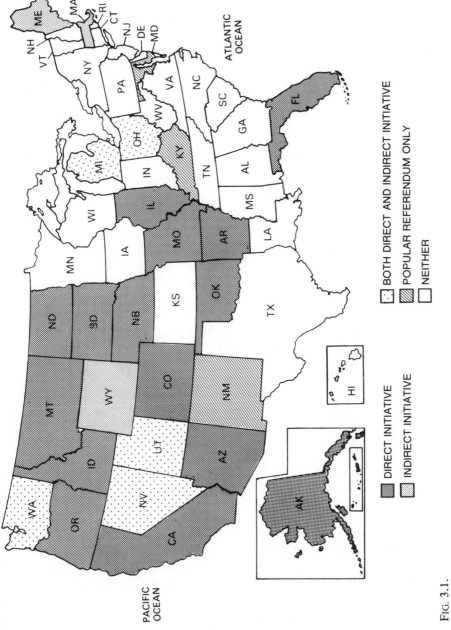

Fig. 3.1.
Provisions for Initiative and Popular Referendum in the United States

DIRECT INITIATIVE
INDIRECT INITIATIVE

BOTH DIRECT AND INDIRECT INITIATIVE
POPULAR REFERENDUM ONLY
NEITHER

37

Table 3.1

STATE PROVISIONS FOR DIRECT LEGISLATION

	Alaska	Arizona	Arkansas	California	Colorado	Florida	Idaho	Illinois
Statutory Initiative								
Year adopted	1959	1910	1909	1911	1910		1912	
Percentage of signatures required [a]	10[b]	10	8	5	5[c]		10	
Geographic distribution of signatures	Y[h]	N	Y[i]	N	N		N	
Legislative review	N	N	N	N[p]	N		N	
Constitutional Initiative								
Year adopted		1910	1909	1911	1910	1978		1970
Percentage of signatures required [a]		15	20	8	5[c]	8[r]		8
Geographic distribution of signatures		N	Y[i]	N	N	Y[t]		N
Legislature review		N	N	N[p]	N	N		
Direct or indirect initiative	D	D	D	D	D	D	D	D
Limit on subjects	Y	N	N	N	N		N	
Preliminary filing	Y	Y	Y	Y	Y		Y	
Form specified by law	Y	Y	Y	Y	Y		Y	
Gubernatorial veto	N	N	N	N	N		N	
Vote necessary	MP	MP	MP	MP	MP		MG[w]	
Restrictions on legislative amendment	Y	Y	Y	Y	N		Y	
Filing deadline (days) [bb]	N	120	120	130	120	90	120	180
Effective date (days)	90	GP	30	I	GP	Jan.	GP	GP
Referendum								
Year adopted	1959	1910	1909	1911	1910		1912	1970
Percentage of signatures required	10[b]	5	6	5	5[c]		10	10
Geographic distribution of signatures	Y[h]	N	Y[i]	N	N		N	
Limit on subjects	Y	Y	N	Y	Y		N	
Preliminary filing	Y	Y	Y	Y	Y		Y	
Form specified by law	Y	Y	Y	Y	Y		Y	
Filing deadline (days) [gg]	90	90	90	90	90		60	78
Vote necessary	MP	MP	MP	MP	MP		MP	
Restrictions on legislative amendment	N	Y	Y	Y	N			
Measures suspended pending referendum [mm]	N	Y	Y	Y	Y		Y	
Provision for voter's handbook [ll]	N	Y	N[nn]	Y	N[nn]	N[nn]	Y	N[nn]
Restriction on paid signature collection	N	N	N	N	Y	N	Y	N
Initiative and referendum extended to localities [mm]	Y	Y	Y	Y				Y

Symbols: Y = yes, N = no, MP = majority of voters voting on propositions, MG = majority of total votes cast for governor, MV = majority of votes, GP = governor's proclamation, and I = immediately.

Sources:
Alaska: State Constitution, Art. VI, Sec. 2–7.
Arizona: State Constitution, Art. IV, Pt. 1, Title 19, 101–44.
Arkansas: State Constitution, Amendment to State Constitution of 1874, Title 2.
California: State Constitution, Art. IV, Sec. 1.
Colorado: State Constitution, Art. V, Sec. 1; Art. XL.
Florida: State Constitution, Art. II, Secs. 3–5.
Idaho: State Constitution, Art. III, Secs. 1, 34 (1801–22).

Table 3.1 *(continued)*

	Kentucky	Maine	Maryland	Massachusetts	Michigan	Missouri	Montana	Nebraska	Nevada	New Mexico	North Dakota	Ohio	Oklahoma	Oregon	South Dakota	Utah	Washington	Wyoming
	1908		1918	1908	1908	1906	1912	1904			1914	1912	1907	1902	1898	1900	1912	1968
	10ᵈ		3+ '1½ᵈ	8ᵈ	5	5ᵈ	7ᵈ	10			2ᵉ	3+ 3ᶠ	8ᵍ	6ᵈ	5ᵈ	5+ 5ᵈ	8ᵈ	15ᵇ
	N		Yʲ	N	Yʰ	Yᵏ	Yˡ	Yᵐ			N	Yⁿ	N	N	N	Yᵒ	N	Yᵐ
	Y		Y	Y	N	Yq	N	Y			N	Y	N	N	Y	Y		

	Kentucky	Maine	Maryland	Massachusetts	Michigan	Missouri	Montana	Nebraska	Nevada	New Mexico	North Dakota	Ohio	Oklahoma	Oregon	South Dakota	Utah	Washington	Wyoming
			1918	1908	1908	1972	1912	1904			1914	1912	1907	1902	1898			
			3+ 1½ᵈ	10ᵈ	8	10ˢ	10ᵈ	10			4ᵉ	10ᶠ	15ᵍ	8ᵈ	10ᵈ			
			Yʲ	N	Yʰ	Yᵘ	Yˡ	Yᵛ			N	Yⁿ	N	N	N			
			Y		N	Y	N	Y				Y		N	N			
	I	I	B	D	D	D	B	D	B	D	D	D	B	B	I			
	Y	Y	N	Y	Y	Y	Y	Y	Y	N	N	N	N	N	Y			
	N	Y	N	N	N	N	Y	Y	Y	Y	N	N	N	Y				
	Y	Y	Y	Y	Y	Y	Y	Y	Y	Y	Y	Y	Y	Y	Y			
	N	N	N	N	N	N	N	N	N	N	N	N	N	N	N			
	MV	MPˣ	MP	MP	MP	MPʸ	MP	MP	MP	MP	MP	MP	MP	MPᶻ	MVʷ			
	N	N	Y	N	N		Y	Y	N	N	N	N	N	Y	Nᵃᵃ			
	50ᶜᶜ			10/ 120	120	120q	120	30/		90	10/			120	360ᵈᵈ	10/	10/	120
	30/ GP		30	10/ 40	GP	270/ 330q	GP	I		30	30	GP	30/ GP	I	5ᵉᵉ	30		90

	Kentucky	Maine	Maryland	Massachusetts	Michigan	Missouri	Montana	Nebraska	Nevada	New Mexico	North Dakota	Ohio	Oklahoma	Oregon	South Dakota	Utah	Washington	Wyoming
	1917	1908	1915	1918	1908	1908	1906	1912	1904	1911	1914	1912	1907	1902	1898	1900	1912	1968
	5	10ᵈ	3ᵈ	2ᵈ	5ᵈ	5	5ᵈ	5ᵈ	10	10	sᵉ	6ᶠ	5ᵍ	4ᵈ	5ᵈ	10ᵈ	4ᵈ	15ᵇ
	N	Yᶠᶠ	Yʲ	N	Yʰ	Yᵘ	Yˡ	N	Yᵛ	N	Yⁿ	N	N	N	Yᵒ	N		Yᵐ
	Y	Y	Y	Y	Y	Y	Y	N	Y	Y	Y	Y	Y	Y	Y	Y		Y
	N	N	Y	N	N	N	N	N	Y	Y	Y	Y	Y	N	N	N		Y
	N	Y	Y	Y	Y	Y	Y	Y	Y	Y	Y	Y	Y	Y	Y	Y		Y
	120	90	30+ 30	90ʰʰ	90	90	120q	90	90	120	90	90ⁱⁱ	90	90ʲʲ	90	60	90	90
	MV	MP	MP	MPˣ	MP	MP	MP	MP	MPᵏᵏ	MPˡˡ	MP	MP	MP	MP	MP	MP	MPᶻ	MVʷ
		Y	N	N	N	N		Y			Y	N	N	N	N	N	Y	
	Y	Y	Y	Y	Y	Y	N	N	N	N	Y	Y	Y	Y	Y	Y		Y
	N	N	Nⁿⁿ	Y	Nᵒᵒ	Nᵒᵒ	Y	N	Nⁿⁿ	Nᵖᵖ	Y	Nqq	N	Y	Nⁿⁿ	Y		Y
	N	N	N	Y	N	N	N	N	N	N	N	Y	N	Y	N	Y		N
		Y	Y			Y		Y			Y	Y	Y	Y	Y			

Illinois: State Constitution, Amendment 7.5, Secs. 3–7; Art. XIV, Sec. 3.

Kentucky: State Constitution, Sec. 132 (subsecs. 100–20), 171.

Maine: State Constitution, Art. IV, Pt. 3, Secs. 17–22.

Maryland: State Constitution, Art. XVI, Secs. 1–5; Art. XI-A, Sec. 7; Art. XXXI, Sec. 23–1.

Massachusetts: State Constitution, Amendment Art. 48, Pts. 1–5.

Michigan: State Constitution, Art. II, Secs. 9, 168 (subsecs. 471–82).

Missouri: State Constitution, Art. III, Secs. 49–53, 126 (subsecs. 011–151).

Montana: State Constitution, Art. III, Secs. 4–8; Art. XIV, Secs. 2, 9, 13–27.

Nebraska: State Constitution, Art. III, Sec. 32 (subsecs. 701–3.)

Nevada: State Constitution, Art. XIX, Secs. 1–6.

Table 3.1 *(continued)*

New Mexico: State Constitution, Art. IV, Sec. 1.
North Dakota: State Constitution, Art. III, Secs. 1–10, Chap. 40–12.
Ohio: State Constitution, Art. II, Sec. I; Art. XVIII, Sec. 4.
Oklahoma: State Constitution, Art. V. Secs. 1–8.
Oregon: State Constitution, Art. IV, Sec. 1, Chaps. 250–51.
South Dakota: State Constitution, Art. III, Sec. 1; Chaps. 9–20; Title 2, Chap. 2–1.
Utah: State Constitution, Art. VI, Sec. 1; Chap. 11, Sec. 20–11.
Washington: State Constitution, Amendments 7, 30, 36; Art. II, Sec. 1; Chap. 29.79.
Wyoming: State Constitution, Art. III, Sec. 52.

[a] Percentage of total vote in preceding gubernatorial election.
[b] Percentage of votes cast in last general election, unless otherwise specified.
[c] Percentage of total vote in preceding election for secretary of state.
[d] Percentage of total vote in preceding gubernatorial election.
[e] Percentage of total population.
[f] Percentage of electors, based on last gubernatorial election.
[g] Percentage of votes cast in last general election for officers receiving highest vote.
[h] Signatures from two-thirds of the election districts.
[i] Signatures from fifteen counties.
[j] More than one-quarter of the signatures may not come from one county.
[k] Signatures from one-third of the counties.
[l] Five percent of the signatures must come from two-fifths of the counties.
[m] Signatures from two-thirds of the counties.
[n] Signatures from one-half of the counties.
[o] Signatures from a majority of the counties.
[p] Legislature holds hearings but may not change or remove from ballot.
[q] Changed in 1981.
[r] Percentage of total vote in preceding presidential election.
[s] Percentage of qualified electors.
[t] Signatures from one-half of the election districts.
[u] Signatures from two-fifths of the counties.
[v] Signaturees from three-quarters of the counties.
[w] In the preceding election.
[x] At least 30 percent of the votes cast at election.
[y] At least 35 percent of the votes cast at election.
[z] At least 33 percent of the votes cast at election.
[aa] No repeal for two years.
[bb] Time before next general election, unless otherwise specified.
[cc] After legislature convenes.
[dd] Constitutional amendments only.
[ee] After governor's proclamation.
[ff] More than one-half of the signatures may not come from one county.
[gg] Number of days after the adjournment of the legislative session in which referendum petitions may be filed.
[hh] After statute has become law.
[ii] After signature of governor.
[jj] After final passage of article.
[kk] Constitutional amendments must be approved by voters at two elections.
[ll] At least 40 percent of the votes cast at election.
[mm] "Yes" means that an explicit mention was made in either the constitution or the codes.
[nn] Several states have no official voter's handbook but require by law that petitioners publish the text of their initiative in newspapers of general circulation in every county at least thirty days before the election.
[oo] State publishes or encourages the publication of the text of each initiative in newspapers of general circulation before the election.
[pp] Constitutional amendment texts provided in sample ballots.
[qq] Voter's handbook was repealed in 1974; state now publishes text of initiatives in newspapers of general circulation.

precondition for placement on the ballot is a petition signed by the number of voters established by law. Signature thresholds are intended to keep the ballot free of frivolous or unreasonably narrow propositions. In every state the number of signatures required to qualify a petition is either a percentage of the total vote cast in the preceding general election or a percentage of votes cast in a previous election for a particular office, usually that of governor. Signature requirements range from a low of 2 percent of the voting-age population in North Dakota to a high of 15 percent of the gubernatorial vote in the preceding election in Wyoming. The median signature requirement is 8 percent of those who voted for governor in the preceding election. The fact that states have set their signature threshold requirements in percentage terms rather than as a set number of valid signatures has affected the practice of direct legislation in the United States. The Swiss constitution calls for a fixed number; as a result, as the Swiss population grows, it should become easier to meet the minimum signature requirement. The consequences of using percentages as thresholds are examined in greater detail below, but these can be briefly summarized here. When the initiative was first established in California, for example, the reformers typically set a percentage of the previous gubernatorial vote as their threshold. In California it was 8 percent, which in 1914 would have been a little over thirty thousand names. Under the Swiss system this would have been the permanent standard. But because the threshold was percentage-based in California, it increased along with the state's population, so that it now takes more than five hundred thousand valid signatures to qualify a consitutional initiative.

Roughly half of the states also require signatures to be geographically distributed. Such distribution requirements are largely motivated by a desire not to allow one urban area in a state to set the agenda in initiatives and referendums. In Massachusetts, for example, no more than 25 percent of the signatures may come from any one county. Almost uniformly, states have stipulated that only registered voters may sign petitions to place initiatives and referendums on the ballot. One notable exception was Colorado, which until very recently allowed all adult citizens to sign petitions. This made the task of signature validation virtually impossible. The Colorado law was amended in 1980 to establish that only registered voters could qualify as petition signers. North Dakota is now the only state that provides that all citizens may sign initiative petitions.

Do low signature thresholds foster increased use of the initiative and referendum and high signature thresholds restrict use? The most frequently cited answer to this question is found in an article by Charles M. Price: "Obviously, there appears to be little relationship between the number of initiatives qualifying and the stringency of a state's qualifying procedures. Indeed, if anything, the results seem to go the other direction, i.e., the tougher a state's qualifying procedures, the more initiatives that tend to get qualified." [3] Price's conclusion that no relationship exists between the stringency of state signature requirements and the number of measures qualifying for the ballot is erroneous. A more thorough analysis demonstrates that the states with the lowest signature thresholds have the highest number of initiatives and popular referendums, while the states with the most restrictive signature thresholds have the lowest number of measures reaching the ballot (see table 3.2).

The seven states with the most restrictive signature requirements are, with the exception of Arizona, among the states with the fewest measures placed on the ballot via petition. Conversely, states such as North Dakota, California, and Oregon, which are among the least stringent states in the number of signatures required, are among the states with the largest number of measures placed on the ballot via petition. Clearly, high signature thresholds will generally limit the number of initiatives qualifying for the ballot, and low thresholds will likely mean that greater numbers of initiatives will qualify.[4]

The statistical relationship between signature thresholds and the number of initiatives and popular referendums qualifying for the ballot is essentially curvilinear. When all initiative and referendum measures placed on the ballot by petition are analyzed, the regression model provides a close fit, with more than one-third of the variance explained. The regression analysis also indicates that the relationship between signature threshold and the number of measures on the ballot is stronger for initiatives than for popular referendums. At the same signature threshold, the number of expected referendums is nine fewer than the number of expected initiatives. Another independent variable that helps to explain the number of initiatives on the ballot is region. At the same signature threshold during this recent period, states in the West averaged about six more initiatives than did states in the rest of the country.[5] In summary, the relationship between signature threshold levels and the number of measures qualifying for the ballot is strong and statistically significant.

In theory, only issues with widespread appeal will be able to meet a signature requirement in the 8–10 percent range. A lower threshold will probably result in an increased number of propositions submitted to the voters, as has been the case in North Dakota.[6] By the same token, a threshold higher than 8 percent will restrict ballot access. Previous studies make clear that most persons who sign petitions do not read the petitions that they are signing and may not even be in favor of the specific proposition that they are petitioning to place on the ballot. Instead, they are more generally in favor of "letting the people vote."[7] This tendency to sign petitions in ignorance is discussed later in this chapter.

It is frequently assumed that high signature thresholds serve to keep off the ballot those initiatives that are frivolous or lacking in widespread appeal. This assumption can be tested by asking whether states with high signature requirements also have higher initiative passage rates. The presumption is that in states where there are high thresholds, those measures that make it onto the ballot are more likely to be acceptable to voters. In states where

Table 3.2

STRINGENCY OF SIGNATURE REQUIREMENTS AND NUMBER OF INITIATIVES AND REFERENDUMS
QUALIFYING FOR BALLOT, 1950–80

| | Signature Requirements | | | |
	Statutory Initiative	*Constitutional Initiative*	*Popular Referendum*	*Initiatives and Popular Referendums since 1950*
North Dakota	2%	4%	2%	67
Maryland			3	12
California	5	8	5	48
Colorado	5	5	5	39
Kentucky			5	0
Massachusetts	5	5	2	18
Missouri	5	8	5	16
Montana	5	10	5	30
South Dakota	5	10	5	14
Ohio	6	10	. 6	17
Oregon	6	8	4	52
Nebraska	7	10	5	14
Arkansas	8	10	6	27
Florida		8		2
Illinois		8	10	3
Michigan	8	10	5	24
Oklahoma	8	15	5	28
Washington	8		4	51
Alaska	10		10	12
Arizona	10	15	5	63
Idaho	10		10	6
Maine	10		10	7
New Mexico			10	2
Nevada	10	10	10	12
Utah	10		10	8
Wyoming	15		15	0
Median	8%	10%	5%	

Sources: The numbers of initiatives and referendums on the ballots since 1950 were obtained from Graham, *A Compilation of Statewide Initiative Proposals on Ballots through 1976,* and from correspondence or interviews with election officials in every state except Maryland. The Maryland data were provided by David Warner, Maryland Legislative Research Office, 24 May 1982. The signature requirements were taken from the relevant sections of the state constitutions or election codes, except for North Dakota, where the required ten thousand signatures equaled less than 2 percent of the 1970 voting-age population. For specific sections see the source listings for table 3.1.

Notes: The table includes all twenty-six states that have the direct or indirect statutory or constitutional initiative or the popular referendum.

Twelve of the states listed provide a slightly lower signature threshold for statutory initiatives than for constitutional initiatives. Eight of the states have a lower threshold for popular referendums than for either form of initiative. In none of the states is there a low threshold for one type of measure and high thresholds for the others. For example, North Dakota imposes a 2 percent threshold for statutory initiatives and popular referendums, and the requirement for constitutional initiatives is only slightly higher at 4 percent. At the other end of the list, Wyoming imposes a 15 percent threshold for statutory initiatives and for popular referendums.

For each state the signature threshold levels are given for each direct legislation type. The states are arranged from less stringent to more stringent thresholds for the statutory initiative, when it is available, since statutory initiatives have been the most frequently used form of direct legislation.

measures are allowed easier access to the ballot, voters may have to reject more of them as narrow or irresponsible.

In states with minimum signature thresholds at or below 8 percent, initiatives that have appeared on the ballot since 1950 have had about one chance in three of approval (35 percent passed). Initiatives in states with higher minimum signature requirements have had about one chance in two of approval (47 percent passed). This relationship between signature thresholds at 10 percent and above and voter approval may be the result of reduced voter fatigue and negativism as a result of fewer initiatives on the ballot, or it may be that initiatives in high-threshold states are generally more acceptable to voters. In either case, the signature threshold plays a role in the success rate.

Legislative Review, Subject Limitations, and Prescribed Format

In states that have the indirect initiative, the legislature may act on a popular petition before submitting it to the voters. In most states, however, the legislature cannot intervene in the initiative process. For example, California requires that the legislature hold hearings on proposed statutes and constitutional amendments after they have been certified for the ballot, but the legislature may not stop the proposition from appearing on the ballot. For a constitutional amendment to appear on the Massachusetts ballot via the initiative procedure, the proposal must receive an affirmative vote of one-fourth of the legislature for two consecutive sessions prior to its submittal to the voters.

Statewide initiatives typically are decided in general elections. Some states allow initiatives on the primary election ballots, and some provide for special elections to decide initiatives or popular referendums. In all states, voting for initiatives, like voting for candidates, is by registered voters in person on election day. During the coming years, however, there may be increased pressure for mail ballots or for the kind of televote process described in chapter 1.

Mail ballots have been used in local elections in California, most notably San Diego's special election in May 1981. The San Diego vote concerned a proposed $224 million convention center. Ballots were mailed to 430,211 city residents who were registered voters, and 261,433 residents returned them, generally by mail. The latter figure represents a response rate of more than double the normal turnout in municipal special elections. In addition to high turnout, advocates of mail-ballot elections argue that the process is less expensive by at least 20 percent and that the election can be held more quickly. Elected officials already prefer special elections on controversial issues, at least partly to avoid having to take a stand that may alienate some supporters. Perhaps mail-ballot elections, which are less expensive and have a high response rate, will become part of state-level initiative politics during the 1980s.

Most of the states that provide for popular referendums restrict the subject matter of legislation that may be referred to the voters; only Arkansas, Idaho, and Nevada do not have such restrictions. Most commonly, emergency legislation and appropriations are exempted from the referendum. Also, slightly less than half of the states with the initiative restrict the subject matter open to popular vote. The most common restrictions are that initiatives must cover only a single subject and that they must not concern the judiciary.

Can the initiative be used to appropriate funds from general tax revenues? In California, the initiative has normally been used to create agencies to be financed by fees imposed on those directly benefited. But more recently initiatives have proposed agencies whose programs would be financed from general tax revenues. The California state constitution would appear to conflict with such initiatives, since it requires that state legislators consider the competing demands for limited state revenues. In the wake of Proposition 13, as groups press for their programs, this will be an important area of judicial decision making.

Other Limitations

California presents an interesting case study of how the process of direct legislation has been modified by changes in constitutional provisions and the election code, as well as by judicial decisions. Many of California's procedural changes arose in the 1940s, when pension and retirement schemes were particularly prevalent. Three of these changes — the use of petitions for one election only, restriction of initiatives to a single subject, and the stipulation that individuals cannot be appointed to office via initiatives — are of particular interest.

In California, signatures on petitions that fail to qualify for one general election cannot be used in the next general election. Circulators failed to meet the signature threshold in 1940; however, because of the low turnout in the 1942 gubernatorial election, the number of signatures gathered in 1940 would have been sufficient to meet the threshold for 1944. The state supreme court blocked this attempt, however, stating that the proponents would have to circulate new petitions to qualify for the 1944 ballot.[8]

California's provision restricting initiatives to a single subject resulted from a 1948 "pension bill of rights" initiative.[9] Among the subjects covered in this initiative were gambling, state senate reapportionment, retirement pensions, fish and game, and surface mining. This omnibus proposal, containing more than twenty thousand words, met the signature requirement; but the state supreme court decided that it constituted a revision of the state constitution rather than an amendment to it and was therefore unconstitutional.[10] A "single-subject rule" constitutional amendment was subsequently adopted prohibiting such multisubject initiatives. The standard for determining whether an initiative meets the single-subject rule was laid down in the case of *Perry* v. *Jordan,* where the court ruled that all parts of the initiative must be reasonably germane.[11]

The California constitution also prohibits naming any individual to an office by initiative, and a 1964 legislative constitutional amendment prohibits mentioning any private corporation by name in a proposed constitutional amendment.[12] The prohibition against naming individuals to office by initiative resulted from the passage in 1948 of a pension plan initiative that removed the incumbent director of the State Department of Social Welfare and designated his successor by name. That initiative was repealed by another one adopted as a constitutional amendment in the 1949 special election. The prohibition against referring to private corporations by name in a proposed constitutional amendment was a reaction to a 1964 initiative that proposed both a state lottery and a specific corporation, the American Sweepstake Corporation, to administer it. Not only was this proposition defeated by a 70–30 margin but in the same election California voters approved a constitutional amendment, proposed by the legislature, that prohibited mentioning any private corporation by name in initiatives. By adopting this legislative proposal, the voters not only rejected the lottery but also made unconstitutional any future propositions identifying particular corporations.

Vote Necessary for Passage and Means of Future Amendment

As I will discuss fully in chapter 5, sometimes as many as 25 percent of those who turn out to vote for candidates in a statewide election do not vote on the state propositions on the ballots. Perhaps in response to this tendency, six states have initiated special requirements for passage beyond approval by a simple majority of those voting on the proposition. In Massachusetts, Nebraska, and Washington, not only must there be more affirmative votes than negative notes but the the affirmative votes cannot be less than 30 percent, 35 percent, and 33 percent, respectively, of those who turn out to vote. Idaho's requirement is a majority of the number of votes cast for governor, and Maine requires an affirmative vote of a majority of those who turn out. Wyoming has the most unusual requirement, mandating an affirmative vote equal to at least 50 percent of the total vote in the preceding general election. The apparent rationale for a requirement such as this one is to preclude the voters in a low-turnout election from deciding statewide propositions unless the affirmative vote is as high as it would have been in a higher-turnout election.

Majority rule is a widely accepted principle of democratic government. A majority is normally 50 percent plus one, of either the total vote cast or the total number of citizens. The theoretical basis for majority rule is that it is an easily recognizable means to resolve political contests, it is commonly accepted in practice, it maximizes the legitimacy of the decision, and it constitutes an expression of the popular will. While majority rule is a widely accepted democratic election rule, not all democratic decisions result from this rule. In most candidate elections in the United States, for instance, only a plurality is needed to win an election; elected officials may win with less than 50 percent of the vote if they receive more votes than their opponents. Nevertheless, many citizens consider majority rule to be fundamental to democratic government.

Despite the theoretical clarity of simple majority rule, some states require more than a simple majority affirmative vote (usually 55–75 percent) on a referendum in order for it to be approved. The rationale for such rules is that some referendums should require an unmistakably popular and unequivocal verdict. Such extraordinary majority requirements occur most commonly in referendums on bonded indebtedness. At the local level, extraordinary majorities have been required to amend a home-rule charter or to incorporate a town. These requirements have been challenged as violating the equal protection clause of the Fourteenth Amendment; however, the U.S. Supreme Court has ruled that extraordinary majority requirements are not inherently unconstitutional.[13]

The Supreme Court has also left its mark on the direct legislation process by striking down the requirement that only taxpayers be allowed to vote in school elections.[14] Prior to this decision in 1970, fourteen states limited suffrage to "taxpayers." In one Louisiana city this meant that 60 percent of the registered voters were ineligible.[15] The Supreme Court rejected the rationale that only taxpayers have a stake in bond elections.

One indication of the distrust of legislatures felt by many proponents of initiatives is that roughly half of the states restrict the ability of the legislature to amend statutory initiatives. In many cases, the amendment must be subjected to a popular vote. Further, despite the fact that governors are generally provided the veto power over legislative statutes, no provision exists for a gubernatorial veto over statutory initiatives. In most states, successful initiatives are automatically implemented within ninety days of the election (assuming that there are no pending legal challenges to the initiatives).

THE COURTS AND DIRECT LEGISLATION

Opponents of the initiative and referendum have always resorted to the courts either to exclude the initiative and referendum entirely or to declare certain outcomes unconstitutional. As early as 1912, the process of direct legislation was challenged as being inconsistent with a republican form of government and therefore unconstitutional.

The Republican Guarantee Clause

The U.S. Constitution guarantees to every state a republican form of government: "The United States shall guarantee to every State in this Union a Republican Form of Government, and shall protect each of them against Invasion; and on Application of the Legislature, or of the Executive (when the Legislature cannot be convened), against domestic Violence." [16] Based upon the assumption that the initiative and referendum are inconsistent with a republican form of government, the Pacific Telephone and Telegraph Company refused to pay an annual 2 percent licensing tax that had been authorized by a 1906 Oregon initiative. A suit brought against the company by the state of Oregon resulted in the landmark U.S. Supreme Court decision of *Pacific States Telephone and Telegraph Company* v. *Oregon.* [17] Relying on a previous decision, *Luther* v. *Burden,* the Court declared the constitutionality of direct legislation to be a political question best resolved by the Congress. [18]

> Under this article of the constitution it rests with congress to decide what government is the established one in a State. For, as the United States guarantee to each State a republican government, congress must necessarily decide what government is established in the State before it can determine whether it is republican or not. And when the senators and representatives of a State are admitted into the councils of the Union, the authority of the government under which they are appointed, as well as its republican character, is recognized by the proper constitutional authority. And its decision is binding on every other department of the government, and could not be questioned in a judicial tribunal. [19]

By defining the *Pacific States* case as a political question, the Court avoided being forced to decide whether it felt that the initiative and referendum were appropriate forms of representative government. While the Supreme Court did not comment on the merits of the argument that the initiative and referendum are organs of direct democratic government rather than representative government, the decision in the *Pacific States* case has been widely interpreted to mean that initiatives and referendums fall within the confines of the U.S. Constitution. [20]

More recently, opinions from state and federal courts have indicated a judicial deference towards direct legislation. An example of this is found in the language of a recent opinion of the California Supreme Court about the 1911 amendment to the state's constitution: "Drafted in light of the theory that all power of government ultimately resides in the people, the amendment speaks to the initiative and referendum, not as a right granted to the people, but as a power reserved by them. . . . *It has long been our judicial policy to apply a liberal construction to this power* wherever it is challenged in order that the right be not improperly annulled. If doubts can reasonably be resolved in favor of the use of this reserve power, courts will preserve it." [21]

The U.S. Supreme Court has also recently stated its view on the direct legislation process and more specifically the California experience with the initiative. In the case of *James* v. *Valtierra* the Court concluded that "California's entire history demonstrates the repeated use of the referendums to give citizens a voice on questions of public policy. . . . Provisions for referendums demonstrate devotion to democracy. . . ."[22]

The Equal Protection and Due Process Clauses of the Fourteenth Amendment

While the courts have sung the praises of direct legislation, on several occasions they have found some provisions of the implementation of direct legislation in violation of Fourteenth Amendment protections. In *Hunter* v. *Erickson,* for instance, the Court ruled unconstitutional the Akron, Ohio, city ordinance that prohibited "the city council from implementing any ordinance dealing with racial, religious, or ancestral discrimination in housing without the approval of the majority of voters of Akron."[23] The explicit racial classification and the recognition that the public referendum placed a special burden on minorities were two of the reasons why the Court declared this form of direct legislation unconstitutional. Another area of judicial intervention has been that of state or local provisions restricting voting participation on ballot propositions and the question of extraordinary majorities (requiring an affirmative vote of more than 50 percent of the total).

Prior to the 1870s, referendums and bond elections were generally decided by a simple plurality. But the problems of municipal indebtedness were exacerbated by the depression of 1873, and many localities had to default on their bonds. Subsequently, many states amended their constitutions to establish debt ceilings and extraordinary majority requirements.[24] To date, the courts have not been willing to abolish extraordinary majority requirements, even though these requirements have been challenged on the grounds that they violate the equal protection clause of the Fourteenth Amendment, that they establish a special burden on proponents of propositions, and that they may contradict the one-man, one-vote principle.

In a decision quite distinct from subsequent federal court decisions, however, the California Supreme Court in 1970 declared unconstitutional the two-thirds majority requirement for city, county, or school district general obligations bonds.[25] After recognizing the historical explanation for extraordinary majorities and the adverse financial position of local governments in the late 1800s and early 1900s, the court found that the two-thirds requirement meant that the voters who opposed the proposition had disproportionate power. Finding such a classification discriminatory and unrelated to any "compelling state interest," the court held the requirement unconstitutional.[26]

In a similar case, the West Virginia Supreme Court relied on the equal protection clause to declare unconstitutional the state's 60 percent requirement for education bonds.[27] But on appeal to the U.S. Supreme Court, the West Virginia decision was overturned.[28] In a seven-to-two decision, Chief Justice Burger, writing for the majority, argued that the one-man, one-vote principle did not apply in this case because the 60 percent requirement did not dilute the voting power of any geographic location.[29] While the U.S. Supreme Court agreed that extraordinary majorities made it "more difficult for some kinds of governmental action to be taken," such difficulties did not constitute a violation of the equal protection clause because the 60 percent requirement did not discriminate against any identifiable class.[30]

In reaching decisions on the constitutionality of extraordinary and concurrent majority voting requirements, the U.S. Supreme Court has distinguished between elections for legislative officials and referendums.[31] In the case of elections for legislative office, the Court has adopted a one-man, one-vote rule, the logical outcome of which is a strict majority rule.[32] In sharp contrast to the legislative election decisions, however, the referendum decisions have legitimized voting rules inconsistent with the one-man, one-vote or simple majority requirements. In a 1976 decision the Supreme Court gave the reasons for this distinction:

> The equal protection principles applicable in gauging the fairness of an election involving the choice of legislative representatives are of limited relevance, however, in analyzing the propriety of recognizing distinctive voter interests in a "single-shot" referendum. In a referendum, the expression of voter will is direct, and there is no need to assure that the voters' views will be adequately represented through their representatives in the legislature. The policy impact of a referendum is also different in kind from the impact of choosing representatives — instead of sending legislators off to the state capitol to vote on a multitude of issues, the referendum puts one discrete issue to the voters.[33]

The central concept connecting these referendum decisions is a concern that individual, group, or community interests could be adversely affected by a simple majority rule.[34] For most referendums and bond elections, however, the courts have struck down restrictions on who can vote.[35] Thus, the courts desire that the electorate be diverse, while at the same time they are willing to accept local decisions about how large a majority is required to decide a referendum issue or bond proposal. The most recent concurrent majorities case recognizes this same desire to protect the identifiable interests of rural residents in a consolidation dispute. In a unanimous decision, the U.S. Supreme Court dismissed the argument for a simple majority of the total vote cast and retained instead the requirement that a majority in both the city and the noncity areas must approve the consolidation.[36]

In addition to these decisions on the equal protection question of the extraordinary majority cases, the Supreme Court has been asked to decide the constitutionality of a California provision requiring approval in a local referendum before a state public body can develop a federally financed low-rent housing project.[37] A three-judge appeals court had declared the mandatory referendum unconstitutional because it denied the plaintiffs equal protection. As in *Gordon* v. *Lance,* Chief Justice Burger dismissed the equal protection claim.

The issue of the legitimacy of referendums as instruments of public policy arose again in *City of Eastlake* v. *Forrest City Enterprises, Inc.*[38] Here the city charter had been amended to require that changes in land use agreed to by the city council be approved by a 55 percent vote in a referendum. A real estate developer sued, seeking to have the charter amendment declared invalid because it was an unconstitutional delegation of legislative power and therefore a violation of his due process rights. Chief Justice Burger, writing again for the majority, dismissed the argument that referendums are delegation of legislative authority by arguing that the real delegation flows from the people to the legislature and that the people can reserve to themselves the power to decide matters of public policy. Burger then dismissed the due process claims by arguing that the referendum process "ensures that all the people of a community will have a voice in a decision which may lead to large expenditures of local governmental funds for increased public services."[39]

THE FREE SPEECH ISSUE IN PETITION CIRCULATION AND CAMPAIGN SPENDING CASES

The courts have also been called upon to assess the constitutionality both of specific direct legislation procedures in cases involving signature collection in shopping centers and of restricting campaign contributions and overall spending in ballot proposition campaigns. In 1970, in *Diamond* v. *Bland,* the California Supreme Court ruled that petition circulators could not be denied access to the Inland Center, a San Bernardino shopping complex.[40] Citing preceding cases in which shopping centers had been ruled quasi-public, the California court decided that anyone opening private premises to the public must allow such public activities as the circulation of petitions. The U.S. Supreme Court refused to hear the appeal of this decision, and petition circulation is now commonplace in California shopping centers.

As will be shown in chapters 7 and 8, direct legislation campaigns are among the best-financed statewide elections in the United States. Campaign spending on ballot measures is often higher than on statewide races for the U.S. Senate or the governorship. Frequently, one side substantially outspends the opposition, raising questions about the fairness of the outcome or the integrity of the electoral process. The state and federal courts have been called on to decide several cases arising out of this dispute. In so doing, they have established a limited scope of state intervention in this area, especially when it interferes with expression of political speech.

The most important ruling in the area of campaign financing has been the decision in *Buckley* v. *Valeo*. The U.S. Supreme Court upheld the Federal Election Campaign Act's limitation of one thousand dollars on contributions to candidates for federal office but invalidated restrictions on expenditures by or on behalf of candidates. The Court held that the contribution and expenditure of money for political expression were the equivalent of pure speech. Hence, statutory limits on that speech must come under the Court's strict view, and expenditure ceilings impose significantly more severe restrictions on protected political expression than do limitations on financial contributions. The Court argued that a restriction on expenditures "necessarily reduces the quantity of expression by restricting the number of issues discussed, the depth of their exploration, and the size of the audience reached." [41] Construed narrowly, *Buckley* applied only to candidate elections; in fact, the Court drew a distinction between candidates and referendums.

The *Buckley* decision has proven very important in the subsequent decisions on the constitutionality of campaign spending regulation in direct legislation. The California Supreme Court adhered to the structure of the *Buckley* decision when it decided to invalidate expenditure limitations on campaigns to pass ballot propositions [42] and qualify them. [43]

Two recent U.S. Supreme Court decisions further clarify the scope of permissible regulation in this area. In *First National Bank of Boston* v. *Bellotti,* the Court overturned a Massachusetts statute prohibiting corporations from making any expenditure or contribution, directly or indirectly, to influence the vote on ballot measures. [44] Here again the Court saw the regulation as infringing on fundamental First Amendment rights and therefore ruled the statute unconstitutional. Using a similar rationale, the Court overturned a California Supreme Court decision permitting a $250 contribution limitation in local initiative campaigns. [45] Here again the value of free speech took precedence.

Throughout these cases the U.S. Supreme Court has taken a consistent stand on the constitutionality of initiatives and referendums. The Court is not willing to assume that initiatives and referendums are inherently unrepresentative or prone to bias. As Justice Black stated in *James* v. *Valtierra,* "provisions for referendums demonstrate devotion to democracy, not to bias, discrimination, or prejudice." [46]

THE WILLINGNESS OF THE COURTS TO DECLARE SUCCESSFUL INITIATIVES UNCONSTITUTIONAL

While the courts have accepted the constitutionality of direct legislation in general, they have not hesitated to declare a particular initiative in conflict with the state or federal constitution. Perhaps for that reason, successful initiatives are almost always challenged in the courts. From 1960 to 1980 six of the ten initiatives approved by the California electorate were struck down in whole or in part by state or federal courts. In 1982 the California Supreme Court significantly cut back the power of a seventh successful initiative, the Jarvis-Gann property-tax initiative (Proposition 13). In two different opinions, the court ruled that the 1978 property-tax-cutting initiative's requirement of a two-thirds vote for new taxes does not apply to governmental entities that do not have the power to assess property taxes. Other cases are still pending on Proposition 13, the more recent appropriations limitation initiative, and the initiatives that passed in 1980 and 1982.[47] The courts have thus played a significant role in modifying the degree of implementation of all but three of the ten successful ballot initiatives in California's past twenty years. In addition, items of direct legislation concerned with school busing, capital punishment, and open housing in particular have fared poorly in the state and federal courts.[48] The legal decisions for the successful California initiatives, 1964–1979, are presented in Appendix A.

Perhaps the best-known judicial veto of an initiative occurred in 1964 after California voters approved Proposition 14, repeal of the Rumford Act. The initiative was worded as follows: "SALES AND RENTALS OF RESIDENTIAL REAL PROPERTY. Initiative constitutional amendment. Prohibits State, subdivision, or agency thereof from denying, limiting, or abridging right of any person to decline to sell, lease, or rent residential real property to any person as he chooses. Prohibition not applicable to property owned by State or its subdivisions; property acquired by eminent domain; or transient accommodations by hotels, motels, and similar public places."[49] Proposition 14 passed by a wide margin, with 65 percent of the voters deciding in effect to repeal open housing. As with most successful initiatives, the outcome was subsequently challenged in the courts. The California Supreme Court ruled that the proposition violated the equal protection clause of the Fourteenth Amendment and was therefore unconstitutional. Further, the state court found that the intent of Proposition 14 was to place state authorization behind private discrimination. The U.S. Supreme Court upheld the decision of the California Supreme Court, agreeing that Proposition 14 violated the equal protection clause.[50] The decision in this case established the principle that in a conflict between a constitutional protection and a popular vote, the constitutional protection prevails.

THE ROLE OF STATE AND LOCAL GOVERNMENTS

Many states require the secretary of state, the attorney general, and county election officials to become actively involved in administering the process of direct legislation. All states except Maine prescribe the format for initiative propositions and for the description of the initiative on signature petitions.

Proponents of initiatives are generally required to file with the secretary of state the complete text of the proposition, often before any signatures are collected. Also, to maximize fairness and honesty, the attorney general is often required to give the proposition its title. Even when the attorney general titles initiative propositions, however, the result can be misleading. In 1972, for instance, California's attorney general titled the environmentally oriented proposition on air pollution "The Pollution Initiative." In the ensuing campaign, opponents exploited the theme: "Vote no on Pollution; vote no on Proposition 9." In truth, a vote against the proposition was a vote for pollution, but the title of the initiative played into the hands of the opponents.[51] In states that do not require a preliminary filing, the petition initiators are generally allowed to title and describe their own propositions.

The procedural requirement of a preliminary filing protects individuals who sign petitions by guaranteeing that the petition they sign is the one to be voted on. After the filing, no changes can be made in the proposition. In a recent case in Dade County, Florida, proponents of a tax-cutting initiative omitted a key word, thereby reducing taxes by 99.95 percent rather than by the intended 50 percent.[52] The mistake was discovered after the signatures had been collected, and the court ruled that the initiative must be voted on as written. Miami voters defeated the proposal overwhelmingly.

In some states, either election officials or the state legislature may assign propositions positions on the ballot. Even in states such as California — where the law mandates that bonds appear first, legislative proposals next, and popular initiatives last — the election official or state legislature may specify which bond proposal is designated Proposition 1, for example. Some academic research, as well as the conventional wisdom among campaign firms, indicates that having the designation "Proposition 1" improves the chances of passage.[53]

But ballot location is significant for all measures, not just the first one. Drawing from data provided by the Office of the California Secretary of State, I have compared the success rates for ballot locations 1 through 25 (see table 3.3).[54]

The relationship between ballot location and passage is negative and statistically strong — that is, propositions appearing later on the ballot are less likely to pass. For each successive ballot location there is a decrease of 0.85 percent in the likelihood of passage. Some ballot locations appear to be lucky — notably numbers 7, 20, 23, and 25 — while others seem to be unlucky — notably numbers 5, 18, and 24.

Observers of California politics have long noted the greater success of those propositions appearing earlier on the ballot. Campaign consultants Herbert Baus and William Ross argue that in 1966 the secretary of state designated as "Proposition 1" a measure that enabled public employee retirement funds to be invested in common stocks because his reelection might be helped if the public employees were happy.[55]

Table 3.3

BALLOT LOCATION AND PASSAGE

Ballot Location	Number of Observations	Observed Percentage of Success	Predicted Percentage of Success
1	45	67%	63%
2	45	62	62
3	45	67	61
4	45	53	60
5	45	44	60
6	44	59	59
7	43	74	58
8	42	67	57
9	40	63	56
10	39	51	55
11	36	47	54
12	32	59	54
13	30	47	53
14	29	52	52
15	29	41	51
16	26	58	50
17	26	46	49
18	21	29	48
19	18	39	48
20	16	63	47
21	12	42	46
22	11	46	45
23	10	60	44
24	8	25	43
25	7	57	42

Source: March Fong Eu, "A Study of Ballot Measures: 1884–1980" (Sacramento: Office of the California Secretary of State, 1980, Photocopy).

More generally, however, the order of ballot propositions is determined by the order in which the propositions are qualified. This decision rule for election officials operates in cases where initiatives appear before legislative referendums, as in Washington, and in cases where initiatives follow bonds and legislative referendums, as is now the case in California.

John Mueller's research on patterns of ballot proposition voting confirms the popularly held notion that voter decisions on propositions are affected by the propositions that precede them.[56] Mueller characterizes this as an election mood. Initiative proponents often attempt to exploit voter moods. Baus and Ross present the example of a 1958 right-to-work initiative which labor feared. In order to establish a negative voter mood, "labor moved with speed and cunning to qualify a maudlin [*sic*] proposition which would have imposed a state income tax of up to 49 percent."[57] Labor was successful in qualifying its proposition ahead of the right-to-work proposition and was assigned position 17, making right-to-work Proposition 18. Labor guessed correctly, as business fought the tax measure intensively, reminding voters again and again to vote no on 17. Meanwhile labor forgot its stalking horse and built upon the "no" mood to defeat Proposition 18.

Most states impose a deadline for submitting the completed petitions to county or state officials for certification and counting. These deadlines are motivated by the time constraints of signature validation and ballot preparation. In all but six states the petitions for referendums must be submitted within ninety days of the adjournment of the state legislature; even more restrictive deadlines exist in Illinois (within seventy-eight days) and in Idaho, Maryland, and Utah (within sixty days). In California, because the deadline is much less restrictive for initiatives than for referendums, many groups choose the initiative as the means to correct what they see as legislative errors.

The most difficult and expensive aspect of direct legislation for states and localities is petition signature validation, which in most states is handled by the county clerk or registrar. To ease the work load, some states require the proponents of the initiative to provide the number of the voting precinct for each person who has signed the petition; but because most voters do not know their precinct number, either volunteers or professional firms must complete this task. The work of the county clerk is complicated by the fact that he must not only validate voter registration for petition signatures but also prevent the counting of any multiple signatures. The county clerk of Los Angeles County currently estimates that it costs the county twenty-nine cents to validate each signature for which the precinct number is provided.[58] In 1978 California required nearly five hundred thousand valid signatures to qualify a constitutional initiative. The task of signature validation has recently become even more time-consuming in California, both because more initiatives were filed and circulated in the 1970s and early 1980s and because the number of required signatures has increased as the population has increased. Given these contraints, beginning with the 1978 election, California now makes only a random sample of petition signatures for valid voter registration. Overall, the Office of the California Secretary of State estimates that 8–8.5 percent of all signatures are examined.[59]

The secretary of state qualifies an initiative or referendum upon certification from the county clerks that the signature requirement has been met. The imposition of fees in order to get petitions considered has generally been ruled out to avoid restricting the use of the process to wealthy interests. An additional expense is incurred by nine states that publish a voter's handbook, mailed to the homes of registered voters three to four weeks before the election. California's secretary of state estimates that in her state these handbooks cost about $2 million per election for printing and postage.[60] While the format varies from state to state, these handbooks contain an official description of each proposition and, frequently, arguments prepared by proponents and opponents of each proposition. The arguments for and against the propositions are the opinions of the authors and are not checked for accuracy by any official agency. Frequently arguments in the handbook become issues in the ensuing campaign. For instance, the question of evidence for and against the effects of secondhand cigarette smoke on nonsmokers' health was debated both in the handbook and during the Proposition 5 anti-smoking initiative campaign. (The extent to which voters use the handbooks, as well as their format and readability, is discussed in chapter 7.)

Several states have no official voter's handbook but require that the petitioners publish the text of their initiative in newspapers of general circulation in every county at least thirty days before the election. Three states — Michigan, Missouri, and Ohio — bear the costs of publishing the texts of proposed initiatives in general-circulation newspapers. California has recently instituted a reform that may foster voter awareness: the legislative analyst is required to estimate the probable cost to the state of enforcement of the proposition, and this cost estimate is published in the voter's handbook. Analysis of this sort is intended to help the interested voter better understand the implications of his vote.

Even with a voter's handbook, the task of understanding propositions and deciding how to vote can be difficult, and many voters have become confused. Confusion on initiatives and referendums derives from at least three sources. First, propositions are often lengthy and written in technical or legal language. For instance, the 1976 farmworkers' initiative — a typically long and complicated proposition — required more than six double-column pages in fine print in the voter's handbook. The equally long and complicated law that it would have repealed was also printed in the handbook. Second, propositions may be written to disguise what a yes or no vote means. An example of this problem was the 1976 California nuclear initiative, where a yes vote meant in effect a no vote on the future development of nuclear power. (The problems of proposition complexity, length, and wording are explored in greater detail in chapter 7.) Finally, the nature of the issues themselves may be confusing, as in the case of regulation of nuclear power plants. Given these factors, many voters are understandably confused by ballot propositions. The voter's handbook is an effort by the state to lessen such confusion.

Many states also provide voters with information about the amounts spent by both sides in a direct legislation campaign. While this poses an additional cost to state government, it is usually justified in terms of the importance of letting voters know who is spending money on each side and in what amounts. In some states the spending levels on controversial propositions can rival or exceed the amounts spent on the governor's race. (The effects of spending on proposition contests are discussed in chapter 8.)

One final fiscal consideration for administering direct legislation is the option of allowing special elections for the express purpose of deciding initiatives. California provided such special elections in 1973 and 1979. Beyond the obvious costs of staffing the polling places are such expenses as validating signatures and preparing and distributing a special voter's handbook. The Office of the California Secretary of State estimates that the 1979 special election cost the state $6.7 million.[61]

CONCLUSIONS

Do initiatives and referendums provide for an expression of popular sovereignty or are they an additional tool in the hands of the special interests? This is a central issue in the debate over direct legislation. In this chapter I have provided evidence on the degree of open access that is part of the assumption of greater popular sovereignty accorded to direct legislation. A more complete assessment of the popular sovereignty issue must await the analysis of survey data in subsequent chapters. Based upon the evidence presented in this chapter, however, it is clear that in order for initiatives and referendums to meet signature thresholds, legal challenges, and campaign costs, their sponsors must have substantial political resources (money and manpower). Organized interests clearly have an advantage over most individuals in overcoming these hurdles. Thus, if a test for the popular sovereignty of initiatives and referendums is equal access in placing an issue on the ballot, the initiative and referendum fail.

Much of the litigation over the initiative and referendum discussed in this chapter is concerned with another persistent issue in the debate over direct legislation: Is the initiative and referendum's penchant for direct democracy consistent with the Constitution's prescription that we shall have a representative form of government? The courts, including the U.S. Supreme Court, have consistently ruled that the initiative and referendum are permissible under the U.S. Constitution. In other words, a mixture of direct and representative forms of government is constitutionally permissible at the subnational level. The courts have also addressed the question of popular sovereignty in direct legislation by ruling that a simple majority rule is not universally applicable. Thus, the people may decide an issue, but in some cases an affirmative decision may require an extraordinary majority, a position that some may consider inconsistent with popular sovereignty and political equality.

□□□□□□□□□□□□□□□□□□□□□□□□□□□

The Initiative Industry, the Petition Process, and the Increased Usage of Direct Legislation

n 1982, voters in American states voted on more initiatives than at any time since the Great Depression. As noted in chapter 1, the renewed interest in the initiative may be part of a widespread and growing distrust of government among citizens. More specifically, some critics claim that the flurry of initiative activity is related to public frustration with state legislatures. Recently, Patrick McGuigan, editor of Washington, D.C.'s *Initiative and Referendum Report,* described "voter frustration on both sides of the political spectrum, and in the middle too, with the non-responsiveness of legislatures." [1]

The experience of the 1970s teaches that the initiative can be the route to political fame and glory. But for Proposition 13 in California, few Americans would ever have heard of Howard Jarvis. Similarly, Paul Gann would have been at best a long shot for the U.S. Senate nomination from California had he not cosponsored Proposition 13 with Jarvis and then succeeded in sponsoring his spending limitation measure, the primary issue of the November 1979 special election. Aspiring politicians have used the initiative idea in noninitiative states as well. Gubernatorial candidates Al Quie of Minnesota and William Clements of Texas proposed adoption of the initiative as part of their successful campaigns.

In this chapter I examine the recent resurgence of initiative activity. All of the explanations for this increased usage are tested. Especially important to understanding the initiative process in the 1980s is the initiative industry, which makes money by assisting groups and interests in obtaining the necessary petition signatures, overcoming legal and procedural challenges, and then managing the campaign. In this chapter I describe the methods used by the initiative industry and assess the efforts of some states to restrict its power. I conclude with an analysis of the number and kinds of questions voted on and the success rate for different kinds of issues.

THE POLITICS OF GETTING AN INITIATIVE ON THE BALLOT

An initiative is drafted by the individual or group that wishes to see a particular proposition adopted. A review of recent California statewide propositions suggests at least three methods by which initiatives are drafted:

1. *The defeated-legislation method.* One of the most common ways to draft an initiative is to draw from pending or recently defeated legislative bills. The coastal zone initiative of 1972 was taken almost verbatim from legislation that had been introduced previously in the California legislature.[2]

2. *The public-hearing method.* While the original text of California's 1974 fair political practices initiative was the result of negotiations between Secretary of State Edmund G. Brown, Jr., the People's Lobby, and Common Cause, the proposed text of the proposition was the subject of sixty Common Cause public hearings throughout California. Thus, the political reform initiative was drafted in a manner consistent with the Common Cause penchant for open meetings and accessible decisionmakers.[3]

3. *The private-special-interest method.* If a group or interest has sufficient resources, it can employ a political consultant to draft its proposition. Many initiatives are prepared by special campaign consultants whose business is to draft a proposition with maximum chances of electoral success. Examples of such propositions are the 1972 farmworkers' initiative and the 1976 greyhound racing initiative.

While initiative advocates are not generally permitted to title their proposition, they can title the committee or group sponsoring the initiative, just as opponents may title their sponsoring group. Much thought is devoted to naming committees both pro and con. A sample from the 1978 elections would include Defend Our Children (California), Committee Against Tax Discrimination (Massachusetts), Citizens' Committee to Protect Our Land (Oregon), and Nebraskans for Freedom of Choice (Nebraska).

Clearly, many groups choose to title their campaign when titling their committee for or against a proposition; they also try to establish a broad appeal by cloaking themselves in an admired cause. The titles that groups choose may often be misleading. For instance, Alaskans for Litter Control and Recycling was in fact a group of bottlers and brewers who opposed an initiative to require a deposit on all beverage cans and bottles; similarly, Nebraskans for Freedom of Choice was a group of businesses opposed to an initiative for a mandatory deposit on beverage containers. By adopting titles such as these, opponents attempt either to diffuse the support of the proponents by confusing the issue or to establish their own support by redefining or distorting the issue. Committee names may also shield the true identity of committee members. By choosing a name like "Oregonians Opposed to . . ." or "Citizens Opposed to . . . ," the campaign committee attempts to communicate a broad-based opposition. Almost all of the money for the Oregonians Opposed to Nonsupervised Dentistry came from the American Dental Association; a more accurate title for the group would have been "American Dentists Opposed to Denturism." One might assume that the Citizens Opposed to a Nuclear Ban had originated in a town meeting; in reality, it was overwhelmingly composed of energy interests. Clearly, proponents and opponents of initiatives deliberately name their groups so as to maximize electoral support. How could one vote against common sense, litter control, freedom of choice, our land, or supervised dentistry?

Once the initiative has been drafted by one of these three means, it must next receive popular support in the form of petitions signed by citizens. A major hurdle for any initiative proponent is to collect enough signatures to qualify the proposal for the ballot. How is this done?

Meeting the Signature Requirements

Most successful California initiative petitions are placed on the ballot with the assistance of professional signature collectors, whose business is to help special-interest groups obtain a place on the ballot. Groups wishing to place issues on the ballot not only must meet the signature threshold but must do so within a specified time — generally between 90 and 120 days. In several states an "initiative industry" has developed to help groups overcome these hurdles. While some groups have been successful in placing measures on the ballot without professional assistance, the initiative industry is responsible for the more typically successful petition drives. Even the California State Employee Association (CSEA), which has over 100,000 members, employed a signature-gathering firm to place a proposition providing for increased benefits to public employees on the 1972 ballot.[4] Clearly, the leaders of the CSEA doubted that the membership would circulate and return petitions in sufficient numbers to qualify the proposition.[5]

The 1970s have witnessed a rapid growth in the number of firms engaged in signature collection. Until the 1970s, "the late Joe Robinson, a close ally of California's then-Secretary of State Frank Jordan, had a near-monopoly on the signature collection business in the state."[6] More recently, the industry has expanded to include other signature-collection firms.[7] Charles M. Price, after studying the California petition firms, summarized their organizational structures as follows: "Petition firms have networks of contacts (crew chiefs) in the major cities of California who, in turn, hire petition solicitors who are paid 25¢ per signature. The solicitors fan out to supermarkets, shopping centers, movie theater lines, or street corners. The usual advice to the professional petition pusher is to look for people who are moving slowly. F. G. Kimball has noted, 'The best all-time place for us (to gather signatures) was the King Tut exhibit.'"[8]

The paid signature collector employs a variety of approaches to obtain the maximum number of valid signatures with a minimum amount of effort. In the initial approach the circulator summarizes the initiative in the most appealing way possible: "Sign this petition and lower food costs!" or "Sign this petition and lower taxes!" In Price's study of petition firms, he learned that the experience of most "crew chiefs" is that most people will sign petitions. If people appear hesitant, "solicitors are told to emphasize that signing the petition does not mean the person agrees with the initiative; signing just helps get the measure on the ballot so that the public can have the right to vote." [9] There is, of course, no guarantee that the circulators' summaries of propositions are accurate. In 1972 former Secretary of State Edmund G. Brown, Jr., presented evidence at a legislative hearing that some professional circulators intentionally conceal the true content of an initiative:

> Here is a petition that was used to obtain signatures for Proposition 22. Now, as you can see, over the Attorney General's summary, which is at the top of the page, is inserted this card, which is called, very appropriately, a dodger card, and this card says, "For lower food prices." There were a number of these dodger cards. That was one that was used quite extensively. Then there was a pink card that also fit under the second page of the petition — this one talks about preventing inflated food prices. Then there was another dodger card that was originally used about the unfair secondary boycotts and that was abandoned because they felt it was not effective enough. [10]

Volunteer signature gatherers have also developed approaches to signature collection that raise questions about the extent to which the signer knows what he is signing. Because of the time constraints imposed upon signature collection, volunteers are often instructed not to waste time answering questions. Common Cause, self-described as an organization dedicated to citizen understanding of government, took shortcuts in explaining Proposition 9 during its 1974 efforts to qualify the Fair Political Practices Act. Kenneth L. Smith, the California executive director of Common Cause in 1974, describes the signature-gathering process as follows:

> The people out front were salespeople — pitchmen — their commission was a signature, and the fewer words they had to use, the greater their commission.
> Once at the table anyone who wished to read the document was ushered to the side and given a copy so as to not block the petition itself. Antagonists were ignored or asked to move on. . . . People with questions about the content were given information to read, but not discussion time from the workers. . . . The singular objective was 500,000 signatures in five months. Education on the issues would have to wait until after the measure was qualified. [11]

The practices of both volunteer and professional petition circulators lead to the same question: Do those citizens who sign petitions actually read what it is they are signing? The answer is generally no. Most people trust the petition circulator's description of the proposition to be accurate, and they desire to comply with the request for assistance. The *Los Angeles Times* report on signature collection for the 1980 rent initiative concluded that "voters who signed petitions rarely bothered to read what they were signing." Many of the circulators "misunderstood what it was they were asking people to sign." The petition circulators who understood the proposition "frequently kept silent when uninformed signers drew the wrong conclusion," and in some cases they "lied to voters about what the initiative was intended to do." [12] Social psychologists studying the process of signature solicitation have determined that both situational factors — how and where someone is approached — and inner convictions about the initial question predict the likelihood of signing. [13] Petition circulators in both the Common Cause and the farmworkers' cases framed the requests so as to maximize the likelihood of signing: "Want to stop corrupt politics?" and "Want to help the farm workers?" In an effort to play upon the conforming tendencies in most people, circulators also encourage quick signing rather than discussion.

Signature gathering has been prone to abuse in California. Use of the "dodger card," deceptive tactics, and illegal practices such as the employment of children to gather signatures have been part of the initiative process in California. [14] Abuses similar to these have led to restrictions on paid signature collection in Colorado, Idaho, Massachusetts, Ohio, South Dakota, and Washington. It is clear, however, that even when the signature collection procedures are not deceptive, many persons do not take the time to learn what they are signing.

One of the most blatant cases of deception and fraud in signature gathering occurred recently in Colorado. Proponents of a measure to legalize casino gambling submitted petitions on which signatures — including that of a Denver judge — had been falsified and the circulators' signatures had been fraudulently notarized; and some circulators admitted to being drunk in a public park at the time they signed the petitions. The Colorado secretary of state invalidated twenty-five thousand of the signatures because of evidence of "flagrant and pervasive fraud." In the judgment of Mrs. Buchanan, the Colorado secretary of state, the circulators' efforts were an "unprecedented insult to the people of Colorado." [15]

The available evidence indicates that only about half of those who sign petitions will actually vote for the proposition. Herbert Baus and William Ross relate an experiment by Dorothy Corey, a California pollster, who had been asked by a client whether "we can count on those who signed our petitions." Corey answered that she didn't think so, but she surveyed the petition signers and found that most could not remember signing any petition, and "about half were for the measure they qualified for the ballot and half against it!" [16]

Corey's findings are consistent with those of Allen R. Wilcox and Leonard B. Weinberg, who studied the voting intentions of persons who had signed petitions to place George Wallace on the 1968 presidential ballot. Wilcox and

Weinberg found "that Wallace failed to receive majority endorsement even from those individuals who signed his petition, and, in fact, finished second to Richard Nixon." [17] The fact that most people seem not to read the petition they are signing might lead to the conclusion that gathering enough signatures to qualify an initiative is easy. This is not the case, however, because obtaining a signature does not mean that the signature is valid; a person who has signed may not have given the correct address or may not be registered to vote. The most difficult hurdle is the half-million signatures required to qualify an initiative. Success in placing an initiative on the ballot in a populous state requires a substantial expenditure of money or a corps of highly motivated and disciplined volunteers.

Signature-gathering firms in California currently charge from five hundred thousand to one million dollars to place a proposition on the ballot. [18] In 1978 the usual rate per valid signature gathered was one dollar, of which thirty cents went to the individual petition circulator. [19] The remaining seventy cents went to the signature firm for expense, overhead, and profit. Charles Price has noted that because the costs of an all-paid signature drive are so high, "most petition firms are hired to provide a supplementary batch of signatures — 50,000 or 75,000 names — to go along with the volunteer effort by initiative proponents." [20] Apparently the most expensive signature drive was the computerized approach for the Jarvis income-tax initiative of 1980.

Until very recently, the task of signature collection involved face-to-face contact between an initiative petition circulator and a petition signer. But in 1980 the campaign-management firm of Butcher-Forde instituted a radically new approach to signature collection for Proposition 9, the Jarvis income-tax initiative. On this proposition the traditional face-to-face signature-collection method was replaced with a direct-mail computer-letter petition form and a request for a campaign contribution. This effort was highly successful; it obtained more than eight hundred thousand signatures and $1.8 million in campaign contributions. The direct-mail approach, relying on computer lists of likely supporters, has been used quite successfully in candidate elections, fundraising, and marketing. [21] Robert Kuttner compares the signature phase of the 1980 Jarvis income-tax initiative with that of the Jarvis-Gann property-tax initiative as follows: "Proposition 13, fueled by a true voter panic, was qualified for the ballot by thousands of little people volunteering their time; it cost Jarvis about a nickel a signature. There was no populist revolt in the campaign for Proposition 9. Jarvis bought the signatures — at an average of $2.53 each." [22]

The process of direct-mail signature solicitation is expensive, costing between $750,000 and $1 million, depending on the size of the initial mailing, among other factors. It is therefore roughly double the price now being charged for in-person signature collection. On those issues where the public is likely to respond to simultaneous fundraising appeals, however, direct-mail solicitation will probably become the preferred method because of the high financial return. The technology of directed mailings allows proponents to select persons who are likely to be receptive to petition appeals and who will contribute to the campaign. This new campaign technology in the initiative process may induce others to take their message to the people in this way.

Campaign Management

Not only the number of firms collecting signatures but also the number of firms handling initiative campaign management has grown. Until recently, signature collection and campaign management were handled by separate firms. Now, however, some firms handle both aspects of the direct legislation process. Furthermore, successful initiative managers usually handle partisan/candidate contests as well. Both Whitaker-Baxter and Spencer-Roberts, the two nationally known firms, built their reputations in initiative campaigns of the 1930s and 1940s.[23]

There are now at least a dozen California campaign-management firms active in the initiative industry.[24] They include long-established firms such as Whitaker-Baxter and Spencer-Roberts, as well as such newcomers as Russo-Watts. Some firms specialize in certain subject matter, such as rent control, taxes, or nuclear power. Other firms have expertise in the application of campaign technology to initiatives. An example of this is the use of direct-mail signature collection by Butcher-Forde. Many of the California firms are involved in ballot proposition campaigns in other states as well. For instance, the firm of Weiner and Company managed the successful campaign to legalize gambling in Atlantic City, New Jersey. Other firms have expanded their operation to candidate campaigns. Woodward, McDowell, and Larson successfully managed the elections of S. I. Hayakawa (R–Calif.) and Gordon Humphrey (R–N.H.) to the U.S. Senate, as well as those of two New Hampshire congressmen.[25]

Thus, the California initiative industry appears to be booming. Firms handle not only initiatives but candidate contests as well. Their business is most intense during elections; but because California decides initiatives in primary, general, and special elections, there appears to be year-round business. While firms are not quick to discuss profits, they often make 50 percent or more on signature collection; and campaign management is probably equally lucrative.[26]

SUCCESSFUL AND UNSUCCESSFUL PETITION CIRCULATION EFFORTS

Drafting a proposition and establishing an organizational structure are only the beginning steps in the initiative and referendum process. The real test of the commitment and resource of the petitioners comes in the signature-gathering phase. While those groups with money can purchase the services of professional petition circulators, many groups cannot afford to patronize the initiative industry and must handle this task themselves. Of all initiatives filed with and titled by the secretary of state in California since 1960, less than 20 percent have obtained sufficient signatures to qualify for the ballot. Table 4.1 summarizes the percentages of direct initiatives introduced, qualified, and adopted in California since 1912.

The data in table 4.1 indicate that since the 1970s the initiative has experienced renewed usage. During the two previous decades there was a drop in the number of initiatives appearing on the California ballot. This trend was reversed in the 1970s as Californians voted on more than double the number of initiatives than in either the fifties or the sixties. Additional evidence of an initiative explosion is the fact that over 180 proposed initiatives were titled during the seventies. This is nearly triple the number for any previous decade. The trend appears to be continuing, as there were 107 initiatives titled in 1980–82.[27]

That proponents of initiatives have been increasingly unsuccessful in qualifying their initiatives for the California ballot is also demonstrated in table 4.1. In the first two decades after the initiative was established in 1912, more than two-thirds of the titled initiatives obtained sufficient signatures to qualify for the ballot. While the proportion of initiatives qualifying for the ballot diminished somewhat after 1929, the most dramatic decline in successful petition drives has occurred since 1960. The 1970s had the highest number of propositions titled but the lowest success rate in qualifying those petitions. What accounts for this increasing inability to qualify propositions?

One explanation for this increasing failure rate is that the increased size of the California electorate may make it more difficult for groups to meet the signature requirement. As states increase in population, the number of signatures needed also increases. The number of signatures required for propositions in California in selected years from 1910 to the present is presented in table 4.2.

Because the number of California voters has increased so dramatically since 1910, the number of required petition signatures has also increased. While less than seventy-five thousand valid signatures qualified an initiative in the 1912–20 period, petitioners have needed more than five hundred thousand since 1970. It is important to remember, however, that the proportion of gubernatorial votes required to qualify an initiative has not increased since the initiative was established. Petition circulators operate under no larger percentage requirements in 1982 than in 1914.

Most students of direct legislation have concluded that although the percentages have remained constant, the larger number of signatures actually required accounts for the declining success rate in qualifying propositions. In short, according to conventional wisdom, the critical threshold is one of numbers rather than of percentages. V. O. Key and Winston Crouch argue that "at the time the system was originally adopted, these figures were small

Table 4.1

CALIFORNIA DIRECT INITIATIVES TITLED, QUALIFIED, AND ADOPTED, 1912–79

Decade	Number Titled[a]	Qualified for Ballot		Adopted		
		Number	Percentage of Titled	Number	Percentage of Qualified	Percentage of Titled
1912–19	45	30	67%	8	27%	18%
1920–29	51	35	69	10	29	20
1930–39	66	35	53	50	26	14
1940–49	42	19	45	6	32	14
1950–59	17	10	59	2	20	12
1960–69	44	9	20	3	33	7
1970–79	181[b]	22	12	7	32	4
1980–82	107	13	12	5[c]	38	5
Total	553	173	36%	50	29%	9%

Sources: March Fong Eu, "A Study of Ballot Measures: 1884–1980" (Sacramento: Office of the California Secretary of State, 1980, Photocopy), 3; interview with Barbara Lee, Elections Division, Office of the California Secretary of State, 5 August 1982.

[a] Titled initiatives include all proposals officially submitted to the attorney general prior to circulation of the petition, regardless of whether the proposal subsequently qualified for the ballot.

[b] Two of those titled were withdrawn prior to circulation.

[c] In the 1982 primary there were two initiatives on the gift-and-inheritance tax; both passed, and the one with the most votes became law.

Table 4.2

SIGNATURES NECESSARY FOR INITIATIVE AND REFERENDUM PETITION IN CALIFORNIA, 1912–82

Election	Total Gubernatorial Vote	Signatures for Constitutional Initiative (8%)	Signatures for Statutory Initiative[a]	Signatures for Referendum (5%)
1912–14	385,713	30,857	30,857	19,286
1923–26	965,787	77,263	77,263	48,289
1935–38	2,329,722	186,378	186,378	116,487
1947–50	2,558,399	204,672	204,672	127,920
1959–62	5,255,777	420,462	420,462	262,789
1963–66	5,853,232	458,259	292,662	292,662
1971–74	6,510,072	520,806	325,504	325,504
1979–82	6,922,378	553,790	346,119	346,119

Sources: Eu, "A History of the California Initiative Process," 13; correspondence with Edward Arnold, Elections Assistant, Office of the California Secretary of State.

[a] From 1912 to 1966 the signature requirement for statutory initiatives was 8 percent; in 1966 it was reduced to 5 percent.

enough to create no difficulty in using the initiative and the referendum, but the rapid increase in the size of the electorate has made the circulation of petitions a tremendous task." [28]

As discussed previously, in the period since 1960 there has been a dramatic decline in the percentage of initiatives that qualify for the ballot. Before that time, 45–69 percent of all titled initiatives met the signature requirements. Since 1960 only 20 percent or less of the titled initiatives have met the signature threshold. At least part of the reason for this decline may be the growth in the number of signatures required. In 1960, constitutional initiatives required more than 400,000 signatures to qualify for the ballot. This figure constituted an increase of roughly 100,000 signatures over the requirement in the 1955–58 period. Thus, Key and Crouch are correct in asserting that signature requirements based upon fixed percentages of the electorate may reduce the percentage of initiatives that qualify for the ballot. The evidence in tables 4.1 and 4.2, however, indicates that the number of signatures did not really become a barrier until the 1960s, not in the 1930s or 1940s as Key and Crouch predicted.

Perhaps in response to the signature-threshold problem and in order to encourage initiative proponents to sponsor statutes rather than constitutional amendments, the signature requirement for statutory initiatives was reduced in 1966 from 8 percent to 5 percent. This reduction, however, has not improved the success rate for statutory initiatives. In the period 1950–64, 47 percent of the titled statutory initiatives qualified for the ballot. Since the percentage requirement was reduced to 5 percent in 1966, only 25 percent of the titled statutory initiatives have gathered sufficient signatures to qualify for the ballot. What factors explain this declining rate of statutory initiative petitions qualifying for the ballot?

A primary reason for having signature thresholds is to keep frivolous and excessively narrow propositions from the ballot. One important consequence of the increased failure rate in the 1970s is that the total number of ballot propositions per election has been kept under thirty. Of the twenty-nine propositions given titles by the California attorney general in 1975 and 1976, only three had sufficient signatures to qualify for the state's 1976 primary- and general-election ballots. If titled initiatives had had the same success rate in 1976 as they did in the period 1912–29, over twenty initiatives would have appeared with the twenty-six other propositions on the 1976 ballots.

The 1970s in California have been a period of increasing efforts to qualify initiatives of all kinds. While the half-million-signature requirement is the primary reason for the failure of many initiative petitions, it is also clear that many proposed initiatives fail because they arise from excessively narrow interests that cannot generate the manpower or resources to gather sufficient signatures. An example is the 1976 statutory initiative to change the parental consent required for medical care of minors. Many such initiatives are titled but fail to generate much of a signature-collection drive.

Why have the 1970s witnessed this dramatic increase in the attempt to place issues on the ballot, and why have the 1960s and 1970s witnessed the dramatic decline in the proportion of titled initiatives qualifying for the ballot? Are the topics of recent proposals more frivolous than those of propositions circulated prior to 1960? To answer these questions, the 476 initiatives titled in

California between 1912 and 1979 can be categorized by topic and examined by decade to determine the relative success of each issue area over time.[29] These proposed initiatives are summarized in Appendix B.

The dramatic rise in the number of titled initiatives in the 1970s results at least in part from the electorate's increased interest in the taxing and fiscal areas; forty initiatives were titled in this decade alone, five of which qualified for the ballot. The remaining initiative proposals in the 1960s and 1970s are widely distributed among such categories as education, gambling, morals, labor, alcohol and drugs, and health.

Were the proposed initiatives of the 1960s and 1970s that failed to qualify for the ballot more frivolous than those that failed prior to 1960? Not significantly. The overwhelming majority of the unsuccessful initiatives of this recent period dealt with serious policy questions. And multiple initiatives were titled in several subject areas; for instance, in 1978 alone, four separate initiative petitions on school busing were being circulated. None of these was successful, but a legislative constitutional amendment on school busing was put on the 1979 special election ballot. Similarly, in 1968–70 four separate initiative petitions to lower the voting age to eighteen were circulated. All four failed to qualify. Not all the topics of proposed initiatives were as broad as these; some of the more narrow issues dealt with bail bonds, elimination of jawed traps, dog racing, and marijuana decriminalization. Yet even these more narrow proposals are hardly frivolous; furthermore, they are at least as central to the public policy concerns of the 1970s as are many of the issues voted on prior to 1960.

The subject matter of successful initiative petitions clearly varies over time; only initiatives dealing with taxes have a continuous and high level of popularity. In every decade since California first established direct legislation there have been initiatives concerning taxes; in most decades there have been four or more such measures on the ballot. Taxing and spending decisions clearly constitute one of the principal applications of direct legislation. Education and elections have also been recurrent issues, although less frequently than taxes. The more typical pattern, however, is for issues and issue areas to be popular for only a short period of time. Not since the 1920s have the voters initiated any bond proposals. Interest in alcohol control was high through the 1930s and then declined, only to return in the 1970s in the form of drug control. Social and welfare aid did not become an issue until the Depression, and the appearance of these issues declined after 1960. Interest in environmental concerns was relatively low until the 1970s, when coastal regulation, dam construction, and wildlife all became subjects of proposed initiatives.

To summarize, during the 1970s and early 1980s there has been an initiative explosion. The number of measures appearing on the ballot by petition in the 1970s was more than double the number in either of the two previous decades. The increase in the number of measures titled has been even more

dramatic. Some groups appear to be capitalizing on anti-governmental sentiment; others claim legislative inaction; and, as we will see, some individuals
and businesses profit from the initiative and therefore have a stake in its
expansion.

USAGE AND ELECTORAL SUCCESS OF DIRECT LEGISLATION

Since the inception of direct legislation in 1898 there have been more than
17,000 statewide propositions. Between 1968 and 1978, 2,315 statewide propositions were placed on the ballot; in 1978 alone, voters decided 334 of
them.[30] (Appendix C provides a complete breakdown, by year and by state,
of the number of propositions for this period.) The use of direct legislation at
the state level is obviously increasing. Ballot propositions at the city and
county levels are even more numerous; for example, Ohio had a total of 1,846
state and local referendums in 1968.[31] And if sufficient signatures are becoming increasingly difficult to obtain to qualify initiatives for the ballot, an even
smaller proportion of initiatives are successfully adopted (see table 4.3).

About one-third of statutory and constitutional initiatives placed on the
ballot have been approved by the voters. Among the states that have voted on
initiatives, Nebraska has the lowest approval rate, 7 percent; and in only six
states have 50 percent or more of the initiatives been approved. Oregon voters
have decided more statewide initiatives than have voters of any other state;
voters in California, the second heaviest user of initiatives, have decided
sixty-seven fewer initiatives than have Oregonians. A careful examination of
table 4.3 also indicates that five states — Oregon, California, North Dakota,
Colorado, and Arizona — have been heavy users of the initiative, having submitted more than one hundred proposals to the voters. Of these five high-use
states, North Dakota is the only state not in the Far West.[32] These five states
account for 58 percent of the initiatives submitted in the twenty-three states
employing the initiative over this seventy-year period. States in the western
region have decided more initiatives because they were among the first to
establish the process, their signature thresholds are relatively low, and direct
legislation has become an accepted part of the western political culture. States
in the western region are also the heaviest users of the popular referendum.
Arizonans, for instance, have decided thirty popular referendums since 1950.
One explanation for such heavy use is that in Arizona the signature threshold
for popular referendums is half that for statutory initiatives and only one-
third that for constitutional initiatives. Another heavy user of the popular
referendum has been North Dakota, where voters have decided twenty-four
popular referendums since 1950. In fact, as indicated in table 3.2, North
Dakota has become the heaviest user of direct legislation, voting on sixty-
seven proposals since 1950.

Table 4.3
STATUTORY AND CONSTITUTIONAL INITIATIVES PROPOSED AND APPROVED BY VOTERS FOR ALL STATES, 1898–1979

State[a]	Statutes			Constitutional Amendments			Total Initiatives		
	Number Proposed	Number Approved	Percentage Approved	Number Proposed	Number Approved	Percentage Approved	Number Proposed	Number Approved	Percentage Approved
Oregon	126	43	34%	101	28	28%	227	71	31%
California	67	19	28	93	27	29	160	46	29
North Dakota	135	55	41	30	18	60	141	65	46
Colorado	50	22	44	75	21	28	125	43	34
Arizona	66	22	33	46	19	41	112	41	36
Washington	74	35	47	—	—	—	74	35	47
Oklahoma	28	7	25	44	11	25	72	18	25
Arkansas	23	11	48	45	24	53	68	35	51
Missouri	15	5	33	34	7	21	49	12	24
Ohio	8	2	25	38	9	24	46	11	24
Michigan	5	4	80	36	14	39	41	18	44
Montana	33	21	64	3	1	33	36	22	61
Massachusetts	28	13	46	2	2	100	30	15	50
Nebraska	14	1	7	15	7	47	29	8	27
South Dakota	23	3	13	2	0	0	25	3	12
Nevada	13	7	54	5	3	67	18	10	56
Maine	16	5	31	—	—	—	16	5	31
Idaho	11	6	55	—	—	—	11	6	55
Alaska	10	5	50	—	—	—	10	5	50
Utah	8	2	25	0	0	0	8	2	25
Florida	0	0	0	2	1	50	2	1	50
Illinois	1	1	100	1	1	100	2	2	100
Wyoming	0	0	0	0	0	0	0	0	0
Total	754	289	38%	572	193	34%	1,326	482	36%

Sources: Data for the period 1898–1976 were obtained from Graham, *A Compilation of Statewide Initiative Proposals Appearing on Ballots through 1976*; data for 1978–80 were obtained from correspondence or interviews with election officials in each state.
[a] States are listed in order of total usage.

In theory the constitutional initiative, being reserved for amendments to the constitution, should be used less frequently than the statutory initiative. A state constitution is generally assumed to contain only essential language on the structure and operation of government. However, initiative sponsors have not been less likely to propose constitutional initiatives than statutory initiatives. In the nineteen states providing both types of initiative there have been nearly as many constitutional initiatives as statutory ones, and in eight of the states listed in table 4.3 there were more constitutional initiatives than statutory ones. Perhaps because of the greater legal significance of constitutional initiatives, voters are somewhat less likely to approve them. From 1950 to 1980 citizens have voted on 264 statutory initiatives and 168 constitutional initiatives, approving 42 percent of the statutory initiatives and only 30 percent of the constitutional.

At least two likely causes for the widespread use of constitutional initiatives can be identified. First, the legal status of a successful constitutional initiative is more secure than that of a statutory initiative. Furthermore, in many states the signature thresholds for the two kinds of initiatives are the same. Thus, sponsors of initiatives have clear incentives to use the constitutional initiative because it is just as easy to use as the statutory initiative and because the constitutional initiative is much harder to overturn once voted in. Second, some states have such long and detailed constitutions that many policy changes require constitutional change. Consequently, proponents of initiatives are compelled to use the constitutional initiative option. The initiative process itself may be one of the causes of long constitutions. In California, for instance, any change to a successful constitutional initiative requires passage of another constitutional initiative.

How successful is the legislative referendum, in which the legislature submits, without popular petition, propositions to the voters? A comparison of the usage and approval data for initiatives and legislative referendums is presented in table 4.4. As this table indicates, voters are much more likely to approve a statute or constitutional amendment proposed by the legislature than one proposed via the initiative. Over 60 percent of the legislative proposals are approved, compared with the 32–37 percent of statutory and constitutional initiatives.

Initiatives are apparently awarded a degree of skepticism not necessarily directed towards legislative referendums. Many voters may believe that the "burden of proof is on the advocate." [33] When an initiative is met by an organized and powerful opposition, the electorate is much less likely to vote yes. In contrast, legislative referendums have arisen from compromise and bargaining and are much less likely to face opposition. In fact, many legislative referendums have been approved unanimously by the legislature, and this information is routinely included in the voter's handbook. Another reason why others favor legislative referendums over initiatives may be that they

Table 4.4

VOTER APPROVAL RATES FOR INITIATIVES AND LEGISLATIVE PROPOSITIONS FOR ALL STATES, 1898–1978

State	Proposed by Legislatures			Proposed by Popular Petition		
	Number Proposed	Number Approved	Percentage Approved	Number Proposed	Number Approved	Percentage Approved
Statutory proposals						
Alaska	4	2	50%	6	3	50%
Arizona	14	6	43	71	28	39
Idaho	4	3	75	11	5	45
Maine	124	89	72	12	4	33
Michigan	7	3	43	4	3	75
Montana	43	25	58	26	15	58
Nebraska	11	5	45	9	1	11
Ohio	16	3	19	6	2	33
Oklahoma	11	9	82	26	6	23
Oregon	35	18	51	119	39	33
Subtotal	269	163	61%	290	106	37%
Constitutional proposals						
Arizona	105	67	64%	46	19	41%
Arkansas	79	37	47	56	27	48
California	476	294	62	90	24	27
Michigan	93	59	63	34	8	23
Nebraska	243	167	69	15	7	47
Ohio	113	74	65	38	8	21
Oklahoma	159	73	46	42	10	24
Oregon	238	138	58	88	28	32
Subtotal	1,506	909	60%	409	131	32%
Total proposals	1,775	1,072	60%	699	237	34%

Sources: Austin Ranney, "United States," in Butler and Ranney, *Referendums,* 77. Much of Ranney's data are drawn, in turn, from Graham, *A Compilation of Statewide Initiative Proposals Appearing on Ballots through 1976.*

are more trusting of elected representatives than of the special-interest or public-interest groups that generally propose initiatives.[34]

In the eleven states listed in table 4.4, over 72 percent of the propositions voted on had a legislative origin. For these states the prime instigator of ballot propositions is the state legislature. In some states the proportion of legislative referendums is even higher. For example, 84 percent of the constitutional amendments voted on in California since 1912 were placed on the ballot by the legislature.[35] In Alabama, Georgia, and Louisiana, none of the statewide ballot propositions are the result of the initiative or popular referendum, yet these states often have as many as thirty-five statewide propositions. (Appendix C provides a state-by-state breakdown of the number of statewide propositions since 1968.)

While table 4.4 allows comparison of the success rates of legislative referendums and initiatives, it does not provide information on how one-sided or competitive initiatives are. The percentages of yes and no votes for each initiative that appeared on the California ballot between 1960 and 1980 are given in table 4.5. In the literature on candidate elections the result is generally considered one-sided or noncompetitive if one candidate gets more than 60 percent of the vote.[36] This same standard was used against the initiatives given in table 4.5, and the resulting percentages of both competitive and one-sided elections appear at the bottom of the table.

According to the 60 percent rule, more than two-thirds — 69 percent — of the initiatives voted on in California since 1960 have been one-sided. The single most competitive initiative, the 1962 senate reapportionment initiative, lost with 47 percent of the vote. From table 4.5 it is evident that most California initiatives are overwhelmingly defeated.

The scope of subject matter presented to voters in initiatives is quite broad. In the 1978 and 1980 elections alone, voters decided initiatives on such diverse subjects as casino gambling, a state lottery, tax and spending limitations, the drinking age, branch banking, right to work, obscenity, beverage container deposits, apportionment, land-use planning, the death penalty, school busing, the hunting of mourning doves, milk prices, and abortion. Absent from this list are issues that would arise from groups lacking the financial resources or organizational skills necessary to meet the signature requirements. In recent years there have been few initiatives to increase welfare expenditures, provide mass transit, or require building access for the handicapped. Because the initiative process requires a special kind of political activity — obtaining petition signatures — persons who lack these resources cannot play as great a role in determining what issues are placed on the election ballot. Some groups, especially political minorities, the poor, and the less educated, are likely to find access to the legislature far less restrictive than access to the ballot.

Across the country, the subject matter of initiatives on the ballot in recent elections has varied somewhat from that evident in previous elections; however, the general array of interests represented is consistent with previous years. A categorization of the more than twelve hundred initiatives voted on since 1898 would reveal that the subject matter of initiatives both in California and in other states is fairly evenly distributed across such issue categories as health, welfare, housing, business regulation, revenue and taxes, and public morality. The subject areas most apt to result in initiatives are governmental processes and revenue and taxes. Voters in states other than California have been more likely to vote on initiatives concerning government organization, the environment, and education. Californians have decided more initiatives concerning public morality, health, welfare, and housing.[37]

My analysis of the subject content of initiatives thus far has been limited to the breakdown by topic of all statewide propositions since 1898. But what types of initiatives does the electorate find interesting? While there have been many more initiatives concerning government organization than business or labor, perhaps the latter category most interests the voter. Survey items from

Table 4.5

COMPETITIVENESS OF INITIATIVE MEASURES ON THE CALIFORNIA BALLOTT, 1960–80

Year	Subject	Percentage Voting Yes	Percentage of Voters[a]
1960	* Senate reapportionment	36%	81%
1962	Senate reapportionment	47	80
	Control of subversive activities	40	84
1964	* Repeal of Fair Housing Act	65	96
	* Prohibition of pay television	66	95
	* Lottery	31	93
	* Control of railroad train crews	61	93
1966	Obscenity regulation	44	88
1968	* Property-tax limitation	32	92
1970	* Tax shift for schools and social welfare	29	93
1972	* Air pollution control	35	93
	* Property-tax limitation	34	93
	* State employee salaries	33	91
	* Highway patrol salaries	39	91
	* Death penalty	68	94
	* Obscenity regulation	32	94
	* Marijuana decriminalization	34	96
	Coastal-zone conservation	55	93
	* School-busing limitation	63	93
	Agricultural labor relations	42	93
1973	Tax and expenditure limitations	46	99[b]
1974	* Political reform	70	90
	Protection of wild and scenic rivers	47	88
1976	* Nuclear power plant restrictions	33	95
	* Greyhound racing	25	94
	* Agricultural labor relations	38	96
1978	* Jarvis-Gann tax measure	65	97
	Smoking	46	96
	Homosexual teachers	42	95
	* Death penalty	71	88
1979	* Appropriation limitation	74	93[b]
1980	* Jarvis income-tax reduction	39	96
	* Uniform standards for rent control	35	94
	Oil Surtax	44	94
	Smoking and No Smoking sections	47	95
Percent Competitive		31 (11)[c]	
Percent One-Sided		69 (24)[c]	

Source: Office of the California Secretary of State, *Statement of the Vote, 1960–80* (Sacramento, 1960, 1962, 1964, 1966, 1968, 1970, 1972, 1973, 1974, 1976, 1978, 1979, 1980).
Note: Propositions preceded by an asterisk were one-sided.
[a] Percentage of those voting in the election who marked their ballots on this measure.
[b] Special election.
[c] Number in parentheses indicates number of propositions comprising percentage indicated.

the 1968 and 1970 Center for Political Studies American National Election Studies indicate what types of initiatives are most interesting to voters. Respondents were first asked if there were any propositions in which they were particularly interested; those answering yes were then asked what those propositions were.

While there was some variation, voters were most interested in the kinds of propositions that they decide most often — government organization and revenue and taxation questions. More than half found these questions interesting. Respondents were surprisingly uninterested in civil rights questions. Propositions concerning health, education, and welfare were apparently much more interesting to voters in 1970 than in 1968. In 1970, 22 percent found these topics interesting — double the percentage from 1968.

CONCLUSIONS

Successful direct legislation petition drives are becoming more and more dependent on the initiative industry or upon a cadre of committed volunteers. Although in California more ideas are being submitted to the secretary of state for their official title, a declining percentage of them makes it past the signature-collection phase. Thus, the issues placed before the voters reflect the interests of groups with money or highly motivated volunteers.

As the initiative industry grows, it may begin to seek out and encourage initiative and referendum business. Groups who would not otherwise use the process may be contacted and offered a bargain rate for an initiative campaign all the way from petition drive to legal challenge in the courts. Such sponsorship raises serious questions about the issue agenda of direct legislation in the future. The bias towards well-financed groups or those with small but active followings will likely grow even larger. Equally important to the future of direct legislation is the probable growth in politicians' perception of the initiative as the means to elective office. Political entrepreneurs may sponsor initiatives as a means of winning in a crowded primary field or in order to solidify support among one single-issue following or another.

Are initiative and referendum proposals unsound and frivolous? Or do they deal largely with issues in the general welfare and of widespread interest? The major problem is how to define these terms. Oregon's 1978 vote on denturism — whether to allow nondentists to fit dentures — may seem frivolous or unsound to some but of central concern to others. It is indisputable, however, that over time most of the issues presented to voters have been serious public policy questions. It is also clear that the issue concerns of initiatives and referendums have changed considerably over time.

The initiative and referendum, like most political processes, can be two-edged swords. Throughout their history they have been used for a variety of issues, but for the most part only organized groups have had the resources to use them effectively. Thus, claims that the process reduces the power of special interests and pressure groups seems questionable. At the level of the voters, the process poses special problems of understanding and comprehension. In chapters 5, 6, and 7, I will look at the experience of voters with direct legislation in order to learn who votes on propositions, why they participate, and how informed they are about those propositions.

Who Votes on Ballot Propositions?

An important aspect of politics in any society is how often and in what ways citizens participate in the decisions made by government. Political processes vary in the extent to which citizens of different skills and backgrounds can effectively participate. Advocates of the initiative and referendum have generally argued that direct legislation allows more voters to make their voices heard more effectively. For example, in the congressional hearings on the proposed national initiative, Ralph Nader argued that use of the initiative and referendum would politically activate "people who ordinarily would not be part of the political process" and that "the best antidote to cynicism in a civil sense is to endow the cynic with power." Senator James Abourezk (D–S.D.), the chief sponsor of the proposed constitutional amendment to provide a national initiative process, argued that "the voter initiative provides a concrete means for citizen participation. . . . Perhaps most importantly, it would lessen the sense of alienation from Government to which millions of Americans now profess." [1]

It is frequently argued that establishment or expansion of the initiative process will increase citizen participation in elections and thereby reduce alienation from government. However, very little evidence has been presented to demonstrate higher rates of voter participation resulting from the process. As I documented in chapter 2, disputes about who votes on propositions and why, as well as other related issues, recur frequently in the debate over direct legislation and seem never to have been empirically resolved. In fact, very little is known about the aggregate rates of participation on propositions.

Citizen participation in politics is generally achieved through popular elections structured in ways that may affect the amount of popular participation. Not all states have the processes of direct legislation; of those that do, some allow propositions to be voted upon only in general elections. Fewer states, most notably California, also provide for initiatives in primary and special elections. [2] On such matters as rates of turnout, representativeness of electorates, and levels of voter information, general elections differ from primary elections, just as partisan elections differ from nonpartisan elections. Even the form of ballots has been shown to affect participation in candidate elections.[3] To what extent do the type of election, its timing, and its format affect who votes on ballot propositions? In this chapter I will explore these questions by analyzing who votes on ballot propositions.

Participation in Initiative /Referendum Elections

Voting levels in proposition elections can by determined by comparing rates of turnout with rates of actual voting on propositions in primary and general elections. Turnout is defined as the proportion of the voting-age population that goes to the polls, while participation on propositions is defined as the proportion of voters that actually votes on ballot propositions.[4] Statewide propositions are usually voted upon at the same time as are candidates in presidential and midterm elections (and in California in primary and special elections as well). Therefore, an important first step is to examine rates of participation in presidential, midterm, primary, and special elections in order to see to what extent the average rates of voting on propositions vary by type of election.

Do the different rates of turnout in presidential and midterm elections affect rates of voting on propositions in those years?

A substantial literature on levels of national and statewide turnout already exists.[5] However, none of these studies is concerned with ways in which differences in turnout might affect participation on statewide propositions. For the analysis in this chapter, data on turnout and participation on propositions were gathered for California, Massachusetts, and Washington for the years 1960–82. These states were selected because of their long experience with direct legislation, their reputations as heavy users of the initiative process, and the availability of aggregate and survey data. The rates of turnout in presidential and midterm elections for the three states were derived from the U.S. Census Bureau's *Statistical Abstract of the United States* and from each state's *Official Statement of Vote* for the years indicated. The turnout rates for the three states and for the entire United States for the period 1960–82 are summarized in figure 5.1. There was a higher rate of turnout for presidential elections, and Massachusetts and Washington generally had turnout rates higher than those for California. From 1960 to 1982 turnout in presidential elections in Washington averaged seventeen percentage points higher than in midterm elections, while turnout in Massachusetts and California averaged ten percentage points higher.

The fluctuation in turnout between presidential and midterm elections, as summarized for these three states in figure 5.1, has long been recognized by

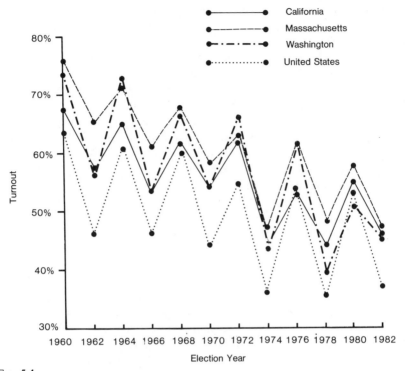

FIG. 5.1.

TURNOUT IN PRESIDENTIAL AND MIDTERM GENERAL ELECTIONS FOR CALIFORNIA, MASSACHUSETTS, WASHINGTON, AND THE UNITED STATES IN GENERAL, 1960–80. Data from U.S. Bureau of the Census, *Statistical Abstract of the United States: 1972,* 375–77, *1980,* 497–523, *1983,* 490 (Washington, D.C.: U.S. Government Printing Office, 1972, 1980, 1983); State of California, *Statement of the Vote,* 1960–82 (Sacramento: Office of the Secretary of State, 1960–82); Commonwealth of Massachusetts, *Election Statistics,* 1960–82 (Boston: Office of the Secretary of the Commonwealth, 1960–82); and State of Washington, *Abstract of Votes,* 1960–82 (Seattle: Office of the Secretary of State, 1960–82).

political scientists.[6] However, of concern to this study is whether those who vote on propositions differ in important ways from presidential to midterm elections.

WHAT KINDS OF CITIZENS TURN OUT TO VOTE?

A citizen must make at least three decisions about voting in an election: whether to go to the polls at all; whether to vote on a proposition; and finally, how to vote. A growing literature discusses the voter's decision of whether to turn out, its causes, and its consequences.[7] Those who do decide to go to the polls must then decide on which candidate or proposition contests to vote. Not all of those who turn out actually vote in all candidate races or on all ballot propositions.

Previous voting studies have found that the most important independent variables affecting turnout are education, income, and age. Some previous studies have also presented evidence of a strong relationship between "socio-economic status" and turnout. While education and income are parts of this status, it is conventionally defined to include occupation and perceived social class as well. As Sidney Verba and Norman Nie conclude, "Citizens of higher social and economic status participate more in politics. This generalization . . . holds true whether one uses level of education, income or occupation as the measure of social status." [8]

While the high correlation between occupation, income, education, age, race, and perceived social class on the one hand and turnout on the other hand is well known, political scientists have been uncertain about which variable has the largest effect upon turnout. Precise assessment of the effects of these independent variables has been difficult because of the small size of the usual national sample. [9]

The sample size problem has been overcome: Raymond E. Wolfinger and Steven J. Rosenstone have analyzed the Bureau of the Census's *Current Population Survey for 1972,* which provides a large enough number of respondents to allow precise estimates of the effects on turnout of the independent variables mentioned. They found that education has the largest impact on turnout. In fact, high levels of income and high-status occupation have minimal effects on turnout except among people with little formal schooling. [10]

Other than education, only age has a significant independent effect on turnout. Because younger or less educated citizens are less likely to turn out, they are disproportionately absent from the pool of voters who decide propositions. This bias in who turns out to vote is important to keep in mind in the following exploration of which kinds of voters actually vote on propositions. Also of importance, however, is the fact that Wolfinger and Rosenstone were examining *national* turnout data. By comparing a California Poll sample of California voters from 1972 with the Wolfinger/Rosenstone national sample, it is possible to determine the extent to which voters in this important initiative state fit the national patterns of participation. [11]

Education is associated with turnout both in California and in the entire United States. In the national sample only 52 percent of those persons with less than an eighth-grade education reported that they had voted, compared with 69 percent of high school graduates, and 86 percent of college graduates. For the California sample, the same relationship between education and turnout exists. While even relatively uneducated California voters turn out at higher rates than in the nation as a whole — averaging 6 percent higher for each category — the effect of increased education upon participation is again consistently evident. [12]

Why does education have such a significant effect upon turnout? Wolfinger and Rosenstone argue that education provides experience in dealing with bureaucracy which helps citizens overcome procedural hurdles; instills a sense of citizen duty which includes the obligation to vote; and increases the individual's knowledge about politics and his sense of confidence in dealing with complicated or abstract subjects. [13] Given the importance of education in determining who votes, it is important to examine the relationship between education and participation in voting on ballot measures.

The different levels of turnout in presidential and midterm elections having been established, an important question remains to be explored: Do the same relationships of education and age to turnout persist in nonpresidential elections? Despite the importance of voting in midterm elections, remarkably little research has been done on who votes in them. Until very recently, most assumptions about midterm election turnout were based on Angus Campbell's study of the 1956 and 1958 elections. [14] Drawing on a much more recent and larger sample, Rosenstone, Wolfinger, and McIntosh compared turnout in the 1972 and 1974 general elections. They found "few substantial differences between the two groups [of voters]. . . . Midterm elections, however, have many fewer young voters." [15]

Unfortunately, the Rosenstone-Wolfinger-McIntosh data for 1974 do not include state of residence as a variable. Because not every state has direct legislation, state-level data are needed to determine the differences in who votes in presidential and midterm elections. If the composition of the two electorates is different (as has been assumed on the basis of Campbell's work), this could have important consequences for rates of voting on statewide propositions. Fortunately, such state-level data do exist for California; and the following comparison of presidential and midterm elections is based on the California Poll's post-election surveys for the 1970, 1972, 1974, 1976, and 1980 California general elections. The bivariate relationships of education, income, occupation, race, and age with turnout for California presidential and midterm elections are summarized in table 5.1.

On the average, turnout in California presidential elections was 14 percent higher than in midterm elections during the 1970–80 period. The greatest decline in turnout occurred between the 1972 and 1974 elections. The relationship between age, education, and turnout found by Wolfinger and Rosenstone is again evident in this table. Turnout dropped in the midterm years for all categories of education, income, occupation, race, and age; but there was a greater than average drop in the turnout of those working as laborers or in service occupations, as well as of the less educated and the poor. There was also a disproportionate decline in turnout between the presidential and midterm elections for all respondents under age forty-five; younger voters

Table 5.1

Turnout Rates for California General Elections, 1970–80, by Demographic Category (In Percent)

Demographic Category	Turnout					Average Turnout		
	1970	1972	1974	1976	1980	Midterm	Presidential	Decline
Education								
0–8	58%	59%	50%	54%	78%	54%	64%	10%
9–11	42	61	42	61	61	42	61	19
12	60	74	56	60	64	58	66	8
Some college	66	86	63	73	78	65	79	14
Degree	75	92	71	75	89	73	85	12
Advanced degree	76	93	91	87	92	84	91	7
Income								
$0–4,999	52	61	44	58	72	48	64	16
$5,000–9,999	55	72	52	55	66	54	64	10
$10,000–19,999	68	83	63	68	73	66	75	9
$20,000+	71	90	76	79	83	74	84	10
Occupation								
Service/laborers	47	66	37	56	72	42	65	23
Craft/operative	57	67	45	60	61	51	63	12
Clerical/sales	59	85	65	69	80	62	78	16
Professional/managerial	69	88	64	65	82	72	82	10
Race								
White	62	81	64	73	80	63	78	15
Nonwhite	57	60	39	56	64	48	60	12
Age								
18–29	39	67	42	53	61	41	60	19
30–44	63	80	57	70	81	60	77	17
45–59	74	84	74	82	84	74	83	9
60+	79	82	75	80	89	77	84	7
Total	62%	78%	60%	69%	77%	61%	75%	14%

Sources: California Polls 7008, 12–17 November 1970; 7207, 7–18 November 1972; 7408, 6–17 November 1974; 7609, 13–24 November 1976; and 8101, 13–23 January 1981, provided by The Field Institute through the State Data Program, University of California, Berkeley.

were much less likely to participate in the midterm elections than in the presidential elections.[16] The data in table 5.1, including those that show a decline in turnout for the young in midterm elections, are consistent with the findings of Wolfinger, Rosenstone, and McIntosh. Based upon their larger national sample, they found that, as in presidential years, education was the most important predictor of the vote. The dropoff between the two elections was significantly greater among the youngest cohort. Other than the difference in turnout among the young, the demographic composition of the two electorates was almost identical.[17]

In terms of partisan divisions, the general election data from the 1970s and 1980s show little deviation from one election to the next. There is, however, some important variation on the ideology question. The breakdown of about 30 percent liberal, 45 percent conservative, and the remainder moderate is consistent across the three midterm elections; but the profile of voters in presidential years is more conservative. On the average, over half of those who voted in presidential election years reported that they consider themselves to be conservative. The proportion of liberals among voters was about the same in midterm and presidential years, but the number of moderates declined in the presidential years. Therefore, ballot measures that are appealing to conservatives should be more likely to do well in presidential election years.

Having established the differences between general election types, we can now move on to a related question: Is the proportion of voters who cast votes on propositions lower in presidential elections than in midterm elections? The literature on the kinds of voters who turn out in the two situations leads to contradictory conclusions.

The conventional view of citizens who participate in presidential elections has been that they include less interested, less involved, and less knowledgeable voters than those who participate in midterm elections.[18] However, Robert Arsenau and Raymond Wolfinger have recently demonstrated that this is not so. They find, instead, that "off-year congressional electorates are not substantially more knowledgeable, interested, or partisan than presidential year electorates."[19] The Arsenau-Wolfinger finding of equal levels of interest and knowledge in presidential and midterm electorates leads to a second hypothesis: there will be roughly equal levels of voting on statewide propositions in both types of elections.

Before these opposing hypotheses about the nature of participants in midterm and presidential elections can be tested, a standard measure of participation on propositions must be developed. Such a standard measure is "dropoff," the proportion of voters who cast ballots but who do not vote in a particular candidate race or on a proposition. Some previous research on candidate elections has used a similar concept of "rolloff" or "falloff," the proportion of voters who vote for the office listed first on the ballot but do not vote in a subsequent candidate race.[20] Dropoff, the measure used in this research, includes persons who turn out but do not vote for the highest office, whereas rolloff does not. Generally speaking, 2–3 percent of those who turn out do not vote on the first office listed; it is important to include these persons in the calculus of dropoff.

Dropoff in presidential and midterm elections for California and Massachusetts from 1970 to 1982 and for Washington from 1960 to 1982 is compared in tables 5.2, 5.3, and 5.4. Contrary to the surge-and-decline hypothesis, dropoff on propositions is not greater in presidential election years. Indeed, the dropoff on propositions tends to be almost identical in midterm elections, in which the more interested and involved "core voters" participate. For these three states, dropoff averaged 16 percent in presidential elections and 15 percent in midterm elections. In California the differences between the two types of elections is even more dramatic, with dropoff on propositions being twice as high in the 1970 and 1974 midterm elections as in

Table 5.2

CALIFORNIA GENERAL ELECTION TURNOUT AND DROPOFF, 1970–82
(IN PERCENT)

	1970	1972	1974	1976	1978	1980	1982	Average
Turnout	54%	62%	44%	53%	44%	55%	49%	51%
Dropoff								
President		3		3		2		3
Governor	2		2		3		2	2
Lieutenant governor	3		5		5		5	5
Secretary of state	3		5		8		6	6
Controller	5		7		9		7	7
Treasurer	4		6		9		7	7
Attorney general	4		5		6		7	6
Board of equalization	8		11		16		13	12
Senator	2		4	8		5	3	4
Congress	5	6	8	8	9	7	6	7
Assembly	6	6	9	10	10	9	9	8
Supreme Court	36		33		27		30	32
Average dropoff by								
category of proposition								
Bonds	14 (2)	10 (3)	11 (1)	13 (3)	13 (1)	12 (2)	11 (5)	12 (2)
Legislative proposals	19 (18)	10 (12)	19 (15)	17 (10)	18 (4)	16 (8)	16 (5)	16 (10)
Initiatives		7 (7)	13 (1)	6 (2)	7 (3)	6 (1)	10 (5)	8 (3)
All propositions	19 (20)	9 (22)	18 (17)	14 (15)	13 (8)	15 (11)	13 (15)	14 (15)

Source: State of California, *Statement of the Vote,* 1970–82 (Sacramento: Office of the Secretary of State, 1970–82).

Note: Numbers in parentheses indicate the number of propositions of each type on the ballot.

Table 5.3

MASSACHUSETTS GENERAL ELECTION TURNOUT AND DROPOFF, 1970–82
(IN PERCENT)

	1970	1972	1974	1976	1978	1980	1982	Average
Turnout	58%	63%	47%	62%	49%	60%	48%	54%
Dropoff								
President		2		2		2		2
Senator	5	5		4	3		3	4
Congress	12	14	10	10	11	12	10	11
Governor	9		2		4		3	5
Lieutenant governor	9		2		4		3	5
Attorney general	8		3		4		6	5
Secretary of state	9		6		9		10	9
Treasurer	11		27		9		10	14
Auditor	11		28		10		13	16
Average dropoff								
on propositions	25 (5)	17 (9)	26 (6)	8 (9)	17 (7)	13 (6)	11 (4)	17 (7)

Source: Commonwealth of Massachusetts, *Election Statistics,* 1970–82 (Boston: Office of the Secretary of the Commonwealth, 1970–82).

Note: Numbers in parentheses indicate the total number of propositions on the ballot.

Table 5.4

WASHINGTON GENERAL ELECTION TURNOUT AND DROPOFF, 1960–82 (IN PERCENT)

	1960	1962	1964	1966	1968	1970	1972	1974	1976	1978	1980	1982	Average
Turnout	73%	56%	73%	53%	66%	54%	66%	43%	62%	39%	59%	45%	58%
Dropoff													
President	1		1		1		3		2		2		2
Senator		3	5	6	5		4	6			3	3	4
Congress	11	9	6	6	8	9	14	6	11	5	8	7	8
Governor	3		2	3	3		3		3		2		3
Lieutenant governor	10		7		6		8		8		9		8
Secretary of state	10		7		9		8		10		11		9
Treasurer	13		9		10		10		12		11		11
Auditor	11		11		13		14		15		13		13
Attorney general	13		9		9		7		10		6		9
Superintendent of public instruction	35		50				22		45		40[a]		38
Commissioner for public lands	13		10		10		11		12		10		11
Insurance commissioner	16		13		13		16		11		12		14
Average dropoff by category of proposition													
Initiatives	13 (5)	14 (1)	18 (1)	6 (3)	10 (3)	8 (2)	15 (6)	10 (1)	13 (2)	14 (1)	9 (1)	4 (3)	11
Referendums		16 (2)	16 (4)	15 (3)	16 (3)	10 (4)	14 (8)		13 (2)		14 (2)		14
Legislative constitutional amendments	18 (1)	18 (8)	26 (1)	18 (8)	21 (7)	10 (2)	23 (10)	12 (2)	17 (3)		17 (2)	9 (1)	17
All propositions	14 (6)	17 (11)	18 (6)	15 (14)	17 (14)	14 (8)	18 (24)	11 (3)	15 (6)	14 (1)	14 (5)	5 (4)	14

Source: State of Washington, *Abstract of Votes*, 1960–82 (Seattle: Office of the Secretary of State, 1960–82).

Note: Numbers in parentheses indicate the number of propositions of each type on the ballot.

[a] Unopposed.

the 1972 presidential election. Thus, the surge-and-decline argument clearly does not hold in voting on statewide propositions. Instead, the finding that presidential electorates are not more prone to dropoff is consistent with Arsenau and Wolfinger's more recent analysis.

While there is no increased dropoff in presidential election years, there is a consistent pattern of higher dropoff in those years when voters elect state officials and face longer ballots. California and Massachusetts elect their officials in midterm years, whereas Washington voters face the longer ballot in presidential years. Tables 5.2, 5.3, and 5.4 provide evidence of higher dropoff in elections with longer ballots, a finding that suggests that voter fatigue may be an important variable.

Comparison of dropoff rates across states is made easier by averaging the rate of dropoff by candidate contest and type of proposition for each of the three states. The average general election dropoff in all three states for the six elections held from 1970 to 1982 is summarized in table 5.5.

California, Massachusetts, and Washington have strikingly similar average rates of dropoff. In the contests for president and senator the dropoffs for the three states are almost identical. Massachusetts voters are somewhat more likely to drop off when voting for governor, while California voters are the least likely to drop off when voting for governor; in fact, fewer California voters drop off when voting for governor than when voting for president. In voting on candidates, California voters consistently have the lowest dropoff

Table 5.5

AVERAGE GENERAL ELECTION DROPOFF IN CALIFORNIA, MASSACHUSETTS, AND WASHINGTON, 1970–82, BY TYPE OF CONTEST (IN PERCENT)

	California	Massachusetts	Washington
Dropoff			
President	3%	2%	2%
Senator	4	4	4
Congress	7	11	8
Governor	2	5	3
Lieutenant governor	5	5	8
Attorney general	6	5	9
Secretary of state	6	9	9
Treasurer	7	14	11
Auditor (Controller)	7	16	13
Average dropoff by category of proposition			
Initiatives	8		11
Referendums			14
Legislative propositions	16		17
All propositions	14 (15)	17 (7)	14 (9)

Sources: State of California, *Statement of the Vote,* 1970–82 (Sacramento: Office of the Secretary of State, 1970–82); Commonwealth of Massachusetts, *Election Statistics,* 1970–82 (Boston: Office of the Secretary of the Commonwealth, 1970–82); State of Washington, *Abstract of Votes,* 1970–82 (Seattle: Office of the Secretary of State, 1970–82).

rate, particularly in elections for secretary of state, treasurer, and auditor (controller). In the latter two cases, the Massachusetts and Washington voter dropoff rates are more than double those in California.

Even though the average number of statewide propositions voted on varied in these states, the average dropoff rate on propositions was quite similar. Between 1970 and 1982, the average dropoff on propositions in California and Washington was 14 percent, in Massachusetts 17 percent. Massachusetts's somewhat higher dropoff rate is surprising; voters in that state had less than half as many propositions to vote on as did voters in California. Apparently, having more propositions on the ballot does not necessarily result in a higher rate of dropoff.

Are there differences in rates of voting on propositions among general, primary, and special elections?

Data on differences in rates of voting on propositions among general, primary, and special elections are limited to California, the only state of the three studied that places propositions on the primary ballot. The turnout rates for primary, general, and special elections in California from 1970, when initiatives first began appearing on primary election ballots, to 1982 are compared in figure 5.2. There is clearly a pattern of higher turnout in the presidential elections of 1972, 1976, and 1980. Turnout in the midterm general elections of 1970, 1974, 1978, and 1982 averaged 9 percent lower than turnout in the three presidential elections. With one exception, turnout in primary elections in California was 8–16 percent lower than turnout in the general elections held later the same year. The exception to this pattern was the 1978 primary, which had a relatively high rate of turnout for a primary election; only 2 percent more voters turned out in that year's general election. The 1978 primary did not include a contest for the U.S. Senate, and the incumbent Democratic governor faced no real competition within his party. Given these facts, it is surprising that turnout for the 1978 primary election was higher than that for the presidential primaries of 1972 and 1976 and the 1974 general election. However, one reason for this unusually high turnout for a midterm primary election was the presence on the ballot of Proposition 13, the Jarvis-Gann property-tax initiative. As I will demonstrate in chapter 7, most voters were aware of this proposition and perceived it to be important.

Turnout is generally lower in primaries than in general elections at least in part because the lack of party attachment results in more complicated decisions for voters. In general elections, voters can rely on the party cue to simplify their candidate choices. Because decision making is more difficult and because primary elections are, with the apparent exception of 1978, less salient, voters participate in them less. Those who do turn out in primaries have generally been found to be better educated, more involved in politics,

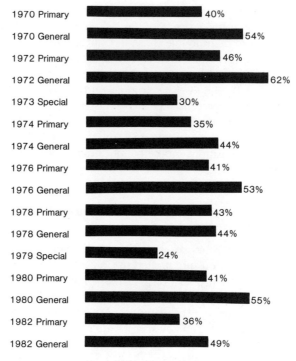

Election	Turnout
1970 Primary	40%
1970 General	54%
1972 Primary	46%
1972 General	62%
1973 Special	30%
1974 Primary	35%
1974 General	44%
1976 Primary	41%
1976 General	53%
1978 Primary	43%
1978 General	44%
1979 Special	24%
1980 Primary	41%
1980 General	55%
1982 Primary	36%
1982 General	49%

FIG. 5.2.
TURNOUT IN GENERAL, PRIMARY, AND SPECIAL ELECTIONS IN CALIFORNIA, 1970–82.
Turnout is defined as the percentage of the voting-age population that cast ballots.
Data from U.S. Bureau of the Census, *Statistical Abstract of the United States: 1978*
(Washington, D.C.: U.S. Government Printing Office, 1979), 522–25; and State of
California, *Statement of the Vote,* 1970–82 (Sacramento: Office of the Secretary of
State, 1970–82).

and more knowledgeable about public affairs.[21] In the special elections in
1973 and 1979, held solely for initiatives, Californians turned out at a rate of
24–30 percent. At 5–11 percent below the turnout for the primary election of
1974, in which approximately one-third of eligible Californians voted, the
1973 and 1979 turnouts were so low that they call into question the legitimacy
of special elections held for ballot propositions.

Voting research has documented that electoral participation is a function
of an individual's psychological involvement in politics. For many citizens,
interest in politics and regularly scheduled elections is quite low. In special
elections for propositions, the stimulus of candidate and party competition is
removed from the election; as a result, only the highly informed and politically knowledgeable will know when and how to participate. Thus, in California special elections examined here, between two-thirds and three-fourths of
the eligible citizens — and a majority of the registered voters — did not vote.

This type of special election is rare in the United States but somewhat more common in Europe. Apparently in response to the problems of low turnout, Denmark, Scotland, and Wales have all established qualified majority requirements whereby 30–67 percent of the electorate (all eligible voters) must vote affirmatively for a measure to pass.[22] If special elections become more common in the United States, such a rule may be needed.

The profile of voters in general elections constructed earlier in this chapter demonstrates that the partisan breakdown was rather constant across the general elections but voters in the presidential years were more likely to see themselves as conservatives than were voters in midterm years. Are similar differences in the types of persons that vote manifested in primary elections? A voter profile of the primary elections between 1970 and 1980 can be compared with the voter profile for general elections.

Voters who decide ballot measures in presidential primaries are more likely to be liberal than voters who participate in midterm primary elections. As in the earlier analysis of general elections, the party breakdown over the period from 1970 to 1980 is remarkably constant. Democrats, however, do appear to have a larger share of the electorate in presidential primaries than in presidential general elections. As in the earlier profile of general electorates, the young constitute a larger share of the voters in presidential years in both primaries and general elections. In addition, those with some college education or with a college degree constitute a larger share of the voters in presidential primaries than they do in midterm elections. The implications of these differences depends on the issues being decided. (In chapter 8 I examine the extent to which party and ideology, among other variables, determine initiative voting.) Proponents of issues with potential liberal support would be well advised to time their campaigns for presidential primary years. Conversely, conservatives enjoy a substantial advantage in all of the electoral situations analyzed; but their advantage is even larger in the midterm elections, both primary and general.

Is dropoff higher in general elections, in which larger numbers of citizens participate? To answer this question I calculated the average dropoff rate for candidates and propositions in the primary and general elections from 1970 through 1982. Despite the difference of 11 percent in average turnout between primary and general elections, California voters drop off in nearly identical proportions when voting on propositions. As noted previously, an important distinction between initiatives and other statewide propositions emerges: popularly proposed initiatives in California had a dropoff rate that was less than half that for all other types of propositions in the same elections, probably because they were proposed by petition and generally received more public attention. Popular initiatives also had a lower dropoff rate than legislative proposals in Washington (see table 5.5), although the difference between these rates was not as pronounced as in California.

While primary voters are not more likely to drop off when voting on propositions, on the average they are more likely to drop off in contests for Congress, governor, secretary of state, treasurer, controller, attorney general, state board of equalization, and state assembly. High dropoff rates in these contests result at least in part from California's primary system, which permits easy access to the ballot. Both parties often have fifteen or more candidates competing for each statewide electoral office, and California voters are asked to choose from among this number of contestants without the economizing device of a party cue. For many California voters, the apparent solution to this situation is simply not to vote for candidates in these races. The dropoff rate for most of these offices in the general elections is about one-third of that found in the primary elections. This difference makes the similarity in dropoff rates on propositions even more striking. In short, primary voters are less likely to drop off when voting on statewide propositions. This means that substantial numbers of primary voters skip voting on some candidate races and then resume voting on statewide propositions.

"Voter Fatigue" and Order of Initiatives on the Ballot

It is plausible that when voters are faced with a lengthy ballot, a higher dropoff rate might occur for those items located near or at the bottom of the ballot. A careful review of the aggregate data in California, Massachusetts, and Washington demonstrated that in candidate races generally, the further down the ballot, the greater the dropoff. Fatigue is not an important factor, however, in voting on initiatives as distinguished from legislatively initiated propositions. For instance, in the 1976 primary election in California the average dropoff for the three categories of propositions was: bonds, 12 percent; legislative proposals, 16 percent; and popular initiatives, 5 percent. Some voters appear to pick and choose the propositions on which they will vote, with popular initiatives eliciting the largest amount of participation. For legislative propositions, generally, the further down the ballot, the greater the proportion of dropoff.

In the 1976 California election, dropoff averaged 6 percent on popular initiatives, 13 percent on bonds, and 17 percent on legislative proposals. Dropoff decreased by 11 percent from legislative Proposition 12 to Proposition 13, a popular initiative. In numbers of voters, close to a million more voters participated in deciding Proposition 13 than participated in deciding Proposition 12. In addition, another legislative proposal, Proposition 15, was placed after two popularly initiated propositions; in this case, dropoff increased by 9 percent from Proposition 14 to Proposition 15. Table 5.6 suggests that some voters vote only on popular initiatives, which generally are the propositions receiving considerable publicity. Further evidence that some voters may vote on only one or two propositions is found in the 1978 California primary election; table 5.7 presents the dropoff percentages from this election.

Table 5.6

VOTER DROPOFF FOR CANDIDATES AND PROPOSITIONS IN CALIFORNIA'S 1976 GENERAL ELECTION

	Vote	*Dropoff*
Office		
President	7,867,117	3%
Senator	7,472,268	8
Congress	7,451,946	8
Assembly	7,291,002	10
Proposition [a]		
1	7,085,780	13
2	7,109,023	13
3	6,983,419	14
4	6,960,551	14
5	6,900,616	15
6	6,678,961	18
7	6,805,801	16
8	6,734,664	17
9	6,670,563	18
10	6,761,962	17
11	6,521,390	20
12	6,785,195	17
13	7,649,347	6
14	7,707,947	5
15	6,972,497	14

Source: State of California, *Statement of the Vote,* 1976 (Sacramento: Office of the Secretary of State, 1976).

Note: The voting-age population was 15,036,317; the voter turnout was 8,137,202, or 53 percent.

[a] Propositions 1–3 were bonds; propositions 4–12 and 15 were legislative constitutional amendments; and propositions 13 and 14 were initiatives.

The differences in dropoff rates between categories of initiatives in the 1978 primary election are consistent with those discussed previously. On Proposition 13, the Jarvis-Gann property-tax initiative, there was a very low dropoff, 3 percent; on bonds, an average dropoff of 15 percent; and on legislative proposals, an average dropoff of 19 percent. What is distinctive about this election is the markedly lower dropoff on Proposition 8, the legislative response to Proposition 13. Opponents and proponents of Proposition 13, the Jarvis-Gann initiative, argued that the two propositions should be paired, since acceptance of one required rejection of the other. The rate of dropoff on Proposition 8 was probably so low because the two propositions were so closely linked. On legislative proposals other than Proposition 8, the average dropoff was 22 percent; on the propositions directly preceding and following Proposition 8, dropoff rates were 24 percent and 23 percent, respectively. Thus, hundreds of thousands of voters must have voted only on propositions 8 and 13. Voting on property taxes was clearly important to these voters, a point substantiated by the *Los Angeles Times* exit poll. Highly salient issues such as Proposition 13 apparently are not affected by voter fatigue (see table 5.7). In fact, although Proposition 13 came at the end of the

Table 5.7

Voter Dropoff for Candidates and Propositions in California's 1978 Primary Election

| | Dropoff | | |
	Democratic	Republican	Total
Office			
Governor	12%	4%	9%
Lieutenant governor	16	11	14
Secretary of state	31	26	29
Controller	23	25	24
Treasurer	19	24	22
Attorney general	16	17	17
Congress	22	21	23
Assembly	26	28	28
Board of Equalization	29	41	34
Superintendent of Public Instruction [a]			21
Proposition [b]			
1			14%
2			15
3			15
4			22
5			25
6			21
7			24
8			8
9			23
10			21
11			23
12			23
13			3

Source: State of California, *Statement of the Vote,* 1978 (Sacramento: Office of the Secretary of State, 1978).

Note: The voting-age population was 15,098,508; the voter turnout was 6,842,936, or 45 percent, of which 6,447,807 were registered with a political party.

[a] Nonpartisan.

[b] Propositions 1 and 2 were bonds; propositions 3–12 were legislative constitutional amendments; and proposition 13 was an initiative.

ballot, over 350,000 more voters marked their ballot for the proposition than for governor, the first ballot choice.[23]

Writing about the 1964 election, John E. Mueller argued that controversial propositions can increase participation rates on noncontroversial propositions: "The abstention rate for the most controversial proposition is also a highly significant contributor to abstention on the non-controversial propositions: When the abstention on this proposition decreases by two percentage points, the average abstention on the non-controversial propositions goes down by well over one percentage point. Controversial propositions appear to draw the voters' attention and interest to the proposition part of the ballot."[24] While controversial propositions may have increased participation on noncontroversial propositions in the 1964 election, the data from 1978 seem to argue just the opposite. In 1978 some voters apparently turned out solely to vote on propositions 8 and 13, and there is no evidence of increased voting on the other propositions because of the controversial nature of the Jarvis-Gann Proposition 13.

In order to assess the extent to which California voters differ from voters elsewhere, I have tabulated aggregate dropoff data from two other states, Massachusetts and Washington. California is the most advantageous state in which to study dropoff because Californians decide propositions more often. In the six general elections between 1970 and 1980, California averaged sixteen propositions per election. By comparison, voters in Washington faced, on the average, ten propositions per election — roughly three-fifths as many propositions as California voters faced. During the same period, Massachusetts voters voted on an average of seven statewide propositions per election. Interestingly, many observers in Massachusetts expressed concern over the possibility of high dropoff rates in the 1976 election because voters faced an unusually long ballot of nine statewide propositions. Given these differences in frequency of voting on propositions, what are the patterns of dropoff in Washington and Massachusetts? How do these states differ from California in dropoff rates? Data on Washington and Massachusetts presented in tables 5.3 and 5.4 shed some light on these questions.

It is worth repeating that the amount of dropoff in candidate races in California and Washington was quite similar and that in Washington a lower dropoff occurred on initiatives and referendums than on legislative proposals. Washington voters exhibited a fairly consistent average rate of dropoff on initiatives: excluding the 1974 election, which had only three propositions, the average dropoff on propositions ranged from 14 percent to 18 percent, with 16 percent being the overall average. Even though overall turnout varied from presidential to midterm elections, the rate of dropoff was not related to low or high overall turnout. During the high-stimulus presidential-gubernatorial elections of 1960, 1964, 1968, 1972, and 1976, the rate of dropoff was no higher than in the low-stimulus midterm elections.

For Washington voters, the candidate races at the top of the ballot generally elicited greater levels of participation than did popular initiatives. This same pattern was present in the California data. In the ten Washington elections under review, only rarely did a proposition have a dropoff rate as low as that for any of the contests for statewide elective office. In 1970, 5 percent of those who turned out did not vote for senator, and the same percentage did not participate in the referendum on abortion. On the average, voters in Washington showed a greater dropoff rate when voting on initiatives than when voting for president, senator, congress, governor, lieutenant governor, and secretary of state. Assuming that dropoff is an accurate measure of voter interest, these data support the conclusion that for Washington voters, propositions are less important than most candidate races; only the race for superintendent of public instruction was an exception.

Is there evidence of voter fatigue in Washington? As already discussed, Washington voters decide almost all statewide candidate races in presidential election years. If voter fatigue is present, than a higher dropoff rate should occur in presidential election years, when voters face the long ballot. But, as is revealed in table 5.5, dropoff on statewide propositions averages only 2 percent higher in presidential election years. Hence, voter fatigue from deciding candidate races does not appear significantly to affect the dropoff on statewide propositions. Does having more propositions on the ballot lead to higher dropoff on propositions in Washington? In 1972 Washington voters faced twenty-four statewide propositions in addition to the already long ballot of national and statewide offices. The average dropoff rate on all propositions was 18 percent, one of the highest in the period under study; but the dropoff rate was the same in 1964, when only six propositions were on the ballot.[25] Thus, the length of the ballot did not consistently lead to higher dropoff.

In an earlier study of voting behavior on propositions in Oregon, Joseph La Palombara and Charles Hagan also found that ballot length did not necessarily lead to higher voter dropoff:

> An analysis of the behavior of the Oregon electorate over the last ten years has
> indicated that voter fatigue has not operated as might be expected. The greatest
> popular participation, excluding special elections, has taken place in those
> instances when the greatest number of proposals have appeared on the ballot.
> Nor is there any indication that the voter will be less inclined to mark a complete
> ballot as the number of proposals increases. Most of the measures which received
> the largest number of total votes appeared in the last three ballot positions.[26]

Thus, in Washington, Oregon, and California, voters searched the ballot for the controversial propositions and voted on them, whether they were listed before other propositions, as in Washington, or after all of the other propositions, as in California and Oregon.

On legislative propositions, however, the tendency for the dropoff rate to increase further down the ballot has been demonstrated with California aggregate data.[27] When Jerome Clubb and Michael Traugott examined dropoff in forty-four states having statewide propositions, they also found a significant relationship between ballot length and voter fatigue.[28] Appendix C provides a complete breakdown of the total number of statewide propositions in each state since 1968. The Clubb-Traugott analysis includes states with a large number of legislative propositions and no initiatives. Since 1968 the following states have had 80 or more legislative propositions: Alabama (80), Georgia (142), Louisiana (150), Rhode Island (80), and Texas (88). Thus, their finding is quite consistent with those reported here: voter fatigue is a factor explaining dropoff on legislative propositions but not on initiatives or popular referendums.[29]

Massachusetts presents an interesting contrast to the states already described because its citizens do not vote on as many state candidate races. As noted earlier, in Massachusetts, as in Washington and California, the average dropoff for propositions is higher than that for most state offices (see table 5.3). However, Massachusetts is different from the other states discussed in that voters typically decide fewer propositions. An exception to this was the 1976 election, when Massachusetts voters faced an unusually long ballot including nine statewide propositions; the state's 1970–80 average dropoff rate of 17 percent on propositions is lowered by the high rates of voting on these nine propositions. When these propositions are removed from the calculation, Massachusetts voters had an average dropoff rate of 19 percent for that period. The more normal tendency of Massachusetts voters to drop off at higher rates on propositions is found in 1970, where the lowest dropoff rate for the propositions – 23 percent – was nearly double that for the state office of auditor, with its 12 percent dropoff. Over a third of the 1970 Massachusetts voters did not participate in the balloting on Question 4, apportioning the legislature.

As shown, the amount of dropoff in comparable candidate races in California, Massachusetts, and Washington is quite similar. Ballot length varies, however: Massachusetts has the shortest, while Washington has the longest. Not counting justices of the Supreme Court, Washington voters elect two more state executive officers than California voters and three more than Massachusetts voters. Not surprisingly, voters faced with so many decisions may decide simply not to vote in the contests for offices such as superintendent of public instruction. In 1964 only 50 percent of the Washington voters actually voted for superintendent of public instruction, and eight years later only 55 percent cast votes for this office.

EFFECTS OF INITIATIVES ON OVERALL RATES OF TURNOUT

Advocates of the initiative and referendum frequently assert that if citizens were allowed to decide issues directly by voting on ballot propositions, turnout would increase. Part of this assumed increase in participation would come from the activation of presently alienated voters – a hypothesis that is fully tested in chapter 8. Proponents of a national initiative process for the United States have also argued that adoption of the initiative would activate presently indifferent citizens, motivating them to turn out. In his testimony before the Senate subcommittee considering the proposed national initiative, Larry L. Berg said,

> It [the proposal] will permit people to act rather than respond. It will permit people to do rather than react to something. . . . I would suggest that being unable to take such action is related to the continued drop in the percentage of turnout in voting. The initiative will have a positive impact on that for a variety of reasons. One is the ability to act and have some of the control in their own hands and to take action themselves. I think it will help to restore some of the confidence in elections and government that obviously is very much lacking.[30]

Berg is not alone in asserting that a national initiative would lead to increased citizen participation in politics and higher levels of turnout. In a post-election editorial on the 1978 general election, the *New York Times* stated, "Direct democracy offers another benefit: It is a powerful stimulus to political participation. Nobody said democracy has to be dull. People are more likely to vote when issues capture their interest." [31] In a similar vein, Senator Mark Hatfield, a current sponsor of the national initiative constitutional amendment, has argued that "voter turnout appears to be significantly increased by the appearance of initiatives on the ballot." [32]

Do initiatives and referendums increase turnout? Answering this question is difficult because in most elections where initiatives are decided, candidate contests also appear on the ballot. It is therefore difficult to determine whether increased turnout results from the presence of initiatives or the coincidental candidate contests. One way to avoid this problem is to study special elections, in which there are no candidate races. In such elections, as has been shown, turnout is very low; items of direct legislation by themselves have not activated more than 30 percent of the voting-age population in any state studied. But there are so few cases of special elections that studying them does not provide a sufficient answer to the question.

The only survey data that directly address the effect of initiatives on turnout are from a 1962 California Poll. Respondents were asked if there were any special candidate races or ballot propositions that made them want to turn out to vote. [33] Nearly half of the respondents indicated that a particular candidate contest or proposition interested them. Of that group, 75 percent stated that the governor's race between Richard Nixon and Edmund G. "Pat" Brown was their motivating interest. In sharp contrast, less than 2 percent named any of the statewide propositions as important in their decision to turn out to vote. [34] This indication that propositions clearly were not a motivating force for turnout in 1962 is amplified by the fact that 7 percent listed the contest for superintendent of public instruction as a special reason to turn out. Unfortunately, no similar item was included in any more recent California polls. In the June 1978 *Los Angeles Times* exit poll, when those who had just voted were asked, "Would you have come here today if Proposition 13 were not on the ballot?" 7 percent answered no. Thus, even when there was a proposition as controversial and well publicized as Proposition 13, 93 percent of those who voted reported that they would have come to the polls without this initiative. [35] On the basis of self-reported vote intentions, it appears that propositions do not appear to increase turnout significantly, contrary to the frequent assertions by advocates of the process. In addition, ballot propositions as controversial and salient as Proposition 13 are rare; if turnout was increased by only about 7 percent because of this proposition, the effects of other initiatives must be even less.

David H. Everson has effectively demonstrated that over time there is no relationship between initiatives and turnout. [36] A summary comparison of

Table 5.8

AVERAGE TURNOUT IN NORTHERN STATES, WITH AND WITHOUT THE INITIATIVE 1960-80

	Presidential Years						
	1960	*1964*	*1968*	*1972*	*1976*	*1980*	*Average*
All northern states with initiatives	68% (9)	66% (7)	66% (6)	61% (9)	59% (13)	57%	63%
All northern states without initiatives	71% (25)	67% (27)	65% (28)	60% (25)	59% (21)	58%	63%
Difference	−3%	−1%	+1%	+1%	0%	−1%	0%

	Midterm Years			
	1970	*1974*	*1978*	*Average*
All northern states with initiatives	51% (6)	44% (9)	44% (14)	46%
All northern states without initiatives	51% (28)	45% (25)	41% (20)	46%
Difference	0%	−1%	+3%	0%

Sources: Everson, "Initiatives and Voter Turnout: A Comparative State Analysis"; and idem, "Initiatives and Voter Turnout: The Case of 1978," 10.

Notes: Turnout is the percentage of the voting-age population casting ballots for president in 1960, 1964, 1968, 1972, and 1976; and for congress in 1970, 1974, and 1978.

The table excludes the fifteen southern states, identified by the U.S. Census Bureau as follows: Alabama, Arkansas, Delaware, Florida, Georgia, Kentucky, Louisiana, Maryland, Mississippi, North Carolina, Oklahoma, South Carolina, Texas, Virginia, and West Virginia.

Numbers in parentheses indicate the number of states comprising the percentages.

turnout since 1960 in all northern states, comparing states having the initiative with those without it, is provided in table 5.8. Contrary to assertions of the initiative's proponents, states with initiatives on the ballot do not have higher turnout. In fact, their turnout is on the average the same as that of noninitiative states. In his more detailed analysis, Everson shows that even though noninitiative states have relatively less educated populations and more restrictive registration requirements — two factors that have been shown to produce lower turnout — they still have the same average rates of turnout as states with the initiative. Thus, the added electoral stimulus of ballot propositions does not typically lead to higher voter turnout.

Roger Telschow, director of Initiative America, a lobbying organization seeking to establish a national initiative process, has argued that the 1978 election demonstrated that initiatives will increase turnout.[37] While Telschow did not document his methodology, he clearly included the South, and his finding was thus substantially affected. Because few southern states have initiatives and because the region also has the lowest average turnout, inclusion of these states in his sample "spuriously pulls down the average of states not holding initiatives."[38] Once statistics from the South are deleted from the 1978 data, the findings more closely resemble those of table 5.8.[39] Furthermore, both Telschow and Everson ignore the potential effect of the concurrent candidate elections in 1978. Of the sixteen states deciding an initiative in 1978, only two did not have a contest for U.S. senator or governor. In half of these initiative states, there were contests for both offices.[40] A comparison of initiative states with noninitiative states in 1978 indicates that the initiative states were more likely to have elections for governor that year than were the noninitiative states (75 percent and 70 percent, respectively). Given these factors, it is quite plausible that in 1978 voters in initiative states were responding to the stimulus of candidate contests and not initiatives.

In sum, over the last twenty years, turnout generally has been the same whether or not states had the initiative process. These aggregate findings are confirmed by the 1962 and 1978 survey data and by the low turnout for special proposition elections. No evidence exists for the claim that initiatives will increase voter turnout over time.

CONCLUSIONS

A careful review of electoral participation in candidate races and on ballot propositions in California, Massachusetts, and Washington has demonstrated important differences in overall rates of participation, both between candidate races and propositions and among different types of propositions. In general elections, participation on propositions is lower than in many candidate races; for propositions placed on the ballot by the legislature, participation is considerably lower than in most candidate races. However, in states where voters decide propositions in primary elections, participation on propositions is generally higher than for about one-half to two-thirds of the candidate races. In fact, in the 1976 and 1978 California primary elections the highly contested nuclear power and property-tax initiatives had lower dropoff than any of the candidate elections. Whether propositions are decided in primary, general, or special elections has an effect on the total number of participants but, interestingly, does not appear to affect dropoff.

Analysis of aggregate data has also revealed high rates of voter participation on initiatives and popular referendums, whether they appear first on the ballot, as in Washington, or last, as in California. Fatigue, therefore, does not interfere with participation on either an initiative or a referendum. On other types of statewide propositions, however, dropoff generally tends to increase as one proceeds down the ballot; and for these types of propositions dropoff is quite high, often with more than one-fourth of the voters not participating. In candidate races for controller, secretary of state, and treasurer, the effects of fatigue are also apparent. One of the most interesting regularities found in this chapter is the relatively constant rate of dropoff on propositions across the three states. Voting on fewer propositions, as in Massachusetts, does not lower the dropoff rate.

Despite widespread variation in turnout and ballot length, the dropoff level on statewide propositions is relatively constant. As has been demonstrated, dropoff on propositions varies less from state to state and by type of election than does the dropoff on candidate races that come earlier on the ballot. Consistently, 75–80 percent of those who turn out cast votes on statewide propositions. Thus, many voters appear willing to vote on propositions, regardless of how little they may know about them. In chapter 7 I will address the question of voter knowledge, but it is important to note here that voters are more willing to vote on a proposition, on which they have no ballot cues, than they are to vote for a nonpartisan office such as that of superintendent of public instruction. As has been noted, dropoff is consistently much lower for initiatives than for other types of statewide propositions. Furthermore, voters appear willing to search the ballot to find initiatives.

It is clear that as many as a third of those who turn out do not vote on some statewide propositions; yet to be addressed is the important question of which voters drop off. If dropoff is randomly distributed throughout the electorate, then it may be of little consequence. But if some types of voters tend consistently to drop off, the representativeness of the electorate is further biased. In chapter 6 I will examine the degree of representativeness of initiative and referendum voters.

The Representativeness of Voters
Who Decide Statewide Propositions

Data on the levels of voter participation in elections having statewide propositions show that on the average 15–18 percent of those who turn out do not vote on statewide propositions. But are some of these voters more likely to drop off than others? The rather constant rate of dropoff on propositions found in presidential, midterm, and primary elections suggests that there may be an explanation for dropoff across elections. Another important finding discussed in chapter 5 is the fact that dropoff is much lower on initiatives than on other types of statewide propositions. The evidence is clear that some people vote on certain propositions but not on others.

Which voters drop off, and why? Are there segments of the population that are more likely to drop off on propositions? To what extent are proposition electorates representative? Because the concept of representation is so all-encompassing, it is important to specify clearly the population or populations to be represented and to provide comparisons of representativeness in other contexts or electoral situations. The population to be represented in proposition elections can be the body of voters who turn out to vote, or, more broadly, the electorate. As has been noted, proponents of initiatives frequently assert that the decisions reached by referendum are more representative than those made in candidate elections. This argument rests in part on the assumption that initiatives provide a more accurate transmission of public opinion than do legislators. But part of the argument also stems from the fact that propositions presumably activate a more representative electorate. Thus, the primary comparative referent to be used here will be candidate voters. Are proposition voters more representative of the citizenry than candidate voters?

Representation as used in this context employs the concept of descriptive representation rather than other concepts such as authority or accountability. The most thorough treatment of the concept of representation is that of Hanna Pitkin. According to Pitkin, descriptive representation focuses on "the representative's characteristics, on what he *is* or *is like,* on being something rather than doing something. The representative does not act for others; he "stands for" them, *by virtue of a correspondence or connection between*

100

them, a resemblance or reflection. In political terms, what seems important is less what the legislature does than how it is composed." [1] Descriptive representation has at its core the assumption that persons stand for others "by being sufficiently like them." [2] Students of voting and legislatures have frequently used the concept of descriptive representation. To what extent does a legislator resemble the constituency? Do the attributes of voters correspond to those of the electorate? The research reported in this chapter compares the extent to which those who vote in candidate contests or on ballot propositions are representative of the larger population, including those who turn out and the total electorate. In chapter 5, I examined the nature of those who vote in special, primary, and general elections. In this chapter I compare the rates of voting for candidates and for propositions to determine whether there is an added education, age, or class bias in proposition voting beyond the general bias documented in chapter 5. In this chapter I also explore possible explanations for voter dropoff on ballot propositions.

Voting on initiatives is often more complicated than voting for candidates. Not only is the voter faced with often complex and technical issues but the traditional economizing device of a party cue is absent. What types of voters, if any, are advantaged by this type of electoral arrangement? Some voters, because of their educational resources and political experience, may be more able to determine how their own interests are affected by propositions and to vote accordingly. But not all voters have these important political skills. Despite the clear relevance of who does and does not vote on propositions, little empirical study of these questions has previously been done.

A brief review of what is known about the "representativeness" of voters in similar electoral situations — nonpartisan local elections and direct primaries — will provide insights into the problem of representation when voters are called upon to make decisions without the aid of a party cue. As has been demonstrated, direct primaries and nonpartisan electoral systems grew out of the same reform era as the initiative and referendum and reflect the same perspective on government. How representative are the voters who participate in direct primaries and nonpartisan local elections?

Representativeness of Voters in Nonpartisan and Primary Elections

The literature on the origins of nonpartisanship in city politics documents effectively the motivations of the reformers to reduce the influence of political bosses and political parties. [3] The literature on the effects of the reforms and, more specifically, on which parties or groups benefited from the reforms is extensive. [4] While the studies vary in locale and method, it appears that nonpartisanship typically enhances the probability that Republicans will win local elections.

One of the most frequently cited studies on this subject is Eugene C. Lee's *The Politics of Nonpartisanship.* Lee presents evidence that Republicans benefited from nonpartisanship and were overrepresented in city government. For the period 1931 to 1955, in the cities Lee studied Republican registration averaged 42 percent, but 69 percent of the mayors and councilmen were Republicans. In Pomona, California, for instance, 50 percent of the voters were registered as Republican, but 85 percent of the mayors and councilmen were Republican.

Writing several years later, Willis D. Hawley found strong evidence of a Republican bias in nonpartisan elections held in cities with populations of more than sixty thousand:

> If only cities above 60,000 are considered, the relationship between city size and the Republican bias of nonpartisanship becomes more pronounced. In these cities the average Republican bias is 35.1 percent; that is, *Democrats would have won more than a third more of the races for councilmen and mayor in these cities than they did between 1957 and 1966 had elections been partisan rather than nonpartisan.* It might be noted that the average partisan bias for all cities regardless of size was a Republican bias of 5.16 percent.[5]

Hawley also found that in cities of under sixty thousand the effect of nonpartisanship was small and worked to the advantage of Democrats almost as often as it worked to the advantage of Republicans. Socioeconomic status accounted for about one-fourth of the variance in the bias of nonpartisanship; in cities whose residents were poorer, less educated, and engaged in working-class occupations, Republicans were more likely to win in nonpartisan elections.[6]

In direct primaries also, the voter is unable to use the organizing device of party identification. Descriptions of both the origins and development of primaries confirm that the reformers who established direct primaries had the same ethos as those who established nonpartisan local elections and direct legislation.[7] Several attempts have been made to assess the levels of participation in primaries and the extent to which participants were representative.[8]

In general, citizens who participate vigorously are more likely to see their preferences fulfilled. James Lengle demonstrates that the citizens who actually participated in the California primaries of 1968 and 1972 were demographically unrepresentative of the party identifiers within the state. Lengle also demonstrates a high correlation between socioeconomic status and participation in presidential primaries. He finds that nonparticipation in primaries may alter the outcome. Differences in rates of participation were important in 1972 because the nonparticipants had a clear preference for Humphrey, while the participants preferred McGovern. Had the primary been a perfect transmitter of the feelings of party identifiers, Humphrey, instead of McGovern, would have won the 1972 California primary and perhaps the nomination.[9]

Lengle's findings of unrepresentativeness in primary electorates are quite different from those of Austin Ranney. In his study of 1966 primary voters in

Wisconsin, Ranney found that in terms of issue position or candidate preferences, "primary voters are not significantly unrepresentative of the general party following." [10] Ranney's findings run counter to the conventional wisdom, which had held that "in states with a modicum of inter-party competition primary participants are often by no means representative of the party." [11] While studies of primary electorates in different states may reach opposing conclusions about whether participants are unrepresentative in issue or candidate preference, they typically find, as shown in the preceding chapter, that voters in primaries are better educated, more affluent, and more interested in politics. In chapter 5 I also demonstrated that in California liberals constituted a larger proportion of those voting in the presidential primary years than of those voting in non-presidential primary elections.

One of the principal arguments of the progressive reformers was that the traditional devices of representative democracy did not give the citizen an adequate voice in public affairs. Thus, the reforms of "direct democracy" — the initiative, referendum, recall, nonpartisan elections, and direct primaries — were envisioned as allowing more citizens to participate more effectively. But to what extent do the initiative and referendum fulfill the goal of effective representation for more citizens? In this chapter I attempt to find out.

WHICH VOTERS ARE MORE LIKELY TO VOTE ON PROPOSITIONS?

Students of direct legislation at the local level, where there have been numerous propositions on a wide variety of issues, also have found voters who participate on local propositions to be unrepresentative. Howard Hamilton, after examining the evidence on participation in local referendums, concluded, "Comparisons of the voters and nonvoters confirms that direct democracy also has a distinct social bias. Because of low turnout, local referenda are likely to have more class bias than major elections." [12] To what extent are Hamilton's findings true at the state level?

In a survey conducted in 1976 by Research Analysis for the *Boston Globe,* six hundred Massachusetts citizens who reported that they intended to vote were asked if they usually took time to read and vote on proposed constitutional amendments and state laws. Twenty percent of Massachusetts voters reported that they "tend to skip voting" on propositions — a figure that is close to the average dropoff in voting on propositions in Massachusetts. [13] But this dropoff is not evenly distributed among all groups. Low-income respondents indicated high rates of dropoff, while respondents with incomes of over twenty thousand dollars, Republicans, liberals, and males were much more likely to indicate that they voted on propositions. [14]

National election studies conducted in 1970, 1972, and 1974 by the Center for Political Studies at the University of Michigan reveal a strikingly similar pattern to that found in the Massachusetts data. Voters were asked, "If you had state or local propositions on the ballot, did you vote on all, most, some, or none of these propositions?" The percentage of voters who voted on all or most propositions is reported in table 6.1. Level of education has a strong impact on the likelihood of voting on all or most propositions. For these three elections, on the average 90 percent of the voters with college degrees reported voting on all or most propositions. In contrast, under two-thirds of those with less than an eighth-grade education reported voting on all or most of the propositions. These data provide a partial answer to the question of who participates in deciding propositions. In general, the likelihood of full participation increases with education.

While the difference in voting rates between categories of income is less pronounced than the difference due to educational level, it is nevertheless evident that poorer respondents are less likely to report voting on all or most of the propositions on the ballot. Thirty percent of the respondents with an income under five thousand dollars reported voting on only some or none of the propositions. The effect of income on the likelihood of voting on all or most ballot propositions persists after controlling for education. Thus, both education and income play a role in whether a voter will vote on all or most propositions. Blacks are much less likely to participate fully in the process than whites. While the differences between categories of subjective social class are less marked, they are consistent with the other data suggesting a connection between low socioeconomic status and nonparticipation on propositions.[15]

As I demonstrated in chapter 5, the number of propositions presented to voters varies considerably from state to state. Massachusetts generally has less than half as many statewide propositions as California or Washington. In 1976, however, Massachusetts voters were faced with nine statewide propositions, and this unusually large number of measures for Massachusetts voters prompted speculation that many voters would not vote on all of the propositions.[16]

In response to an item in the Massachusetts Poll, nearly two-thirds of Massachusetts voters reported that they would vote on all of the statewide propositions. The proportion so reporting — 65 percent — was very close to the 67 percent of the national sample from 1972, which also indicated participation on all measures. In both polls, there is clear evidence of the effect of socioeconomic status on the reported rate of voting on propositions. Looking at income, for instance, we see that only half of the Massachusetts Poll respondents with incomes under five thousand dollars intended to vote on all propositions, while 68 percent of the high-income respondents indicated that they would read and vote on all nine propositions.

Data from the 1970–74 Center for Political Studies National Election Studies and from the 1976 Massachusetts Poll support the conclusion that

Table 6.1

PERCENTAGE OF VOTERS IN THE UNITED STATES WHO VOTED ON ALL OR MOST BALLOT
PROPOSITIONS, 1970–74, BY DEMOGRAPHIC CATEGORY

Demographic Category	1970	1972	1974	Mean
Education				
0–8	65%	62%	61%	63%
9–11	71	79	74	75
12	77	80	77	78
Some college	90	88	89	89
Bachelor's Degree	86	94	89	90
Income				
$0–4,999	66	70	73	70
$5,000–9,999	75	80	74	76
$10,000–14,999	83	86	81	83
$15,000–24,999	92	88	83	88
$25,000 +	83	99	91	91
Occupation				
Professional	86	94	88	89
Managerial	78	83	86	82
Clerical	79	82	81	81
Sales	80	88	87	85
Craft	83	78	58	73
Operative	72	75	60	69
Service	61	79	62	67
Laborer	70	63	66	66
Race				
White	81	84	81	82
Black	45	62	65	57
Sex				
Male	82	83	83	83
Female	76	82	77	78
Party Identification				
Strong Democrat	77	77	77	77
Weak Democrat	71	77	79	76
Independent Democrat	74	82	83	80
Independent	87	86	77	83
Independent Republican	85	88	82	85
Weak Republican	80	86	81	82
Strong Republican	83	83	81	82
Total	78%	82%	80%	80%

Source: American National Election Studies for 1970, 1972, and 1974, Center for Political
Studies, Inter-university Consortium for Political and Social Research, University of
Michigan, Ann Arbor, Michigan.

poorer, less educated people vote less often on initiatives and referendums.
Yet, as we have learned, these groups are also less likely to turn out to vote
generally. The question therefore arises, are poorer and less educated people
underrepresented in the initiative process simply because they are less likely to
turn out, or are they doubly underrepresented — less likely to turn out and less
likely to vote on ballot measures if they do turn out?

WHO VOTES ON BALLOT MEASURES AND IN CANDIDATE CONTESTS?

It has already been established that certain kinds of people — specifically those who are young, black, or female or who have less education or income — are less likely than other citizens to go to the polls. The Massachusetts data just analyzed provide evidence that even when members of these relatively non-participatory groups do turn out, they are less likely to report having voted on all propositions. These data, however, do not provide the necessary information for a comparison between participation on propositions and participation in candidate contests. It is important to know whether the voters who participate in candidate contests are any more or less representative than those who vote on statewide propositions.

Official election returns show precisely how many voters mark their ballots in the candidate races and on the propositions. Thus, aggregate election data provide accurate estimates of overall levels of dropoff; but because they have been aggregated, they do not reveal what kinds of people are most likely to drop off. To discover what kinds of people are most likely to drop off, I analyzed post-election survey data from eight California primary and general elections. These data allow us to view rates of voting and dropoff for a variety of offices and propositions. The percentage of voters who indicated that they skipped voting for a particular candidate contest or ballot measure is presented in table 6.2. Voters who did not remember how they voted are not included in this measure of dropoff; if those persons had been included, the percentage would be much larger.

Voters indicate that on ballot propositions they drop off at rates roughly double the rates for candidate races. The range of reported dropoff in candidate races is from 1 percent to as high as 5 percent in a primary election contest. The range of dropoff for propositions is much larger: from a low of 1 percent on Proposition 9, the 1980 Jarvis income-tax initiative, to 17 percent on Proposition 4, a 1974 constitutional amendment proposed by the legislature to alter the number and length of terms of members on the University of California board of regents. The sample of propositions covered, however, contains the most controversial and best-publicized initiatives. As I documented in chapter 5, dropoff is lowest for these measures, and measures such as Proposition 4 may therefore be more representative of noninitiative ballot propositions. There is also some variation in the type of candidate contest for which post-election data were available. The candidate dropoff data include contests for the presidency in both primary and general elections and other well-publicized contests such as for governor and U.S. senator. At the same time, the data summarized in table 6.2 include contests for lieutenant governor and attorney general — contests in which more overall dropoff is evident.

Less educated, blue-collar workers, nonwhites, and those over age sixty-

VOTERS' SELF-REPORTED DROPOFF, 1972–80, BY DEMOGRAPHIC CATEGORY, IN PERCENT

	1972 Gen: House of Rep.	1972: Prop. 2	1974 Gen: Governor	1974: Prop. 4	1976 Prim: President	1976 Prim: Senator	1976: Prop. 15	1976 Gen: President	1976 Gen: Senator	1976: Prop. 13	1976: Prop. 14	1978 Prim: Prop. 8	1978 Prim: Prop. 13	1978 Gen: Governor	1978 Gen: Lt. Governor	1978 Gen: Attorney General	1978: Prop. 5	1978: Prop. 6	1980: Prop. 9	1980: Prop. 10	1980: Prop. 11	Average Candidate	Average Proposition
Education																							
0–11	5	16	3	44	8	15	3	1	3	12	5	17	10	1	3	5	6	8			5	5	13
12	2	8	2	21	4	11	2	2	1	2	3	10	11	0	2	3	3	4			3	3	7
Some college	6	9	4	13	5	10	2	0	5	5	2	6	6	1	3	2	1	3			4	4	5
B.A. degree or more	2	2	4	7	3	5	0	1	3	3	2	6	3	2	5	1	1	2			3	3	3
Income																							
Lowest	4	14	3	29	11	10	2	2	7	7	3	12	6	1	4	6	3	6	2	3	5	5	7
Medium/low	7	13	3	11	8	13	2	0	3	8	1	11	7	1	4	3	3	4			3	5	7
Medium/high	3	5	3	18	1	7	1	1	4	5	4	7	6	1	3	3	2	3	1	1	3	3	5
Highest	1	7	3	7	3	8	0	1	2	3	2	4	6	1	2	2	1	1	2	2	3	3	3
Occupation																							
Service/labor	7	7	0	31	7	24	6	6	4													7	12
Craft/operative	3	7	3	27	1	9	2	1	2													3	10
Clerical/sales	6	5	3	9	3	10	1	3	0													4	5
Professional/managerial	2		5	3	12	3	4	1	4													3	6
Race																							
White	4	8	7	4	7	5	1	1	3	3	3	5	3	3	3	1	3	1	2	2	4	4	5
Nonwhite	3	9	6	2	6	6	5	3	3	3	3	6	3	3	3	6	8	4	5	8	4	4	8
Age																							
18–29	7	7	3	16	1	1	1	1	6	6	2	5	4	1	7	5	1	3	2	3	2	4	4
30–44	3	6	1	15	4	11	2	1	3	3	3	6	5	3	3	3	2	2	1	3	3	3	4
45–64	2	7	1	13	4	9	0	3	1	6	2	8	3	2	2	2	5	3	1	2	3	3	4
65+	2	16	5	32	10	13	2	0	3	6	2	17	11	1	2	2	3	1	1	3	4	4	11
Total	4	8	3	17	5	6	2	1	3	4	3	11	8	1	3	2	3	2	1	2	4	4	7

Sources: California Polls, 1972–80, The Field Institute, San Francisco, California; Survey of Attitudes on Nuclear Power, June 1976, Rand Corporation, Santa Monica, California; CBS News/*Los Angeles Times* exit polls, 1978–80.

Note: Because of inflation in the 1970s, it is necessary to present these data in terms of relative position rather than in actual dollars.

five are much more likely than other voters to drop off on ballot propositions. Voters in these same categories are not more likely to drop off in candidate contests. The relationship between education and dropoff on ballot propositions is especially strong. Nearly half of those who had not finished high school dropped off when voting on Proposition 4 in 1974, but only 3 percent of these same voters dropped off when voting for governor in the same election. As education increases, the amount of reported dropoff decreases. These data are consistent with the data analyzed from Massachusetts and present a strong case that those who vote on ballot measures have a socioeconomic and educational bias beyond that normally found in turnout. Additionally, older voters are significantly more likely to drop off, especially on ballot propositions.

The data just analyzed give us a sense of which voters drop off and in what situations. The extent of bias represented by these figures, however, is not summarized in the preceding tables. In order to measure the degree of over- or underrepresentation present in those who vote in candidate contests and on ballot propositions, the ratio of representation for each category of independent variables can be computed. The proportion of voters who went to the polls is compared with the proportion of voters who reported voting for a proposition or in a candidate race in tables 6.3 and 6.4. These ratios reveal both the direction and the magnitude of overrepresentation or underrepresentation for each category of socioeconomic or demographic variables.[17] The formal definition of the measure for any category is:

$$RR = \frac{Y_i - X_i}{X_i} \times 100,$$

where RR = the ratio of over- or underrepresentation; X_i = the percentage of all voters comprising the category; and Y_i = for the same category, the percentage that actually voted in the candidate or proposition contest. This measure of over- or underrepresentation is identical to the one employed by Sidney Verba and Norman Nie in *Participation in America* and similar to the one employed by Robert A. Dahl in *A Preface to Democratic Theory.*[18] The rates of turnout and vote on Proposition 4 and the ratios of representation for the statewide proposition and the gubernatorial election are presented in table 6.3. In 1974, people with eight years or less of education comprised 8 percent of all voters but only 4 percent of the Proposition 4 voters. Thus, persons with less than an eighth-grade education were underrepresented in the voting on Proposition 4 by a ratio of − 50. In the vote on Proposition 4, the less educated segment of voters was clearly underrepresented, while the well educated were overrepresented. It has been demonstrated previously that persons with lower socioeconomic status are less likely to turn out, but according to the data in table 6.3, if voters are asked to decide ballot measures in addition to choosing candidates, the problem is only compounded. Citizens with

RATIOS OF REPRESENTATION FOR PROPOSITION 4 VOTERS AND FOR GUBERNATORIAL VOTERS, 1974 CALIFORNIA GENERAL ELECTION, BY DEMOGRAPHIC CATEGORY

	Percentage of Turnout (%) (N)		Percentage of Proposition 4 Voters (%) (N)		Percentage of Gubernatorial Voters (%) (N)		Ratio of Representation for Proposition 4 Voters	Ratio of Representation for Gubernatorial Voters
Education								
0–8	8%	(50)	4%	(20)	8%	(47)	−50	PR
9–11	8	(48)	6	(25)	8	(48)	−25	PR
12	26	(161)	23	(105)	26	(158)	−12	PR
Some college	33	(210)	36	(160)	33	(196)	+9	PR
Degree	15	(95)	17	(78)	15	(92)	+13	PR
Advanced degree	11	(67)	14	(63)	10	(63)	+27	−9
Income								
$0–4,999	12	(68)	6	(25)	11	(66)	−50	−8
$5,000–9,999	20	(116)	20	(86)	20	(113)	PR	PR
$10,000–14,999	21	(125)	22	(93)	21	(120)	+5	PR
$15,000–19,999	21	(126)	22	(95)	21	(123)	+5	PR
$20,000 +	27	(157)	30	(129)	27	(153)	+11	PR
Occupation								
Service/labor	7	(41)	5	(25)	7	(41)	−29	PR
Craft/operative	19	(113)	16	(70)	19	(110)	−16	PR
Clerical/sales	17	(99)	19	(82)	16	(96)	+12	−6
Professional/managerial	41	(240)	44	(188)	40	(231)	+7	−2
Race								
White	91	(570)	91	(408)	91	(550)	PR	PR
Nonwhite	9	(59)	9	(42)	10	(58)	PR	+11
Age								
18–29	19	(120)	21	(93)	19	(116)	+11	PR
30–44	28	(173)	29	(129)	28	(171)	+4	PR
45–60	27	(171)	29	(132)	27	(165)	+7	PR
60 +	26	(166)	21	(96)	26	(157)	−24	PR

Source: California Poll 7408, The Field Institute, San Francisco, California. 6–17 November 1974.

Notes:

Ratio of Representation = $\dfrac{\text{Percentage of Proposition 4 voters} - \text{Percentage of turnout}}{\text{Percentage of turnout}} \times 100$

PR = perfect representation.

lower socioeconomic status not only are less likely to come to the polls but also are less likely to vote on many statewide propositions if they do come. Citizens at the other end of the socioeconomic ladder enjoy a double advantage: they are both more likely to turn out to vote and more likely to register a preference on the proposition.

Data for the categories of income in table 6.3 present the same overall picture as that discussed for education: the poor are significantly underrepresented, with citizens earning less than five thousand dollars having a − 50 ratio of underrepresentation. Older voters were also significantly underrepresented in voting on Proposition 4. The underrepresentation of less educated and low-income groups is substantial, and the overrepresentation of high-education categories is especially pronounced.

But is this pattern also true of voting in candidate races? It is clear from the data in table 6.3 that the gubernatorial electorate is almost perfectly representative of those who turned out. The contrast between the representativeness of proposition electorates and that of candidate electorates (columns 3 and 4 in the table) is stark. Fewer voters dropped off in the governor's contest, and those who did tended to be randomly distributed across the voting population. Those who dropped off on the proposition, on the other hand, tended to come from the less educated, low-income segments of the voting population. These findings are consistent with those of Clubb and Traugott, who, after examining a national sample of referendum voters in the 1968 election, conclude that "referenda voting was even more closely associated with income, education, and subjective social class than was voting in partisan races."[19]

The contrast between the representativeness of those who voted on the proposition and that of those who voted on the candidate race in 1974 is significant. For purposes of comparison, the ratio of representation for the same variables for all of the candidate contests and ballot propositions for which data are available are tabulated in table 6.4. The table also contains an average column for both candidate and proposition elections to facilitate comparison of the two types of voting. A comparison of turnout and actual voting reveals that the less educated, poorer, blue-collar, and older voters are underrepresented in voting on ballot propositions. Underrepresentation of the less educated and poorer voters is much less manifest in the voting in candidate contests, where blue-collar and older voters are not underrepresented at all. It is important to note that the baseline population used in computing these ratios is the number who turned out to vote; if adult population had been used as the baseline, the ratios would be much larger.[20]

In every proposition election but one the less educated were significantly underrepresented, yet in half of the candidate races they formed the same proportion of actual voters as they did of the total who reported that they had turned out. Again in table 6.4, the underrepresentation of the older voters on propositions is manifest; but they are not underrepresented in the voting in candidate contests.

The Massachusetts and California data can be compared with data from Florida. The Policy Science Program at Florida State University conducted a post-election survey of Florida voters from which the ratios of representation for several propositions and a candidate race in a single election can be computed. In the 1978 general election Florida voters decided propositions as controversial as the equal rights amendment and legalized gambling and as bland as executive reorganization and the establishment of a public service commission. The ratios of representation of voters on the governor's race and on eight statewide ballot propositions are compared in table 6.5. The results of the Florida election survey indicate that of those who turn out, the less educated, the nonwhites, and the blue-collar workers are consistently underrepresented in deciding statewide ballot propositions but not in deciding the governorship. If the baseline population were all adults, rather that just those who turned out, these groups would of course be even more underrepresented. The degree of underrepresentation was nearly identical across all propositions, with two exceptions — the propositions on legislative apportionment and creation of a state board of education. Unlike in California, none of the Florida propositions came close to the candidate races in the level of representation. These data confirm that the underrepresentation of some groups in deciding statewide propositions is a problem across states; indeed, it may be even more widespread than the California data indicate.

POSSIBLE EXPLANATIONS FOR VOTER DROPOFF ON BALLOT PROPOSITIONS

Regrettably, none of the available surveys asked questions directly addressing the issue of why voters drop off. It seems reasonable, however, that voters with less education are less likely to have opinions on issues and are more reliant on a political party and on candidates for office to structure the political world. When less educated voters are asked to vote on complex and often technical issues, they are less able to connect their political opinions and choices with a vote and therefore are less likely to participate.

Does the wording of ballot questions affect dropoff? Presumably, the less educated and the poor may be less able to read and understand questions. The 1976 Massachusetts data permit assessment of the effect of ballot wording on support for an issue. Respondents were first asked whether they favored or opposed the general issue for each of five statewide propositions coming before voters that November. Later in the same survey, respondents were asked to read the actual propositions and then report their vote. For each of the five issues, the percentage supporting the general idea and the

Table 6.4

Ratios of Representation for Candidate Elections and Ballot Propositions in California, 1972–80, by Demographic Category

	Candidates	1972, President[a]	1972, U.S. House[a]	1974, Governor[a]	1976, President[b]	1976, Senator[b]	1976, President[a]	1976, Senator[a]	1978, Governor[b]	1978, Governor[a]	1978, Lieutenant Governor[a]	1978, Attorney General[a]	1980, President[b]
Education													
0–11	−	− 6	−	−	− 6	− 7	− 7	−	−	−	−	−	− 8
12	−	−	−	−	− 4	− 4	−	− 4	−	−	−	−	−
Some college	+ 3	−	−	− 3	−	+ 3	−	−	−	−	−	−	−
B.A. degree or more	−	+ 5	− 4	+ 4	+ 7	−	−	+ 3	−	− 3	−	−	−
Income[c]													
Lowest	−	− 8	− 8	−	−	−	− 0	−	−	− 7	− 7	−	−11
Medium/low	− 4	− 4	−	−10	−10	−	− 7	−	−	−	−	−	−
Medium/high	−	−	−	+ 3	+ 3	−	−	−	−	−	−	−	+10
Highest	−	+ 6	−	+ 3	+ 3	+ 2	+ 2	−	−	−	−	+ 4	− 8
Occupation													
Service/labor	+13	−	−	−	−18	−	−						
Craft/Operative	−	− 5	−	−	−	−	+ 4						
Clerical/sales	−	+ 7	− 6	− 6	− 6	−	−						
Professional/ managerial	+ 3	−	− 2	−	+ 4	−	−						
Race													
White	− 1	− 1	−	−	−	+ 1	−	− 1	−	−	− 1	−	
Nonwhite	−	−	−	−	− 6	− 6	−	+ 7	−	−	+ 6	−	
Age													
18–29	−	− 4	−	−	+ 5	+ 4	−	− 5	−	− 5	− 5	−	+12
30–44	+ 3	+ 3	−	+ 4	−	−	−	− 3	−	−	−	−	+ 4
45–64	− 4	−	−	−	−	− 4	−	+ 4	−	−	−	−	+10
65 +	−	−	−	− 4	−	−	−	−	−	−	−	−	−

Sources: California Polls, 1972–80, The Field Institute, San Francisco, California; Survey of Attitudes on Nuclear Power, June 1976, Rand Corporation, Santa Monica, California; CBS News/*Los Angeles Times* exit polls, 1978–80.

[a] General election.
[b] Primary election.
[c] Because of inflation in the 1970s, it is necessary to present these data in terms of relative position than in actual dollars.

percentage who would vote yes after reading the actual ballot wording are presented by income category in table 6.6.

Data for four of the five issues examined in the Massachusetts Poll show a decline in favorable responses after the respondent had read the ballot propositions. On the income-tax and flat-rate electricity measures, support for the issue declined by 17 percent and 18 percent, respectively. These measures, because of their fiscal nature, were more technical and difficult to com-

Table 6.4 *(continued)*

1980, Senator[b]	1980, President[a]	Average	Propositions	1972, Prop. 2[a]	1974, Prop. 4[a]	1976, Prop. 15[b]	1976, Prop. 13[a]	1976, Prop. 14[a]	1978, Prop. 8[b]	1978, Prop. 13[b]	1978, Prop. 5[a]	1978, Prop. 6[a]	1980, Prop. 9[b]	1980, Prop. 10[b]	1980, Prop. 11[b]	Average
	−3	−17	−39	−7	−14	−7	−13	−	−8	−8						−12
	−1	−	−12	−	−	−	−	−	−4	−4	−4					−3
−2	−	+3	+9	−	−	+3	−	−	−	−						+2
+3	−	+18	+19	−	−	−	−		+3	+3	+3	+3				+5
−5	−	−4	−15	−50	−6	−9	−	−	−	−1	−7	−5	−	−5		−9
	−3	−8	−	+4	−7	−	−4	−	−	−4						−2
−	+1	+6	+5	−	−	−3	−	−	−	−			+7	−		+1
−	+2	+1	−	+11	+8	+2	−	+3	−	+4	+4	+3	−10	−		+4
	−1	−	−29	−	−											−5
	−	−5	−16	−	−											−3
	−1	+7	+12	−	−											+3
	+1	+8	+7			−2	−									+2
+1	−	−	−	−	−	+1	−	+1	−1	+1	+1		+1	+1	+1	+1
−11	−	−7	−15	+11	−	−6	−	−7	−7	−6	−6		−11	−11	−11	−6
+12	−	+1	+8	+11	−	−	+4	−	−	−	−		+18	+18	+18	+6
+7	−	+1	+3	+4	−	−	−	+3	+3	−	−		+6	+6	+6	+3
−21	−	−3	−4	+7	−	−	−	−4	−4	+7	−3	−	−17	−21	−21	−5
	−	−	−11	−24	−9	−	−	−13	+7	−	−6					−6

prehend as actual ballot propositions than some of the other propositions. In contrast, the straightforward wording of the propositions on the equal rights amendment, handguns, and nonreturnable containers quite closely reflected actual voter sentiments on the general issues and therefore appeared to present fewer problems of comprehension. Only on the nonreturnable-containers measure was there an increase in favorable responses after the proposition was read. The absence of a drop in support for this proposition is explained in part by the relative simplicity of the proposition. Dropoff appears to have been highest on the more complex and technically worded propositions.

Does the electoral mechanism of statewide ballot propositions effectively translate public opinion on an issue into public policy? Being in favor of the

Table 6.5

RATIOS OF REPRESENTATION IN THE GOVERNOR'S RACE AND IN EIGHT STATEWIDE PROPOSITIONS FOR THE 1978 FLORIDA GENERAL ELECTION, BY DEMOGRAPHIC CATEGORY

	Governor	Proposition 2, Equal rights amendment	Proposition 3, Legislative apportionment	Proposition 4, Executive reorganization	Proposition 5, Establishment of public service commission	Proposition 6, Judicial elections	Proposition 7, Tax laws	Proposition 8, State board of education	Proposition 9, Casino gambling
Education									
0-8	PR	-25	-25	-50	-25	-25	-25	-50	-25
9-11	PR	-11	-22	-11	-11	-11	-22	-22	PR
12	PR	PR	-3	-3	-3	-3	-3	-6	PR
Some college	PR	PR	+4	+4	PR	+4	-4	+4	-4
Advanced degree	PR	PR	+13	+13	+13	+13	+13	+13	PR
Occupation									
Semiskilled	PR	-8	-15	-8	-8	-8	-8	-8	-8
Skilled	PR	PR	-11	-22	-11	-11	-11	-11	-11
Clerical	-3	PR	PR	PR	PR	+3	PR	PR	+3
Managerial	-8	PR	+8	PR	PR	+5	PR	PR	PR
Professional	+5	+9	+5	+9	+5	+5	+5	+9	+5
Housewife	PR	PR	+16	PR	+11	PR	PR	+17	PR
Race									
White	+1	+3	+3	+4	+4	+3	+3	+4	+3
Nonwhite	-9	-27	-27	-36	-36	-27	-27	-36	-18

Source: Florida State University Poll, 8–20 November 1978, Policy Science Program, Florida State University.

Notes: The sample was limited to those who cast ballots; therefore, the ratio of representation is based on turnout rather than voting-age population. Number of respondents = 786.

PR = perfect representation.

Table 6.6

MASSACHUSETTS VOTERS' ATTITUDES ON GENERAL ISSUES AND INTENDED VOTE ON PROPOSITIONS, 1976, BY LEVEL OF INCOME

Percentage Yes Response to (1) General Issue and (2) Ballot Proposition Wording

Income	Graduated Income Tax			Flat-Rate Electricity			E.R.A.			Handguns			Containers			Total	
	(1)	(2)	Change	(1)	(2)	Change	(1)	(2)	Change	(1)	(2)	Change	(1)	(2)	Change		
$0-4,999	68%	36%	-32%	61%	22%	-39%	59%	53%	-6%	48%	29%	-19%	54%	58%	+4%	11%	(59)
$5,000-9,999	63	41	-22	45	29	-16	75	73	-2	43	43	—	36	43	+7	17	(91)
$10,000-14,999	69	50	-19	47	32	-15	76	72	-4	39	38	-1	44	47	+3	27	(144)
$15,000-19,999	57	45	-22	50	30	-20	80	73	-7	39	39	—	47	48	+1	21	(109)
$20,000-24,999	55	35	-20	55	36	-19	74	82	+8	42	41	-1	52	58	+6	12	(66)
$25,000+	38	40	+2	38	35	-3	78	70	-8	46	49	+3	44	51	+7	12	(63)
Total	60%	43%	-17%	49%	31%	-18%	75%	71%	-4%	42%	40%	-2%	46%	49%	+3%		

Source: Massachusetts Poll, Research Analysis, Boston Globe, 29 September-3 October 1976.

principle of a graduated state personal income tax is one thing; voting yes on the proposed constitutional amendment may be quite another. Although 60 percent were in favor of the idea in principle, the positive response on the proposed amendment as written was 17 percentage points lower, at 43 percent.

Unfortunately, the Massachusetts Poll did not ascertain the respondents' level of education; thus, the effect of ballot wording on those with less education cannot be measured using this survey. However, table 6.6 does contain evidence that the greatest effect of ballot proposition wording was upon poorer voters. While those with incomes under five thousand dollars were among the most supportive of the idea of a graduated state income tax, much of that support dissipated when these persons were asked to vote after reading the actual ballot wording. Persons in the lowest income category were the most likely to state that they could not vote on this proposition either because it was too long and complicated or because they did not understand what a yes or no vote would mean. Even though this is the kind of issue that benefits persons having low socioeconomic status, these persons were apparently unable to act in their self-interest in this context. In sharp contrast, the response of those earning over twenty-five thousand dollars to the actual ballot proposition almost perfectly mirrored their attitudes on the general issue of a graduated income tax. For respondents earning between five thousand and twenty-five thousand dollars, the support for the idea of a graduated income tax declined by about 20 percent between general issue and actual proposition. Clearly, wealthier people were better able to use the mechanism of direct legislation to express their policy preference and their economic self-interest.

The same general pattern is found on the question of flat-rate electricity. Sixty-one percent of respondents earning less than five thousand dollars supported the idea of flat-rate electricity. But when asked to vote on the actual proposition, only 22 percent stated that they would vote yes. As in the case of the proposition on a graduated income tax, poor people were more likely to state that they would skip voting on the proposition because it was too long and complicated or because they did not know what a yes or no vote implied. Respondents in the lowest income category were the most supportive of the idea of flat-rate electricity, but they were the least likely to vote yes on the ballot proposition. In sharp contrast to the case of poorer respondents, the policy preference of high-income respondents was almost perfectly mirrored by their reported vote on the actual proposition.

Further evidence of low-income respondents' inability to translate their issue preference into votes on propositions is found by comparing position on the issue with intended vote on the handgun-registration proposition. For all but the lowest-income respondents, the reported vote on the proposition very closely approximated the position on the general issue. On the remaining two issues, the low-income respondents were no more prone to have difficulty translating issue position into vote than any of the other respondents. Thus,

Table 6.7

EFFECT OF PROPOSITION WORDING ON DROPOFF IN MASSACHUSETTS, 1976

Percentage Who Would Skip Voting Because the Ballot Was Too Long
and Difficult to Understand

	Graduated Income Tax	Flat-Rate Electricity	E.R.A.	Handguns	Containers	Total	
Party Identification							
Democrat	23%	19%	19%	12%	12%	49%	(295)
Republican	19	18	15	10	5	16	(95)
Independent	19	17	17	7	3	32	(193)
Ideology							
Liberal	17	18	10	6	6	21	(125)
Conservative	22	15	22	8	7	21	(128)
Middle of the road	20	17	16	9	6	49	(291)
Don't know	43	36	36	30	25	9	(56)
Sex							
Male	16	15	16	4	6	50	(301)
Female	27	22	20	16	10	50	(299)
Income							
$0–4,999	36	32	29	24	17	11	(59)
$5,000–9,999	31	28	21	12	8	17	(91)
$10,000–14,999	18	13	19	7	7	27	(144)
$15,000–19,999	15	19	19	7	5	21	(109)
$20,000–24,999	21	12	9	5	6	12	(66)
$25,000 +	6	6	13	3	2	12	(63)
Total	21%	18%	18%	10%	8%		

Source: Massachusetts Poll, 29 September–3 October 1976, Research Analysis, *Boston Globe*.

Note: Respondents were asked: "If the November election were being held today, would you vote 'Yes,' 'No,' or would you skip voting on this law because it is too long and hard to understand?"

on simpler issues such as the equal rights amendment and nonreturnable containers, low-income voters apparently were not confused. But on the more complicated measures, the mechanism of ballot wording acted to underrepresent considerably this group's viewpoint.

Additional evidence of the effect of proposition wording is found in table 6.7, in which the proportions of respondents who reported that they would skip voting because the proposition was too long and complicated or that it was too hard to understand what a yes or no vote meant are presented. The tendency to skip voting on propositions is clearly related to income. As income increases, the proportion of respondents voting also increases. On the economic issues of graduated income tax and flat-rate electricity, 32–36 percent of the low-income respondents simply did not participate. In sharp contrast, only 6 percent of those with high income reported that they would skip voting on these propositions. Women were consistently more likely than men to skip voting on propositions.

In a study of the office block and party column ballots, Jack Walker came to similar conclusions about the effects of ballot complexity upon participation: "Our analysis does suggest that poorly educated voters, who are presumably also the most apathetic, marginal participants, are the ones most directly affected by complicated ballots. Those with the lowest sense of involvement and personal political efficacy are most likely to neglect possible choices or leave portions of the ballot blank. . . ." [21] It is clear that the same problems Walker found with more complicated ballot patterns are also found when poorer or less educated voters are faced with long and complicated propositions. These voters, therefore, are the most likely to drop off.

The Readability of Ballot Titles and Descriptions

Generally the complete text of a proposition must be filed with the secretary of state, often before any signatures are collected. Many states also require that the attorney general give the proposition its title. [22] Most states also provide for a short ballot summary of each proposition. Does the wording of the proposition title and short summary limit participation on ballot propositions? To what extent are voters able to read and understand the proposition title and short summary? The Massachusetts data analyzed above lead to the conclusion that some voters have difficulty understanding the ballot description printed on the ballot. How readable are the ballot descriptions in Massachusetts and other states? Are the short titles understandable to most voters? The analysis that follows uses three standard readability formulas to ascertain the readability of ballot descriptions and the proposition titles.

Readability formulas calculate the probable difficulty of any text by measuring the variables of vocabulary (or word difficulty), sentence length, complexity, and conceptual difficulty. Additionally, formulas may include in their overall estimate of difficulty the size of type, legibility of type, quality of paper, and effective use of illustrations. With advances in computer technology, even complex readability formulas can now be computed, providing valid and reliable estimates of textual difficulty. All of the readability formulas used in this book have been independently validated by comprehension test scores and, given the size of the samples examined, should lead to reliable estimates of readability. A more detailed description of readability assessment, together with the actual formulas, is found in Appendix D.

The readability of ballot descriptions — the questions as they are printed on the ballot — for California, Massachusetts, Oregon, and Rhode Island during the 1970s is summarized in table 6.8. The ballot descriptions for propositions in California and Oregon were readable at approximately the eighteenth-grade level (the bachelor's degree plus two additional years); the ballot descriptions in Massachusetts and Rhode Island were somewhat more readable, at approximately the fifteenth-grade level (third year of college).

What proportion of each state's citizenry has sufficient reading ability to comprehend ballot descriptions such as these? The educational breakdown

Table 6.8

READABILITY OF BALLOT DESCRIPTIONS IN CALIFORNIA, MASSACHUSETTS, OREGON, AND RHODE ISLAND, 1970–79

State	Average Number of Words in Sample	Average Number of Words per Sentence	Readability		
			Fry[a]	Dale-Chall[a]	Flesch[b]
California	8,121	21.4	17.9	17.3	24.5
Massachusetts	4,414	30.4	15.0	14.5	32.9
Oregon	3,779	21.2	17.9	16.3	25.4
Rhode Island	1,588	41.8	15.0	14.5	32.9
Mean		24.0	17.2	16.3	25.5

Sources: State of California, *California Voter's Pamphlet,* 1974–80 (Sacramento: Office of the Secretary of State, 1974–80); Commonwealth of Massachusetts, *Massachusetts Information for Voters,* 1974–80 (Boston: Office of the Secretary of the Commonwealth, 1974–80); State of Oregon, *State of Oregon Voter's Pamphlet,* 1970–80 (Portland: Office of the Secretary of State, 1970–80); State of Rhode Island, Voter Information on Statewide Referenda, 1976–79 (Providence: Office of the Secretary of State, 1976–79).

[a] The figures in this column represent the readability grade levels. For more information see Appendix D.

[b] The figures in this column represent the readability scores on the Flesch readability index (0 = very difficult, 100 = very easy). For more information see Appendix D.

for these four states and for the United States as a whole is given in table 6.9. In terms of formal schooling, less than one-fifth of the adults in California, Massachusetts, Oregon, and Rhode Island would have the capacity to read and understand the actual ballot question and description printed on the ballot. However, as I will demonstrate in chapter 7, it is the better educated segment of the electorate that is the most knowledgeable about ballot questions and likely to utilize multiple sources of information. The less educated, less knowledgeable segment of the electorate is much more likely to arrive at the voting booth knowing very little about the propositions. Based upon the high readability level needed to understand the ballot descriptions, it is unlikely that the often large numbers of uninformed voters will be able to learn about the ballot propositions after entering the voting booth.

WHAT ARE THE CONSEQUENCES OF OVER- OR UNDERREPRESENTATION?

The preceding analysis has demonstrated that people who vote on most statewide propositions are demographically very unrepresentative both of the voting-age population and of those who turn out to vote. Demographic unrepresentativeness on salient initiatives or in candidate elections is due largely to the fact that some groups turn out in larger proportions than others. On noncontroversial propositions, however, the data demonstrate an additional class and education bias, less educated and lower-income voters being much more likely to drop off.

Table 6.9

LEVELS OF EDUCATION FOR ADULTS IN CALIFORNIA, MASSACHUSETTS, OREGON, RHODE ISLAND, AND THE UNITED STATES AS A WHOLE, 1976

Years of School Completed	California	Massachusetts	Oregon	Rhode Island	Whole United States
0–8	13%	14%	11%	20%	17%
9–11	13	14	13	18	16
12	34	37	38	33	36
Some college (13–15)	23	18	22	14	17
B.A. degree or more (16+)	17	17	15	15	14
Mean year of school completed	13	13	13	12	13

Source: U.S. Bureau of the Census, *Statistical Abstract of the United States, 1981* (Washington, D.C.: U.S. Government Printing Office, 1981), 144.

What are the consequences of underrepresentation in elections to decide propositions? In the case of the California propositions analyzed in this chapter, outcomes were not significantly altered by the representativeness of the participants, because most were very one-sided.[23] This cannot be said of all states or for years beyond the 1970s, however. The Massachusetts data clearly indicate substantial variations in intended vote by categories of income. Thus, the unrepresentativeness of low-income groups undoubtedly played a part in the defeat of the propositions for graduated income tax and flat-rate electricity. The underrepresentation of groups of low socioeconomic status plays a part in the success or failure of propositions for which the outcome is close.

CONCLUSIONS AND IMPLICATIONS

How representative are those who decide statewide propositions? Advocates of the initiative, both during the Progressive era and currently, have argued that direct legislation would inject more popular participation into government. Further, the reformers assert that the establishment of an initiative process leads to more representative decisions than arise in candidate elections. Despite the central importance of these claims to the policy debate about the initiative process, the question of representation in this context has not been widely studied. The analysis in this chapter provides important evidence on the issue.

Despite the differences in turnout between presidential and midterm elections, the average rate of dropoff on propositions in California, Washington, and Massachusetts is not higher in presidential election years. Further, despite the higher rate of dropoff for candidate races in primary elections, the average rate dropoff on propositions in primary and general elections is strikingly similar. Thus, even with substantial differences in electoral stimulus, on the average almost a fifth of those who vote do not participate on some propositions.

Evidence of a significant underrepresentation of groups of lower socioeconomic status and an overrepresentation of groups of higher socioeconomic status has been found in voting on legislatively proposed statewide propositions and some initiatives. The California data analyzed here cover an entire decade and a wide variety of issues. Therefore, the findings of a socioeconomic bias in ballot proposition voting have considerable weight. Survey data from Massachusetts confirm that poorer people are less likely to participate even on highly salient measures such as the graduated income tax.

The evidence presented in this chapter disputes the claim that direct legislation fosters more effective citizen participation or more adequately expresses the public sentiment than conventional devices of representative democracy such as candidate elections. Persons with low education and income are underrepresented in deciding most propositions. On controversial initiatives, the voters are typically no more representative than those who vote in candidates races for governor, U.S. senator, U.S. Congress, or President. In Florida, voters deciding salient propositions were less representative than those who voted for governor.

The data presented raise questions about the extent to which the processes of direct legislation can be seen as an expression of public sentiment on issues. The institutional hurdle of ballot proposition wording limits the participation of many voters. While a majority of Massachusetts voters favored the graduated tax, when confronted with a long and complicated proposition, a significant proportion of supporters of the general issue indicated that they would skip voting on the proposition. There is only a remote chance that voters who do not know the substance of ballot questions before entering the booth will be able to comprehend the ballot title and description provided at the polling place.

Many proponents of direct legislation assert that use of direct legislation processes will lessen apathy and alienation. It may even be argued that some voters find expressive satisfaction in deciding issues. Given the technical and legal language of ballot propositions, however, it is apparent that poorer or less educated citizens who turn out are frustrated by their inability to understand the ballot propositions. Thus, while direct legislation may lessen the alienation of some, it may serve to heighten the sense of alienation and frustration for others. In the absence of party cues or economizing devices, poorer and less educated voters confronted by most statewide propositions are less likely to participate and do not have their preferences recorded. For these citizens, at least, voting on propositions does not lead to a more accurate representation of the popular will than the traditional candidate elections.

□□□□□□□□□□□□□□□□□□□□□□□□□□□□

CHAPTER 7

Direct Legislation and Voter Rationality

When voters choose from among competing candidates in partisan/candidate elections, their decision is simplified by cues provided by political parties during the campaign and, typically, as part of the ballot format. A party cue not only identifies a candidate with a party but reinforces the standing attachments most Americans feel towards one of the major parties.[1] In addition, party affiliation usually is reinforced by the campaign focus on candidate attributes. Sometimes voters choose to defect from their party attachment because their party's candidate is unappealing or because the other party's candidate is more appealing.[2] Voters also consider issues when choosing from among candidates, and issues appear to have become more important in recent elections.[3] Very rarely, however, do partisan/candidate elections resemble referendums on a single issue, because the intervening factors of party and candidate make these elections focus on several issues in addition to party and candidate images.

An assumption made by proponents of direct legislation, both during the Progressive Era and today, is that voters are or will become sufficiently involved, interested, and informed to pass judgment on laws, in addition to choosing among candidates. As noted above, voting on ballot measures requires more interest and information than does voting for candidates. Existing studies of candidate elections indicate that the assumed high levels of interest and information do not exist. Most studies of voting in partisan/candidate contests indicate that many voters are poorly informed, uninterested, and rarely involved in politics.[4] Thus, the untested faith that many reformers have in the electorate's capacity to assimilate complex and often technical information on proposed laws of constitutional amendments runs counter to the scholarly literature about citizen interest in candidate elections and in politics generally. Most studies of voting behavior, however, have focused solely on candidate elections; they do not speak directly to the issue of voter interest in deciding ballot propositions. In this chapter I examine the extent to which voters are interested, informed, and knowledgeable about ballot propositions.

As I discussed in chapters 1 and 2, a central issue in debates over the establishment of direct legislation has been the extent to which voters would participate effectively in deciding ballot propositions. Most advocates of direct legislation have claimed that voters would be interested in the propositions and at least as informed about them as they are about candidate contests. Some advocates of direct legislation do not dispute the low interest and involvement of the electorate. They argue instead that citizens, because they do not feel a sense of personal efficacy in the traditional candidate elections, become apathetic about elections and politics. If voters were able to decide issues directly, these advocates assert, they would demonstrate more interest and involvement and would become more informed about issues and government generally.[5]

More specifically, in the debates over direct legislation, proponents of the process have asserted that voters will (1) be interested in the propositions on the ballot; (2) be knowledgeable about the propositions on the ballot; (3) not depend on any single source of information when deciding how to vote on propositions; (4) be attentive to the major issues of the ballot measure campaign; (5) read and use the voter's handbook; and (6) be able to translate their policy preferences on the general issue into their actual vote on a proposition.

Opponents of direct legislation generally argue that most voters are not interested in most propositions. Even though many voters may support the general idea of ballot propositions, when the time arrives actually to vote on them, they will not bother to inform themselves about the propositions. According to this argument, outcomes of ballot propositions are a reflection more of luck or voter whim than of reasoned judgment. In addition, because of their general disinterest, voters will be especially susceptible to the advertising gimmicks or emotional campaigns of special interests. The extent to which voters actually become more interested and involved in politics is a very important part of the debate over direct legislation.

Voter Interest in Statewide Propositions

According to V. O. Key, "For most Americans issues of politics are not of central concern."[6] More recent studies of voter interest have also concluded that "voters have limited interest in politics" and that the characteristic most predictive of interest in politics or campaigns is education.[7] One of the earliest voting studies put it succinctly: "The better educated have more political interest."[8]

While several studies have explored the topic of voter interest generally or in the context of candidate elections, very few have examined how interested voters are in statewide propositions. In a 1982 California survey, respondents indicated slightly greater interest in propositions than in candidate contests.[9] One measure of interest in direct legislation is the extent to which voters cast ballots on propositions. In chapter 5, I demonstrated that there is considerable variation in the overall rates of voting on propositions. Voters appear to be equally interested in initiatives and contests for governor or U.S. senator. On most propositions, however, and especially on those placed on the ballot by the legislature, the level of participation is considerably lower. Based on this evidence, voters generally appear to be less interested in propositions than in candidate contests but about equally interested in initiatives and statewide candidate contests. But aggregate rates of participation are not a good measure of interest for the reasons presented in chapter 6. Because of complex wording, some types of voters are more likely not to participate, even on initiatives.

Another indication of the comparative interest levels of most voters for candidate and proposition elections is the timing of their voting decision. California voters were asked when they made up their minds about how they would vote for governor in the 1978 general election; for president in the 1980 primary election; on Proposition 13, the property-tax reduction, in the 1978 primary election; and on Proposition 15, the nuclear power initiative, in the 1976 primary election. Voters in candidate contests generally decided their vote early in the campaign, while voters on propositions generally decided much later. Nearly 70 percent of those who voted in the June 1980 primary election reported that they knew their candidate choice for President several months before, and over half of the voters had decided their gubernatorial vote months before the 1978 general election. In contrast, over one-fourth of all Proposition 15 voters decided their vote on the last weekend. Even on the contested Proposition 13, the property-tax initiative, 39 percent reported that they decided in the last week. Only 14 percent of the presidential voters and 22 percent of the gubernatorial voters decided their vote in the last week. There are important differences between the two decision-making contexts. Voters face a more complicated task in deciding how to vote on propositions because parties rarely take a stand and elections rarely focus on the individual attributes of proposition advocates. In sum, information costs are much higher for voters in the ballot-measure context.

A more direct comparison of interest in proposition and candidate contests is found in a statewide survey of Florida voters in 1978, the first year the state used the direct legislation process. The Florida voters were asked the extent to which they were interested in politics, the governor's race, and the constitutional revisions (propositions). The topics of the propositions ranged from legalized gambling and the equal rights amendment to more technical propositions dealing with government organization and taxes.

Florida voters reported being more interested in candidate contests than in ballot propositions. In 1978 nearly two-thirds of the Florida voters surveyed were very interested in the governor's race. Slightly more than half of those surveyed were very interested in the ballot propositions. Given the newness of the process of direct legislation in Florida and the controversial nature of the equal rights amendment and legalized gambling propositions, it is surprising that voters were clearly more interested in the governor's race than in the ballot propositions. At least in part because of the stimulus of a campaign, Florida voters expressed considerably less interest in politics than in election contests.

Other studies have also documented clear differences in citizen interest in different types of political races.[10] Studies of voting in partisan/candidate elections have shown that involvement in an election depends substantially on education[11] and socioeconomic status[12] and that partisans and independents who lean towards a particular party are more interested in campaigns and more concerned about the outcomes than are pure independents.[13] In one of the few studies of proposition electorates, Howard Hamilton concludes that "manifestly most of the public paid little attention to the campaign."[14] Hamilton's study is helpful in demonstrating the broad contours of public interest in a proposition election, but he does not address the question of which kinds of citizens are interested in this mode of politics. Are the same types of citizens who have been shown to be more interested in candidate elections – the well educated, those of high socioeconomic status, and partisans – also more interested in statewide propositions? Florida voters in 1978 who were very interested in politics, the governor's race, and the constitutional revisions are compared in table 7.1. Voters with less than a twelfth-grade education, nonwhites, and strong Democrats showed the greatest decline in expressed interest between the governor's race and the propositions. The only category that showed an increase in expressed interest on propositions was the pure independents. Such evidence, of course, runs counter to the assertion that the main reason for the apathy and lack of interest of the mass electorate is the blandness of candidate elections.[15] Based on the Florida experience in 1978, there is little reason to assume that adding issues to the ballot will increase to a significant degree the overall level of interest in elections or politics.

Fortunately, the Florida data permit a more direct measure of the extent to which those voters who were uninterested in candidate elections were interested in the new opportunity to vote on statewide propositions. Of those who were not interested in the governor's race, over 70 percent also had little or no interest in the constitutional revisions. Are the same respondents interested in both types of elections?

Persons who are interested in one form of election are also interested in the other; almost all of those who are very or somewhat interested in one type of election are very or somewhat interested in the other. Voters who are not interested in candidate elections are also not interested in ballot propositions. These data offer little support to those who see more widespread use of direct legislation as a means of increasing citizen interest.

Previous research on voting indicates that about one-fifth of the electorate is attentive to politics and likely to follow it closely.[16] The public has been

Table 7.1

Florida Voters Very Interested in Politics, the Governor's Race, and the Ballot
Propositions, 1978

	Percentage Very Interested			Difference between Interest in Constitutional Revisions and in Governor's Race	Number of Respondents in Category
	Politics	Governor's Race	Constitutional Revisions		
Percentage Total	41%	64%	54%	−10	484
Education					
0–8	34	78	56	−22	18
9–11	38	55	38	−17	42
12	35	61	53	−8	139
Some college	45	69	58	−11	138
Bachelor's degree or more	49	65	59	−6	133
Occupation					
Semiskilled/skilled	32	63	47	−16	104
Clerical	44	66	61	−5	160
Managerial/Professional	47	64	51	−13	160
Race					
White	42	65	56	−9	425
Nonwhite	32	59	39	−20	51
Party Identification					
Strong Republican	46	68	58	−10	40
Weak Republican	42	61	49	−12	86
Independent Republican	40	59	56	−3	34
Independent	32	58	67	+9	40
Independent Democrat	32	58	48	−10	31
Weak Democrat	40	66	58	−8	152
Strong Democrat	52	73	48	−25	79
Don't know	26	46	45	−1	11
Liberal/Conservative					
Conservative	40	62	51	−11	274
Moderate	51	67	58	−9	66
Liberal	38	63	56	−7	115
Don't know	27	68	50	−18	25

Source: Florida State University Poll, 8–20 November 1978, Policy Science Program, Florida State University.

found to be somewhat less attentive concerning state issues than concerning national or local concerns.[17] To what extent does the electorate express interest in statewide propositions? The preceding analysis of the Florida data shows that interest in propositions was generally lower than for the candidate races at the top of the ballot. This was true despite the fact that Florida voters decided such controversial propositions as the equal rights amendment and legalized gambling.

The most recent California Polls, taken in 1982, find that voters report giving about the same amount of review to propositions and candidate contests.

In June 1976 California voters decided the nuclear power initiative, a proposition that provides an interesting test case of voter attentiveness. This particular campaign was intensive, well financed, and highly publicized in the news media. California voters were asked in 1976 how much attention they had paid to the campaign on Proposition 15, the nuclear power initiative. Even in an extremely politicized campaign on a controversial issue such as nuclear power, only 19 percent reported devoting a lot of attention to the campaign. An equal percentage reported paying no attention to the campaign, while nearly two-thirds of the voters (63 percent) reported that they had paid some or a little attention to the campaign.

Voters appear to see proposition campaigns as they see most matters of government: they pay only limited attention, leaving to the activists and other attentive members of the public the task of closely monitoring politics. Voters are not very interested in most propositions — including some controversial ones, such as the nuclear power initiative or the equal rights amendment; they become very interested in only a few initiative propositions. Examples of this type of proposition are California's open-housing initiative in 1964 and the property-tax initiative in 1978.

How Informed and Knowledgeable Are Voters about Propositions?

Previous voting studies have documented the fact that the average voter is uninformed about politics and is rarely knowledgeable even about major public issues. In the 1948 presidential election, candidates Dewey and Truman debated the Taft-Hartley Act throughout the entire campaign, and the two parties took opposite positions. Even so, at the time of the election 30 percent of the voters had never heard of the act or had no opinion about it.[18] Eugene McCarthy's near-victory in the 1968 New Hampshire primary was widely interpreted as a vote against the Vietnam War. McCarthy had been an outspoken dove on the war, and many attributed President Johnson's withdrawal from the race to McCarthy's strong showing. Yet more than half of those who voted for McCarthy were hawks.[19] In 1978, in the midst of the energy crisis, 40 percent of adult Americans did not know that the United States imported oil.[20] Some disagreement exists among political scientists about the extent and importance of issue voting, but most would agree that in the 1970s a greater sensitivity to specific issues developed among voters. Some of the more recent issues upon which voters have strong opinions are amnesty for draft evaders, government health insurance, busing of school children, unrestricted abortions, and legalization of marijuana.

The public is equally as ignorant about institutions as it is about issues. Less than one-third of the adult population can explain the electoral college,[21] and generally only 50–60 percent of the adult population can identify correctly which party has a majority in the House of Representatives. In addition, less than 50 percent of the adult population can recall the name of their congressman, and only 60 percent can name even one of their U.S. senators.[22]

Many citizens are equally uninformed about candidates. In 1976, for example, only 41 percent of the voting-age population stated that they could name both of their district's candidates for Congress, and only 52 percent stated that they could name both of their state's candidates for U.S. Senate.[23] When asked actually to name the candidates, the percentages who could do so were even lower. Knowledge of issues and candidates, even though clearly related to voting choice, may be too stringent a standard by which to judge the electorate. It could be argued that issue voting occurs when voters do not like an incumbent's policies. But in ballot proposition elections there are no incumbents or candidates to evaluate. Given these low levels of voter knowledge in politics, it is logical to expect that voters will not be any more knowledgeable about ballot propositions.

Of course, voters with limited knowledge about public events can rely on simplifying or economizing devices such as party identification, the psychological attachment to a political party. Party identification allows voters to act where party cues are available without fully knowing the particulars of an election. But on statewide propositions, where there is no party cue, the presence of an uninformed electorate is more problematic than in partisan/candidate elections.[24]

One of the distinguishing features of many statewide proposition elections is the comparatively large proportion of voters who drop off. One reason dropoff is so high is that many voters have not even heard of the ballot propositions before voting. Over one-third of those Californians who turned out to vote in 1972 did not remember having heard anything about Proposition 2 before the election. Interestingly, all registered voters in California have the opportunity to learn about all of the statewide propositions by reading the *Voter's Handbook,* which is mailed to voters' homes at the state's expense.

Substantial proportions of the electorate report not having seen or heard anything about even very controversial or highly publicized propositions. For example, on California's November 1976 Farmworkers' proposition there were major expenditures and media efforts on both sides; yet only six weeks before the election, 54 percent of the eligible California voters had not seen or heard anything about the proposition. In his study of the June 1972 environmental initiative, Proposition 9, Carl Lutrin found that "a little over five weeks before the election over 67 percent of the voters had not heard of the proposition." He concluded, "Because of the numbers, complexity and legal jargon of the measures on the ballot, between one- and two-thirds of the voters were unaware or undecided about the proposed initiatives (environmental) until the last few weeks before the election."[25] Voters do appear to know about some of the most controversial initiative propositions, such as Proposition 14, open housing (1964), or Proposition 13, property-tax reduction (1978).[26] Once again, this distinction between highly salient propositions and all others is important. But what kinds of voters are more attentive and informed about propositions, and what sources of information are used by voters?

The question of how informed voters are was put directly to Colorado voters, who were asked, "When you vote on ballot issues, in general do you feel very informed, somewhat informed, or not too informed about the specifics of the issue?"[27] Seventy-eight percent of the Coloradans surveyed considered themselves either somewhat informed or not too informed about ballot propositions. At the same time, however, most of the less educated and lower-income voters considered themselves either not too informed or not at all informed about ballot propositions. When voters evaluate how informed they are, the data closely mirror the general findings of chapter 6. Direct legislation is a political process best understood and utilized by those voters who are better educated or better-off financially.

The mass media, it is frequently argued, influence the formation of attitudes towards political issues and set the agenda of a political campaign. The significance of the media in opinion formation on propositions, it may be hypothesized, is even greater than in candidate races. In candidate elections, information from the mass media must be filtered through the perceptual screen of party identification and the subjective response to the candidate personally.[28] Such filters are generally absent in proposition elections. Of course, on issues such as capital punishment, legalization of marijuana, or gun control, the voters are likely to have *standing opinions* in much the same way that party identification is a *standing decision*. But the vast majority of voters have no set opinions on most ballot questions and are usually unaware of the proposition until late in the campaign. Based upon the data of California's 1972 Proposition 2 campaign, it is reasonable to assume that 35 percent or more of those who turn out will not be aware of the less controversial but more common propositions.

In California in every recent election, and in many other direct legislation states, one or more propositions – typically initiatives – received widespread media attention. These propositions were also vigorously contested, increasing the likelihood that voters would be aware of them. How attentive was the public to this media coverage? One of California's most controversial and highly contested propositions was the 1976 nuclear power initiative, Proposition 15. In a post-election survey, respondents were asked how much attention they had given to the news about Proposition 15. Close to one-fifth of those who voted in California's June 1976 primary election reported that they had paid little or no attention to the news about Proposition 15. Education was clearly associated with attentiveness to the news about this proposition: voters who had not attended college or who earned less than seventeen thousand dollars a year were significantly more likely to report that they had paid little or no attention to the news about the initiative.[29]

A frequent issue in direct legislation campaigns is an effort by the legislature to short-circuit an initiative by passing a more moderate, less drastic measure. In both the 1976 and 1978 California primary elections the state legislature passed compromise legislation in an effort to impede the more drastic initiative proposition. The theory that the legislature can affect mass behavior on propositions assumes that (1) the electorate knows of the legislative action and (2) such knowledge changes voters' intentions. Before the June 1976 election the legislature hastily passed bills on nuclear safety that were touted as more moderate than Proposition 15. News of the legislative consideration of these bills received substantial coverage in the press. To what extent had the electorate heard of the bills? What did voters know about them? [30]

Even though the "legislative solution" to the nuclear safety question was a major focus of attention in the Proposition 15 campaign, only half of those who voted in the June election had heard of the legislative bills. Of these persons, only half claimed to know anything about the bills. Thus, less than a quarter of the June 1976 voters had heard of the legislative bills and knew something about them; further, there is no evidence that this knowledge altered their vote on the proposition. These data do not permit an assessment of the role that these bills played among the political elite, campaign activists, and contributors; but among voters, the legislative bills had no discernible effect.

The attention given to Proposition 15 by the mass media and the record-breaking campaign expenditures for this proposition provide one of the best possible tests of how interested and informed voters can be on statewide propositions and on some of the issues in the campaign. If voters are not interested and informed about a proposition as publicized and contested as the nuclear power initiative, they cannot be expected to be informed about the more routine, less conflictive, less publicized propositions. The evidence from propositions 2 and 15 in California and the self-assessment of Coloradans make clear that on both routine legislative propositions and controversial initiative propositions the voters may not follow the campaign or have much interest in it and hence do not generally consider themselves very informed about the issues they are deciding.

SOURCES OF INFORMATION USED BY VOTERS

Information about politics comes from a wide variety of sources, including television, radio, newspapers, magazines, and, in the case of propositions, the voter's handbook. Voters may also gain information from friends, family members, work associates, and fellow members of groups or organizations. From the available data on direct legislation campaigns, it is possible to determine the sources of information used by voters.

In June 1978 California voters decided Proposition 13, the Jarvis-Gann property-tax initiative. In a post-election interview a representative sample of Californians were asked, "What was the most important source of your information about Proposition 13?" Three-fourths of California voters learned about Proposition 13 from the newspapers and television. One-fifth relied on friends, relatives, work associates, or other persons for information. California voters were unusually aware of Proposition 13: nearly all of the voters indicated that they had heard of the proposition, and more than 75 percent knew it dealt with taxes.

In a 1979 survey, Mervin Field asked Californians about interpersonal contact concerning the ballot, without reference to any specific proposition or candidate race. He asked, "Do you generally talk to other people about the candidates or propositions on a ballot or does this subject usually not come up in your conversations?" To this question over 70 percent indicated that they did talk to others about their ballot decisions. Once again, education is the best predictor of political involvement. While 57 percent of those with less than a high school education said that they talked to others about candidates or propositions, over 90 percent of those with advanced degrees talked the ballot over with others.[31] However, discussing ballot issues and candidates with others, and those discussions being the most important source of information are very different matters. While most people apparently engage in discussions about the ballot, only a few consider these to be their most important source of information.

The most popular source of information on Proposition 13 was the newspaper: 39 percent gave it as their primary source. A close second was television: 36 percent gave it as their primary source. The importance of newspapers as the source of information was found in a 1982 California Poll. Respondents in this survey indicated that newspapers were the most important source of information in candidate contests as well. Studies of direct legislation campaigns have generally attributed widespread influence to newspapers, and the data in the 1978 and 1982 surveys confirm their continued influence. Edward Banfield and James Wilson argued that "when voters pass on a multitude of referenda, the newspaper acquires added influence."[32] Joseph Harris, writing about the California electorate, stated, "It appears that most voters rely upon the recommendations of the newspapers they read."[33] Dean McHenry asserted that newspapers would have an even greater impact on less salient measures: "The more obscure the office (contest), the greater the influence of the press."[34] More generally, about half of Californians indicated that they very often read articles about state or local affairs in the newspaper. When asked a similar question about television, 59 percent indicated that they very often watched television news stories or other programs about state or local affairs.[35]

John Mueller tested many of these arguments about the importance of newspapers in his study of the 1964 California open-housing initiative. From a sample of absentee ballots, Mueller compared voting patterns with the patterns of newspaper endorsements. When subjected to empirical testing, the assumed relationship between newspaper endorsements and voting does *not* exist. Mueller concluded that "evidence for believing that newspapers exercise little influence on the vote for propositions seems quite persuasive." [36]

Mueller's criterion for influence — ballot patterns' matching newspaper endorsements — is probably too rigid. Because California voters decide so many propositions and because most people value their independence, voters may not choose to vote in patterns uniformly consistent with the printed newspaper endorsements. Even though few voters may vote the newspaper line, the possibility remains that newspapers are influential on some or even most of the ballot propositions. The survey data on Proposition 13 indicate that for over one-third of the June 1978 California voters, newspapers were the most important source of information about the proposition. Thus, even on the most salient of propositions, newspapers are reported as the most important source of information.

Additional evidence that newspapers are influential in proposition elections can be found on less salient propositions as well. In November of 1972 California voters decided Proposition 2, a health science bond measure. On a relatively inconspicuous issue such as Proposition 2, it is not surprising that more than a third of the voters — 37 percent — responded that they did not remember seeing or hearing anything about it before the election. Among the voters who had heard of the measure the electronic media was more widely used (40 percent) than newspapers (25 percent). The 1972 data also measured the relative importance of advertisements, editorials, and news stories. In the electronic media, advertisements were more important than editorials — 23 percent and 11 percent, respectively. The opposite was true for newspapers. Only 7 percent listed newspaper advertisements as a source of information, while 18 percent cited newspaper editorials or stories. Proposition 2 voters reported considerably more use of the voter's handbook than did Proposition 13 voters, with one-third listing it as a source of information. (Use of the voter's handbook is discussed later in this chapter.)

Further evidence of the importance of television and newspapers as primary sources of information for voters deciding propositions can be found in the June 1976 California campaign on Proposition 15, the nuclear power initiative. Nearly half — 46 percent — of those who voted on Proposition 15 reported that they had gotten information on the proposition from television news or advertising. Radio was also reported to be an important source of information. Nearly one-third of the Proposition 15 voters — 31 percent — reported newspapers as a source of information. But one of the least used sources of information was the voter's handbook; only 13 percent reported having gotten information on the proposition from this source. Similarly, relatively few people made use of interpersonal sources of information such as friends or relatives, labor unions, employers, or people campaigning for or against the proposition. When asked a more general question in 1982, a significantly higher proportion of Californians — 27 percent — reported using the handbook; only 4 percent had made use of interpersonal sources of information.[37]

In proposition elections, voters rely almost entirely upon the mass media for information about propositions. This is true both of well-publicized measures such as initiative propositions 13 and 15 and of relatively obscure legislatively initiated measures such as the health science bond, Proposition 2. The analysis thus far has focused primarily on propositions. As has been demonstrated, partisanship and candidate appeal make voting on candidates quite different from voting on propositions. Two recent California surveys asked voters what their most important information sources were in candidate and proposition elections.

Between 75 and 80 percent of all voters surveyed reported that newspapers and television were their most important sources of information in both candidate and proposition elections. More voters see newspapers as the most important source for deciding propositions (45 percent), while more voters see television as the most important source for deciding among candidates (44 percent). Voters in proposition elections are almost twice as likely to list as their most important sources of information word of mouth or other nonmedia sources such as the voter's handbook (8 percent for propositions, 4 percent for candidates). But even for propositions, over 80 percent of the voters reported that their most important source of information was television, radio, or newspapers.

Do different kinds of voters use different sources of information? The types of information sources used by voters in deciding how to vote on Proposition 13, the June 1978 Jarvis-Gann property-tax initiative, and in candidate and proposition contests generally are shown in table 7.2. In addition to the general finding that proposition voters are somewhat more likely to use newspapers than they are television, the sources of information most likely to be used by voters in the different categories of education, voting frequency in statewide elections, income, and race are shown. The better educated, affluent, frequent voter is much more likely to list newspapers as his most important source of information and will use newspapers somewhat more in deciding on ballot propositions than in deciding on candidate races. As education increases, reliance on television as the most important information source decreases. For ballot issues, about half of those with less than a twelfth-grade education mentioned television as their primary source of information, while only about 20 percent of those with advanced degrees did so. These same relationships between education, race, and income recurred in the more recent 1982 California survey.

Do voters generally have more than one source of information, or do most people rely entirely on a single source of information, such as television news? For the November 1972 election, the number of different sources listed

Table 7.2

SOURCES OF INFORMATION FOR CALIFORNIA VOTERS ON PROPOSITION 13, 1978, AND ON BALLOT PROPOSITIONS AND CANDIDATE RACES GENERALLY

| | Most Important Source of Information | | | | | |
| | For Proposition 13 | | For Propositions Generally | | For Candidate Races | |
	Tele-vision	News-paper	Tele-vision	News-paper	Tele-vision	News-paper
Education						
0–8	60%	21%	52%	36%	65%	26%
9–11	67	14	43	33	63	27
12	51	27	39	35	54	27
Some college	37	38	30	42	43	41
Bachelor's degree	28	48	24	61	30	60
Advanced degree	21	53	17	58	26	57
Voting Frequency in statewide elections						
Every time			24	50	37	46
Most of the time			27	46	45	42
Half the time			46	33	57	32
Less than half the time/Never			46	34	56	29
Income						
$0–9,999	52	22	47	29	59	25
$10,000–19,999	44	32	34	42	45	37
$20,000–29,999	41	38	28	48	45	43
$30,000 +	33	45	22	50	34	50
Race						
White	39	36	30	45	42	41
Nonwhite	56	27	41	36	54	33
Total	43%	34%	32%	43%	45%	40%

Source: California Polls 7807, 12–18 August 1978, 7904, 12–19 November 1979, The Field Institute, San Francisco, California.

by each respondent has been summarized.[38] More than one-third of the voters in the 1972 general election reported using no sources of information on Proposition 2, the health science bond. Despite the wide array of information sources available, only 28 percent of the voters listed two or more sources of information. A measure such as Proposition 2 does not have the salience of many other propositions, but it is still somewhat surprising that 72 percent of the voters who voted on Proposition 2 listed none or only one of the information sources. The majority of those voters who remembered seeing or hearing anything about the proposition reported information from a single source; and the most frequently mentioned source of information on this proposition was the electronic media.

Are better educated voters more likely to mention multiple sources of information? The analysis in chapters 5 and 6 on voter participation would lead us to assume so. A tabulation of the number of sources mentioned according to the education, income, race, economic level, and occupation of

Table 7.3

NUMBER OF SOURCES OF INFORMATION USED BY CALIFORNIA VOTERS IN THE PROPOSITION 2
CAMPAIGN, 1972

	Number of Respondents in Category	Number of Sources Reported			
		0	1	2	3+
Education					
0–8	106	41%	52%	5%	3%
9–11	169	39	47	7	7
12	363	26	53	12	9
Some college	326	15	61	16	8
Bachelor's degree	147	8	66	15	10
Advanced degree	75	7	45	24	24
Income					
$0–4,999	175	40	45	10	5
$5,000–9,999	299	29	53	11	7
$10,000–19,999	496	18	56	14	12
$20,000+	153	11	63	18	9
Occupation					
Professional/managerial	419	13	58	17	12
Clerical/sales	158	15	61	16	8
Craft/operative	291	34	51	9	7
Service/laborer	114	34	51	7	8
Student/unemployed	38	47	40	5	8
Retired	170	22	57	12	9
Race					
White	997	19	57	14	10
Nonwhite	193	40	47	7	6
Economic Level					
Lower	80	48	36	15	1
Lower middle	245	31	53	8	7
Middle	677	19	57	13	11
Upper middle	150	15	60	18	7
Upper	38	11	68	11	11
Total		23%	55%	13%	9%

Source: California Poll 7207, 7–18 November 1972, The Field Institute, San Francisco, California.

Proposition 2 voters is presented in table 7.3. Education and income are the variables that most account for voters' use of multiple sources of information on ballot propositions. Nearly half of those with advanced degrees mentioned two or more sources of information. In contrast, voters with less than a high school education or an income under five thousand dollars were much more likely to have used none of the available information sources.

The data analyzed thus far are useful in determining those sources of information used by voters in deciding how to vote on statewide ballot propositions. Voters in statewide proposition elections report a heavy reliance on television and newspapers for information about such highly publicized propositions as California's property-tax and nuclear power initiatives. On less controversial ballot propositions such as the University of California health facilities bond and other propositions placed on the ballot by the state legislature, many more voters cannot remember seeing or hearing anything about the proposition. Among voters who can remember hearing about a proposition, only the better educated or more affluent can mention more than a single source of information. Partly in response to charges of limited information about some propositions and widespread voter ignorance, some states have initiated a voter's handbook or voter's pamphlet.[39] This handbook provides the ballot title, a summary description of the proposition, and arguments both for and against the proposition. It is mailed to the household of every registered voter shortly before each election that includes statewide ballot propositions.

How widely read are the handbooks? The existing literature on direct legislation presents widely differing answers to this question. Donald Balmer, Eugene Lee, and John Mueller assert that the handbooks are widely read, but they offer no empirical evidence to support their claim.[40] Robert Benedict reports that many campaign managers from California estimate that 50 percent of the voters employ the handbook.[41] Joseph La Palombara's early study of this subject comes to a very different conclusion: he finds that "in Oregon, the Voters Pamphlet is read by only a small percentage of the population."[42] Unlike those who believe that the handbook is widely read, La Palombara offers empirical evidence to substantiate his claim. His data are somewhat dated, however, being limited to the 1948 Oregon election.

Survey research on recent California elections reported earlier in this chapter indicates that 13–33 percent of voters listed the handbook as a source of information for their decisions about voting on propositions. This evidence clearly disputes the claims by Balmer, Lee, Mueller, and Benedict that the handbook is an important source of information to many proposition voters. In highly contested proposition elections, the pamphlet ranks well behind television, newspapers, and often the radio as a source of information. Even on the less contested propositions, no more than one-third of the voters reported using the handbook as a source of information. Thus, the available survey evidence indicates that most voters do not read the handbook or use it as a source of information for decisions on propositions.

To what extent do the handbooks have an effect on the level of knowledge among proposition voters? Again, the existing literature is long on specula-tion voters. In highly contested proposition elections, the pamphlet ranks nia, Eugene C. Lee concluded that an important source of information was the handbook mailed by the state to every voter.[43] Lee's conclusion had been previously asserted by John Mueller, who argued that the voter's handbook could be "quite important in influencing opinion, at least on the non-controversial propositions."[44] Similarly, Donald Balmer, writing about Oregon's experience, gave the voter's handbook high marks.[45] Hugh Bone, writing about voter usage of the handbook in Washington state, has found that "voters who mention the pamphlet as their first source of information are significantly better informed." [46] It is possible, of course, that voters who use the handbook also attend to other information sources on propositions and that these voters are part of an attentive segment of the electorate who would know about the propositions with or without the voter's handbook. Given the finding presented earlier in this chapter that well-educated voters are more likely to use multiple sources of information, Bone's finding stems not so much from a positive effect of the voter's pamphlet as from the greater likelihood that well-educated voters will have read the pamphlet and will be generally better informed. To test this hypothesis, education, income, occupation, and race of respondents have been cross-tabulated with use of the handbook as a source of information in the November 1972 election.

Voters who are the most likely to be informed about and interested in propositions are also the most likely to read the handbook. Only 7 percent of those with less than an eighth-grade education mentioned the handbook as a source of information, but 44 percent of those with advanced degrees remembered seeing something about the proposition from this source. As has been demonstrated, the well-educated are more apt to have multiple information sources, so it is not surprising that they are also better informed. In sum, respondents who read the pamphlet are better informed about propositions, not so much because of the pamphlet itself but because they are apt to be better educated and somewhat more attentive to multiple sources of information about both the propositions and government generally.

One early dissenter from the prevailing view that handbooks have an important effect on voters was Joseph La Palombara. He argued that in order for the handbook to have an effect, the voters had to comprehend the arguments presented in it. La Palombara found that of the small percentage who bothered to read the Oregon voter's handbook, an even smaller percentage understood the real meaning of many of the proposals. La Palombara substantiated his argument by citing an experiment in which he had polled seventy college students and college graduates and found that "not one of them, after reading the pamphlet, understood the nature of more than fifty percent of the proposals presented at the general election of 1948." [47] La Palombara's experiment can be expanded by testing the readability levels of ballot handbooks. Having examined survey data to learn which voters use the handbook, we can now examine one possible explanation for the low levels of readership: that the text is too complicated for most voters to comprehend.

As I discussed in chapter 6, the extent to which a person understands written material depends upon both his reading ability and the readability of the text itself. An individual's reading ability depends upon his intelligence, education, environment, and interest and purpose in reading. The readability of textual material depends upon the number of ideas expressed and their complexity; the vocabulary, syntax, and organization of the prose; and the format and typography.[48] La Palombara's experiment was a test for comprehension, an attribute of readers; in this research I will examine readability, an attribute of texts.

I introduced and applied the methodology of readability assessment in chapter 6, where I found that the short titles and descriptions that often appear on the ballots were written at the fifteenth- to the eighteenth-grade level, depending on the state. This at least partly explains both the rather high rates of dropoff and the lower representation of less educated and lower-income voters in decisions on ballot measures. The primary point of interest here is the extent to which voters can be expected to be able to read and comprehend the voter's handbook.

Voters' handbooks constitute one of the largest governmental efforts at both mass communication and civic education. The costs range from over $350,000 per election in Massachusetts to over $2 million per election in California. The voter's handbook frequently contains for each ballot proposition the short title; the official ballot description; an analysis or explanation, typically prepared by the legislative analyst, the attorney general, or the secretary of state; arguments for and against the proposition, typically prepared by the proposition's sponsors and opponents; and the actual text of the proposition. The readability of these sections of the handbook is summarized in table 7.4. According to table 7.4, the least readable section of the voter's handbook is the official description. These descriptions, frequently included in whole or in part on the ballot, will be comprehended by only a few voters. While the remainder of the handbook is more readable, citizens still need a reading level equivalent to that of a third-year college student in order to understand the document. As I demonstrated in chapter 6, this means that more than two-thirds of those who receive the document cannot read it. To give a better sense of this relative reading difficulty, I compared the readability levels of random samples of text from recent editions of four popular magazines: *Time, Newsweek, People,* and *Reader's Digest.*

Unlike the voter's handbook, popular magazines such as *Time, Newsweek,* and particularly *People* and *Reader's Digest* are readable for most people. Rather than being limited to an audience with a reading capacity at the fifteenth- to the seventeenth-grade level (one year less than the B.A. degree) or higher, these magazines range between the ninth- and twelfth-grade levels in reading difficulty and fall closer to the Flesch "standard" reading-ease score of 50.[49] Given these findings, it is evident that compared with other widely disseminated written material, the descriptions of ballot propositions are much more difficult to read. The only portion of the handbook that comes even close to the popular magazines' readability is that including the pro/con arguments written by proponents and opponents of each proposition, and even here the readability level would effectively exclude half of the potential voters from readership.

These findings of a high level of reading difficulty in the voters' handbooks support the California survey research data discussed earlier which revealed

Table 7.4

READABILITY OF VOTERS' HANDBOOKS IN CALIFORNIA, MASSACHUSETTS, OREGON, AND
RHODE ISLAND, 1970–80

Handbook Section	Number of Words in Sample	Average Number of Words per Sentence	Readability		
			Fry[a]	Dale-Chall[a]	Flesch[b]
Official description					
California	8,121	21.4	17.9	17.3	24.5
Massachusetts	4,414	30.4	15.0	14.5	32.9
Oregon	3,779	21.2	17.9	16.3	25.4
Rhode Island	1,588	41.8	15.0	14.5	32.9
Analysis/explanation					
California	9,528	23.3	15.4	14.5	36.6
Oregon	5,830	23.7	15.1	14.6	37.3
Arguments pro/con					
California	14,327	18.8	13.9	12.8	44.2
Actual proposition					
California	2,725	45.4	15.3	16.1	19.2

Sources: State of California, *California Voters' Pamphlet,* 1974–80 (Sacramento: Office of
the Secretary of State, 1974–80); Commonwealth of Massachusetts, *Massachusetts Information for Voters,* 1974–80 (Boston: Office of the Secretary of the Commonwealth, 1974–80);
State of Oregon, *State of Oregon Voters' Pamphlet,* 1970–80 (Portland: Office of the Secretary
of State, 1970–80); State of Rhode Island, *Voter Information on Statewide Referenda,*
1976–79 (Providence: Office of the Secretary of State, 1976–79).

[a] The figures in this column represent the readability grade levels. For more information see
Appendix D.

[b] The figures in this column represent the readability scores on the Flesch readability index (0
= very difficult, 100 = very easy). For more information see Appendix D.

that less than one-third of those who received the handbook reported reading
it. The readability data also call into question the higher reported readership
findings of Balmer, Lee, Mueller, and Benedict. Responses to a survey
research question about voter's handbook usage are almost certain to include
some overreporting because of social desirability. Given these readability
scores, the vast majority of voters who received the handbook could not
effectively use it.[50] Having examined the sources of information used by
voters, we can now assess how knowledgeable voters are about the propositions they are asked to decide.

HOW KNOWLEDGEABLE ARE VOTERS ABOUT BALLOT PROPOSITIONS?

In the analysis thus far, I have demonstrated that rates of participation,
representativeness of the electorate, and reliance on information sources are
different for candidate and proposition elections. A further distinction exists
between initiatives and all other propositions. But how knowledgeable are
voters regarding statewide propositions? Because party cue and candidate
evaluation are absent, voters may need greater knowledge than in a par-
tisan/candidate election. The decision of how to vote on propositions is made

even more difficult by the large number of issues on the ballot and by the length and technical language of most propositions. In chapter 6, I demonstrated that the less educated voters have a more difficult time overcoming the twin hurdles of ballot length and proposition complexity.

Previous studies of voting behavior generally presented a picture of an apathetic, uninterested, and politically ignorant citizenry. Philip Converse found that voters seldom integrated their positions on issues into a consistent conceptual framework and that individual voters' opinions on issues were rarely stable over time: "The rank order correlation between what a voter thinks about that issue in two years is very low."[51] Other scholars, most notably Christopher Achen, attributed this absence of continuity in individual responses to unreliable and poorly worded questions.[52] The preponderance of evidence, however, indicates a general absence of ideology and a fluidity of issue opinions. Commenting directly on ballot propositions, Mervin Field said, "Voters seldom have clearly defined opinions about ballot measures."[53] Given the evidence from studies about voters in other contexts, there is little reason to believe that voters will be knowledgeable about the substance of measures when deciding ballot questions.[54] (In chapter 8, I examine the process of opinion change in greater detail.)

Because ballot propositions often deal with complex issues, it is important to differentiate between the voters' knowledge about the broad issue involved and their knowledge about the proposition itself. Even with widespread coverage, very few voters could become knowledgeable about a subject as complex as nuclear power during the course of an election campaign. Expecting voters to know about the content of ballot propositions is, however, a very different question. Determining the extent of the voters' knowledge about the propositions they are deciding is essential to an evaluation of the quality of mass participation in direct legislation. It can be presumed that in order to be minimally knowledgeable about propositions, voters will have to attend to the news media; the voter's handbook; friends, relatives, and work associates; or other information sources. But as already demonstrated, many voters do not attend to any of these sources of information, especially on the less controversial ballot measures. A few days before the 1962 California general election, persons who planned to vote were asked whether they had seen or heard anything about the statewide ballot propositions. Only 11 percent reported having seen or heard about the controversial Francis amendment, a proposition that prohibited subversives or communists from public employment. Even fewer voters had seen or heard anything about Proposition 23, concerning the state senate reapportionment.[55] In their analysis of voting on Proposition 15, the nuclear power initiative, Deborah and Carl Hensler estimated that between 10 and 33 percent of the voters were well enough informed to make educated judgments about the advantages and disadvantages of nuclear power.[56]

Another way to determine how knowledgeable voters are about propositions is to ask them for their own opinions about how informed and knowledgeable they are on a particular proposition. In June 1976 California voters were asked: "On election day how much did you feel you knew about Proposition 15, the Nuclear Safeguard Initiative?" Most voters reported that they knew something about the initiative.[57] In an exit poll following the Proposition 13 property-tax vote in 1978 the *Los Angeles Times* asked voters whether they felt that they understood the provisions of Proposition 13. An impressive 89 percent reported that they did.[58] In both surveys the better educated voters were more confident that they knew something about ballot propositions. At the other end of the education scale, almost a third of those with less than a high school education felt that they knew little or nothing about the nuclear initiative. Proposition 15, as has been noted, was a well-publicized and highly contested initiative proposition which would have limited future nuclear development in California. As education and income increase, so does the likelihood that voters will think they know something about an initiative. After controlling for the two variables of income and education, it is clear that education is the more important explanatory variable.[59]

Voter opinion on these two recent California propositions indicates that most voters felt that they understood the provisions of the ballot measures. But both of these propositions were the subject of considerable controversy and large advertising campaigns, and the news media may have given as much attention to them as to the candidate races on the ballot at the same time. In a more general question, the Colorado Poll asked, "When you vote on ballot issues, in general, do you feel very informed, somewhat informed, not too informed, or not at all informed about the specifics of the issue?" To this more general question, over half of the Colorado voters felt that they were somewhat informed (51 percent), and 19 percent indicated that they felt very informed about ballot issues. At the same time, 30 percent indicated that they felt not too informed or not at all informed. As was the case in California, lower-income and nonwhite voters were much more likely to indicate that they generally felt uninformed.[60]

Voter knowledge about propositions means very little if it is not effectively translated into a yes or no vote consistent with the voter's opinion on the issues. To what extent is this translation process accomplished? There are at least three sources of possible interference or confusion in this translation process. First, the length of the proposition and the technical nature of the language may lead to dropoff or confusion. Second, the nature of the issues themselves may be confusing; even experts in the field of nuclear engineering could not agree on the merits of the nuclear power initiative proposition. Finally, voters may be unclear about what a yes or no vote means. For instance, in the case of the nuclear power initiative, was a yes vote a vote to limit future development (correct) or a vote for nuclear development itself (incorrect)?

To What Extent Does the Process of Direct Legislation Confuse Voters?

Do lengthy and technically worded propositions lead to confusion and non-participation? As I have demonstrated, voters deciding statewide propositions may be confused both by the complexity of the language in the measure and by the length of the proposition. Some voters who have opinions on the substance of an issue, such as graduated income tax or nuclear power, may not be able to translate their policy preferences into a vote on the proposition. In chapter 6, I demonstrated that for some Massachusetts voters, especially low-income voters, the length of the ballot and the technical nature of the language were so overwhelming that they dropped off and did not vote on propositions dealing with taxes or utilities. Not only may the wording of a proposition be technical and lengthy but the question may not tell the voter what the effect of a yes or a no vote will be. Even when the issue is concise and fairly straightforward, voters may be confused about whether they are voting to repeal something or to enact it.

Not all voters who are confused or overwhelmed by the technical nature of propositons decide to drop off, however. Some voters feel that when they are confused or undecided they had better vote no. Duane Lockard commented on a common campaign practice: "Campaigners raise doubts on the basis of the inherent complexity of an issue and then urge a negative vote in view of these doubts. An advertisement run late in a Salt Lake City campaign said simply: 'Confused? Many are. Play it Safe — When in Doubt, Vote No!'" [61] (In chapter 8, I examine in greater detail the typical opinion shift from a yes to a no vote.)

Do voters consider themselves confused by technical or complex propositions? In one California survey more voters considered themselves somewhat or very confused by Proposition 15 (56 percent) than a little or not confused (44 percent). The consistency of subjective voter confusion on Proposition 15 cut across all educational and socioeconomic strata. Only 26 percent of the California electorate reported that they did not find Proposition 15 at all confusing. Thus, on a technical ballot proposition like Proposition 15 there is nearly universal willingness to express some confusion. Evidence examined previously indicated that this is not the case on all ballot issues. In chapter 6, I demonstrated that poorer Massachusetts voters were considerably more likely to express confusion on ballot propositions. In the Massachusetts case many of the confused voters apparently dropped off; but in the California case there was uniformly low dropoff on Proposition 15.

To what extent are voters confused by what a yes or no vote means? Do many voters cast incorrect ballots as a result of this confusion? Previous studies of voting on statewide propositions have generally found that 10 percent or more of the voters cast incorrect or confused ballots. [62] Dennis Anderson's study of Ohio voters deciding the election-day registration issue found 15 percent whose stated position was at variance with how they said they had voted.[63] John Mueller analyzed the patterns of voting on two propositions concerning lotteries and found that for at least one of the two measures, about 60 percent of the ballots were marked capriciously.[64] Previous studies have not all found widespread voter confusion. In some cases, even though there may have been confusion about the wording, almost all voters clearly understood what they were voting for or against. Raymond Wolfinger and Fred Greenstein found in their study of the 1964 open-housing referendum in California that very few voters were confused about what a yes or a no vote meant.[65]

Fortunately, data on statewide propositions exist that will allow the nature and the effect of voter confusion to be tested. In pre- and post-elecion surveys, respondents were asked what a yes vote meant on Proposition 15, the nuclear power initiative. Respondents who felt that a yes vote would continue or speed up construction of nuclear power plants were confused. One month before the election, 18 percent incorrectly answered the question about what the proposition would do. In the post-election survey the proportion of confused voters had dropped slightly, to 14 percent.[66] But who were the confused voters, and how did they affect the outcome? Using different data, Alexander Groth and Howard Schultz found that the poorer, less educated, and older citizens were more likely to be confused and to have voted contrary to their opinions.[67] The proponents of nuclear power appeared to have been more confused than the opponents. But the Groth and Schultz sample was drawn from the Sacramento metropolitan area and thus was not representative of the statewide electorate. The Rand statewide data on the nuclear power vote indicated that less educated, nonwhite, and lower-income respondents were far more likely to cast confused ballots. Over 35 percent of those with less than an eighth-grade education cast confused votes, compared with only 3 percent confusion among college graduates. After controlling for the independent effects of other variables, it is clear that the important variable is education. Thus, the real determinant of the amount of voter confusion is the level of education.[68] A higher proportion of voters who voted yes were confused, which supports Groth's earlier finding that confused voters were more likely to vote yes because they thought that a yes vote was a vote for nuclear development.

Another example of significant voter confusion on a recent California ballot proposition is the June 1980 rent-control initiative. Its title might imply that a yes vote was a vote in favor of rent control, and a no vote a vote against it; it was just the reverse. The proposition was sponsored by landlords in an effort to restrict further extensions of rent control, especially at the state level, and to require that all existing rent-control measures at the local level be subjected to a periodic vote of the people for extension. The initiative was the subject of an intense campaign. Understandably, tenant groups were its most vocal opponents. Based upon its exit poll, the *Los Angeles Times* concluded that "voters apparently ended up confused and suspicious of the proposition." [69]

I have cross-tabulated the exit survey responses to the questions of how residents voted and what they thought the proposition would do. I found that most California voters were confused about the effects of Proposition 10, the rent-control initiative. Over three-fourths of the California voters did not match up their views on rent control with their votes on the measure. Twenty-three percent wanted to protect rent control but incorrectly voted yes, and 54 percent were opposed to rent control and incorrectly voted no. Those who were not confused by the proposition were more evenly divided: 12 percent wanted to protect rent control and voted no; 10 percent were opposed to rent control and voted yes. In this case the confusion benefited the no side, since 82 percent of the no voters were confused, apparently thinking that they were voting against rent control when in effect they were voting for it. [70]

The extent to which voters are confused when voting on statewide ballot propositions depends in large part on the nature of the proposition. In past elections, on very salient issues such as open housing and property taxes very few voters were confused. But on other salient propositions some voters were clearly confused and cast incorrect ballots or chose not to participate at all. Propositions in this category would include California's nuclear and rent-control initiatives and the Massachusetts vote on a graduated income tax. On propositions where confusion exists, some types of voters are more confused than others. Not surprisingly, the less educated voters are least able to comprehend the proposition and vote effectively on it. Voters face serious problems understanding ballot propositions and can cast confused ballots.

I conclude this chapter as I did the chapters on participation and representation: by observing that the process of direct legislation is prone to considerable misrepresentation. Generally, only the better educated can understand the issues, endure the length and complexity of the wording, and cast knowledgeable votes. The universalist ethic of the early and modern advocates of direct legislation is not supported in practice. Less educated voters are less likely to participate on propositions, and the reasons for their lower levels of participation are now partially apparent: they are confused by the propositions and unable to cope with the task of informing themselves about them. This conclusion does not apply to candidate contests, where voters appear to be more effective in translating their preferences into votes. For many voters, direct legislation can be a most inaccurate barometer of their opinions.

The Role of Campaign Spending, Elite Endorsements, and Alienation in Ballot Proposition Voting

Voting behavior on propositions has three essential components: first, whether an individual will vote in an election at all; second, whether an individual will vote on a proposition; and third, whether the voter will vote yes or no on the proposition. In many cases, 20 percent or more of those who turn out do not vote on a given proposition. On California's Proposition 13, however, people who voted were as representative of the voting population as those who cast a ballot in any candidate contest. Compared with voters generally, people who typically vote on propositions are disproportionately well educated, affluent, and white. This bias is amplified by the fact that persons with less education and low income and persons from minority races are less likely to turn out to vote at all.

Most voters give a low priority to following and even voting on propositions. Most do not follow the campaign, and less than one-third read the widely disseminated voters' handbooks. Why voters decide to vote yes or no on propositions is the question addressed in this chapter. Because interest and information are so low, the question of why voters vote as they do is very important to an overall assessment of the process of direct legislation. Voters are not able to reduce their information costs on propositions as they are on candidates through party cues and candidate appeal. In this chapter I examine three possible explanations for proposition voting.

The literature on direct legislation suggests three hypotheses or models that may help explain voter decision making on propositions generally: (1) voters cast their ballots for the side that spends the most money in statewide proposition campaigns; (2) voters rely on elite and media endorsements when deciding how to vote on statewide propositions; and (3) alienated citizens turn out to vote on propositions but vote no as a way of getting back at the establishment. While each referendum may have special features, it appears that the level of campaign spending, the presence of media and elite endorsements, and the influence of alienated voters may help to explain voting patterns for all referendums.

145

LEVELS OF CAMPAIGN SPENDING AND VOTING CHOICE ON PROPOSITIONS

The possible relationship between campaign spending and election outcome has long concerned observers of democratic government. If spending more money than your opponent guarantees victory, then elections are for sale to the highest bidder, and the qualities of the candidates and the way they stand on the issue are secondary or minor. If spending more than the opposition on propositions guarantees victory, then statutory and constitutional changes are also for sale to the highest bidder.

Campaign spending in candidate contests is an important determinant of electoral success but not the sole determinant. Alexander Heard concluded that "there is no neat correlation between campaign expenditures and campaign results." [1] Heard's summary has generally held true in contests for the presidency, the U.S. Senate, and statewide elected offices. In contests for lesser offices or in primary elections, however, greater campaign expenditures have been shown to make a difference. [2] John Owens and Edward Olson found that "expenditures are the most significant determinant of the vote" in state assembly races. [3]

In theory, greater expenditures will make the most difference in contests for lesser offices, in primary elections, or on ballot propositions. This is because voters are more in need of information about these contests, and so the side that can spend more has the advantage. In elections for president, U.S. senator, and governor, voters are more likely to know the candidates and to have formed judgments about them. Moreover, in general elections for these offices, voters can rely on party identification as a cue to help determine their vote and evaluate political advertising.

Proposition elections provide a clearer test than do candidate elections of the effect of campaign spending on election outcomes. Other factors such as party affiliation, incumbency, and name recognition typically are not part of initiative campaigns. Voters on propositions are more susceptible to campaign spending than are voters in candidate elections. Campaign spending can be important in candidate elections as well, especially in building name recognition and a positive candidate image. [4] As I have noted, however, most voters begin the campaign knowing little about most propositions, a situation quite different from that in candidate contests. Data on one aspect of campaign activity — expenditures for and against propositions — have been available in California for more than twenty years. Despite the availability of these data, however, no empirical attention has been paid to the effects of expenditures on proposition success or failure. Some authors have speculated that "the side with the most money can obtain the best publicity and will usually win the election." [5]

Studies of the initiative by Eugene Lee and Larry Berg have relied on 1970s spending data to show that spending is more likely to be successful if it is on the negative side of the proposition. Both of these scholars are tentative in their analysis, perhaps because of their restricted data base. Lee concludes, "Opponents who spend the most tend to be successful, but proponents who spend more often fail." Similarly, Berg finds that "money can make a difference in defeating initiatives."[6]

To answer more conclusively the question of the extent to which campaign spending determines the outcome of statewide propositions, spending data were gathered on all fifty-one propositions that appeared on California ballots between 1954 and 1982. Of these, 31 percent were adopted. The effects of spending on initiative outcomes are presented in table 8.1. The initiatives are divided into three categories: initiatives where proponents' spending was equal to 67 percent or more of the total expenditure on the proposition; initiatives where there was near parity in expenditure (with neither side spending more than 66 percent); initiatives where opponents' spending was equal to 67 percent or more of the total expenditure. In the first and third categories, one side outspent the other by a ratio of two to one or greater.

By spending considerably more than the opposition, can a group pass an initiative into law? If the answer is yes, then direct legislation becomes a means of legislative enactment reserved for well-financed groups or interests. The best available evidence indicates that this is typically *not* the case. Proponents of initiatives who outspent opponents by a two-to-one margin or larger were more likely to fail than to succeed in getting their initiatives adopted. In such cases 48 percent of the initiatives were adopted. While this percentage is higher than the overall success rate of 31 percent, it demonstrates that proponents cannot spend an initiative into law, especially if there is organized opposition. Proponents of initiatives, regardless of the amount they spend, face a great disadvantage because, as is demonstrated in table 8.1, it is harder to pass a proposition than to defeat one. Proponents must convince voters to vote for a change from the status quo, something that many voters apparently resist.

While proponents of initiatives are generally unable to obtain passage of their initiatives by outspending the opposition, it is equally evident that groups or interests opposed to an initiative can virtually guarantee the defeat of an initiative if they significantly outspend the proponents. In cases where initiative opponents' spending was equal to two-thirds or more of the total expenditures, they were successful in defeating the proponents 87 percent of the time. The only two initiatives that survived this level of financial opposition were Proposition 20, the coastal zone initiative (November 1972), and Proposition 5, on gift and inheritance taxes, in the 1982 primary election. In the latter case neither side spent much money. The opponents spent $57,373, more than 2.5 times the proponents' $22,572. For most of the defeated initiatives, however, more money spent by opponents made a difference in their defeat. Successful propositions typically address a timely issue, such as prop-

Table 8.1

EFFECTS OF EXPENDITURES ON CALIFORNIA PROPOSITION OUTCOMES, 1954–82

	Amount of Spending			
Outcome	67% or More by Proponents	Rough Parity	67% or More by Opponents	Total
Adopted	48% (11)	23% (3)	13% (2)	31% (16)
Failed	52 (12)	77 (10)	87 (13)	69 (35)

Sources: Spending data for the period 1958–78 are from the California Fair Political Practices Commission, *Campaign Costs;* data for 1954–56 are from the brief filed in the case of *Citizens for Jobs and Energy* v. *Fair Political Practices Commission* by the firm California Research. Data for propositions in 1972 and 1974 were gathered from primary sources, State of California Archives. Data for candidates and propositions since 1976 are from the Fair Political Practices Commission official spending reports.

erty taxes in a period of inflation (Proposition 13, 1978 primary election) or political reform after Watergate (Proposition 9, 1974 primary election). Also important to the success of these propositions and the coastal zone initiative were their highly motivated and skilled campaigners, who in many cases were volunteers.[7]

Money can make a difference in the outcome of ballot propositions. But what is the range of total expenditures on initiatives? All the initiatives and popular referendums that appeared on the California ballot between 1954 and 1982 are ranked by actual expenditure in Appendix E. Most initiative campaigns are well financed. In 1978, for instance, over $7 million was spent on the campaign for the clean indoor air initiative. This was more than the amount spent on most statewide general election campaigns, including the gubernatorial contest between Governor Brown and Evelle Younger. At least $1 million in each instance was spent on roughly two-thirds of these propositions.

A comparison of campaign spending on propositions over time requires adjustments for inflation. Expenditures for each of the fifty propositions, using 1958 as the baseline year, are given in the far righthand column of Appendix E; campaign costs in all other years have been adjusted according to consumer price indices derived by the California State Department of Finance.[8] These standardized figures show that roughly half of the measures involved expenditures in excess of $1 million in 1958 dollars. Of these, over 10 percent were very hotly contested, with expenditures in excess of $2.5 million in 1958 dollars.[9] Propositions on which there was a relatively low level of campaign spending usually involved issues upon which voters had standing opinions, such as legalization of marijuana, school busing, and the death penalty. Thus, on most competitive initiatives the level of total expenditures was quite high.

While the levels of campaign expenditures on single initiatives demonstrate that most initiatives are taken seriously, the data analyzed thus far do not per-

Table 8.2

TOTAL REPORTED ELECTION EXPENDITURES IN ACTUAL DOLLARS FOR CONSTITUTIONAL OFFICES,
THE STATE LEGISLATURE, AND BALLOT PROPOSITIONS IN CALIFORNIA, 1958–82

	Reported Expenditures				
Year	*Constitutional Offices*	*State Legislature*	*Total Candidate*	*Propositions*	*Total*
1958	$ 4,220,505	$ 1,372,899	$ 5,593,404	$ 6,158,601	$ 11,752,005
1960		1,850,519	1,850,519	1,270,193	3,120,712
1962	6,725,239	2,329,559	9,054,798	1,150,909	10,205,707
1964		2,489,929	2,489,929	5,363,313	7,853,242
1966	9,615,394	6,337,689	15,953,083	916,788	16,869,871
1968		4,865,282	4,865,282	1,577,224	6,442,506
1970	9,129,364	6,094,418	15,223,782	1,407,387	16,631,169
1972		7,875,673	7,875,673	10,618,963	18,494,636
1974	17,886,696	10,638,591	28,525,287	2,248,938	30,774,225
1976		14,749,893	14,749,893	12,655,974	27,405,867
1978	22,416,273	20,243,595	42,659,868	14,734,322	57,394,190
1980		17,541,448	17,541,448	4,532,494	22,073,942
1982	40,517,443	43,251,642	83,769,085	36,073,536	119,842,621

Sources: Data for 1958–70 are from John R. Owens, *Trends in Campaign Spending in California, 1958–1970* (Princeton: Citizens Research Foundation, 1973), 57. Owens's 1970 figures are in error; therefore, the data used here are from a brief filed in the case of *Citizens for Jobs and Energy* v. *Fair Political Practices Commission* by the firm California Research. Data for candidates in 1972 and 1974 are from the California Fair Political Practices Commission, *Campaign Costs,* 2. Data for propositions in 1972 and 1974 were gathered from primary sources, State of California Archives. Data for candidates and propositions since 1976 are from the Fair Political Practices Commission official spending reports.

mit a comparison of proposition and candidate expenditures over time. How much money is spent on propositions, and how does that compare with the amount spent on elections for constitutional offices and the state legislature? Data for the 1958–82 period are presented in table 8.2. The level of reported expenditures on propositions varies widely from year to year. Much higher expenditures were reported for all propositions in 1958, 1964, 1972, 1976, 1978, and 1982 than in other years. Such variations are generally explained by the presence or absence of controversial initiatives. For instance, in 1978 nearly half of the $14 million expended on all propositions was expended on a single proposition: the anti-smoking initiative, Proposition 5. In years of controversial initiatives the level of spending on propositions rivals and sometimes surpasses the level of spending in all state legislative races.

Spending on constitutional offices generally surpasses spending on statewide propositions. It is clear from table 8.2, however, that propositions in recent elections have become increasingly expensive. While expenditures on propositions show no continuous trend, expenditures for both constitutional offices and the state legislature have risen continuously since 1958. Since 1970, expenditures for state legislative races have risen from $6 million to over $40 million. But what portion of this increase is due to inflation? This question can be answered by standardizing the data for increases in the cost of living.

With control for inflation, it is clear that the 1958, 1964, 1972, 1976, and 1978 elections had roughly equivalent levels of campaign spending on propositions. But even after control for inflation, the 1982 election clearly surpassed any previous election in the level of campaign spending on ballot propositions. In constant dollars, $10,360,320 was spent in 1982, compared with a previous high of $7,338,606 in 1972. After 1966, contestants for the state legislature spent more money; and this trend accelerated after 1974. In constant dollars, the 1982 total candidate expenditures were about five times as high as those in 1958.

For initiatives and for all statewide races, the bulk of these expenditures were on electronic advertising. The large disparity in expenditures between the two sides on many initiatives was one of the motivations behind the Fair Political Practices Act, Proposition 9, in June 1974. After its passage, the expenditure-limitation provisions of this proposition were declared unconstitutional. But the courts left intact the disclosure provisions, so that voters can now learn how much money is donated by whom to which side. The authors of this political reform initiative presumed that voters would include information on campaign contributions and overall levels of spending in their electoral calculus. This presumption, however, appears not to be borne out by actual experience. When asked, few voters know which side spent more money, and even fewer think that it is important.[10]

The June 1976 California nuclear initiative, Proposition 15, is a clear example of an initiative on which one side spent significantly more money. Proponents of this initiative to limit future nuclear development spent $1,257,132, while opponents spent $4,033,590.[11] Opponents thus outspent proponents by a ratio larger than three to one. During the campaign, the initiative's proponents argued again and again that they were at an economic disadvantage and that the opposition was financed by the energy industry and public utilities. Despite the large difference in expenditures and the importance of the difference as a campaign issue, only 37 percent of those who voted on the proposition knew that there had been more advertising on the negative side. Better educated and richer voters were more likely to know which side had spent more on this campaign. Even among such voters, however, less than half knew which side had spent more in the case of Proposition 15. To most voters, therefore, knowing the differences in campaign spending was unimportant in their decision of how to vote.

Still, knowing which side spends the most money does not keep campaign spending from having an effect on voting intentions. The changes in voting intentions on propositions, which generally coincide with disparities in campaign spending, lead to the conclusion that on issues where voters do not have standing opinions, more spending by opponents of an initiative will generally lead to its defeat.

The typical pattern of change in voting intentions on propositions moves from widespread support – often by as much as two to one – early in the campaign to one-sided rejection on election day, often by the same margin. The decline in the degree of support appears to begin as the opposition launches its well-financed advertising campaign, as in the 1972 California pollution initiative, the 1976 Massachusetts handgun registration question, and California's 1978 anti-smoking and 1982 beverage container initiatives. In each of these cases, as the campaign developed, support for the proposition declined (see Appendix F). While the disparity in campaign expenditures is certainly not the only reason for the defeat of these propositions, the effect of the campaigns against them was great.

THE ROLE OF MEDIA AND ELITE ENDORSEMENTS

In campaign literature, much disagreement exists over how large a role media and elite endorsements play in determining the outcome of proposition elections. Some scholars have argued that press endorsements are the most helpful of all elite endorsements because they are printed on marked ballots and can be taken to the polls.[12] Similarly, Edward Banfield and James Wilson conclude that "when voters must choose among many obscure candidates or pass on a multitude of referenda issues, the newspaper acquires added influence."[13] After studying a local referendum campaign, Reo Christenson inferred that when voters lack certainty, a newspaper endorsement – in this case by the *Toledo Blade* – can carry the day.[14]

Not all studies of direct legislation, however, have concluded that newspaper endorsements affect the outcome of proposition elections. Howard Hamilton and Sylvan Cohen argue that "the power of the press in referenda is considerably myth."[15] John Mueller, in his study of over a thousand actual ballots in Los Angeles, found that "no one marked the ballot according to the *L.A. Times'* recommendations, and only 8 percent of the absentee voters followed the newspaper endorsements with three or fewer deviations." Mueller concluded that newspapers exercise only minimal influence on the vote for or against propositions.[16]

A less stringent way to measure newspaper influence is to measure the extent of congruence between electoral endorsements and voting results collectively. Using this methodology, James Gregg found that the electorate agrees with newspaper endorsements over 80 percent of the time. Gregg also found that endorsements are more influential on propositions and in primaries than in candidate races.[17]

Thus, scholars disagree on what role, if any, newspaper endorsements play in the success of propositions. All agree, however, that newspaper endorsements of propositions are most likely to have an impact when voters have few sources of information. One such case was in the voting on Proposition 2 decided by California voters in 1972, which would have provided bonds for health science facilities. Only 14 percent of those who voted on this proposition listed newspaper editorials as a source of information. Even though relatively small amounts were spent on television advertisements, 15 percent reported such advertisements as a source of information.

Data in chapter 7 revealed that few voters rely on newspapers as their primary source of information on propositions. Voters were typically uninterested in the propositions, knew little about the main campaign issues, and relied on advertising as their primary source of information. In contrast to voters on such salient measures as propositions 13 (property taxes) and 15 (nuclear power), voters on Proposition 2 (health sciences bond) were more likely to rely on the voter's handbook. Even so, only one-third reported using the handbook mailed to each household. Many voters decided their vote without prior exposure to either the substance or the content of the measure. Even on critical and vigorously contested propositions, rarely more than 30 percent report using more than one source of information. Moreover, only a few voters report ever using more than two sources of information. In light of low voter interest and scanty attention to the media, it is difficult to see newspaper endorsements as determining the outcome of propositions. Evidence clearly supports Mueller's earlier finding that voters rarely rely on newspaper endorsements.

Most California propositions are relatively noncontroversial measures placed on the ballot by the state legislature. If newspapers and other political elites agree on how to vote on propositions, how often does the electorate follow suit? Because most voters do not inform themselves about propositions, possibly most voters would disagree with even a unified elite position. In order to assess the level of elite consensus, I tabulated widely disseminated elite endorsements on all statewide propositions in California from 1970 to 1982 (see table 8.3). This sample of elites comprised six major daily newspapers, two statewide labor organizations, a statewide business organization, two statewide taxpayers' associations, and a public interest group. Elite opinion was considered unanimous if all twelve of the groups agreed, and consensual if only one source among the twelve disagreed; if two or more of the twelve sources disagreed with the remaining sources, the elite opinion was considered divided.

California elites have demonstrated significant agreement on almost two-thirds of all ballot propositions since 1970. Such widespread consensus is surprising given the diversity of groups in the sample. According to table 8.3, most propositions are much less conflictual than one might expect. When the twelve elite groups were in agreement, the outcome of the vote on the proposition was consistent with their position 75 percent of the time. In other words, even on propositions where elites representing a wide spectrum of interests can agree, a majority of voters choose to vote the other way 25 percent of the time.

Table 8.3

ELITE CONSENSUS ON CALIFORNIA PROPOSITIONS, 1970–82

	Degree of Elite Consensus						Total Number of Endorsements
Election	*Unanimous*[a]		*Consensual*[b]		*Divided*[c]		
1970 Primary	13%	(1)	50%	(4)	38%	(3)	8
1970 General	45	(9)	35	(7)	20	(4)	20
1972 Primary	50	(5)	10	(1)	40	(4)	10
1972 General	23	(5)	32	(7)	45	(10)	22
1973 Special					100	(1)	1
1974 Primary	67	(6)	11	(1)	22	(2)	9
1974 General	41	(7)	24	(4)	35	(6)	17
1976 Primary	27	(4)	40	(6)	33	(5)	15
1976 General	47	(7)	27	(4)	27	(4)	15
1978 Primary	54	(7)	15	(2)	31	(4)	13
1978 General	50	(4)	25	(2)	25	(2)	8
1979 Special	25	(1)	25	(1)	50	(2)	4
1980 Primary	27	(3)	27	(3)	46	(5)	11
1980 General	9	(1)	18	(2)	73	(8)	11
1982 Primary	0	(0)	25	(3)	75	(9)	12
1982 General	27	(4)	33	(5)	40	(6)	15
Mean	34%	(64)	27%	(52)	39%	(75)	

Sources: Printed endorsements of the *Los Angeles Times, Oakland Tribune, Sacramento Bee, San Diego Union, San Francisco Chronicle, San Francisco Examiner,* the American Federation of Labor–Congress for Industrial Organization, California State Employees Association, California State Chamber of Commerce, California Taxpayers Association, United Taxpayers Association, and Common Cause.

[a] All twelve elite endorsements were in agreement.
[b] Only one of the twelve elite endorsements is different from all others.
[c] Two or more elite endorsements differed from the others.

Apparently voters are more hesitant than elites to change the status quo. With the exception of the property-tax propositions of 1978, the propositions on which California elites and voters disagreed generally involved narrow constitutional questions, such as whether one county could tax property owned by another county (Proposition 11, 1978 primary election). In 80 percent of elite-voter disagreements the elites supported the constitutional changes and the voters did not. In other words, the elites recommended a yes vote, but the majority of those casting ballots voted no.

Voters' disagreement with elite consensus is difficult to understand in view of the fact that on many of these propositions there was no opposition during the campaign. Thus, electoral choice flowing in the opposite direction — usually in opposition to the proposition — suggests that many voters decide propositions in the voting booth, on the basis mainly of snap judgments and a hesitation to vote for change.

It is evident from these data that even with a broad base of support or opposition, propositions are often decided contrary to that consensus. This finding runs counter to some previous studies. Gordon Baker found that the success of a reapportionment vote in Oregon resulted from a broad basis of support.[18] Thomas Henderson and Roger Rosenbaum argue that elites are important to successful local consolidation votes.[19] Both studies, however, were single cases, and neither examined a large number of measures over time. More complete data make it evident that even elite consensus on some measures does not guarantee that voters will agree.

As I have noted, there is widespread speculation about the potential effects of endorsements by political elites for and against propositions. Campaign organizations often assemble a "line-up" of notable experts, politicians, and community leaders. To what extent do endorsements by such notables influence the outcome of propositions? In his study of a reapportionment referendum in Oregon, Gordon Baker argued that the activities of the League of Women Voters in support of the proposition added prestige to the campaign.[20] One of the most frequently cited types of referendum in which elite opinion becomes an issue is one on fluoridation. Even on such a technical subject, both sides provide claims of scientific expertise. Harvey Sapolsky describes the role of experts in fluoridation campaigns:

> The health officials believe that fluoridation's safety and efficacy are technical public health problems, for which they represent the only legitimate scientific position. They do not perceive the anti-fluoridationists to be experts in public health problems and on this basis easily dismiss their arguments. The opponents, however, number among themselves persons with scientific or professional credentials. In most communities there is at least one doctor, dentist, university science professor or Ph.D. research scientist who will speak out against fluoridation. Several of these persons have gained a national reputation through their fight against fluoridation, and are active in referendum campaigns throughout the country. While the public health officials may consider these anti-fluoridationists to be marginal at best in their scientific profession, and to be speaking outside their particular field of competence, the voters may well consider them to be qualified to discuss the technical issues and to be granted the status of fluoridation experts.[21]

Unfortunately, Sapolsky was unable to assess the actual role of elite endorsements in voters' decision making on fluoridation referendums. Did the voters recognize, understand, and incorporate these endorsements in their voting choice? What role do scientific experts play in technical propositions? Do politicians or elected officials have much influence?

One recent proposition in which both sides attempted to exploit elite endorsements and expertise was California's nuclear power initiative, Proposition 15 (June 1976). This proposition dealt with a highly complex question: How safe are nuclear power plants? In an effort to simplify the decision process for voters, both proponents and opponents attempted to demonstrate that important elite opinion was on their side.

Among the groups and individuals who endorsed Proposition 15 and its restrictions on the development of nuclear power were physicist Harold Urey, who authored a statement in the voter's handbook, and Ralph Nader, a long-time critic of nuclear safety and a leader of Critical Mass, the organization that supported anti-nuclear initiatives in eight states in 1976. Tom Hayden, running in the Democratic primary election for the U.S. Senate, also endorsed the proposition. Environmental groups and the Sierra Club played an active role in defending the initiative. Among the groups and individuals who opposed the initiative, thereby supporting the continued development of nuclear power, were nuclear scientist Edward Teller, Ronald Reagan, Edmund G. "Pat" Brown, electric utility companies, many business organizations, and most labor unions.

Both sides claimed the support of "the experts." Proponents of the initiative claimed identification with the Union of Concerned Scientists and attempted to exploit the resignation of three nuclear engineers from a General Electric nuclear power facility. The "No on 15"·Committee produced a list of fifty-two hundred nuclear experts who opposed the measure and argued that nuclear power was safe. Probably the most notable figure to oppose the measure was Edward Teller, known for his work in developing weapons and winner of numerous awards in physics.

How much influence did elite endorsements have on the voters' decision on Proposition 15? This is a difficult question to answer because we cannot learn all the influences that play a role in any voting choice. But we can assess the extent to which voters (1) knew of the endorsing group or individual, (2) trusted the endorser, and (3) thought the endorser had taken a position. The responses of voters intending to vote on Proposition 15 to each of these aspects of elite influence on proposition voting are summarized in table 8.4. Some illuminating details about mass perceptions of elite opinion on a particular ballot proposition, the nuclear power initiative, are presented in this table. Politicians were clearly the best-known individuals involved in the Proposition 15 campaign. Gerald Ford, Ronald Reagan, Edmund G. Brown, Sr., Edmund G. Brown, Jr., and John Tunney were all known by 90 percent or more of the voters. The only nonpolitician with this kind of name recognition was Ralph Nader. In contrast, few voters knew of Harold Urey, Edward Teller, or the Energy Research and Development Administration (ERDA). Between these extremes, most but not all voters knew of the League of Women Voters, the Sierra Club, Tom Hayden, and the California State Energy Commission.

Among the most trusted groups and individuals were scientists, nuclear engineers, Edward Teller, and Ralph Nader. Groups and individuals for which 25 percent of the voters expressed "no trust at all" included Ronald Reagan, Tom Hayden, labor union leaders, religious leaders, Edmund G. Brown, Sr., Gerald Ford, and John Tunney. Groups and individuals per-

Table 8.4

VOTER PERCEPTIONS OF POLITICAL ELITES DURING THE CALIFORNIA NUCLEAR INITIATIVE CAMPAIGN, 1976

I

	Ralph Nader	Edmund G. "Pat" Brown	Harold C. Urey	Edward Teller	Sierra Club	President Gerald Ford	California State Energy Commission	Ronald Reagan	Governor Jerry Brown	Tom Hayden	Senator John Tunney	League of Women Voters	ERDA
Have you heard about [group/person]?													
Yes	91%	91%	13%	22%	71%	100%	64%	99%	98%	67%	91%	74%	29%
No	9	9	87	78	29	—	36	1	2	33	9	26	71
How much would you trust what [group/person] might say about nuclear power plants?													
A lot	29	11	22	45	17	14	21	16	25	4	10	18	26
Some	33	30	27	26	34	34	41	27	40	23	31	34	43
A little	21	30	16	13	24	27	21	21	20	24	30	26	17
Not at all	10	22	7	8	18	20	9	32	9	31	22	13	5
Don't know/not sure	7	7	28	9	7	5	9	5	5	18	7	10	10
Do you think [group/person] is for or against nuclear power plants?													
For	11	28	26	62	7	47	57	43	28	12	24	9	64
Against	49	10	16	14	75	4	7	9	15	36	14	26	4
Neither	7	9	6	2	2	10	10	7	14	6	10	13	10
Don't know/not sure	34	52	53	23	16	39	26	41	43	46	53	52	22
Has [group/person] taken a position for or against Proposition 15?													
For	23	8	13	12	42	8	17	11	10	22	9	13	14
Against	13	12	9	37	20	12	26	18	12	12	12	11	28
Has not taken position	3	5	1	3	1	13	6	6	13	2	6	4	6
Don't know/not sure	61	75	77	48	37	67	51	66	65	64	73	72	53

II

	California Legislators	Electric Utility Companies	Business Leaders	Labor Union Leaders	Environ- mentalists	Nuclear Engineers	Scientists	Religious Leaders
How much would you trust what [group] might say about nuclear power plants?								
A lot	8%	15%	6%	6%	18%	40%	45%	12%
Some	41	33	33	20	37	36	38	28
A little	35	29	33	34	26	13	11	26
Not at all	12	21	23	35	13	6	2	25
Don't know/not sure	6	3	5	5	6	5	4	9
Do you think [group] is mostly *for* nuclear power plants, mostly *against* nuclear power plants, or *divided?*								
Mostly for	20	64	36	34	8	67	44	4
Mostly against	4	17	5	9	63	3	3	19
Divided	57	9	42	33	17	22	43	45
Don't know	19	10	16	24	13	9	11	32
Do you think [group] is mostly *for* Proposition 15, mostly *against* Proposition 15, *divided,* or *has no position?*								
Mostly for	8	23	9	11	46	22	14	9
Mostly against	11	51	26	25	18	39	23	7
Divided	56	10	40	28	16	22	43	38
No position	3	1	6	7	2	2	4	12
Don't know	22	15	20	29	19	16	16	34

Source: Survey of Attitudes on Nuclear Power, May–June 1976, Rand Corporation, Santa Monica, California.

ceived as favoring the proposition (opposed to nuclear development) included environmentalists, the Sierra Club, Tom Hayden, and Ralph Nader. Groups and individuals perceived as opposing the proposition (favoring nuclear development) included Edward Teller, the California State Energy Commission, and ERDA.

As informative as these data are about how voters saw political and scientific elites on an important proposition, they do not answer satisfactorily the question of which elites influenced voting on the proposition. If the voters did not know anything about Edward Teller or the Sierra Club, then these elites most likely did not exercise much influence. Similarly, if the voter did not trust the endorser, then their endorsement was probably of little consequence. Even if the voter knew and trusted the endorser, in order for the endorsement to influence the vote, the voter had to perceive the endorser as being in favor of or opposed to the proposition. Finally, because we want to assess the maximum potential elite influence on voting for or against Proposition 15, it is important to control for mixed perceptions. For instance, 5 percent of the voters on Proposition 15 knew Senator Tunney, trusted him, and thought he favored the proposition, but 6 percent knew him, trusted him, and thought he opposed the proposition. Thus Senator Tunney's adjusted influence against the proposition could have affected 1 percent of the vote at most. The adjusted elite influence for and against Proposition 15 is shown in table 8.5.

The electorate perceived elite opinion to be solidly against Proposition 15. Nearly half of the voters knew of nuclear engineers and utility companies involved in the campaign, trusted them, and perceived them to be opposed to this initiative. On the positive side, the only group with widespread recognition and trust was the environmentalists. In the battle to claim scientific expertise, the opposition clearly won. While some voters thought scientists and engineers favored Proposition 15, many more voters put them clearly in opposition.

An equally interesting fact in these summary data is that politicians played a minor role in shaping the perceptions of the electorate. The politicians' comparatively low level of influence stems in part from their untrustworthy image. Even more important was the fact that the electorate had trouble identifying the politicians' positions on the proposition. Finally, among those voters who knew and trusted the politicians, there were often significant differences in perceptions of their positions on the proposition.

These findings that politicians and candidates have relatively little influence are consistent with an earlier study of the 1962 subversives initiative, the Francis amendment. Paul Hoffman and Jenniellen Ferguson found that "only 37 percent thought they knew whether Governor Brown favored or opposed Proposition 24 and 11 percent of these (4 percent of the total sample) misperceived his position. Only 38 percent thought they knew whether Mr. Nixon favored or opposed Proposal 24 and 34 percent of these (13 percent of the total sample) misperceived his position." [22] Had Hoffman and Ferguson

Table 8.5

INDEX OF MAXIMUM ELITE AND GROUP INFLUENCE FOR AND AGAINST THE
CALIFORNIA NUCLEAR INITIATIVE, 1976

| | Voter Perceptions of Elite Endorsements | |
Elites Involved	In Favor of the Proposition	Opposed to the Proposition
Electric utility companies		48%
Nuclear engineers		48
Environmentalists	41%	
Scientists		31
Business leaders		29
Labor leaders		15
Ralph Nader	15	
Sierra Club	15	
California State Energy Commission		10
Ronald Reagan		10
California legislature		9
Edward Teller		9
ERDA		8
Tom Hayden	6	
President Gerald Ford		5
Edmund G. "Pat" Brown		4
Religious leaders	3	
League of Women Voters	2	
Governor Jerry Brown		2
Senator John Tunney		1
Harold C. Urey	1	

Source: Survey of Attitudes on Nuclear Power, May–June 1976, Rand Corporation, Santa Monica, California.

controlled for whether the electorate trusted Brown and Nixon, their potential influence on the proposition would probably have fallen in the 10–15 percent range.

ALIENATED VOTERS AND DIRECT LEGISLATION

Few concepts in the social sciences are as unbounded as political alienation. Some of the most frequently cited aspects of political alienation are distrust, feelings of personal inefficacy, unhappiness, dissatisfaction, and anomie. In short, almost any feeling of dislike for or discontent with the political system or public institutions has been taken to constitute political alienation. Such conceptual ambiguity fosters confusion and uncertainty and makes it very difficult to compare different studies on what may be an important political attitude.

An example of an all-encompassing definition of the alienated voter is provided by Murray B. Levin and Murray Eden:

> Alienated voters are hostile to politicians and disenchanted with the political process. They are wary of candidates who spend large sums of money during campaigns. They are skeptical of those who are endorsed by powerful "public" figures, and they tend to believe that campaign promises and platforms are empty verbiage. If they vote at all, it is against the "greater evil," against the "politician," against the well-financed, and against the powerful. They do not really vote "for" anyone.[23]

Other scholars have argued that in the context of referendums, alienated voters are less likely to turn out; and of those who vote, most vote no in an effort to get back at the local establishment.

Distrust of political leaders is typically seen as characteristic of alienated voters.[24] But partisan/candidate elections provide only limited opportunities to express discontent. Referendums, however, are seen as a means of registering protest, of getting back at the establishment, and of expressing discontent.[25] A critical question, however, is whether *alienation* correctly describes all those who are to a degree distrustful, discontented, or eager to communicate a message to government. If the answer is yes, then the concept of political alienation is all-inclusive.

If the concept of political alienation is to be useful to scholars, a more bounded definition is desirable. Jack Citrin, Herbert McClosky, Merrill Shanks, and Paul Sniderman provide a means to distinguish alienation from other attitudes towards the political system.

> What distinguishes the allegiance/alienation continuum from other attitudes toward the political system is its explicit reference to feelings of *closeness/ distance, attachment/separation,* or *identification/rejection.* To be politically alienated is to feel a relatively enduring sense of estrangement from existing political institutions, values and leaders. At the far end of the continuum, the politically alienated feel themselves outsiders, trapped in an alien political order; they would welcome fundamental changes in the ongoing regime.[26]

Political alienation, however defined, is theoretically important to the student of direct legislation for two quite different reasons. First, some scholars and elected officials have argued that if we extend to new jurisdictions the process of direct legislation, most notably the establishment of a national initiative, current political alienation will diminish. Second, several studies of local referendums have found that alienated voters cast negative ballots, which perhaps accounts for the defeat of propositions.[27]

A rallying call for the establishment of direct legislation has frequently been that alienated and disenchanted voters would gain a greater sense of systemic attachment and personal political efficacy if permitted to vote on initiatives and referendums. This assumption was expressed in the U.S. Senate hearing on the proposed national initiative. Senator James Abourezk, sponsor of the legislation, argued that "providing a national initiative will lessen the sense of alienation from government now felt by millions of Americans."[28] Harlan Hahn, author of several studies of local referendums, also argued that a national initiative would reduce alienation.[29]

Because there has not been direct legislation at the national level in the United States, it is difficult to know whether Hahn, Abourezk, and other advocates of direct legislation can correctly argue that a national initiative process would reduce alienation. But if the argument is correct, political alienation should decline after states adopt direct legislation. Do alienated voters think that adding initiatives and referendums to ballots gives citizens more control over government? During the 1970s the citizens of Florida amended their constitution to provide direct legislation at the state level; thus, Florida can be a test case.

In a statewide survey in 1978, Florida voters were asked whether they felt that propositions gave citizens more control over government. The results of this survey, conducted by the Florida State University, give us an example of how alienated voters viewed their first extensive statewide experience with direct legislation. Alienated and distrustful voters in the Florida sample were the least likely to think that propositions gave them more control over government. This finding is exactly the opposite from that predicted by such advocates of direct legislation as Abourezk and Hahn. Direct legislation appears not to have lessened the sense of alienation.[30] Further evidence that alienated Florida voters were not activated by propositions is given in table 8.6, where the extent of over- or underrepresentation among voters in each category of the alienation scale in voting on propositions and for governor is given.

The data from table 8.6 demonstrate that alienated voters are not more likely to vote on propositions than for candidates. In some cases the proportion of alienated persons voting perfectly represents their proportion among all those who voted. The Florida data also reveal that on some propositions alienated voters are more likely to drop off than nonalienated voters. For propositions 2 through 9, the alienated had an average dropoff rate of 14 percent, while the nonalienated had an average dropoff rate of 11 percent.

While the reduction of the widespread political alienation in American society has been seen by some as a reason to extend the use of direct legislation, even more typically it has been treated as an independent variable used to explain outcomes of propositions. In study after study, alienated voters have been identified as a force in opposition to particular referendums. This profound "negativism" among the alienated is itself a syndrome thought to accompany political alienation.

Presumably, alienated citizens are more suspicious of political elites and lack confidence in their own ability to influence community decision through normal channels; therefore, they vent their frustration by rejecting those elites through the only channel open to them: a direct vote on a referendum. This perspective on alienated voters and referendum voting is widespread in the literature. The alienated are seen as participating in politics only when

Table 8.6

Degree of Over- and Underrepresentation in Voting on Ballot Propositions and for Governor of Alienated and Nonalienated Florida Voters, 1978

Trust/Alienation Scale Category[a]	Degree of Over- and Underrepresentation in Voting on								
	Governor	Proposition							
		2	3	4	5	6	7	8	9
0	−	+5	+10	+4	−	+5	−	+5	+5
1	−7	+7	+4	+7	+4	+7	+7	+7	+4
2	−3	−3	−	−3	−3	−3	−3	−3	−
3	−	−	−11	−	+6	−6	+6	−6	−

Source: Florida State University Poll, 8–20 November 1978, Policy Science Program, Florida State University.
[a] 0 = very trusting, 3 = very distrusting.

they can register a protest by saying no.[31] John Horton and Wayne Thompson state this position as follows:

> Research on local referendums shows a consistent pattern of negative voting among the socially and economically deprived segments of the population. The research reported here tests the hypothesis that referendums may serve as institutional outlets for protest, that voting against local issues may be an expression of political protest on the part of the powerless and ordinarily apathetic members of the community. The findings from a study of defeated school-bond issues in two communities show a consistent relationship between powerlessness and negative votes in those cases where a feeling of powerlessness took the form of alienation from certain symbols of power in the community. This relationship holds independently of economic self-interest and related variables. Evidence suggests that voting down local issues does not represent an organized, class-conscious opposition, but a type of mass protest, a convergence of the individual assessments of the powerless who have projected into available symbols the fears and suspicions growing out of their alienated existence.[32]

There are several problems with the methodology employed both by Horton and Thompson and by many of the other scholars who have found an association between alienation and negative voting on propositions. Much of the literature makes the implicit assumption that negative votes on propositions are the result of alienation. But as already noted, on most propositions most voters vote no. The reasons for negative voting are numerous; for example, many confused voters vote no because of their uncertainty about the meaning of the proposition (chapter 7). The assumption that negative voting is the result of alienation is even more troubling when we learn that some of the characteristics frequently used to define alienation are low socioeconomic status and a low level of education. It is true that these segments drop off more (chapter 5) and are more likely to be confused (chapter 7), but the effects of low socioeconomic status on proposition voting may have nothing to do with alienation.

Horton and Thompson offer little independent empirical support for their assertion that these voters are more likely to vote negatively because of alienation, and what evidence they do offer is methodologically flawed. For example, they assume that agreeing with the statement "The school board is just as much a special-interest group as any other group in town" indicates alienation.[33] It should not surprise us to learn that the persons who agree with the statement—the alienated—are also more likely to vote no on school bond measures.

Of all the studies linking alienation to negative voting, those by Horton and Thompson are the most frequently cited. But the authors do not maintain a distinction between alienation and negativism. James Wright, commenting on their muddled conceptualization, states that "the footnote to the 1960 article which describes the measures to be employed begins, 'Negative (alienated) responses are . . .' (1960:192). And in the 1962 article, the concepts are again conflated: 'in the university town, the most negative politically conscious would be those persons *who felt alienated* in a town dominated by the university and who were critical of education.'"[34] Unfortunately, almost all studies linking alienation to negative voting suffer from similar methodological problems or have been proven false in subsequent studies. Students of fluoridation referendums often asserted that negative outcomes were "convenient devices for registering protest."[35] Because such proposals are supported by community and scientific elites, a negative vote was assumed to reflect political alienation. Harvey Sapolsky, however, demonstrated that both sides in fluoridation campaigns "line up" experts. He further showed that a more plausible explanation for the defeat of fluoridation measures is voter confusion.[36]

Another frequently cited implication of the assumed connection between alienation and negativism is the argument that as turnout increases, the likelihood of passage decreases.[37] Clarence Stone, relying on eighteen cases rather than on Boskoff and Zeigler's single case, finds "little evidence to support the generalization that 'no' voting increases as turnout rises."[38]

Even though the alienation/negativism hypothesis has major flaws, it is widely cited. On the basis of the Florida data described above, I have tested the voting behavior on eight Florida propositions to determine whether alienated voters were more likely to vote no. These data are presented in table 8.7. On seven of the eight Florida propositions, alienated voters were not more likely to vote no. In fact, on propositions 2, 5, 7, and 9 they were more likely to vote yes. The conceptual linkage between alienation and negative voting does not bear empirical scrutiny.[39] If alienated persons are not more likely to turn out and vote no, then either they are not activated by referendums generally or they are not discontented. One final problem with the

Table 8.7

Voting Behavior of Alienated and Nonalienated Voters on Florida's
1978 Ballot Propositions

Vote on:	Trust / Alienation Scale Category [a]				
	0	1	2	3	Total
Proposition 2					
Yes	40%	51%	50%	31%	41%
No	56	45	45	60	50
Dropoff	4	4	6	10	6
Proposition 3					
Yes	31	43	34	23	34
No	56	42	52	51	49
Dropoff	14	16	14	26	17
Proposition 4					
Yes	17	16	18	15	17
No	74	78	70	71	73
Dropoff	10	6	11	15	10
Proposition 5					
Yes	29	15	19	23	21
No	56	75	68	67	67
Dropoff	15	11	12	10	12
Proposition 6					
Yes	43	57	39	25	43
No	44	35	48	58	45
Dropoff	13	8	13	17	12
Proposition 7					
Yes	21	34	22	30	27
No	61	55	61	58	59
Dropoff	18	11	16	12	15
Proposition 8					
Yes	24	16	19	17	19
No	64	75	68	65	68
Dropoff	13	10	13	18	13
Proposition 9					
Yes	18	9	29	30	21
No	78	89	69	66	76
Dropoff	4	2	2	5	3
Total sample	22%	29%	31%	19%	

Source: Florida State University Poll, 8–20 November 1978, Policy Science Program,
Florida State University.
[a] 0 = very trusting, 3 = very distrusting.

alienation hypothesis is that on some measures a negative vote supports "the
establishment." Thus, even if a majority votes no, it is not necessarily an anti-
establishment message. Voters have clearly discovered that voting no means
different things on different propositions. John Mueller found that of 1,293
ballots he studied in 1964, only 1 was marked negatively for all of the propositions.[40] In short, adding direct legislation to a political system will not lead
to greater participation among the alienated; and the alienated will not vote
more often on propositions than for candidates, nor will they see propositions as a means of greater political control.

CONCLUSIONS

Explaining the behavior of large numbers of citizens on hundreds of referendums is a difficult task, and most of what has been written about this process appears to be inaccurate. The most frequent problem in the literature is the penchant to overgeneralize from a single issue to all propositions. While this chapter does not explain the outcome of any single election, it demonstrates that voters responded more favorably to campaign appeals on the no side of an issue and that massive spending to support a proposition holds little promise of success.

The role of elites in the process of direct legislation is limited. Newspaper, scientific, and partisan endorsements will not hurt, but relatively few voters attend to these cues, and hence, they do not guarantee electoral success.

Finally, the presumption of negative voting among the alienated is false. Moreover, substantial evidence refutes the assumption that more widespread use of direct legislation will reduce alienation.

Voting Behavior on Ballot Propositions

Free and open elections are the most important institution of popular control of government. Through the electoral mechanism, the public has the opportunity to choose its rulers and indirectly set policy. In some jurisdictions, voters may attempt to set policy directly through use of the initiative and referendum. Understanding elections requires first an assessment of the structure and operation of the electoral process. In chapters 3 and 4, I demonstrated that the way in which a state structures the initiative or referendum will affect the operation of the process. For instance, a low signature threshold is likely to foster more widespread use, while a high signature threshold will do the opposite. Because of the American practice of voting on proposed statutes or constitutional amendments, ballot measures are difficult to summarize in nontechnical language. As a result, only a small fraction of the citizenry can read and understand the ballot measures, voters' handbooks, or actual propositions. Understanding the mechanical operation of the initiative and referendum process is an important first step to explaining voting behavior.

A second step to explaining voting behavior is to determine who votes on ballot measures. Rates of voting vary dramatically between presidential and midterm elections, between primary and general elections, and between special and regularly scheduled elections. Not all voters who go to the polls actually vote on the propositions or in particular candidate contests. Even though many more voters will participate in initiative voting in presidential general elections, the rate of dropoff for initiatives is about the same regardless of the electoral context. Voters who drop off are typically poorer, less educated, and nonwhite.

Having established the structural implications of the process and the nature of participants in it, I now turn to a third concern: How do people come to vote as they do? [1] Much of the work of modern political science has focused on this question, but rarely has attention focused on voting in contexts other than that of candidate/partisan elections. In chapter 8, I demonstrated that alienation does not lead to higher turnout, nor are the alienated likely to vote as a block. My examination of the effects of campaign spending on the outcome of proposition elections has shown that it is unlikely that a group could buy passage of a measure. However, the evidence indicates that voters respond to disproportionate spending on the negative side of a measure.

In chapter 7, I demonstrated that voters tend to decide their voting intentions for initiatives much later than for candidates, and they rarely know much about the substance of the measure being decided. Even in well-publicized campaigns, few voters can recall campaign controversies that received attention in the media. The voter's handbook is so complex and technical that it can inform only a few voters. For these reasons, political elites and the mass media can make a difference in the outcome of some proposition elections. But the electorate appears to differentiate among measures according to their salience. On controversial issues where elites and experts appear divided, many vote no, apparently feeling that when there is reasonable doubt, they should vote no. As discussed above, on the less publicized and less controversial measures the tendency is to vote yes, and the earlier on the ballot the measure appears, the greater are its chances of success.

THE NEGATIVE BIAS IN INITIATIVE VOTING

In votes on legislatively sponsored constitutional amendments or bonds most voters tend to vote yes. (This tendency is partly a function of ballot location, since the chances of passage negatively correlate with location further on down the ballot.) This is just the reverse in the case of initiatives, most of which are defeated by the voters. On issues other than those on which voters have standing opinions, there is a predictable movement from general support for the proposition in the early campaign to its rejection as the campaign proceeds. This pattern of opinion change in the direction of the negative vote is an important aspect of many initiative campaigns. Initially, the issue being decided has an appeal that accounts for the early support. As the campaign begins and the voters learn that the proposition has some shortcomings, the appeal of the measure begins to fade. Once the voters begin to learn reasons to vote no, the proportion of negative voters in the cross-sectional surveys begins to increase, and by election day the initiative is often defeated.

The shift to negative votes will be larger if that side has money to spend for advertising. Few voters have mastered the substantive intricacies of the ballot measure; their voting decision is typically based on reactions to advertising, elite and media endorsements, or a generalized sense of the measure. On less salient measures voting takes place in an informational vacuum, where voting becomes a form of electoral roulette. On the more salient, contested, and

controversial propositions, voters' decision processes appear to be more structured by the campaign appeals of the two sides, as well as their overall
presence in the campaign, as measured by spending and elite and media
endorsements.

THE SIDE THAT DEFINES THE PROPOSITION USUALLY WINS THE ELECTION

A successful ballot proposition campaign sets out to define the measure in
such a way as to increase the chances of victory on election day. By deciding
which issues to raise and on which themes to focus, each side seeks to structure the debate. In the absence of the party cue, voters are more dependent on
the two sides to simplify the choice and help organize the electoral decision.

The battle over defining the proposition is one of the most important
aspects of initiative politics. It is not uncommon in a statewide initiative campaign for the campaign to focus on only a very small part of the proposition.
After the grass-roots organizers had succeeded in qualifying the clean indoor
air initiative – a proposition that would have established nonsmoking sections in public buildings, businesses, and restaurants – the opponents, principally tobacco companies, responded by structuring their campaign around
themes such as "Big Brother [government] is at it again" and "This measure is
another example of excessive government regulation." The "No on 5" Committee wanted the voter to think about big government's intrusion into personal decisions and not to focus on what the proponents used as campaign
themes: recent research on the harmful effects of second hand smoke and
nonsmokers' rights. Had the proposition become a referendum on nonsmokers' rights rather than on excessive government interference, the opponents would have had a more difficult time defeating the measure. But
because the opponents successfully defined the measure, the outcome was
much less a vote on smoking in public places than it was a vote on governmental intrusion into private activity.

A primary substantive issue in the campaign was the complexity of the law,
not the problem it was designed to correct. This flaw worked to the advantage
of the opponents as they effectively used television and radio advertisements
to point out that restaurants would be required to establish nonsmoking sections but bars would not, that in the same arena smoking would be prohibited
at basketball games but not at boxing matches. Not only were these distinc-
tions hard for most voters to understand and remember but the advertisements also effectively communicated a sense that the proposition was going
too far.

A second example of the importance of defining the question to be decided
by the voters is the 1978 California vote on homosexual teachers. The tide of
previous anti-homosexual referendums at the municipal level makes the
defeat of the California statewide initiative surprising. This defeat was not,

however, a vote in favor of the homosexual life style, as some interpreted it to be.[2] Instead, it was the result of widespread concern over specific elements of the proposition that were perceived as extreme and unnecessary. Opponents of the measure won the battle of defining the proposition by successfully calling attention to the probability that due-process protections would not be afforded to school teachers accused of homosexuality or of encouraging that life style. According to the opponents, under the proposition, a person could be subject to immediate suspension and a disciplinary hearing even if the charges against him were the result of hearsay evidence. The opponents of the measure also argued that the measure was unnecessary because local school districts already had sufficient means to solve the problem, if it existed. Using these themes, the opponents of the initiative diverted attention from the issue of homosexuality or homosexual teachers — a referendum they would probably have lost — to a vote on an unnecessary, poorly drafted measure whose constitutionality was questionable.

These are only two of many examples that make the point that the side that defines the issue will win the election. Howard Jarvis and Paul Gann were successful in making the June 1978 Proposition 13 a referendum on high property taxes, while the opponents failed to establish their perspective, which was that the measure was excessive and would likely lead to financial ruin. The opponents of the nuclear power initiative, the 1976 Proposition 15, were successful in focusing attention on jobs and a safe nuclear industry, while the proponents failed to focus the campaign on the need for tougher safety standards. Had the vote occurred after the Three Mile Island incident, their campaign theme might have been more successful.

Agenda setting is, of course, very different from defining the proposition once it appears on the ballot. There are two important phases in the initiative process. The first phase, setting the agenda, involves qualifying measures for the ballot. In this phase, groups with money, or dedicated volunteers, can sometimes overcome the signature-collection hurdle and put a proposition on the ballot. But the proposition that qualifies for the ballot will not necessarily be defined for the voters by the proponents. As we have seen, it is not uncommon for the opponents to emerge with a very different view of the central issues involved and to focus public attention on their own agenda. Antismoking groups put clean indoor air on the ballot, but that was not the focus of the subsequent campaign. During the phase of the campaign when the proposition is defined for the voters, campaign spending and elite mobilization are critical and may prove decisive. As discussed above, opponents of initiative campaigns appear to enjoy somewhat of an advantage in this phase. However, it is important to learn what, if any, stable predispositions help voters decide how to vote on statewide propositions.

A key to understanding whether such predispositions exist is to examine the electorate's voting intentions on propositions over the course of a campaign. Given low levels of interest and information, widespread opinion change can reasonably be expected during the campaign, as the voters learn more about the issues. On what kinds of propositions are a person's voting intentions most likely to change? On what kinds are opinions stable? Are voters more likely to change their voting intentions in regard to propositions than they are their intentions in regard to candidates?

Change in Voting Intentions on Propositions

Most voters are willing to state a preference for or against a proposition even if they know very little about it. In an initial cross section of voters surveyed three to four months before the election, rarely will more than 20 percent of those who have seen or heard of the proposition say that they are undecided or have no opinion. This widespread willingness to state an opinion on a proposition does not mean, however, that voters are unwilling to change their voting intentions as the campaign proceeds. Substantial changes in aggregate voting intentions that occur during many proposition campaigns almost certainly reflect a degree of measurement error. Some respondents, when asked about their intended vote, will indicate a positive or negative preference even though they know nothing about the proposition. The number of nonattitude, or inaccurate, responses should decline as the campaign nears completion.[3]

A careful study of the more than twenty-five statewide propositions for which at least three separate surveys are available reveals three distinct patterns in the stability of voting intentions during a ballot proposition campaign:

1. *Standing opinions* — the aggregate of voters' opinions changes very little throughout the campaign.
2. *Uncertain opinions* — there is variation in support for the proposition but the side that has led all along wins.
3. *Opinion reversals* — there is substantial variation in support of the proposition and the side that was at one time far behind wins.

Examples of all three patterns from California and Massachusetts are presented in Appendix F.

Even before the campaign on the proposition begins, most voters have their minds made up on issues such as the death penalty, legalized use of marijuana, and the equal rights amendment. Propositions on these subjects pass or fail on the basis of voters' standing opinions on the issues. The stability of voting intentions on these issues results from a deeper attachment to their opinions than is the case for voting intentions on issues like subversive activities, handgun registration, and homosexual teachers.[4] On some issues, the cross-sectional data reveal a greater degree of opinion fluidity than is found on issues where many voters have standing opinions. This second type of proposition — dealing with issues upon which voters have uncertain opinions — is exemplified by the California nuclear power and property-tax initiatives. During the campaign, more voters were consistently either for or against these propositions, but considerable variance was found in the degree of electoral support or opposition over time. The remarkable stability of voting intentions demonstrated on issues such as the death penalty is not evident here. Issues on which voters have uncertain opinions are those on which they may experience more cross pressures but on which ultimately they appear to follow their initial opinions.

One of the most dramatic and interesting aspects of statewide propositions is the degree to which intended voters interviewed late in the campaign have voting intentions very different from those of voters interviewed early in the campaign. In each of these cases, persons surveyed in the early stages of the campaign were very supportive of the proposition, often by a margin of more than two to one. But later in the campaign more people opposed the proposition than supported it, and on election day the proposition was defeated by a substantial margin.

An example of aggregate opinion reversal is the 1972 tax reduction measure. As with most propositions, in the initial survey very few persons said that they were undecided or did not know how they would vote on the proposition. By the second survey, however, the ranks of the undecided had more than doubled. By election day the measure was soundly defeated. It appears that opinion change on this measure was a two-step process. The aggregate data suggest that voters moved from initial support for the tax cut to undecided about it. As the campaign proceeded, the number of undecided voters declined and the number of opposition voters increased.

In the other examples of reversal in the intended vote among the cross sections, the proportion of undecided did not grow as the campaign progressed. Rather, on issues such as subversive activities, handgun registration, and restriction of smoking in public places, the proportion of contrary voters in each successive cross section grew, and the actual no vote was typically larger than in the last pre-election survey.

But on what proportion of propositions is there widespread change in voting intentions? Is greater stability of voting intentions manifested in surveys for candidate races than in those for propositions? To answer these questions, I examined all California candidate contests and propositions in the period 1960–82 in which at least three cross-sectional surveys were available in addition to the actual vote.

The same three patterns of voting intentions emerged from these data. In some cases there was little opinion change, with roughly the same division of the vote throughout the entire campaign. In a second category of propositions and candidate races there was moderate change in voting intentions. In these cases significant changes in the margin of preferences occurred over time, but the side that won had led all along. In the third category of proposi-

Table 9.1

Stability of Voting Intentions in California Candidate and Proposition Contests, 1960–82

Change in Voting Intentions	Type of Election				Total	
	Candidate		Proposition			
Little [a]	77%	(27)	28%	(10)	51%	(37)
Moderate [b]	11	(4)	19	(7)	16	(11)
Significant [c]	14	(5)	53	(19)	33	(24)

Source: California Polls, 1960–82, The Field Institute, San Francisco, California.

[a] Roughly the same margin of preferences persisted throughout the campaign.

[b] There were significant changes in the margin of preferences, but the side that led all along won.

[c] There were significant changes in voting intentions as the campaign proceeded; the side that had at one time been far behind won.

tions and candidate races there was substantial variation in voting intentions. Generally, one side led by 60 percent or more in early surveys only to lose by a similar margin. The degree of change in voting intentions for candidates and for propositions is presented in table 9.1.

Voting intentions are much more likely to change during a proposition campaign than in a candidate contest. Significant aggregate opinion changes were more than three times as likely in proposition campaigns: there were widespread fluctuations in only 14 percent of the candidate races but in 53 percent of the proposition campaigns. While there was little change in voting intentions in 77 percent of the candidate contests, this was the case in only 28 percent of the proposition campaigns. In sum, in roughly three-fourths of all proposition campaigns studied there was moderate or widespread change in voting intentions.

The fact that voting intentions of the electorate change so dramatically on ballot propositions and so rarely in candidate races confirms an earlier finding in chapter 7: voters on propositions are less sure of their voting intentions, less knowledgeable about the proposition contests, and probably more susceptible to campaign appeals. In candidate contests, party identification acts as a standing decision and a simplifying device. In contrast, only a few issues covered by ballot propositions have the kind of standing decision so typical of candidate contests. Perhaps the best example of an apparent standing decision on a ballot proposition is the death penalty. In California the vote in favor of the death penalty is predictably 65–70 percent. Another reason for the greater stability of voting intentions in candidate contests is the fact that the candidates either have run for office before or are well known for other reasons. For example, in the 1962 governor's race in California between Edmund Brown, Sr., and Richard Nixon, voting intentions were remarkably stable over time. Voters knew the candidates before the formal campaign began. In sharp contrast voters knew very little about nuclear power, flat-rate electricity, or reapportionment before those campaigns began. Even if candidates are less well known in the primary election, by the time they run in the general election they have the benefit of prior coverage, while the general-election propositions are new to the voters. Finally, part of the widespread change in voting intentions on propositions among the electorate is probably due to "instant opinions" or nonattitudes. When voters are asked several months before the election for their intended vote, surprisingly few respond "undecided" or "don't know." This almost certainly means that they are expressing an instant reaction or opinion to the idea of the proposition. As the campaign heats up, these instant positive opinions typically change to expressions of opposition. The electorate's original voting intentions are neither deeply rooted nor stable.

CORRELATES OF VOTING CHOICE IN PROPOSITION ELECTIONS

Most studies of voting behavior on propositions have focused on a single issue, such as fluoridation in Cambridge, Massachusetts; urban mass transit in Atlanta, Georgia; or open housing in California.[5] As a result, most of what has been written about voting on propositions has not been generally applicable. Age, religion, and parental status help to explain voting on school bonds.[6] On economic issues, social class has been a useful predictor.[7] On open-housing propositions, which have been the subject of considerable scrutiny, occupation, party identification, race, socioeconomic status, education, and intrastate regional breakdowns all have been shown to be significant.[8] A debate has arisen over the extent to which economic self-interest is important in referendum voting.[9] In a recent study of a casino gambling vote, religion was shown to be an important factor in the outcome.[10]

Depending on the subject matter of the particular initiative being studied, scholars have identified such variables as education, social class, occupation, income, region, religion, and sex as being important in explaining election outcome. While each of these variables has predictive power for a given issue, it is doubtful that they have general applicability to all propositions. On the propositions where I was able to analyze post-election survey data, I found that none of these independent variables consistently correlated with voting choice.[11] For instance, while religion makes a difference in voting on an initiative to legalize gambling, it does not make a significant difference on most propositions.

Two other variables – party identification and ideology – may play an important role in structuring the vote on ballot measures. Party identification is generally acquired in childhood from parents and, in comparison with other variables, is remarkably stable. Voters in a sense have made a standing decision to be a Democrat or a Republican, and they vote consistently with that partisanship. Even most of the nominal independents have partisan leanings and vote accordingly. In short, in partisan/candidate elections, party identification, more than any other variable, helps voters make electoral choices. However, in other electoral contexts, most notably in primary elections, voters cannot rely on party cues, and party identification thus has limited utility.

One reason why party identification is important in the context of partisan elections is that it simplifies the decision-making task for the voter. Voters apparently assume that candidates of their own party more accurately reflect their concerns and interests and vote accordingly. In the absence of a compelling reason to vote against their standing decision, most voters will rely on the party cue.[12] In voting on statewide propositions, however, the party cue is generally absent both on the ballot itself and in the campaign.

There are good reasons for political parties to avoid stands on ballot measures. Foremost is the fact that a proposition rarely means any payoff to the electoral fortunes of the party candidates in the election. In the case of the California nuclear power initiative, it has already been demonstrated that candidates for the presidency and the U.S. Senate, as well as notable party and community leaders, were not widely perceived as having taken stands on the subject. This is at least in part the result of the realization on the part of the candidate or the party that every party stand on a proposition may alienate some voters. Occasionally, however, propositions are translated into partisan issues. Examples of two such propositions are California's 1964 Proposition 14, on open housing, and its 1973 Proposition 1, the Reagan tax initiative. Raymond Wolfinger and Fred Greenstein found that party identification was among the most important variables predicting the vote on open housing in California.[13] The battle over this issue assumed partisan overtones because of the salience of the issue and the involvement of Lyndon Johnson, Pierre Salinger, and Pat Brown. A similar partisan split occurred in 1973 when Ronald Reagan championed a tax-cutting initiative, Proposition 1. Here again, the parties and their leaders did not hide the partisan implications of the vote. To what extent do party followers divide on statewide propositions? The partisan divisions of the vote on twenty California propositions that have appeared on the ballot since 1972 for which there exist either post-election survey data or pre-election data from a survey made within a few days of the election are presented in table 9.2.

On most propositions voters from both parties came down on the same side of the issue, but with differing levels of support or opposition. For instance, 80 percent of the Democrats voted yes on the health sciences bond, but 62 percent of the Republicans did as well; only 24 percent of the Republicans intended to vote to decriminalize marijuana in 1972, and less than half (42 percent) of the Democrats had the same intention. On some propositions the two parties were even less divergent. Democrats and Republicans had almost identical voting intentions on the wild-rivers initiative, and only nine percentage points separated the two parties on the rent-control initiative of 1980.

Table 9.2

PARTY IDENTIFICATION AND THE VOTE ON BALLOT PROPOSITIONS IN CALIFORNIA, 1972–80

% Affirmative Votes among Those Who Had Made Up Their Minds or Had Voted on the Proposition

Party Identification	Prop. 2 (1972), Health Sciences Bond	Prop. 17 (1972), Death Penalty	Prop. 18 (1972), Obscenity	Prop. 19 (1972), Marijuana	Prop. 20 (1972), Coastal Zone	Prop. 21 (1972), School Busing	Prop. 22 (1972), Agricultural Labor Relations	Prop. 1 (1973), Reagan Tax Cut	Prop. 4 (1974), Board of Regents	Prop. 17 (1974), Wild Rivers
Republican	62%	82%	47%	24%	46%	68%	65%	73%	54%	54%
Democrat	80	57	27	42	67	54	37	27	76	55
Independent/declined to state/other	71	48	13	79	74	52	23	54	64	60
Total	72%	67%	33%	36%	59%	60%	42%	46%	67%	54%

Party Identification	Prop. 15 (1976), Nuclear Power	Prop. 8 (1978), Legislative Property-Tax Measure	Prop. 13 (1978), Property Taxes	Prop. 5 (1978), Smoking	Prop. 6 (1978), Homosexual Teachers	Prop. 9 (1980), State Income Tax–Jarvis	Prop. 10 (1980), Rent Control	Prop. 11 (1980), Oil Company Tax
Republican	20%	36%	77%	43%	49%	49%	38%	32%
Democrat	43	57	53	47	33	29	30	55
Independent/declined to state/other	39	47	58	51	38	39	29	46
Total	35%	49%	62%	46%	38%	38%	34%	44%

Sources: California Polls, 1972–80, The Field Institute, San Francisco, California; Survey of Attitudes on Nuclear Power, June 1976, Rand Corporation, Santa Monica, California; CBS News/Los Angeles Times exit polls, 1978–80.

In some instances, however, there was a clear partisan division of the vote. Six examples emerge from the data in table 9.2: Proposition 20, the coastal zone initiative; Proposition 22, on agricultural labor relations; Proposition 1, the Reagan tax initiative; Proposition 8, the Behr property-tax initiative; Proposition 9, the Jarvis state income-tax initiative; and Proposition 11, the oil company tax. In all cases, there was more than a 20 percent difference between the two parties. In the case of the 1972 agricultural-labor-relations initiative, two-thirds of the Republicans voted to limit the union-organizing power of farmworkers; only one-third of the Democrats supported the same proposition. The partisan split was even more evident on the Reagan tax initiative, Proposition 1. In a survey conducted immediately before the election, Republicans overwhelmingly favored the measure: 73 percent of those with their minds made up reported an intended yes vote. Most Democrats, however, came to the opposite conclusion: only 27 percent reported an intended yes vote.

Referendums such as these are not typical, however. Parties and candidates usually avoid stands on propositions, and the voters are left to their own resources. One resource voters may use is an ideological predisposition. If voters are able to translate a ballot measure into liberal or conservative terms, their decision-making task will be simpler. To what extent does self-identification with a liberal or a conservative ideology affect the vote on propositions?

To a surprising extent, ideological self-classification appears to determine voting behavior. While 88 percent of the strong conservatives reported an intended affirmative vote on the death penalty, Proposition 17, only 20 percent of the strong liberals intended to vote yes. This same general pattern emerges on several of the propositions. With only three exceptions, these propositions are initiatives rather than legislatively sponsored referendums. Hence, it would be a mistake to overgeneralize from these data. But on most initiatives since 1972 the California electorate has apparently relied on ideological predispositions to help determine their vote.

The bivariate analysis suggests a relationship between party identification and the vote on some ballot questions, and an even stronger relationship between ideological self-identification and ballot proposition voting. Thus far, however, I have not assessed the independent effects of these variables, nor have I controlled for possible spurious relationships. On propositions for which I have post-election vote data, I have conducted a multiple regression analysis to determine which independent variables are related to voting choice and their relative strength. The most straightforward technique is a linear estimation operation using dummy variables. The dependent variable is dichotomous — an affirmative vote being counted as one, a negative vote as zero.[14] I hypothesized that an individual's vote would to varying degrees respond to the independent variables of party identification, ideological self-identification, education, income, race, occupation, and age. Using a stan-

Table 9.3

IDEOLOGY AND THE VOTE ON BALLOT PROPOSITIONS IN CALIFORNIA, 1972–80

% Affirmative Votes among Those Who Had Made Up Their Minds or Had Voted on the Proposition

Ideological Identification	Prop. 2 (1972), Health Sciences Bond	Prop. 17 (1972), Death Penalty	Prop. 18 (1972), Obscenity	Prop. 19 (1972), Mari-juana	Prop. 20 (1972), Coastal Zone	Prop. 21 (1972), School Busing	Prop. 22 (1972), Agricultural Labor Relations	Prop. 1 (1973), Reagan Tax Cut	Prop. 4 (1974), Board of Regents	Prop. 17 (1974), Wild Rivers
Strong conservative	57%	88%	55%	17%	35%	70%	61%	88%	51%	39%
Moderate conservative	61	83	42	21	52	65	52	59	58	56
Middle	77	67	30	34	66	61	40	42	68	42
Moderate liberal	85	45	21	60	67	56	33	27	74	60
Strong liberal	89	20	15	84	85	27	22	14	83	73
Don't know	63	74	36	27	44	53	33	40	100	77
Total	72%	67%	33%	36%	59%	60%	42%	46%	67%	54%

	Prop. 15 (1976), Nuclear Power	Prop. 8 (1978), Legislative Property-Tax Measure	Prop. 13 (1978), Property Taxes	Prop. 5 (1978), Smoking	Prop. 6 (1978), Homo-sexual Teachers	Prop. 9 (1980), State Income Tax—Jarvis	Prop. 10 (1980), Rent Control	Prop. 11 (1980), Oil Company Tax
Conservative	25%	29%	79%	46%	49%	54%	39%	29%
Middle	33	51	63	45	40	37	33	46
Liberal	48	65	43	49	23	21	27	62
Total	35%	49%	63%	46%	38%	38%	34%	44%

Sources: California Polls, 1972–80, The Field Institute, San Francisco, California; Survey of Attitudes on Nuclear Power, June 1976, Rand Corporation, Santa Monica, California; CBS News/Los Angeles Times exit polls, 1978–80.

dard dummy-variable design, I also dropped missing data from the estimation. (The formal equation and the multiple correlation coefficients for the independent variables are presented in Appendix G.)

The regression analyses determine both the degree and the direction of influence of each significantly related independent variable on the dependent variable, the percentage of affirmative votes. The interpretation of the data will best be done by use of an example, say Proposition 5 in 1978, the anti-smoking initiative. When all independent variables are held to a value of zero, the expected affirmative vote is 51 percent. (This is the constant term in the table.) As each of the various independent variables is analyzed, we can gain a better understanding of its relative influence. For instance, smokers are significantly less likely to vote yes on this proposition; knowing that a person is a smoker reduces the expected yes vote to only 12 percent. If a person is a Republican and a smoker, the predicted yes vote is 45 percent less than if he is not (39 percent plus 6 percent). For each of the propositions summarized in Appendix G, the independent effect on the expected vote either up or down is indicated. Comparing across propositions, it is clear that party and ideology are the most consistent variables. Home ownership, for instance, matters very little on measures other than tax votes.

Using this technique, the propositions for which I obtain the best predictions are Proposition 13, the Jarvis-Gann property-tax initiative, and Proposition 9, the Jarvis income-tax initiative. In contrast, the variables in the equation explain very little of the vote on the University of California health sciences bond in 1972. For most of the propositions the multiple correlation coefficients are not very high. To gain a sense of their relative strength, I have done a multiple regression with the same independent variables for candidate elections in the same time period (see Appendix G).

The multiple correlation coefficients are much higher for the candidate races than for the propositions in the same period. Nearly two-thirds of the variance in the California vote for president is explained by the independent variables in the equation. Again, party and ideology are the variables consistently most significant, but in this case they have an even greater impact than they did on the propositions.

On the basis of this comparison between the two types of voting situations, it is apparent that voters have a much less structured voting situation on ballot measures than in candidate contests. Even the tax votes, which are more influenced by these independent variables, are far less structured than candidate contests in general-election settings. Voting in primary-election candidate contests also appears to be uninfluenced by these independent variables. All the variables that one could reasonably assume might play a role in voter decision making were included in the equation, yet they appear to have relatively little explanatory power. Voting on ballot propositions appears to be more structured by party and ideology than by other factors, but each measure has a marked random and ad hoc nature. Therefore, predicting initiative voting across issues is very difficult, even when measures such as party and ideology are included; it is even more difficult in the case of noninitiative ballot measures.

CONCLUSIONS

The individual voter faces a sizable decision-making challenge when confronted by ballot propositions. On the noncontroversial measures, most voters face an informational vacuum, and it is difficult to explain why people vote as they do. It appears that most voters make snap judgments on the measure in the voting place. Even on the contested and controversial measures — typically initiatives — voters can rarely rely on a party cue, and the only remaining decision strategy is to attempt to translate the issue into an ideological predisposition. On some issues the question is poorly focused for such an analysis — how can one translate basic problems with the drafting of a measure into ideological terms? On occasion, however, ideology appears to orient voters, and if one variable is going to work across measures, it will be this one.

Independent variables such as party, ideology, education, race, income, and so on, have a larger impact on voting choice in partisan/candidate general elections. Voting in primary elections resembles voting on propositions in that the independent variables have little predictive power and the voting decision appears to be more random. Studies have found that voting on local and state propositions is largely idiosyncratic decision making, where different forces are at work, depending on the issue. This is the first study to compare issues over time and across subject areas. Great variability in ballot proposition voting exists at the state level as well. This finding is especially important when the importance of party, ideology, and the other variables in partisan/candidate contests is compared with their importance in ballot propositions.

CHAPTER **10** □□□□□□□□□□□□□□□□□□□□□□□□□

The People Rule?

Should voters or legislators initiate and decide questions of public policy? If voters decide such questions, should they be limited to statutory decisions, or should they also be able to alter the Constitution by popular vote?[1] Should the values of popular participation be given greater weight than values ascribed to the legislative process? These questions are indicative of a fundamental disagreement over when and in what ways voters should act as legislators. Proponents of direct legislation advocate direct democracy as an essential supplement to the policy-making process. Opponents prefer indirect democracy, the process by which voters elect legislators, who then initiate and decide questions of public policy.[2] Each side argues that its preferred process will allow the people to rule more effectively.

The political division of labor between citizens and representatives is a recurrent issue in debates over other forms of direct democracy as well. Should presidential candidates be chosen by a convention of unconstrained delegates or by the outcomes of primary elections? Should candidates for state and local offices be chosen by party leaders or by direct primaries? Should the voters choose a President through a direct popular vote, or should the President be elected by the Electoral College? While the various forms of direct democracy differ in important ways, they share a fundamental premise: let the people decide. In short, widespread participation is seen as preferable to decisions' being made by an elected body of representatives.

Letting the people decide on ballot propositions is clearly consonant with majority rule, an important component of democratic government. But does direct legislation have democratic liabilities as well? Is direct legislation open and participatory as originally envisioned? To what extent does direct legislation tend to disrupt the basic social conditions necessary for the maintenance of democracy? While the reformers' call to "let the people rule" rings an immediate and positive chord, the actual experience with direct legislation demonstrates that the process is structured in ways that limit effective participation for some voters, and the agenda of issues may only serve to intensify conflict and lead to a politics of confrontation. In contrast, indirect democracy is generally structured to facilitate compromise, moderation, and a degree of access for all segments of the community. In the previous chapter, I have examined the experiences of several states with the direct legislation process; the next step is to evaluate the claims of greater democracy that are so frequently attributed to this process.

Direct Legislation and Democratic Values

Not only do direct and indirect forms of democracy differ in the institutional arrangements they advocate but they pursue quite different ends and values as well. Direct democracy values participation, open access, and political equality. It tends to deemphasize compromise, continuity, and consensus. In short, direct democracy encourages conflict and competition and attempts to expand the base of participants. Indirect democracy values stability, consensus, and compromise and seeks institutional arrangements that insulate fundamental principles from momentary passions or fluctuations in opinion.[3] While direct and indirect forms of democracy maximize different ends, there are several important dimensions of democratic governance upon which the two can be compared: participation, representation, accountability, accommodation, authority, and deliberation.

Participation and Representation

The case for establishing and enlarging direct legislation has one fundamental premise: all citizens should be able to initiate and decide upon legislation themselves. The people, it is argued, can and should serve as legislators, with the legal opportunity to decide both statutes and constitutional amendments. Proponents of the initiative and referendum see it as a logical extension of free and open government. It would be undemocratic, in the view of the "participationists," to deny the people the right to direct legislation.

Just as direct democracy is central to the argument for the initiative and referendum, the idea of a republic and representation is the central premise of direct legislation's opponents. The "representationists" not only criticize the operation of direct legislation in practice but assert that the people can best rule themselves through regular election of public officials. Opponents of direct legislation challenge the claims that direct legislation is necessary for free and open government and that it fosters better government. They also evoke the views of the founders of the American republic, arguing that those men consciously rejected plebiscitarian democracy as extreme and potentially anti-democratic. They argue that the people can rule most effectively through representative institutions and a republican form of government.

Both the participationists and the representationists would agree with the popular sentiment that the people should rule, but they would have very different views on how the people can effectively rule. The evidence presented in this book permits an empirical assessment of who actually does rule in the direct legislation process, as well as some insights into the accuracy of the claims of both opponents and proponents of direct legislation.

The people who rule in the initiative and referendum process are first and foremost the people who set the agenda for the voters to decide at the next election. Essential to the claim that more democratic government results from direct legislation is the assumption that the issues placed on ballots are representative of the issues people have on their minds and would like submitted to a public vote. Very few voters, however, can spontaneously name any particular issues on which they would like to see the public vote. Those issues that do appear on the ballot are typically not the same issues that voters list as the most important problems facing the state or the nation (see chapter 1). Voters rarely volunteer inflation, unemployment, the economy, or the other most important problems of the day as issues they would like to vote on by ballot proposition. The resolution of these issues is apparently to be left to the elected representatives in the state capitals or in Washington, D.C.

Because of voter disinterest and the signature threshold requirement, the agenda of issues to be decided by voters is determined by proponents' capacity to hire professional signature-gathering firms or by the dedication of issue activists or single-issue groups who desire to place measures on the ballot. At this first critical hurdle, most citizens lack the organizational strength and financial resources to propose laws for direct legislation. When proponents of the process argue that "the people" will rule more completely if given the initiative and referendum, they apparently do not refer to the agenda-setting aspect of the process. In fact, it can be argued that "the people," especially those without plenty of money or an organizational base, will probably get better results from their elected representative, who will almost always respond to the inquiry and may well put it on the legislative agenda.[4]

Important examples of groups with limited financial resources who have been successful in placing initiatives on the ballot are the anti-nuclear, anti-smoking, and utility-reform groups. These issues typically are not mentioned by citizens who are asked about issues they would like to have decided by direct legislation; that is, they are not representative of the issue concerns of "the people." Thus, citizens may express opinions on the propositions placed on the ballot, but that issue agenda usually is not an accurate barometer of the issue concerns of most voters. If approval rate is any measure of voter interest, then the issues voters actually decide rarely strike a responsive chord, because a high proportion of initiatives are defeated. The same opponents who successfully lobbied against these bills in the state legislature can defeat them in the wider electoral arena as well.

Interpreting direct legislation results as mandates or expressions of the "popular will" is also problematic. One problem is that voters are not permitted to vote on alternative bills; another is that voters cannot attempt to amend the proposed legislation to make it more acceptable. An additional problem is that voters are limited to an affirmative vote, a negative vote, or an abstention. Because of the way in which propositions are worded, voters often must choose the least inaccurate expression of their opinion. Some Californians may have desired to restrict the advocacy of homosexuality by teachers in public schools, and in theory an affirmative vote on Proposition 6 in 1978 would have achieved this purpose; but the actual proposition provided for a process of removing or disciplining teachers based upon limited or hearsay evidence, a clear restriction of normal due-process rights. Thus, the expression of popular will on homosexual teachers was encumbered by the framing of the ballot question; voting yes meant rejecting due process and civil rights, while voting no meant casting a vote in favor of homosexuality. Another problem that results from proposition wording is the inability to translate variations of opinion into a single affirmative or negative vote. A majority of voters will have voted one way or the other, but that does not mean that they all feel the same way about the proposition.

Less educated and poorer voters encounter additional problems when voting on propositions because of unnecessarily complex and lengthy propositions and their ballot titles. Even on issues of direct relevance, such as graduated income taxes, these voters cannot surmount the hurdle of proposition complexity. As a result, they often abstain from voting. The 1976 Massachusetts graduated-income-tax vote thus did not include the opinions of one important subset of voters, and as a result direct legislation provided an incomplete reading of the popular will.

Because ballot propositions are decided individually, they are frequently difficult to integrate into any overall assessment of the popular will. A majority of voters may vote to reduce taxes but in the same election may vote to raise the salary levels of public employee groups such as police or forestry service personnel. Students of public opinion have frequently observed this tendency towards inconsistency in opinion across related issues.[5] One of the liabilities of the direct legislation process is that it encourages voting on isolated issues without requiring voters to integrate their opinions on one issue with their opinions on others.

Which people rule in direct legislation? Those who set the legislative agenda and those who actually vote on that agenda. Neither the issues put before the voters nor those voters who actually decide them are representative. The people who rule under direct legislation tend to be those who can understand and use the process. Less educated, poorer, and nonwhite citizens are organizationally and financially excluded from setting the direct legislation agenda because their own issue agendas are less articulated and because they lack the resources and personal efficacy to attempt a petition circulation and direct legislation campaign. These same people are less likely to vote on ballot propositions because they cannot comprehend the wording of the proposition and need the assistance of such ballot-organizing devices as political parties.

Despite the high hopes of reformers that direct legislation would increase turnout and reduce alienation, neither has occurred. In fact, direct legislation has not activated uninterested or alienated voters. These citizens, if asked, support the process of direct legislation, but when it comes time to vote, they continue to stay at home or to vote on only a few very salient propositions or in candidate races. In terms of the dimensions of participation and representation, direct legislation is prone to serious biases; and the process has not lived up to the expectations of the reformers that the people could more effectively rule if granted the initiative and referendum.

Accommodation, Accountability, and Authority

Difference of opinion about public policy will exist in any society. An important characteristic of a democratic system is the presence of institutional structures that reflect public opinion in the determination of public policy and can also resolve conflicts over policy by peaceful accommodation. For instance, in the legislative arena rarely will any one side have its way completely. Rather, the legislative product typically will be the result of compromise, allowing consensus to emerge around a policy choice.

In direct legislation the voter is only partially a legislator. The voter is not party to the drafting and compromising process and can play no part in the determination of the policy choice he will confront. Thus, voters are faced with statutes that they did not help to write and that they must affirm or reject in toto. Direct legislation does not face the procedural constraints of the legislative process: hearings, amendments, markup, scheduling, floor debate, and conference. In contrast, rarely do the sponsors of an initiative circulate their bill prior to the petition phase – and once this phase begins, the language cannot be changed. The process of direct legislation is not built upon the principle of compromise and accommodation but instead forces an all-or-nothing policy decision on the question as formulated by the sponsors alone.

Another important distinction between the two forms of legislation is that the direct means does not permit an assessment of the participants' intensity of opinion. In direct legislation all votes are counted equally, but not all voters feel equally positive or negative about the proposition. Some voters may be only slightly opposed or slightly in favor of the proposition, but their votes have the same weight as the votes cast by those who are sure of their opinions and feel strongly about them. In the legislative process, elected representatives can calculate the varying degrees of intensity and include them in their legislative decisions.[6] This advantage of the legislative process works to facilitate accommodation. The strength of feeling among all partisans to an issue is weighted as legislators arrive at compromises acceptable to a majority of legislators. This is not the case in direct legislation, which helps to explain why direct legislation measures are often more extreme than measures produced by legislatures.

Accommodation is a norm of importance to the successful operation of a legislature as well as to that of a political system generally. Subjecting an unlimited array of issues to popular vote has the detrimental effect of intensifying preexisting differences. By their nature, referendum campaigns appeal to passions and prejudices, spotlight tensions, and result only in greater conflict and disagreement. The most notable example of an area in which referendums have had this effect is that of race relations. Derrick A. Bell, Jr., has described the referendum as democracy's barrier to racial equality.

> Appeals to prejudice, oversimplification of the issues, and exploitation of legitimate concerns by promising simplistic solutions to complex problems often characterize referendum and initiative campaigns. Of course, politicians, too, may offer quick cure-alls to gain electoral support and may spend millions on election campaigns that are as likely to obfuscate as to elucidate the issues. But we vote politicians into office, not into law. Once in office, they may become well-informed, responsible representatives; at the least, their excesses may be curtailed by the checks and balances of the political process.[7]

As I discussed in chapter 3, the courts have often protected fundamental rights by overturning the referendum vote in matters protected by the U.S. Constitution or state constitutions. Even though the courts have not hesitated to reject election outcomes, the more important systemic consequence may be the impact of the campaign, which has had the negative effect of making compromise and conciliation more difficult. The founders of the American constitutional system understood the necessity of providing a government that not only was responsive to public opinion but also encouraged compromise, moderation, and conciliation. They consciously insulated fundamental freedoms and liberties from the whims of momentary majorities. In a country as diverse and heterogeneous as the United States, their insight is equally useful in our time.

Proponents of direct legislation often argue that democratic governments require a means to resolve difficult questions authoritatively. Major institutional changes, constitutional amendments, and treaty ratifications are some of the areas frequently cited as suited to a referendum. While some referendums clearly have achieved these ends, it is also possible that referendums will result in inconclusive results or in a situation where both sides can claim victory. Equally important is the fact that referendums are high-risk efforts at conflict resolution. Not only may the division of votes be inconclusive but the campaign may have intensified conflict and reinforced preexisting divisions, thereby making subsequent resolution very difficult.

Still, direct legislation can be successfully used to resolve a policy dispute definitively. One example of this kind of use is the referendum on British entry into the European Economic Community. The decision had important consequences for the future of the United Kingdom and was of a different magnitude than the normal parliamentary issue. A public referendum on the issue in this case served to resolve the issue, but only because both sides were willing to define the vote as decisive.[8] Had the vote been closer or had one side been only a partially active participant, the question might not have been authoritatively resolved. The referendum device has also been used in an effort to resolve definitively such questions as devolution in Scotland and Wales and separatism in Quebec.[9] It may be used to determine the question of statehood for Puerto Rico. For this device to resolve these fundamental questions requires active participation by the two sides and an acceptance of the electoral outcome.

One of the frequently cited positive consequences of the initiative is that it often stimulates the legislature to take action or, at the least, provides a means to determine in part the agenda of legislative action. Whether the initiative serves as a "gun behind the door"[10] or a legislative "bit and bridle,"[11] most students of the process have concluded that on balance, it fosters legislative responsibility. On at least some issues, however, the initiative serves as an easy way for the legislature to avoid deciding an issue, passing it along instead to the voters. In this respect direct legislation discourages legislative accountability. An additional problem for legislative accountability is the fact that voters can hold only themselves accountable for an unsuccessful initiative. Precisely because of the nature of initiative politics, legislators are legally prohibited from tampering with a successful initiative measure or are politically unlikely to do so.

Deliberation

The legislative process is frequently criticized for being slow, cumbersome, and biased against action. These factors, however, have benefits as well as costs, including the open and deliberative nature of the process. In the legislature, proposed statutes and constitutional amendments are reviewed and modified several times before they are submitted to a final vote. As a measure obtains sponsors, survives hearings, and then is opened for amendment in markup, the expertise and experience of legislators, staff, and interested groups and individuals is brought to bear. These same procedures are repeated in the second house of the legislature in every state except Nebraska, which has a unicameral legislature. The process of drafting and modifying initiatives is not subject to the same open and deliberative review. This frequently puts the voters in the position of deciding a measure with flaws that emerge in the campaign but cannot be changed even if the sponsors desire to make the change.

When comparing tl ℮ more open and public nature of legislative drafting conducted in state le' ɪslatures with the more closed and private drafting of initiatives, it is important to consider not only the final product of the process but also the decision-making process of the participants: the voters, in the context of direct legislation, and the legislators, in the legislatures.

Unfortunately, I do not have comparable data on the levels of knowledge and information most legislators have for their voting decisions; but the data I have reviewed on voter decision making on direct legislation raise serious questions about the operation of that process. Voters rarely use more than one source of information, typically television; they rarely consult with others about the proposed legislation; and they often decide their vote late in the campaign or in the polling booth. There is voter confusion on ballot propositions generally because of the legal and technical language that is so much a part of direct legislation. In short, voters appear to reach their voting decision on most propositions with very little deliberation, discussion, or study.

Legislators face some of the same problems as voters, but they have some resources at their disposal that voters do not have. In addition, legislators have structured the decision-making process on the basis of specialization. The committee system, the seniority principle, and professional staff mean that expertise is brought to bear on legislation in the formative stages. In the final voting phase, legislators call upon the knowledge and experience of their colleagues to inform their vote. For any issue there are legislative specialists on both sides of the question. In addition, there are lobbyists, again on both sides of virtually all issues, who seek the ear of any potentially interested legislator. Legislators have not only these resources but also the time and political interest to study proposed laws. They also know that they may be held accountable for their vote and therefore have a stake in understanding the issue. Modern legislatures with trained professional staffs possess a tremendous advantage over individual voters in the knowledge and information aspects of decision making.

There are, in sum, important differences between direct and representative legislation. The electorate as a whole cannot function as a deliberative assembly in the same way that a legislature can. Voters do not develop expertise in the same way or to the same extent that legislators do. The elected legislator will weigh in his voting calculus his personal views on the issue, his perception of his constituents' views on the issue, and his view of the long-range interest of the polity. In direct legislation, voting is more individualistic. Theoretically, the outcome of direct legislation should reflect the majority will; however, given dropoff and voter confusion, this may not be true in practice. What is true of direct legislation is that the outcome, which may or may not reflect the majority will, is subject to fewer institutional checks and safeguards than the legislative process.

A concern with the relative absence of checks and balances is recurrent in the debate over the initiative process. Opponents of the process often cite this as one of their chief procedural concerns, along with oversimplification and overdramatization. Under direct legislation, the task of safeguarding minority rights from majority tyranny is effectively left to the courts. Elected legislatures guard against majority tyranny by the use of indirect rather than direct popular input, by bicameral checks, and by the executive veto. James Madison argued in number 10 of *The Federalist Papers* that the function of a representative assembly is "to refine and enlarge the public views, by passing them through the medium of a chosen body of citizens." [12] The translation of public views into public policy is more likely to be refined and enlarged under representative systems than under direct democratic systems.

The initiative and referendum permit an authoritarian (publicly accepted) resolution of a difficult policy choice and serve as a safety valve for issues that slip between the legislative cracks. In several other respects, however, direct legislation does not compare as favorably. Under direct legislation the decision is limited to a yes or no response to a typically complex issue. The legislative process provides more room for adjustment and accommodation of competing viewpoints. Direct legislation is a closed and private process until the matter goes out for signatures. The legislative process, especially in the formulative phase, is open and public, particularly since the passage of sunshine laws. [13] Direct legislation presents an agenda of issues that does not represent the issue concerns of the general citizenry, and the process is inflexible, providing little opportunity to correct error. Voter decision making in direct legislation is typically the result of snap judgments based upon superficial emotional appeals broadcast on television. The legislative process is more deliberative, substantive, and rational.

The legislative process is not without problems. Last-minute consideration of bills often lacks deliberation, and the closing rush may mean that legislators will cast votes without understanding the substance of measures. The sometimes dominant role played by interest groups makes the process less democratic. Complexity prompts creation of specialized committees and subcommittees, which in turn may exclude some legislators from influence until the bill is brought to the floor. In short, both direct legislation and the legislative process have shortcomings. Much of what has been written about direct legislation in the past, however, has only focused on the weaknesses of the legislative process, ignoring its strengths.

SINGLE-ISSUE POLITICS, THE INITIATIVE, AND THE DECLINE OF POLITICAL PARTIES

The ascendency of single-issue groups in American electoral politics has been discussed by others, but only in the context of partisan/candidate elections. Recent congressional elections have generated considerable commentary on the power and influence of pro- and anti-abortion groups, pro- and anti-ERA groups, environmental groups, school-prayer groups, and others. These well-funded groups are uncompromising on the issue of central importance to them. Often they work independently of the candidate they prefer; sometimes, in fact, the candidate himself openly discourages them from participation in his campaign.

The uncompromising, highly motivated, single-issue approach to politics is not new. For nearly a century the direct legislation process has been primarily a single-issue-group process. To qualify a measure, groups need money or dedicated volunteers. Single-issue groups often have the strength of commitment to persist in the signature-gathering phase. The initiative process does not require compromise in the drafting phase, and some sponsoring groups are often desirous of getting a "pure" vote on their statute or constitutional amendment. These groups, and often their opponents as well, are not as concerned about implications for the governmental process as they are about getting their way on the issue.

If the initiative process is adopted in new jurisdictions or at the federal level, it is quite possible that the focus of much of the political activity of single-issue groups would shift from partisan/candidate elections to direct legislation. The initiative often allows these groups to focus public attention not just in the jurisdiction having the vote but in a much larger area. Even if the single-issue group's proposition is defeated, by having placed its issue in the limelight, it has won an important victory.

But politics is many issues, and government is more than the sum of single-issue-group concerns. In successful democratic governments there must be an institutional means to reach accommodation, and that is not structurally possible with the initiative and referendum. Political parties can play this role. Not only can parties facilitate accommodation but in a decentralized system such as that of the United States, they alone can work across institutions (the President, the Senate, the House) and jurisdictions (federal, state, local).

The initiative weakens political parties because it allows groups to force public decision on issues framed by the groups themselves. The parties are excluded from participation in drafting the measures and therefore may not play much of a role in interpreting them to the voters. The traditional party roles of weighing competing interests, achieving compromise, and moderating demands in order to appeal to the maximum number of voters are not played by the parties in this process because they are not participants. Single-issue groups may include some of these concerns in their campaign strategy, but there is no institutional means to counter their issue perspective, and the propositions are thus typically more extreme than they would be if they were part of a party platform.

The American government needs strong and effective institutions of political accommodation such as political parties and legislatures. Single-issue groups in jurisdictions that have the initiative process can circumvent these institutions, getting their special issue put before the voters without opposition and without contrasting points of view being voted on at the same time. Such control over the decision process is not possible in parties and legislatures, where all perspectives are likely to be heard and many may be submitted to a vote. A government by single-issue groups will eventually frustrate the people themselves. Because the process accentuates differences between religious, racial, ethnic, and other groups, it has a tendency to foster conflict. The possibility that a group can "get it all" by going to the people will only make working with that group all the more difficult. Government by initiative could well lead to an immobilized and ineffectual government, two shortcomings the process was designed to correct.

DOES DIRECT LEGISLATION HAVE A LIBERAL OR CONSERVATIVE BIAS?

Opponents of direct legislation on both the left and the right have argued that voters have or will exhibit clear ideological biases when voting on ballot propositions. In a 1912 volume, James Boyle, an outspoken critic of the process, argued that the effect of direct legislation would be essentially reactionary, that "the principles and practical effects of the Initiative and Referendum are Reactionary as well as Revolutionary. Those who advocate Direct Legislation are 'Retrogressives', not 'Progressives.'" [14] With equal passion, some advocates of the direct legislation process argue that voters will adopt liberal and progressive measures. Also writing in 1912, Delos F. Wilcox concluded, "Unquestionably, the Initiative will open the door to radical legislation. . . . The people simply want to get things moving by clearing away the artificial obstacles put in the way of legislative progress by the predatory or self-complacent interests that have captured the machinery of representative government." [15]

Contemporary advocates of direct legislation are equally divided on whether the process of direct legislation is liberal or conservative in nature. Conservative supporters such as Senator Larry Pressler (R–S.D.) apparently envision more conservative outcomes on initiatives and referendums. [16] Similarly, liberals such as Ralph Nader and Senator James Abourezk (D–S.D.) are convinced that the good judgment of the people is more to their liking. [17] Common to both groups is the belief that the people, and not the legislature, should decide some of these policy questions. Equally important is the fact that both conservatives and liberals are quick to cite single proposition outcomes to support their case but hesitant to summarize the overall experience.

Is direct legislation, then, predominantly liberal or conservative in nature? Many students of the process argue that it is neither. As Austin Ranney concludes, "The referendum is neither an unfailing friend nor an implacable enemy of either left or right." Ranney goes on to observe that outcomes on referendums are difficult to categorize as either totally liberal or totally conservative because "voters observably lean right on some occasions and left on others." [18] Other students of direct legislation argue that the extreme claims found in the early debates have not held true and that the electorate has been neither irresponsible nor destructive. [19]

Austin Ranney, after examining the winners and losers in those initiative contests from 1945 to 1976 that had a clear liberal-conservative dimension, concluded that "liberal positions on economic questions (right to work and taxation laws) generally won, conservative positions on social issues (death penalty, abortion, and racial discrimination) won, while the environmentalists broke even with the advocates of economic growth on nuclear power issues. This pattern is consistent with the widely held view that American voters are predominantly liberal on economic questions and conservative on social issues." [20] Following the taxpayers' revolt of 1978, Ranney's finding of liberal voting on tax measures must be revised. His view that voters are conservative on social issues does remain true, however. Indeed, one of the most persuasive criticisms of direct legislation is that it allows us to vote our passions and our prejudices.

As I demonstrated in chapter 4, direct legislation since 1960 has frequently been used to deal with issues such as school busing, racial integration, marijuana, abortion, and morality. On these issues Ranney found clear conservative voting. This conservative bias in regard to life-style, moral, and racial issues becomes problematic when it conflicts, as it frequently has, with constitutional doctrine. Derrick A. Bell, Jr., has persuasively argued that direct legislation could become democracy's barrier to racial equality:

> Justice Black's declaration that referenda demonstrate devotion to democracy rather than to bias, discrimination, or prejudice, is in fact almost the opposite of the truth when the issue submitted to the voters suggests, even subtly, that majority interests can be furthered by the sacrifice of minority rights. The failure to recognize the special dangers to minority groups in the referendum process can be attributed to a reluctance to acknowledge either that there are minorities in society or that there is racism. Of course, both exist, and neither is likely to disappear in the near future. For ours is a heterogeneous society. [21]

Returning then to the question of whether direct legislation is a liberal or conservative device, the evidence presented earlier demonstrated that ballot access is restricted to groups who can overcome the signature threshold with financial resources or highly motivated volunteers. Because of this fact, the issue agenda presented to voters has more often reflected conservative interests and therefore has not afforded the opportunity to survey the ideological biases of the electorate. But the data do indicate a tendency to support the status quo by voting no on propositions, and a tendency to vote conservatively on life-style, moral, and racial issues, which have been among the issues most frequently the subjects of propositions in the 1960s and the 1970s.

The Future of the Initiative and Referendum

The decade of the 1970s was one of increased initiative and referendum activity. Not only was there a dramatic increase in the number of measures filed, but the number actually appearing on the ballot was larger than in the two preceding decades. The trend towards increased initiative activity has continued in the 1980s. Several states and the U.S. Congress have considered adopting direct legislation. These developments have important implications for American politics.

Direct legislation has become an important part of the politics of several states, and it is likely to become an important part of the politics of any jurisdiction in which it is adopted. Increasingly, in such states as Massachusetts, Michigan, Ohio, California, and Colorado, the initiative tends to dominate the agenda of state politics. Issues not appearing on the ballot will have a hard time competing for attention. Politicians will structure their strategy around these ballot measures, and their stands on these issues will be the most important issue stands of the campaign.

Not only do initiatives tend to dominate elections in states that have direct legislation but they are important factors in the politics of state legislatures as well. On the one hand, an initiative proposal can prod the legislature into action, as in the cases of California's Proposition 8 – the legislative counter-proposal to Proposition 13 – and the legislative toughening of safety standards for nuclear power facilities shortly before the June 1976 vote on nuclear power in California. In such cases legislators attempt to anticipate the initiative agenda in hopes of modifying or capturing it. The fact that legislators so frequently look over their shoulders to preempt upcoming initiatives means that those who threaten the legislature with an initiative have power not only over the initiative agenda but over the legislative agenda as well. As I demonstrated in chapter 1, the issue agenda of initiative activists is not broadly representative of the issue concerns of most voters, and this bias now affects both direct and representative legislation. In states that have direct legislation, groups that have not discovered the power of a real or threatened initiative are at a disadvantage.

Just as the initiative process can encourage legislative action on some subjects, it can also discourage legislative action. In states that have the initiative, state legislatures duck some issues in order to avoid the political heat associated with them. The initiative process allows elected officials to avoid making a decision, passing it along for a public referendum instead. Thus, in some cases direct legislation encourages the legislature to act, while in other cases it fosters inaction. In both cases it is very much a part of the political process.

An important implication of the initiative process is the role it can play in making issue activists famous and helping their political careers. It is doubtful that Paul Gann would have won the nomination for the U.S. Senate in

California had he not been involved in sponsoring initiatives. Similarly, Jerry Brown used his cosponsorship of Proposition 9, the fair political practices initiative, as an appeal in his 1974 gubernatorial campaign. Politicians in states that do not have the initiative have made adoption of the process a campaign promise in their candidacy for the governorship. Gubernatorial candidates who have advocated the initiative as part of their campaign include William Clements of Texas, Albert H. Quie of Minnesota, and Henry Howell of Virginia. It is distinctly possible that Congressman Jack Kemp's advocacy of a national initiative is related to presidential ambitions and would be part of his campaign platform.

Advocacy of the initiative appears to have helped the careers of Gann, Brown, Quie, and Clements. Not all advocates of a particular initiative or of the initiative process in states that do not presently have it have been so successful, but more aspirants are likely to see sponsorship of an initiative or of the process as the pathway to political fame and glory. The tendency to closely identify a candidacy with an initiative is even more likely to be the case in states where nominations are determined by primaries, where candidates are struggling to establish their own identities and build a distinct following.

Not only are initiatives going to be more and more a part of candidate contests but they are going to be increasingly expensive. For groups desiring to place a measure on the ballot, the services of the initiative industry, especially the direct-mail petition-circulation firms, are going to be hard to resist. It is too soon to tell what the full implications of this very recent development will be, but for groups with followings that can be activated through the mail, it probably means more and more initiatives on the ballot. The services of the initiative industry are expensive, and not all groups can afford them. But even those groups who can qualify a measure using volunteer labor will face ever more expensive statewide media campaigns and the costs of certain legal challenges before and after the election.

Opponents of a measure have the advantage of having to invest large amounts of resources only if a measure qualifies; but once it does, the tendency to spend is irresistible. Groups such as organized labor, public utilities, tobacco companies, and glass and aluminum bottlers may not need to spend as much as they do, but their desire for certain victory leads to expensive campaigns. Their strategic consideration is probably accurate: one loss could spawn a host of other ballot measures and give energy to legislative efforts at the local, state, and even national levels. One needs only to look at Proposition 13 to find evidence of the mandate-setting nature of initiatives. In initiative politics the stakes are high and playing the game requires money — often more money than is needed in candidate politics.

The initiative process is expensive not only for the participants but for the taxpayer as well. After the initiative has been adopted, there is a tendency to schedule direct legislation elections more and more frequently. Signature validation, the production and mailing of voters' handbooks, and election administration, especially of special elections, all cost money, and as elections become more frequent the costs escalate.

Unlike the legislative process, in which bicameral legislatures, decentralized decision making, and the threat of a gubernatorial veto function as checks against unconstitutional or excessive legislation, direct legislation is checked in its excesses only by the courts. The courts have actively policed the process, considering cases about the fairness of the campaign process and reviewing virtually all successful initiatives to determine their constitutionality. At least in California, more often than not they have declared the successful initiative unconstitutional in whole or in part. Because initiatives may cover subjects involving constitutional guarantees and because voters are more concerned with the immediate question than with its constitutional implications, there has been an unfortunate trend for initiatives to be not only unconstitutional but a threat to individual liberties as well. The implications for the courts of expanded use of the initiative are worrisome, not only because of the increased work load but because of the institutional costs to a court when it must overturn a successful initiative. The threatened recall of judges and organized opposition to their ordinarily routine reelection are only two examples of the growing political pressure upon the courts to conform to popular prejudices. But if the courts do not serve as a check on the excesses of the initiative, no one will, and the worst fears of the initiative's opponents may be borne out. Because the initiative is structured so independently of legislative and executive institutions, it is very important that the courts have the integrity and political muscle to declare unconstitutional those initiatives that contravene the Constitution.

IMPROVING THE INITIATIVE PROCESS

One of the areas of initiative politics most in need of reform is the petition-circulation process. In addition to ensuring the validity of signatures, the state has a compelling interest in informing voters of the implications of their signature. The prevailing attitude that a person can sign a petition and let the voters decide may make the petition circulator's job easier, but it will also make for longer ballots and potentially higher dropoff on election day. All petitions should require not only a summary of the proposition but a statement in bold letters reading; "BEFORE YOU SIGN IT – READ IT!" As I showed in chapter 3, signature thresholds are correlated with the extent of usage. States should neither restrict use by making the requirements excessive nor encourage frivolous measures by having low signature thresholds. The stringency of a state's qualifying procedures is measured not only in the percentage requirement but also in geographic distribution and other such requirements.

Presently, the initiative process is much too complicated. Because the Progressives distrusted elected officials, they structured the initiative so as to allow the voters to propose actual laws and constitutional amendments. This resulted in the process's being structured in highly legal and technical language. Ballot titles and summaries written at the fifteenth- to eighteenth-grade level are only necessary if the voters are voting on the actual law. But voters could have profound influence over the issue agenda by means of advisory referendums such as the 1975 British vote on entry into the European Economic Community. The wording of the referendum was short and straightforward. The advantage of this approach is that the public can indicate its preference for general policy and the legislature can handle the statutory or constitutional steps necessary for the implementation and administration of the policy.

If legislatures are to be competent and accountable, they must bear some of the responsibility for the adoption and carrying out of policy. An advisory referendum system like that outlined above would allow for greater legislative responsibility than is the case presently. At present, the initiative weakens legislatures by delegating much of their responsibility to the plebiscite and discourages legislative responsiveness, since some elected officials will always be willing to pass the buck on to the voters if they have the option. Restructuring the initiative to foster greater legislative participation would strengthen the legislative process, and the voters could use the electoral mechanism to ensure that legislators acted on their general policy recommendations. The process already works this way in other nations, and the indirect initiative works this way in part in several states.

Simplifying the wording of ballot propositions, shortening them, and putting them in the form of general policy questions not only would have positive effects upon legislatures but also would remove from the courts the responsibility of deciding upon the constitutionality of specific statutes and amendments adopted directly by the people. The present tension between fundamental rights and popular opinion would be reduced because the courts would not be called upon to rule on the constitutionality of advisory referendums or the indirect initiative.

Changing the function of the initiative from the drafting and consideration of specific laws to a more general policy guidance does not mean that the public voice would be difficult to interpret or follow. I would recommend that in addition to putting the proposition in the form of a simple question, the states consider asking multiple-response questions. Permitting voters to communicate both the direction and intensity of their preference would also help to reduce in part the all-or-nothing problem of initiative voting.

Two additional reforms are needed to maximize participation in the initiative process: (1) a shortened, simplified ballot and (2) the practice of holding direct-legislation elections in conjunction with general elections in order to maximize voter participation. Long, complicated ballots foster greater dropoff, especially among the less educated, poor, and nonwhite voters. The use of special elections and even primary elections reduces the pool of participants — by as much as 50 percent in the case of special elections. If direct legislation is to be something more than a middle- and upper-class exercise, the timing and structure of the process will need to be modified.

CONCLUSION: RECURRENT ISSUES IN THE DEBATE OVER DIRECT LEGISLATION

In chapter 1, I detailed the issues that arise whenever direct legislation is considered as a policy-making process. To repeat, the most important questions and issues are these: Will there be majority tyranny? What effect will direct legislation have on representative institutions, fundamental rights and liberties, and the capacity to govern? Will better laws be enacted because of the process? Will people participate in deciding propositions, and will they vote intelligently? Will issues be overdramatized or oversimplified? Will direct legislation educate the public and lead to a heightened political consciousness? Will direct legislation decrease public apathy and alienation? Will direct legislation cure such ills of representative democracy as the political party machines and powerful special interests?

Much of the analysis in the preceding chapters has addressed specifically these arguments and issues. Direct legislation has been neither as positive in its effect as proponents have frequently asserted nor as dire in its consequences as opponents have predicted. The courts have been active in protecting individual rights, minimizing the harmful effects of short-term majorities on minority and individual rights. Representative institutions have been significantly altered by direct legislation and direct democracy more generally. It would be hard to argue that better laws have been enacted by initiative, because so few have been enacted and because such a high percentage of these have been overturned. Voter dropoff and confusion call into question the rationality of the process, especially given the tendency of initiative campaigns to overdramatize and oversimplify. Direct legislation and direct democracy have had the effect of weakening the parties but not the special interests.

Central to the argument for adopting or expanding direct legislation are the following five assumptions: (1) citizen participation will be increased; (2) representation of voter preferences will be improved; (3) voter interest, information, and knowledge will increase and result in knowledgeable decisions on ballot measures; (4) individual voting preferences are effectively communicated through the yes/no vote on ballot questions; and (5) special interests and party machines will be checked or removed from direct legislation.

Citizen Participation

Direct legislation is a difficult process for most voters to understand. Few citizens are sufficiently motivated by an issue to start a petition campaign, and when they are asked to sign a petition sponsored by a highly motivated or well-funded group, they will rarely read what they sign and as often as not will vote against the proposition they helped to place on the ballot. With few exceptions, issues do not emerge from the vox populi spontaneously but, rather, are extensions of the legislative strategy of interest groups. Citizens do not sponsor initiatives; groups do. And the issue agendas created by groups that sponsor initiatives are narrower than the agendas of most state legislatures.

The assertion that more citizens will vote if offered the initiative is in error. Typically, turnout is not increased by direct legislation, and alienated nonparticipants are not moved to the polls by the initiative and referendum. The level of citizen participation does vary by type of election, but only the educated will be able to master the complicated ballot whenever the election is held. The initiative and referendum process is rarely the motivating force behind participation in politics; salient propositions such as Proposition 13 might encourage turnout, but more frequently it is contested candidate contests such as presidential races that attract the voters. Most people are not very interested in politics most of the time, with or without the initiative.

Representativeness of Direct Legislation

Citizens who actually vote on ballot measures are significantly less representative than those who vote in statewide candidate races. Direct legislation is structured in such a way as to discourage participation by less educated and poorer voters, who lack the knowledge and personal efficacy to survive the complicated ballot, the voter's handbook, and the excessive number of voting decisions. Voters on the most salient initiatives are as representative as in partisan/candidate races, but on many initiatives and other ballot measures the process is quite unrepresentative of those who go to the polls and even less representative of the citizenry as a whole. This fact, when combined with the earlier point that direct legislation alone activates few citizens, means that the process is neither more democratic nor more representative than the candidate electoral process.

Voter Understanding

By their own standards most voters have inadequate knowledge to make their voting choice on ballot propositions. Ballot measures often address technical subjects such as the safety of nuclear power, so it is not surprising that so many are unsure of their understanding of a given proposition. But on this and other measures significant voter confusion exists over the meaning of the vote, which goes beyond uncertainty about the best policy option. In initiative campaigns voters typically decide their vote later in the campaign and are more likely to change their minds, and on some propositions as many as a third state that they neither saw nor heard anything about the measure before entering the voting booth. Some voters will be able to master the initiative process, but those with less than graduate-school reading ability will be unable to read and understand the voter's handbook or the actual description of the measure printed on the ballot. Those who have not learned about the measure before entering the booth will play a form of electoral roulette, casting affirmative and negative votes at random, or will decide not to vote on the measures at all. The majority of ballot measures are decided by voters who cannot comprehend the printed description, who have only heard about the measure from a single source, and who are ignorant about the measure except at the highly emotional level of the television advertising, the most prevalent source of information for those who have heard of the proposition before voting. The absence of straightforward, understandable, rational argumentation in initiative campaigns, combined with what has been discovered about voting decision making in these situations, raises serious questions about the integrity of the direct legislation process.

The expectations of the proponents of direct legislation that voters would read and study ballot propositions and then cast informed ballots have been substantially disproven. Voters are no better informed about propositions than they are about candidates. In fact, on most propositions, voters have not heard much prior to entering the voting booth. When voting for candidates, voters can at least utilize the party label if they possess no other information. Typically, however, voters do know something about state candidates and may know something about their issue positions. On the most salient initiatives voters do tend to be about as informed, interested, and sure of their opinions as in statewide candidate elections. But on the more frequent propositions of low salience, a substantial proportion of voters drop off; and of those who vote, many rely on very limited information or no information at all.

Popular Mandate

On the surface it appears that the outcomes of direct legislation would be much easier to interpret than the outcomes of candidate elections. After all, one of the primary motivations for the initiative and referendum is to let the people rule. As I have shown, however, the participants in ballot propositions are neither representative nor very committed to their vote. While many citizens are willing to express opinions on general policy questions, only a few can survive the institutional hurdles of the direct legislation process. Once dropoff, voter confusion, and emotional reaction to the media campaign are considered, it becomes as difficult to impute a mandate of the people to a direct legislation election as to a statewide candidate contest.

Direct Legislation, Special-Interest Groups, and the Political Parties

It is widely accepted that state legislatures are more "professional" and better organized today than they were at the time of the Progressives. It is equally true that state legislatures are still lobbied by special-interest groups. Direct legislation clearly has not removed special interests from the legislative arena; in fact, special-interest groups are heavily involved in referendum politics. In chapter 8, I demonstrated that it is very hard for special-interest groups – or any group, for that matter – to enact an initiative. But these same spending data demonstrate that special-interest groups frequently may veto an initiative. Thus, special-interest groups are primary participants in direct legislation, and their overall influence remains strong.

While direct legislation has not removed special-interest groups from active participation in legislative politics, it (along with the other reforms of direct democracy) has made the political party a far less potent force in state politics. The declining power of party bosses and party elites is probably more the result of the direct primary election and the reduction in the spoils system, but in many states direct legislation was an institutional arrangement to achieve these other reforms.

The case for direct legislation strikes all of the familiar chords of direct democracy: popular rule, open government, citizen participation, and policy representation. The practice of direct legislation has by and large fallen short of the reformers' expectations and is prone to abuse. The people who rule in direct legislation are those who have mastered the process at the petition-qualification and voting stages. Large numbers of citizens are effectively excluded from participation, and what issue concerns they might have do not reach the direct legislative agenda. Because of the participation biases fostered by the direct legislation process and the inability of many voters to translate their opinions into policy, the process has fallen short of the mark in the areas of participation and representation as well.

Missing from the debate over direct legislation has been an understanding of the voter-legislator, as well as the implication of the structure of the process on its own performance. Political scientists and other observers now know quite a bit about the voter-legislator. Still, many questions about direct legislation, particularly those regarding its effects on political elites, remain unanswered. Additional research into direct legislation is needed; I hope this book will encourage it.

Appendixes

Appendix A

JUDICIAL DETERMINATION OF THE CONSTITUTIONALITY OF SUCCESSFUL CALIFORNIA INITIATIVES, 1964–79

Year	Measure	Declared Unconstitutional in Whole or in Part by:		Not Declared Unconstitutional	Pending in the Courts
		State Court	Federal Court		
1964	Repeal of fair housing[a]	X	X		
	Prohibition of pay TV[b]	X			
	Control of railroad train crews			X	
1972	Death penalty[c]	X			
	School busing limitation[d]	X			
	Coastal zone conservation			X	
1974	Political reform[e]	X			
1978	Jarvis-Gann tax measure[f]				X
	Death penalty[g]	X			
1979	Appropriation limitation				X

Sources:
[a] *Mulkey v. Reitman*, 64 Cal. 2d 529 (1966); *Reitman v. Mulkey*, 387 U.S. 369 (1967).
[b] *Weaver v. Jordan*, 411 P.2d 289, 49 Cal. Rptr. 557 (1967).
[c] *Rockwell v. Superior Court of Ventura County*, 556 P.2d 1101, Sup. 134 Cal. Rptr. 650 (1976).
[d] *Santa Barbara School District v. Superior Court of Santa Barbara County*, 530 P.2d 605, 118 Sup. Cal. Rptr. 637 (1975).
[e] *Citizens for Jobs and Energy v. Fair Political Practices Commission*, 547 P.2d 1386, 129 Cal. Rptr. 106 (1976).
[f] *Los Angeles County Transportation Commission v. Richmond*, 643 P.2d 941, 182 Cal. Rptr. 324 (1982).
[g] *People v. Ramos*, 30 Cal. 3d. 553 (1980).

Appendix B

Number of Initiatives Qualifying for the California Ballot, 1912–79

Issue Category	1912–19 Q	1912–19 F	1920–29 Q	1920–29 F	1930–39 Q	1930–39 F	1940–49 Q	1940–49 F	1950–59 Q	1950–59 F	1960–69 Q	1960–69 F	1970–79 Q	1970–79 F	Total 1912–79 Q	Total 1912–79 F
Bond issues	3	2	1	1	—	—	—	—	—	—	—	—	—	—	4	3
Civil liberties/civil rights	—	—	1	—	—	—	1	1	—	—	3	3	3	8	8	12
Courts/law and order	—	1	1	1	4	2	—	—	—	—	—	—	—	7	5	11
Education	2	1	3	2	3	2	2	—	2	—	—	2	3	13	15	20
Elected official/civil service/compensation	—	—	1	—	—	—	—	—	1	1	—	—	2	7	3	7
Elections	5	1	4	2	1	1	2	4	1	—	2	3	1	6	16	18
Energy	—	—	3	—	—	—	—	—	1	—	—	—	1	4	5	4
Environment	—	1	1	—	3	1	2	—	1	1	—	2	3	6	10	11
Fiscal concerns	2	—	1	—	2	—	—	—	1	—	—	1	1	3	7	4
Gambling	2	—	3	3	1	1	1	2	1	—	1	3	1	16	10	25
Government regulation/unit formation	2	1	1	3	2	4	—	—	—	—	1	4	—	6	6	18
Health/medicine/science	2	1	6	1	3	2	1	2	—	1	—	3	1	8	13	18
Labor	2	1	—	2	4	3	2	1	1	—	—	—	3	11	12	18
Miscellaneous	—	1	5	1	2	5	4	—	—	—	2	2	—	5	13	14
Morality	—	1	—	—	—	—	—	—	—	—	1	5	4	8	5	14
Municipal government	3	—	—	—	2	1	—	—	—	1	—	—	—	—	5	1
Prohibition/alcohol/drugs	7	1	1	—	5	7	2	5	—	1	—	1	1	8	16	23
Social and welfare aid	—	—	—	—	2	3	3	4	3	1	1	2	—	—	9	10
Taxation	5	2	6	2	4	6	2	5	3	—	1	5	4	37	25	57

Source: Eu, *A History of the Initiative Process.* All categories except civil rights and civil liberties are those used by the secretary of state in her report. Initiatives may appear under more than one heading.

Note: Q = the number of initiatives that met the signature requirement and qualified for the ballot; F = the number of initiatives that failed to meet the signature requirement.

Appendix C

NUMBERS OF STATEWIDE PROPOSITIONS, 1968–82, BY STATE

State	1968	1969	1970	1971	1972	1973	1974	1975	1976	1977	1978	1979	1980	1981	1982	Total
Alabama	2	23	1	0	6	11	2	2	0	13	9	0	9	0	13	91
Alaska	11	0	17	0	15	1	13	0	16	0	15	0	13	0	8	109
Arizona	12	0	6	0	11	0	10	0	7	0	3	0	9	0	10	68
Arkansas	7	0	3	0	1	0	4	0	4	0	3	0	5	0	4	31
California	12	0	28	0	32	1	26	0	15	0	21	4	22	0	15	176
Colorado	3	0	5	0	12	0	10	0	10	0	2	0	6	0	7	55
Connecticut	0	0	4	0	1	0	4	0	4	0	0	0	4	0	4	21
Delaware	0	0	0	0	0	0	0	0	1	0	0	0	0	0	0	1
Florida	4	0	7	0	5	0	7	0	9	0	9	0	10	0	2	53
Georgia	23	0	15	0	24	0	16	0	28	0	36	0	16	0	5	163
Hawaii	24	0	4	0	3	0	1	0	2	0	34	0	3	0	2	73
Idaho	9	0	4	0	9	0	3	0	2	0	6	0	2	0	11	46
Illinois	3	0	8	0	0	0	1	0	0	0	3	0	2	0	1	18
Indiana	1	0	3	0	5	0	3	0	1	0	2	0	0	0	0	15
Iowa	6	0	4	0	3	0	2	0	0	0	1	0	2	0	0	18
Kansas	4	0	3	1	8	0	11	0	0	0	0	0	3	0	0	30
Kentucky	0	0	1	1	0	2	0	2	0	1	0	2	0	0	0	9
Louisiana	52	0	53	0	42	0	2	0	0	0	1	3	4	0	8	165
Maine	8	0	11	0	11	5	7	7	6	9	7	0	8	10	5	94
Maryland	4	0	11	0	18	0	14	0	21	0	12	5	5	5	5	100
Massachusetts	5	0	5	0	9	0	6	0	9	0	7	0	6	0	4	51
Michigan	8	0	3	0	8	0	4	0	4	0	11	0	7	1	7	53
Minnesota	2	0	2	0	4	0	3	0	1	0	0	0	5	0	4	21
Mississippi	4	0	0	0	2	0	0	3	1	0	7	2	0	0	4	23
Missouri	2	0	8	0	2	0	3	0	10	0	13	2	4	2	18	64
Montana	5	0	4	0	6	0	3	0	6	0	11	0	5	0	8	48
Nebraska	19	0	17	0	34	0	6	0	9	0	10	0	6	0	6	107
Nevada	4	0	9	0	7	0	4	0	11	0	6	0	9	0	12	62
New Hampshire	10	0	5	0	3	0	7	0	8	0	7	0	5	0	4	49
New Jersey	4	3	2	0	3	2	6	6	7	2	7	2	7	8	5	63
New Mexico	1	0	8	0	4	7	3	0	0	0	4	0	6	0	7	40
New York	0	4	1	0	4	12	1	8	0	10	0	4	0	2	0	46
North Carolina	2	1	0	0	7	3	2	0	0	7	0	0	1	0	2	25
North Dakota	8	0	3	0	3	2	7	0	9	0	16	0	16	0	7	71
Ohio	5	2	3	0	4	11	3	9	7	4	3	1	0	2	1	55
Oklahoma	20	2	8	6	7	0	9	8	5	0	7	1	8	0	3	84
Oregon	10	0	17	0	15	1	20	0	16	15	17	0	14	0	6	131
Pennsylvania	6	0	0	0	1	3	1	2	0	2	0	2	0	2	1	20
Rhode Island	6	0	10	0	15	9	12	0	15	2	11	3	6	0	10	99
South Carolina	19	0	14	0	0	0	6	0	0	0	5	0	2	0	2	48
South Dakota	7	0	11	0	6	0	2	0	6	0	7	0	7	0	4	50

State	1968	1969	1970	1971	1972	1973	1974	1975	1976	1977	1978	1979	1980	1981	1982	Total
Tennessee	5	0	1	0	1	0	0	0	0	0	0	0	0	0	1	8
Texas[a]	17	0	7	0	16	9	3	10	7	7	12	3	9	7	6	113
Utah	6	0	3	0	4	0	5	0	4	0	0	0	6	0	4	32
Vermont	0	0	0	0	0	0	0	0	1	0	0	0	0	0	0	1
Virginia	2	0	4	0	2	0	1	0	6	5	2	0	4	0	3	29
Washington	14	0	8	0	24	7	3	6	6	10	1	6	5	5	4	99
West Virginia	2	0	3	0	4	4	1	0	0	0	2	0	2	1	3	22
Wisconsin	4	0	0	0	0	2	0	4	2	5	2	4	1	0	9	33
Wyoming	2	0	5	0	6	0	3	0	0	0	3	0	1	0	3	23
Total	384	35	349	8	407	92	260	67	276	92	335	44	265	45	248	2,907

Source: Data through 1978 are from "Referenda and Primary Election Materials," Inter-university Consortium for Political and Social Research (ICPSR 0006), University of Michigan, Ann Arbor, Michigan. More recent data are from interviews with election officials in each state.

[a] Texas allows for statewide propositions in the primary elections which are conducted by the political parties. They are included in the figures given here.

Appendix D

READABILITY ASSESSMENT AND THE READABILITY FORMULAS
USED IN THIS BOOK

Most scholars agree that the foundation of modern readability assessment was laid over one hundred years ago by Herbert Spencer in "Philosophy of Style," an article published in the *Westminster Review*.[1] Spencer argued that a reader has limited mental powers for the three tasks necessary for comprehension: (1) understanding the words used, (2) understanding their relationship, and (3) grasping the thought conveyed. Spencer placed great emphasis on economizing the reader's attention; he correctly understood that giving time to decoding words would leave less energy to consider their meaning. Spencer correctly assessed the syntactic and semantic features of readability and suggested four of the variables now used in most readability formulas: syllable length of words, familiarity of words, abstract levels of words, and sentence length.

The Flesch formula. In 1943, Rudolf Flesch published his first formula, which was designed for general adult reading matter.[2] Like many other readability formulas, his was validated using as a standard McCall and Crabb's *Standard Test Lessons in Reading*.[3] Flesch revised his reading-ease formula in 1948 because "his count of affixes was time consuming . . . and the scoring system was unsatisfactory."[4] His revised reading-ease formula included a weighting of the number of syllables per one hundred words and of the average number of words per sentence using the following steps:

1. Select samples of one hundred to two hundred words from the material to be rated.
2. Determine the number of syllables per one hundred words ($w1$).
3. Determine the average number of words per sentence ($s1$).
4. Apply in the following reading-ease formula:
   Reading ease $= 206.835 - 0.846\ w1 - 1.015\ s1$.

Since Flesch was primarily interested in assessing adult reading material, he used a reading-ease index from 0 to 100, with 0 representing the most difficult words and 100 representing the easiest, rather than a grade-level index. Flesch's formula has become the most frequently used of all readability formulas.

The Dale-Chall formula.[5] The second most frequently used readability formula also appeared in 1948 and was designed, as Flesch's revision had been, to correct shortcomings in the original Flesch formula. An important difference between this formula and the Flesch formula is the reliance on a

207

three-thousand-word list rather than on the number of syllables as the measure of word difficulty. The procedure for using this formula is:

1. Select samples of one hundred to two hundred words throughout the material to be rated.
2. Compute the average sentence length in words (x_2).
3. Compute the number of words outside the Dale list of three thousand (x_1, or Dale score).
4. Apply in the following formula:
$$x_{c50} = 0.1579x_1 + 0.0496x_2 + 3.6365,$$
   where x_{c50} refers to the grade level of the text.

The Extended Fry graph. The Extended Fry graph constitutes one of the most straightforward ways of obtaining a readability index. This formula is also readily translated into a graphical description, which allows the user to tell at a glance whether a passage is of more than average difficulty in vocabulary or sentence length. The readability graph may be used as follows:

1. Select samples of one hundred to two hundred words throughout the material to be tested.
2. Count the number of sentences in the sample.
3. Count the total number of syllables in the sample.
4. Enter on the graph the average number of sentences and syllables, and plot a dot where the two lines intersect. The area where the dot is plotted will give the approximate grade level.

The Extended Fry graph has been adapted to the computer using a polynomial equation, and, as in this paper, the calculation can be done without using the actual graph.

The Harris-Jacobson formula.[6] A more recently developed readability formula is the Harris-Jacobson formula, which, like the Dale-Chall formula, includes in the equation both a word-length variable and a word-difficulty variable. This formula is well suited to this study because it was designed to measure more sophisticated texts, such as high school chemistry and physics textbooks. The Harris-Jacobson formula uses a different word list and different constants in the equation. The procedure for using this formula is:

1. Select samples of one hundred to two hundred words throughout the material to be rated.
2. Compute the average number of words per sentence (*wps*).
3. Compute the percentage of words not on the Harris-Jacobson list (*dw*).
4. Apply in the following formula:
$$\text{Grade level} = 0.14 \ (dw) + 0.153 \ (wps) + 0.56.$$

All of these formulas are too complicated to employ except by using a computer.

Total Expenditures for California Ballot Propositions, 1954-82

Rank	Proposition	Election	Side with Most Expenditures	Outcome	Actual Expenditures	Expenditures in Constant Dollars[a]
1	15, Gun control	1982 General	No (72%)	Failed	$9,896,101	$2,842,160
2	5, Anti-smoking	1978 General	No (70)	Failed	7,111,924	3,107,001
3	10, Rent control	1980 General	Yes (97)	Failed	6,833,483	2,331,451
4	15, Nuclear power	1976 Primary	No (76)	Failed	6,562,261	3,317,625
5	9, Peripheral canal	1982 Primary	No (56)	Failed	6,412,963	1,841,803
6	11, Beverage containers	1982 General	No (86)	Failed	6,385,153	1,833,816
7	11, Oil-company surtax	1980 Primary	No (93)	Failed	6,067,356	2,070,064
8	9, Income-tax reduction	1980 Primary	Yes (67)	Failed	5,411,305	1,846,232
9	4, Oil and gas conservation	1956 General	Yes (71)	Failed	4,868,267	4,542,093
10	13, Jarvis-Gann property tax[b]	1978 Primary	Yes (51)	Adopted	4,255,283	1,859,014
11	12, Nuclear weapons	1982 General	Yes (100)	Adopted	3,489,646	1,002,226
12	14, Agricultural labor relations	1976 General	No (57)	Failed	3,257,086	1,646,657
13	18, Right to work	1958 General	No (72)	Failed	3,209,062	3,209,062
14	13, Water resources	1982 General	No (66)	Failed	3,053,549	876,972
15	1, Tax and expenditure limitation	1973 Special	Yes (69)	Failed	2,945,128	1,924,920
16	17, Railroad train crews	1964 General	Yes (68)	Adopted	2,860,613	2,602,924
17	6, Homosexual teachers	1978 General	No (55)	Failed	2,313,533	1,010,718
18	10, 11, 12, Reapportionment	1982 Primary	No (100)	Failed	2,235,828	642,130
19	14, Tax limitation	1972 General	Yes (62)	Failed	2,054,290	1,419,689
20	13, Greyhound dog racing	1976 General	No (66)	Failed	1,968,234	995,063
21	16, Abolition of tax exemption for religious school property	1958 General	No (73)	Failed	1,840,005	1,840,005
22	14, Repeal of Rumford Act	1964 General	No (64)	Adopted	1,834,996	1,669,696
23	13, State employee salaries	1972 General	Yes (99)	Failed	1,804,224	1,246,873
24	9, Environment	1972 Primary	No (86)	Failed	1,609,432	1,112,255
25	20, Coastal zone	1972 General	No (80)	Adopted	1,451,369	1,003,020
26	8, Limitation on use of property tax revenues	1970 Primary	Yes (77)	Failed	1,407,387	1,042,509
27	9, Tax limitation	1968 General	No (82)	Failed	1,255,300	1,026,411

209

Appendix E *(continued)*

Rank	Proposition	Election	Side with Most Expenditures	Outcome	Actual Expenditures	Expenditures in Constant Dollars[a]
28	22, Agricultural labor	1972 General	Yes (81)	Failed	1,185,418	819,225
29	8, Victims bill of rights	1982 Primary	Yes (95)	Adopted	1,082,240	310,819
30	15, Prohibition of pay television	1964 General	Yes (82)	Adopted	1,076,697	979,706
31	18, Obscenity	1972 General	No (84)	Failed	1,040,155	718,836
32	7, Income-tax indexing	1982 Primary	Yes (100)	Adopted	1,022,476	293,655
33	6, Gift and inheritance tax	1982 Primary	Yes (94)	Adopted	949,561	272,714
34	17, Tax rate changes	1958 General	No (100)	Failed	813,965	813,965
35	9, Political reform	1974 Primary	Yes (75)	Adopted	810,537	480,746
36	17, Wild and scenic rivers	1974 General	No (64)	Failed	694,755	412,073
37	7, Death Penalty	1978 General	Yes (98)	Adopted	670,237	292,808
38	9, Textbooks	1982 General	Yes (98)	Failed	605,664	173,946
39	16, Statewide lottery	1964 General	Yes (92)	Failed	596,129	542,429
40	14, Reapportionment commission	1982 General	Yes (100)	Failed	589,580	169,327
41	15, Senate reapportionment	1960 General	No (58)	Failed	570,320	556,293
42	23, Senate reapportionment	1962 General	No (64)	Failed	380,863	358,291
43	16, State highway patrol salaries	1972 General	Yes (100)	Failed	379,445	262,229
44	4, Aid to needy aged	1954 General	No (62)	Failed	352,960	324,017
45	22, Osteopath	1962 General	Yes (80)	Adopted	342,364	322,073
46	19, Legalization of marijuana	1972 General	Yes (97)	Failed	196,614	135,877
47	24, Subversive activities	1962 General	Yes (89)	Failed	117,059	110,121
48	27, Death penalty	1972 General	No (58)	Adopted	104,292	72,075
49	5, Gift and inheritance taxes	1982 Primary	No (72)	Adopted	79,945	22,960
50	21, Prohibition of busing	1972 General	Yes (77)	Adopted	55,600	38,424

Sources: Spending data for the period 1958–78 are from the California Fair Political Practices Commission, *Campaign Costs,* 9, 11. Data for 1954 and 1956 are from the brief filed in the case of *Citizens for Jobs and Energy v. Fair Political Practices Commission* by the firm California Research. Data for 1972 and 1974 were gathered from primary sources, State of California Archives. Data for propositions since 1978 are from the Fair Political Practices Commission official spending reports.

[a] Figures in this column have been standardized to control for inflation, with 1958 as the baseline year, thus, all figures in this column are in 1958 dollars.

[b] Includes expenditures for Proposition 8.

Appendix F

Stability and Change in Voting Intentions on Ballot Propositions

Proposition	Yes	No	Undecided/ Dropoff	Number of Respondents Comprising Percentage
		Standing Opinions		
CALIFORNIA — 1964 general election Proposition 14, Repeal Open-housing law				
23–28 March	48%	33%	19%	1,196
1–9 May	48	31	21	1,189
31 August–5 September	49	38	13	1,165
2–7 October	52	33	15	572
Actual vote	63	33	4	7,233,067
CALIFORNIA — 1972 general election Proposition 17, Death penalty				
10–14 August	65	27	8	471
29 September–7 October	62	26	12	1,113
30 October–1 November	62	31	7	1,355
Actual vote	63	30	6	8,595,950
CALIFORNIA — 1972 general election Proposition 19, Marijuana				
10–14 August	31	63	5	471
29 September–7 October	32	58	11	1,114
30 October–1 November	35	58	7	1,334
Actual vote	32	63	5	8,595,950
CALIFORNIA — 1974 primary election Proposition 9, Political reform				
10 April	64	19	17	664
29 April–4 May	70	18	11	202
27–29 May	69	21	10	1,242
Actual vote	63	27	10	5,128,375
MASSACHUSETTS — 1976 general election Question 1, Equal rights amendment				
Pre-Labor Day**	63	13	24	500
Early October*	75	15	10	600
October*	59	12	29	500
Actual vote	56	37	8	2,594,262

Proposition	Yes	No	Undecided/ Dropoff	Number of Respondents Comprising Percentage
		Standing Opinions		
CALIFORNIA — 1978 general election Proposition 7, Death penalty				
12–28 August	84	9	7	1,049
17–24 September	80	10	10	1,075
30 October–1 November	76	17	7	1,375
Actual vote	63	25	12	7,132,210
		Uncertain Opinions		
CALIFORNIA — 1976 primary election Proposition 15, Nuclear power				
8–15 November	36	41	23	570
21 January–1 February	41	47	12	577
19–31 March	39	46	16	1,034
6–8 May	38	52	10	877
May–June	24	45	31	634
31 May–5 June	31	64	6	1,812
June–July	34	63	4	455
Actual vote	31	64	5	6,323,651
CALIFORNIA — 1978 primary election Proposition 13, Property-tax reduction				
11–23 February	46	39	15	1,217
27 March–3 April	48	45	7	586
1–8 May	48	40	12	1,156
29–31 May	58	34	8	1,309
Post-election — 12–28 August	58	34	8	1,049
Actual vote	63	34	3	6,843,001
		Opinion Reversals		
CALIFORNIA — 1962 general election Proposition 24, Subversive activities				
12–19 July	46	34	20	1,202
13–19 September	67	17	16	1,088
9–14 October	54	19	27	1,179
30 October–1 November	47	30	23	1,558
Actual vote	33	49	17	5,929,602

Proposition	Yes	No	Undecided/ Dropoff	Number of Respondents Comprising Percentage
		Opinion Reversals		
CALIFORNIA — 1964 general election Proposition 16, State lottery				
23–28 March	57	30	12	1,196
1–9 May	42	40	18	1,189
31 August–5 September	42	46	11	1,183
2–7 October	36	44	20	577
Actual vote	29	64	8	7,233,067
CALIFORNIA — 1972 general election Proposition 14, Tax reduction				
10–14 August	67	26	7	561
29 September–7 October	40	20	40	1,113
30 October–1 November	24	51	25	834
Actual vote	31	61	8	8,595,950
MASSACHUSETTS — 1976 general election Question 5, Prohibition of handguns				
June	55	39	6	1,000
Pre-Labor Day**	58	31	11	500
October	51	41	8	1,000
October**	40	49	11	500
October*	40	44	17	600
Actual vote	29	64	7	2,594,262
MASSACHUSETTS — 1976 general election Question 7, Flat-rate electricity				
January	67	18	15	1,000
February	71	17	12	1,000
June	51	35	14	1,000
September	50	39	11	1,000
October	42	42	16	1,000
October*	30	40	31	600
Actual vote	23	69	7	2,594,262
CALIFORNIA — 1978 general election Proposition 5, Anti-smoking				
12–28 August	57	38	5	1,049
17–24 September	47	48	5	1,075

213

Proposition	Yes	No	Undecided/ Dropoff	Number of Respondents Comprising Percentage
	Opinion Reversals			
30 October–1 November	42	56	2	1,375
Actual vote	44	52	4	7,132,210
CALIFORNIA — 1978 general election Proposition 6, Homosexual teachers				
12–28 August	61	31	9	1,049
17–24 September	47	41	12	1,075
30 October–1 November	37	58	6	1,375
Actual vote	40	56	5	7,132,210

Sources: California data marked by a single asterisk (*) are from the Survey of Attitudes on Nuclear Power, Rand Corporation, Santa Monica, California. All other California data are from California Poll, Field Research Corporation, San Francisco, California, and State Data Program, University of California, Berkeley.

Massachusetts data marked by a single asterisk (*) are from the Massachusetts Poll, provided by the *Boston Globe* and Research Analysis, Boston, Massachusetts. All other Massachusetts data are from the Becker Polls, provided by the *Boston Herald American* and Becker Research Corporation and, where marked by two asterisks (**), from WBZ-TV Poll, provided by Decision Research Corporation, Wellesley Hills, Massachusetts.

Appendix G

Presented below are the formal equation and the multiple correlation coefficients for the independent variables. For the multivariate analyses, I am testing the following equation:

$$Y = a + b_1X_1 + b_2X_2 + b_3X_3 + b_4X_4 + b_5X_5 + b_6X_6 + b_7X_7 + b_iX_i + e,$$

where
Y = likelihood of affirmative vote
a = constant
X_1 = party identification
X_2 = ideological self-identification
X_3 = education
X_4 = income
X_5 = race
X_6 = occupation
X_7 = age
X_i = other independent variables
e = error term.

The multiple correlation coefficients for the independent variables that were significantly related to voting yes or no at the 0.05 confidence level are summarized in the table below. Also presented is the adjusted R^2 (adjusted multiple correlation coefficient), which is a measure of the extent to which the independent variables predict the vote.

VARIABLES SIGNIFICANTLY RELATED TO VOTING CHOICE
AND THEIR INDEPENDENT EFFECTS

Election/ Proposition	Regression Data	Standard Error	Constant	Adjusted R^2
	Ballot Propositions			
1972 General	0.14 Conservatives	0.045	0.869	0.09
Proposition 2,	−0.15 Whites	0.051		
Health bond	0.09 Democrats	0.036		
($N = 680$)	0.08 Liberals	0.048		
	−0.12 Service/laborer	0.061		
	−0.08 Craft/operative	0.042		

215

Election/ Proposition	Regression Data	Standard Error	Constant	Adjusted R^2
	Ballot Propositions			
1974 General Proposition 4, Regents bond (N = 408)	−0.14 Republicans	0.05	0.805	0.05
	0.10 Liberals	0.05		
	−0.15 Whites	0.08		
	0.11 Advanced degree	0.06		
1976 General Proposition 13, Dog racing (N = 501)	−0.11 Professional/managerial	0.04	0.247	0.02
	0.12 Low to middle income	0.06		
	−0.08 Clerk/sales	0.048		
1976 General Proposition 14, Farm-workers (N = 507)	−0.33 Whites	0.053	0.83	0.11
	−0.22 High income	0.062		
	0.16 Advanced degree	0.06		
	−0.15 Middle to high income	0.064		
	0.12 Service/laborer	0.072		
1978 Primary Proposition 8, Property-tax alternative (N = 1,744)	−0.09 Republicans	0.088	0.677	0.15
	0.08 Liberals	0.065		
	−0.19 Middle to high income	0.037		
	−0.05 Middle-aged	0.026		
	−0.16 Low to middle income	0.04		
	−0.15 High income	0.04		
	0.13 College degree	0.05		
	0.09 Some college	0.05		
1978 Primary Proposition 13, Property-tax reduction (N = 1,744)	−0.22 Public employee	0.023	0.439	0.20
	0.08 Republicans	0.041		
	−0.11 Liberals	0.027		
	0.17 Whites	0.032		
	−0.13 College degree	0.027		
	0.01 Conservatives	0.026		
	0.21 Middle to high income	0.035		
	0.19 High income	0.036		
	0.14 Low to middle income	0.037		
	−0.05 Some college	0.027		
	0.05 Middle-aged	0.025		
	−0.07 Democrats	0.04		
1978 General Proposition 5, Anti-smoking (N = 1,745)	−0.39 Smokers	0.025	0.514	0.14
	0.12 College degree	0.027		
	−0.06 Republicans	0.024		
	0.08 Older	0.033		
	0.06 Some college	0.028		

Appendix G *(continued)*

Election/ Proposition	Regression Data	Standard Error	Constant	Adjusted R^2
	Ballot Propositions			
1978 General Proposition 6, Homosexual teachers ($N = 1,745$)	−0.11 Liberals	0.028	0.355	0.08
	−0.13 College degree	0.028		
	0.07 Republicans	0.033		
	0.20 Older	0.04		
	0.12 Middle-aged	0.031		
	0.06 Conservative	0.028		
	−0.05 Smoker	0.025		
	0.06 Low to middle income	0.032		
	0.04 Middle to high income	0.024		
	−0.04 Some college	0.029		
	0.04 Democrats	0.03		
1980 General Proposition 9, Income tax (Jarvis) ($N = 1,345$)	0.04 Republicans	0.056	0.158	0.20
	−0.11 Liberals	0.033		
	0.10 Own home	0.031		
	0.12 Conservatives	0.031		
	0.08 White	0.046		
	0.12 Middle to high income	0.041		
	0.08 Middle-aged	0.033		
	0.08 Middle income	0.038		
	−0.09 Democrats	0.054		
1980 General Proposition 10, Rent control ($N = 1,345$)	0.09 Own home	0.03	0.282	0.02
	0.07 Conservative	0.03		
	0.07 Republican	0.028		
	−0.07 White	0.046		
1980 General Proposition 11, Tax oil companies ($N = 1,345$)	0.17 Democrats	0.028	0.429	0.11
	0.15 Liberals	0.033		
	−0.19 Middle-aged	0.041		
	−0.10 Conservatives	0.031		
	−0.07 Middle-aged	0.034		
	Candidates			
1972 General President Nixon ($N = 788$)	0.28 Republicans	0.048	0.598	0.43
	−0.31 Liberals	0.030		
	−0.21 Democrats	0.047		
	0.14 Whites	0.040		

Election/ Proposition	Regression Data	Standard Error	Constant	Adjusted R^2
	Ballot Propositions			
1974 General Governor Brown ($N = 537$)	−0.37 Republicans 0.30 Democrats 0.15 Liberals −0.22 Whites	0.074 0.072 0.073 0.053	0.677	0.502
1976 General President Ford ($N = 517$)	0.27 Whites 0.20 High income 0.19 Clerical/sales 0.12 Professional/managerial	0.056 0.063 0.058 0.051	−0.013	0.097
1976 General U.S. Senator Hayakawa ($N = 509$)	0.25 Whites 0.14 High income 0.11 Some college	0.055 0.043 0.050	0.23	0.069
1978 Governor Younger ($N = 511$)[a]				
1978 Primary (Democratic) Governor Brown ($N = 942$)	−0.14 Conservatives −0.12 Whites −0.08 High income 0.06 Liberals −0.05 Middle income	0.026 0.032 0.028 0.029 0.026	1.02	0.07
1978 General Governor Brown ($N = 1,745$)	−0.26 Republicans 0.21 Democrats 0.11 Liberals −0.15 Whites −0.12 Conservatives −0.10 High income −0.12 Older (60+ years) −0.37 Middle-aged −0.05 High school graduates −0.04 Some college	0.028 0.025 0.024 0.027 0.025 0.022 0.030 0.021 0.025 0.022	0.79	0.33

Sources: California Polls, 1972–80, The Field Institute, San Francisco, California; Survey of Attitudes on Nuclear Power, June 1976, Rand Corporation, Santa Monica, California; CBS News/*Los Angeles Times* exit polls, 1978–80.

[a] Data are not statistically significant.

Notes

CHAPTER 1

1. Political discourse on the question of direct versus representative democracy has been substantial. One of the most important treatments of the subject occurs in *The Federalist Papers,* especially number 10. In this essay, James Madison not only deals with the subject of faction but also examines the advantages of a republican form of government. Madison argues that "such democracies have ever been spectacles of turbulence and contention; have ever been found incompatible with personal security or the rights of property; and have in general been as short in their lives as they have been violent in their deaths." In contrast, a republican system will "refine and enlarge the public views, by passing them through the medium of a chosen body of citizens, whose wisdom may best discern the true interest of their country, and whose patriotism and love of justice will be least likely to sacrifice it to temporary and partial considerations" (see Fairfield, *The Federalist Papers*).

2. Price, "The Initiative."

3. A major exception was the 1978 Dade County, Florida, referendum on gay rights. This referendum received extensive national coverage and propelled Anita Bryant into the role of chief national campaigner against homosexuality.

4. The best recent review of direct legislation at the national level is Butler and Ranney, *Referendums.* Great Britain did not experience a national referendum until 1975, when British membership in the European Economic Community was put to a national vote.

5. Not only does the Constitution not provide for a national referendum but the writings of the founding fathers indicate that they would have seen such a process as much too direct and susceptible to momentary majorities (see n. 1 above). They valued a more indirect or representative democracy and placed checks on factions or majorities through the separation of powers, a bicameral legislature, indirect election of U.S. senators, staggered terms of office, and the electoral college. But some scholars see direct legislation as consistent with the Constitution. For a different view on how the founding fathers would view direct legislation see the testimony of Henry Abraham in Senate Subcommittee on the Constitution, *Voter Initiative Constitutional Amendment,* 66–69.

6. "A Weekly Checklist of Major Issues," *National Journal,* 14 June 1980, 993.

7. "Taxes Overboard," *Economist,* 17 June 1978, 11.

8. "The Big Tax Revolt," *Newsweek,* 19 June 1978, 20.

9. Virtually every nationally syndicated columnist devoted one or more columns to Proposition 13. The following is a selective sample of ten columnists and their columns: Jack Anderson, "Tax Revolt: The Opening of U.S.-Wide Movement," *Deseret News,* 13 June 1978; James Kilpatrick, "The Year of the Taxpayer," *San Francisco Chronicle,* 2 June 1978; Joseph Kraft, "Populist Hedonism," *Washington Post,* 11 June 1978; Anthony Lewis, "Fed Up," *San Francisco Chronicle,* 24 November 1978; Mary McGrory, "California's Social Experiment," *Chicago Tribune,* 12 June 1978; James Reston, "Proposition 13, a Silly Answer to a Silly Question," *Salt Lake Tribune,* 11 June 1978; Daniel Schorr, "Proposition 13 in High Places," *San*

Francisco Examiner, 28 June 1978; Tom Wicker, "A New Revolution," *New York Times,* 9 June 1978; George Will, "Californians Vote to Undo What Has Been Done," *Los Angeles Times,* 8 June 1978.

10. "The Tax-Slashing Campaign," *Time,* 23 October 1978, 12.

11. In addition to the articles listed in n. 9 above see "Is There a Parade?" *Nation,* 14 October 1978; "Conservative Cry: Our Time Has Come," *U.S. News & World Report,* 26 February 1979; and "Why the Shift to Conservatism," ibid., 23 January 1978. Not all commentators agreed that the country was turning conservative or that Proposition 13 was evidence of fundamental shifts in voter attitudes; see, for example, Ladd, "What the Voters Really Want"; Gans, "Conservatism by Default"; Bethell, "The Changing Fashions of Liberalism."

12. Kuttner, *Revolt of the Haves,* 17.

13. The coalition of supporters for establishing direct legislation in New York is typical of the broad spectrum of support found elsewhere. In New York, supporters included "the League of Women Voters, the Conservative Party, the !ocal branch of Ralph Nader's Public Interest Research Group, and an ad hoc organization called V.O.T.E., which is headed by a conservative investment banker who says he hopes to become New York's Howard Jarvis" (Nelson, "Power to the People," 12). Conservative author Brian Crozier argues that direct democracy can tame the excesses of party systems, and he sees Switzerland as a case in point (see Crozier, *The Minimum State,* 142–44). Among the most visible liberal advocates of wider use of direct legislation is the People's Lobby, a group that sponsored anti-pollution and government ethics propositions in California (see Tallian, *Direct Democracy*).

14. The proposal did not require a referendum in the case of attack or invasion. The advocates of the proposal felt that the requirement of a popular vote would keep the chief executive and the defense establishment in check. For a treatment of the entire war referendum question see Bolt, *Ballots before Bullets.*

15. The proposed constitutional amendment stipulates that the national initiative may not be used to declare war, call up troops, or propose constitutional amendments (see Nelson, "Power to the People," 14).

16. Liberal advocates of the national initiative include former Senator James Abourezk (D.-S.D.) and Ralph Nader. Conservative supporters include Abourezk's Senate replacement, Larry Pressler (R-S.D.), Congressman Jack Kemp (R-N.Y.), and columnist Patrick Buchanan. Among the moderates supporting the idea are senators Hatfield (R-Oreg.) and DeConcini (D-Ariz.) and Congressman James R. Jones (D-Okla.).

17. Kemp, *An American Renaissance,* 162, 163.

18. California Poll 8206, 1–4 October 1982, The Field Institute, San Francisco California.

19. California Poll 7904, 12–19 November 1979, The Field Institute, San Francisco, California.

20. Survey of Attitudes on Nuclear Power, May–June 1976, Rand Corporation, Santa Monica, California.

21. For a more complete discussion of the problem of nonattitudes see Converse, "The Nature of Belief Systems in Mass Publics," 206–61.

22. Many students of voting behavior have taken the item "Have you always voted for the same party for president?" as a measure of partisan loyalty. In fact, it is more likely that this item is a measure of the popular value of voting for the man and not the party. For a more extensive discussion see Keith et al., *The Myth of the Independent Voter.*

23. Miller, "Political Issues and Trust in Government"; Miller and Levitin, *Leadership and Change,* 226–29; Campbell, *The American Electorate,* 87–99.

24. American Institute of Public Opinion, survey 991, 6–9 January 1978.

25. Gallup, "National Initiative Favored," 10.

26. The items of the Gallup Poll and of the Center for Political Studies (CPS), American National Election Studies, are not identical. The CPS item simply asks whether the respondent favors having more issues decided by the voters at the polls, and does not specify whether the

issues would be decided in a local, state, or national referendum. The Gallup item explicitly asks whether the respondent favors the establishment of a national initiative. The proportion of Gallup respondents supporting the national initiative was 20 percent lower than the proportion supporting the idea of having more issues on the ballots, as asked by the CPS. A likely explanation for the lower level of support found by Gallup is the fact that voters have not experienced the process at the national level and therefore are more uncertain of its implications. Also, the establishment of a national initiative would require a fundamental change in the political system.

27. The Minnesota general election ballot presented voters with the following proposition: "Shall the Minnesota Constitution be amended to provide for initiative and referendum?" While a plurality of voters came down on the yes side, a majority of those voting in the general election was needed to pass the constitutional amendment. Since nearly 14 percent did not vote on the amendment at all, it fell short of this majority rule (Flanigan, "The Initiative Process in Contemporary America").

28. The fact that widespread disaffection has remained high suggests that citizen displeasure with government was more than a rejection of the Watergate scandal. Research done by Arthur Miller on the subject of citizen trust in government suggests that before Watergate, large sectors of the public were also unhappy with the government's handling of the Vietnam War, the unrest associated with civil rights, and urban riots in the late 1960s and early 1970s (see Miller, "Political Issues and Trust in Government").

29. For more detailed discussions of the decline of parties, the role of single-issue groups, and the general fragmentation of American politics see Fiorina, "The Decline of Collective Responsibility in American Politics"; Robert J. Samuelson, "Fragmentation and Political Uncertainty Litter the Political Landscape," *National Journal,* (20 October 1979); and Clifton McCleskey, "The De-Institutionalization of Electoral Politics," in *A Tide of Discontent: The 1980 Elections and Their Meaning,* ed. Ellis Sandoz and Cecil V. Crabb, Jr., 113–38.

CHAPTER 2

1. Key and Crouch, *The Initiative and Referendum in California,* 423–43; Hays, "The Politics of Reform in Municipal Government in the Progressive Era."

2. Hofstadter, *The Age of Reform,* 257.

3. Ibid., 261.

4. Remarks of California Assemblyman Bledsoe, quoted in Anderson, *California State Government,* 192.

5. Bourne, "Functions of the Initiative, Referendum and Recall," 3.

6. Wilcox, *Government by All the People,* 50–51.

7. Smith, *The Spirit of American Government,* 352.

8. Ranney and Kendall, *Democracy and the American Party System,* 60–61.

9. Historians have disagreed about the origins and composition of the Progressive movement. The most widely held view of the period is expressed by George Mowry: "While not wealthy, the average California progressive was, in the jargon of his day, 'well fixed.' He was more often than not a Mason, and almost invariably a member of his town's chamber of commerce. Finally, he apparently had been, at least until 1900, a conservative Republican, satisfied with McKinley and his Republican predecessors" (Mowry, *The California Progressives,* 88). Richard Hofstadter also shares the view that the Progressive movement was composed primarily of upper-middle class, well-educated, and native-born Americans (Hofstadter, *The Age of Reform,* 131–73). Others have argued that Progressivism grew from a more diverse constituency. Alternative views on the origins of the movement can be found in Buenker, "The Progressive Era"; Thelen, "Social Tensions and the Origins of Progressivism"; and Rogin and Shover, *Political Change in California,* 35–89.

10. Some students of American politics have argued that the United States has two predomi-

nant political traditions – the Yankee-Protestant, or "good government," tradition and the European immigrant, or "political machine," tradition. The most frequently cited exponents of this view are Richard Hofstadter (*The Age of Reform,* 9) and James Q. Wilson and Edward C. Banfield (*City Politics,* 46). Others have argued that the Hofstadter-Banfield-Wilson ethos theory does not explain the structure of city governments (see Wolfinger and Field, "Political Ethos and the Structure of City Government").

11. Commons, "Referendum and Initiatives in City Government."

12. DeWitt, *The Progressive Movement,* 4–5.

13. Mowry, *The Progressive Era, 1900–1920,* 5–14; Hofstadter, *The Age of Reform,* 60–130.

14. Munro, *The Initiative, Referendum, and Recall,* 1.

15. "The Arbitrator," *Nation,* 26 October 1921, 478–79.

16. The Columbus Qube poll on President Carter's speech was criticized by Albert H. Cantril, president of the National Council on Public Polls, as unscientific and potentially very inaccurate (see Shirley, "Criticism for the Columbus Poll"). Joe Dirck summarizes the George Bush Qube poll in "Bush Refuses to Concede Nomination to Reagan." For a discussion of the Hawaii Televote experiment see Becker and Slaton, "Hawaii Televote."

The American Broadcasting Corporation nationalized the Qube/Televote techniques in the fall of 1980 with a televised "call-in-your-vote" poll for the Carter-Reagan presidential debate. The methodological problems with the ABC poll were serious: question wording, sampling bias, and mechanical problems. To the viewer, the ABC poll appeared accurate, was neatly summarized in percentage terms on the screen, and seemed to have a high response rate. The news commentator's reminder that the poll was not scientific almost certainly did not correct the impression that the poll was valid and important.

17. Hofstadter, *The Age of Reform,* 131–73.

18. Beer, "In Search of a New Public Philosophy," 27–28.

19. Munro, *The Initiative, Referendum and Recall,* 2–21; Charles A. Beard, "Introductory Note," in Beard and Schultz, *Documents on the State-Wide Initiative, Referendum and Recall,* 8–10; Eaton, *The Oregon System,* 119; Wilcox, *Government by All the People,* 149–53; Barnett, *Operation of the Initiative, Referendum and Recall in Oregon;* and Pillsbury, "Prophecies of Good and Evil in Relation to Direct Legislation."

20. Key and Crouch, *The Initiative and Referendum in California,* 563; Munroe, *The Initiative, Referendum and Recall,* 2–21; Barnett, *Operation of the Initiative, Referendum and Recall in Oregon,* 4; Bourne, "Functions of the Initiative, Referendum and Recall," 3; John Randolph Haynes, "Statement in Support of Direct Legislation in the Commonwealth Club of California Debate over Direct Legislation, October 11, 1911," in Pitt, *California Controversies,* 123–26; and Eugene C. Lee, "California," in Butler and Ranney, *Referendums,* 87–122.

21. Haynes, "Statement in Support of Direct Legislation," 123–26; Tallian, *Direct Democracy,* 61; Benedict, "Some Aspects of the Direct Legislation Process in Washington State," 67; and Bourne, "Functions of the Initiative, Referendum and Recall," 3.

22. Key and Crouch, *The Initiative and Referendum in California,* 442–43; Munro, *The Initiative, Referendum and Recall,* 2–21; Hyink, Brown, and Thacker, *Politics and Government in California,* 131; Beard and Schultz, *Documents on the State-Wide Initiative, Referendum and Recall,* 12.

23. Typically, ballot questions must qualify for the ballot 3 to 4 months before the election, providing voters up to 120 days to study the proposition. Legislative sessions in most states run between 30 and 60 days.

24. Senate Subcommittee on the Constitution, *Voter Initiative Constitutional Amendment,* 12–15; La Palombara, *The Initiative and Referendum in Oregon,* 87–88; and Bone and Benedict, "Perspectives on Direct Legislation," 335–36.

25. Eaton, *The Oregon System,* 3; Haynes, "Statement in Support of Direct Legislation," 124–25; Baker, "American Conceptions of Direct vis-à-vis Representative Governance"; Anderson, *California State Government,* 181–95; and Bourne, "Functions of the Initiative, Referendum and Recall," 3.

26. Barnett, *Operation of the Initiative, Referendum and Recall in Oregon,* 98; Eaton, *The Oregon System,* 127-28; Key and Crouch, *The Initiative and Referendum in California,* 572; and Showell, "Political Independence in Washington State."

27. Barnett. *Operation of the Initiative, Referendum and Recall in Oregon,* 122-23; and Hyink, Brown, and Thacker, *Politics and Government in California,* 52-53.

28. National Economic League, *The Initiative and Referendum,* 34, 42-43; Lipow, "Plebiscitarian Politics and Progressivism"; and Pillsbury, "Prophecies of Good and Evil in Relation to Direct Legislation."

29. National Economic League, *The Initiative and Referendum,* 33, 38-39; and Lineberry and Fowler, "Reformism and Public Policies in American Cities."

30. Bryce, *The American Commonwealth,* 1:453; Oberholtzer, *The Referendum in America,* 411; and Pillsbury, "The Initiative, Its Achievements and Abuses," 426-27.

31. Bryce, *The American Commonwealth,* 1:453; Boyle, *The Initiative and Referendum,* 18-25; Eaton, *The Oregon System,* 117; Lipow, "Plebiscitarian Politics and Progressivism," 2-5; and Keefe and Ogul, *The American Legislative Process,* 456.

32. Commons, "Direct Legislation in Switzerland and America."

33. Most early advocates of direct legislation in America argued that the Swiss experience demonstrated the utility of the system (see J. W. Sullivan as quoted in Tallian, *Direct Democracy,* 12-13; and Wilson, *The State,* 310-12).

34. Bryce, *Modern Democracy,* 1:371-429; Lobingier, *The People's Law,* 26-39, 88-89, 346; Rappard, "The Initiative, Referendum and Recall in Switzerland"; and Commons, "Direct Legislation in Switzerland and America."

35. Kemp, *An American Renaissance,* 161.

36. Goodhart, 122.

37. Friedrich, *Constitutional Government and Democracy,* 545-49.

38. Butler and Kitzinger, *The 1975 Referendum,* 1.

39. Butler and Ranney, "Summing Up," in *Referendums,* 222.

40. Wright, "France," in ibid., 144-45.

CHAPTER 3

1. Hahn and Morton, "Initiative and Referendum," 926-27.

2. In some cases the legislature's substitute proposal must be very similar to the original indirect initiative in order to survive legal challenge. For instance, the proponents of a handgun registration initiative in Massachusetts successfully challenged a legislative substitute proposal and had it removed from the 1976 ballot (telephone interview with Betty Parnes, Department of the State Secretary, Commonwealth of Massachusetts, 19 May 1980).

3. Price, "The Initiative," 249-50.

4. The major reason that these findings are so divergent from Price's is that his sample included only eight states with both statutory and constitutional initiatives, thus excluding North Dakota, Idaho, Utah, Nevada, South Dakota, and Wyoming. Removing states from both ends of his table greatly skewed his results. As I demonstrate later in this chapter, the distinction between statutory and constitutional initiatives does not warrant exclusion from the sample of states that do not provide both.

5. Election officials in each state were interviewed to obtain the number of initiatives and popular referendums qualifying at each signature threshold. Therefore, in the regression analysis, the percentage requirement for each measure appearing on the ballot is known and is included in the analysis.

The multiple regression model has three independent variables: type of measure (popular referendum or initiative); signature threshold (actually one over the signature threshold); and region. Theoretically, because of its longer experience with direct legislation, the West should be treated as a potential independent variable, having explanatory potential beyond the states' required signature levels. The multiple regression equation is as follows:

$$Y = a + b_1X_1 + b_2X_2 + b_3X_3,$$

where Y = the number of measures appearing on the ballot; X_1 = 1/signature threshold; X_2 = region (1 = West, 0 = other); and X_3 = popular referendums (1 = yes, 0 = no). The regression analysis produced the following result:

$$Y = 1.3 + 50.4 \ (X_1) + 6.4 \ (X_2) - 8.8 \ (X_3).$$

The strength of the relationship between the signature threshold and the number of measures qualifying for the ballot can be summarized by the following statistics: $R^2 = 0.37$; multiple $R = 0.60$; $F = 11.34$; and

	Beta	Standard Error b
b_1	0.51	11.07
b_2	0.35	1.98
b_3	-0.47	2.05

For a thorough treatment of this type of bivariate curve fitting in regression analysis see Tufte, *Data Analysis for Politics and Policy,* 65–135.

6. Hugh Bone, commenting on North Dakota's low signature requirements, states: "Undoubtedly the generous number of initiatives on the ballot is due quite largely to the easiness of obtaining 10,000 signatures" (*The Initiative and the Referendum,* 42).

7. For an analysis of the tendency to sign petitions, often without reading or understanding them, see La Palombara, *The Initiative and Referendum in Oregon,* 108–9; Baus and Ross, *Politics Battle Plan,* 61; and Brestoff, "The California Initiative Process." Social psychologists have gone so far as to suggest the optimum condition for positive response to petition signature appeals (see Blake, Mouton, and Hain, "Social Forces in Petition Signing").

8. *Gage* v. *Jordan,* 23 Cal.2d 794, 147 P.2d 387 (1944). The case relied on California Constitution, Art. IV, Sec. 1.

9. *Perry* v. *Jordan,* 34 Cal.2d 87, 207 P.2d 47 (1949).

10. *McFadden* v. *Jordan,* 32 Cal.2d 330 (1948).

11. *Perry* v. Jordan, 34 Cal.2d 87 (1949). Of the recent single-subject challenges, one of the most interesting arose in the litigation over Proposition 13, the Jarvis-Gann property-tax initiative. In the case of *Amador Valley Joint Union High School District* v. *State Board of Equalization,* 583 P.2d 1281, 149 Cal. Rptr. 239 (1978), the court responded to claims by the proposition's opponents that the measure had more than one subject by arguing that all of the proposition's parts were reasonably germane and therefore constitutional.

12. California Constitution, Art. IV, Sec. 1d.

13. *Gordon* v. *Lance,* 403 U.S. 1 (1971); see also *Mihaly* v. *Westbrook,* 403 U.S. 915 (1971).

14. *City of Phoenix* v. *Kolodziejski,* 399 U.S. 204 (1970).

15. Hamilton and Cohen, *Policy Making by Plebiscite,* 60.

16. U.S. Constitution, Art. IV, Sec. 4.

17. *Pacific States Telephone and Telegraph Company* v. *Oregon,* 223 U.S. 118 (1912).

18. *Luther* v. *Burden,* 42 U.S. 1 (1849).

19. Ibid., 42.

20. Some commentators have expressed the hope that the courts would use the guarantee clause to exclude referendums affecting minority groups (see Seeley, "The Public Referendum and Minority Group Legislation").

21. *Fair Political Practices Commission* v. *Superior Court,* 599 P.2d 46, 157 Cal. Rptr. 855 (1979).

22. *James* v. *Valtierra,* 402 U.S. 141 (1971).

23. *Hunter* v. *Erickson,* 393 U.S. 385 (1969).

24. Lacy and Martin, "The Extraordinary Majority," 562.

25. *Westbrook* v. *Mihaly,* 471 P.2d 487, 87 Cal. Rptr. 839 (1970).

26. Jaffe, "The Constitutionality of Supermajority Voting Requirements," 707.

27. *Lance* v. *Board of Education,* 153 W.Va. 559, 170 S.E.2d 783 (1969).

28. *Gordon* v. *Lance,* 403 U.S. 1 (1971).

29. Justices Black, Douglas, Stewart, White, and Blackmun joined in Burger's opinion. Justice Harlan filed a statement concurring in the result, and justices Brennan and Marshall dissented.

30. Ibid., 6–7.

31. The legislative office distinction is an important one because lower federal courts have upheld a 60 percent voting rule in elections for judges (*Lefkovits* v. *State Board of Elections,* 400 Fed. Supp. 1005 [1975]).

32. *Baker* v. *Carr,* 369 U.S. 186 (1962), established that equality of representation is a justiciable question. This decision was followed by the one-man, one-vote decision of *Wesberry* v. *Sanders,* 376 U.S. 1 (1964), and *Reynolds* v. *Sims,* 377 U.S. 533 (1964).

33. *Town of Lockport, New York* v. *Citizens for Community Action at the Local Level,* 430 U.S. 266 (1976).

34. In most school and revenue bond elections, all registered voters may participate. The following decisions declared unconstitutional the requirement of property ownership in these contexts: *Kramer* v. *Union School District,* 395 U.S. 621 (1969); *Cipriano* v. *City of Houma,* 395 U.S. 701 (1969); and *City of Phoenix* v. *Kolodziejski,* 399 U.S. 204 (1970). But for some decisions, the U.S. Supreme Court has held that the electorate in a special purpose unit of government, such as a water storage district, may be apportioned to give greater influence (more votes) to the groups most affected by the governmental unit's functions (*Salyer Land Co.* v. *Tulare Water District,* 410 U.S. 719 [1973]).

35. *Gordon* v. *Lance,* 403 U.S. 1 (1971).

36. *Town of Lockport, New York* v. *Citizens for Community Action at the Local Level,* 430 U.S. 266 (1976).

37. *James* v. *Valtierra,* 402 U.S. 137 (1971).

38. *City of Eastlake* v. *Forest City Enterprises,* 426 U.S. 668 (1976).

39. Ibid., 678–79.

40. *Diamond* v. *Bland,* 477 P.2d 733, 91 Cal. Rptr. 501 (1970).

41. *Buckley* v. *Valeo,* 424 U.S. 1 (1976).

42. *Citizens for Jobs and Energy* v. *Fair Political Practices Commission,* 577 P.2d 1386, 129 Cal. Rptr. 106 (1976).

43. *Hardie* v. *Eu,* 556 P.2d 301, 134 Cal. Rptr. 201 (1976).

44. *First National Bank of Boston* v. *Bellotti,* 435 U.S. 765 (1978).

45. *Citizens Against Rent Control* v. *City of Berkeley,* 454 U.S. 290 (1981).

46. *James* v. *Valtierra,* 402 U.S. 137 (1971), 141.

47. While to date the California court has not declared any part of the Jarvis-Gann property-tax initiative (Proposition 13) unconstitutional, in the case of *Los Angeles County Transportation Commission* v. *Richmond* 643 P.2d 941, 182 Cal. Rptr. 324 (1982) the court ruled that the Proposition 13 requirement that cities, counties, and special districts had to have a two-thirds voter approval in order to impose special nonproperty taxes did not apply to those special districts that did not enforce property taxes. In a second case, the California Supreme Court further narrowed the application of Proposition 13; the court decided in *Carmen* v. *Alvord* 644 P.2d 192, 182 Cal. Rptr. 506 (1982) that Proposition 13 allows local governments to increase property taxes in order to finance public employee retirement systems (Carlsen, "Top Court OKs Prop. 13 Tax Loophole." See also Hager, "State High Court OKs County's Transit Tax"; and Carrisoza, "High Court OKs LA Transit Tax, Narrows Prop. 13").

48. For a list of the judicial determinations of the constitutionality of successful California initiatives since 1964 see Appendix A. For a more detailed treatment of this subject see Baker, "Judicial Review of Statewide Initiatives in California."

49. Wolfinger and Greenstein, "The Repeal of Fair Housing in California," 755.

50. *Reitman* v. *Mulkey,* 387 U.S. 369 (1967).

51. Proponents of initiatives are often unhappy with the titles assigned them (see Tallian, *Direct Democracy,* 87–88; California Assembly Interim Committee Public Hearings, Los Angeles, 10 October 1972, 21–22; and Hensler and Hensler, "Evaluating Nuclear Power," 147).

52. The initiative's sponsors wanted to reduce taxes from 8 mills per $1,000 of property value to 4 mills per $1,000. However, in their petition, they omitted the words "per $1,000," resulting in a proposed tax reduction of 99.95 percent (see Curry, "Miami Area Voting on Near-Wipeout of Property Tax").

53. Perhaps the best-known academic research on ballot position is Bain and Hancock, *Ballot Position and Voter's Choice.*

54. Ballot positions beyond number 25 were excluded because of insufficient cases. For instance, ballot positions 33–48 occurred only once, all during the same election.

55. Baus and Ross, *Politics Battle Plan,* 345–46.

56. Mueller, "Voting on the Propositions."

57. Baus and Ross, *Politics Battle Plan,* 346.

58. Personal correspondence from Edward Arnold, Elections Assistant, Office of the California Secretary of State, 1976.

59. Legislation permitting the secretary of state to qualify an initiative for the ballot through a random-sample check of signatures was passed in 1976 (California State Elections Code, chap. 248). If the sample technique indicates that 110 percent or more of the required signatures are authentic, the measure qualifies for the ballot. If the random sample predicts that less than 90 percent of the required total are authentic, the measure dies. When the sample estimate is between 90 percent and 110 percent of the required total, each signature is checked for authenticity.

60. Interview with Edward Arnold, 15 July 1981.

61. Interview with Edward Arnold, 28 July 1980. Another study reports that special elections in the early 1970s cost an average of one dollar per voter to administer and that in a ten-year period the Seattle school district spent over one million dollars on referendums (Hamilton and Cohen, *Policy Making by Plebiscite,* 34).

CHAPTER 4

1. McGuigan, "Initiative Process Gains Popularity."

2. Scott, *Governing California's Coast,* 319–63.

3. Smith, "Beating the Big Boys," 40–78.

4. This membership figure was obtained in an interview with Keith Hern, Office of Communications, California State Employee Association, 21 May 1980.

5. For a more detailed discussion of the 1972 signature-gathering campaign in California see "Initiative Makes a Big Comeback."

6. Fitzgerald, "Computer Democracy."

7. Included in this group are Allan Blanchard and Associates, Fred Kimball, and Ed and Larry Phillips. Generally speaking, these firms hire individual collectors or subcontract with smaller firms located elsewhere in the state.

8. Price, "Seizing the Initiative," 19.

9. Ibid.

10. California General Assembly, *Public Hearing on Initiative Process,* 48–49.

11. Smith, "Beating the Big Boys," 105–6.

12. Wood and Hicks, "Rent Initiative."

13. Helson, Blake, and Mouton, "Petition-Signing as Adjustment to Situational and Personal Factors"; and Blake, Mouton, and Hain, "Social Forces in Petition Signing."

14. California General Assembly, *Public Hearing on Initiative Process,* 48–49.

15. "Casino Petitions Voided."

16. Baus and Ross, *Politics Battle Plan,* 61. For data on Oregon see La Palombara, *The Initiative and Referendum in Oregon,* 108–9.

17. Wilcox and Weinberg, "Petition-Signing in the 1968 Election," 731.

18. See Eugene C. Lee, "California," in Butler and Ranney, *Referendums,* 102–7.

19. See Wood and Hicks, "Rent Initiative," 1, 4, 5. Edward Arnold, Elections Assistant, Office of the California Secretary of State, estimates that most signature-gathering firms were charging one dollar per valid signature in 1980 (interview, 16 May 1980).

20. Price, "Seizing the Initiative," 19.

21. Nimmo, *The Political Persuaders;* and Sabato, *The Rise of Political Consultants.*

22. Kuttner, *Revolt of the Haves,* 22.

23. Stuart Spencer, of Spencer-Roberts, managed Gerald Ford's 1976 reelection campaign. For a discussion of the early development of these firms see Kelley, *Professional Public Relations and Political Power.*

24. The following firms are now active in California: Braun and Company, Los Angeles (handled several initiative campaigns, most recently in opposition to Proposition 9, the Jarvis income-tax initiative, in 1980); Butcher-Forde Consulting, Irvine (developed the direct-mail approach for initiatives and managed the successful campaign for Proposition 13, the Jarvis-Gann property-tax initiative); Cerrell Associates, Los Angeles (formerly active in initiatives, now primarily involved in candidate contests); Solem and Associates, San Francisco (have developed a specialty in opposition to rent control); Spencer-Roberts, Los Angeles (among the most famous of the early initiative firms, now primarily involved in candidate contests); Russo-Watts, San Francisco (a relatively new firm which successfully managed the passage of the 1979 spending-limitation initiative, Proposition 4); Weiner and Company, San Francisco (managed a successful campaign to legalize gambling in Atlantic City, New Jersey, but failed with a similar proposition in Florida); Whitaker-Baxter, Los Angeles (the earliest and best-known firm; several other firms are spin-offs of this highly successful firm. Managed several campaigns in the 1930s, the defeats of the Garrison revenue bond act and the "ham and eggs" pension plan being among the most notable); Winner-Wagner and Associates, Los Angeles (managed the defeat of the 1976 nuclear initiative but failed in opposition to Proposition 13, the property-tax initiative); and Woodward, McDowell, and Larson, San Francisco (managed the campaign to defeat the anti-smoking initiative in 1978, with a budget of over $6 million; managed the campaigns for restrictions on rent control and against tax on big oil companies in June 1980).

25. Korda, "Masters of the 'Meta Message,'" 159.

26. Interview with Edward Arnold, 15 May 1980.

27. Interview with William Yee, Attorney, Elections Division, Office of the California Secretary of State, 14 May 1982.

28. Key and Crouch, *The Initiative and Referendum in California,* 542–43.

29. List provided by Eu, "A History of the California Initiative Process."

30. Jerome Clubb and Michael Traugott estimate that over fifteen thousand statewide propositions were on the ballot between 1898 and 1968 (see "National Patterns of Referenda Voting," 137). Data for statewide referendums held since 1968 were tabulated from the Referenda and Primary Election Materials, available from the Inter-university Consortium for Political and Social Research (ICPSR 0006), University of Michigan, Ann Arbor, Michigan.

31. Hamilton, "Direct Legislation," 125.

32. Some states are heavy users of ballot referendums that do not result from voter petitions. In the period 1968–78, Louisiana had a total of 150 statewide ballot propositions and Georgia had 142, but none of these propositions were initiatives or popular referendums. In contrast, for this same period, California had 135 ballot propositions and Oregon had 111. At least part of the reason why some states have so many propositions without the initiative or referendum is that any constitutional change must be ratified by the statewide electorate. For instance, several of Alabama's 34 statewide propositions in 1969 concerned charter provisions in only one county or city, yet the state constitution required statewide voter approval of any constitutional change. For a complete breakdown of the numbers of statewide propositions by state for 1968–78 see Appendix C.

33. Key and Crouch, *The Initiative and Referendum in California,* 450.

34. Austin Ranney, "United States," in Butler and Ranney, *Referendums,* 82.

35. Two causes of the widespread use of constitutional amendments are lengthy and highly specific state constitutions and previously enacted initiatives that require voter approval for amendment.

36. Ewing, "Primaries as Real Elections"; Brady, *Congressional Voting in a Partisan Era,* 105; Turner, "Primary Elections as the Safe Alternative," 197; Wolfinger and Heifitz, "Safe Seats, Seniority, and Power in Congress," 339; Budgor et al., "The 1896 Election and Congressional Modernization."

37. Some issues have interesting longevity. In California five topics have each appeared on the ballot five times, and in Oregon one measure has been submitted twelve times.

CHAPTER 5

1. Senate Subcommittee on the Constitution, *Voter Initiative Constitutional Amendment,* 92, 93, 7.

2. Other states that place initiatives on primary election ballots include Nebraska and North Dakota. Maine has used special elections to decide propositions.

3. Rusk, "Effect of the Australian Ballot Reform on Split Ticket Voting"; and Walker, "Ballot Forms and Voter Fatigue."

4. Participation is frequently defined as turnout, but in this case the definition is much more specific, referring to the voters actually voting on propositions.

5. Kelley, Ayres, and Bowen, "Registration and Voting"; Kim, Petrocik, and Enokson, "Voter Turnout among the American States"; Milbrath and Goel, *Political Participation;* Ranney, "The Representativeness of Primary Electorates"; Salisbury and Black, "Class and Party in Partisan and Non-Partisan Elections"; Verba and Nie, *Participation in America;* Wolfinger and Rosenstone, "Effect of Registration Laws on Voter Turnout"; and idem, *Who Votes?*

6. Campbell et al., *The American Voter,* 89–115; and Campbell, "Surge and Decline."

7. See Downs, *An Economic Theory of Democracy;* Cyr, "The Calculus of Voting Reconsidered"; and Meehl, "The Selfish Voter Paradox."

8. Verba and Nie, *Participation in America,* 125.

9. While most studies have found participation in politics to be highly correlated with education, socioeconomic status, and so forth, Gerald W. Johnson presents evidence of a deviant case — West Virginia — where participation is high despite low aggregate levels of socioeconomic status ("Research Note on Political Correlates").

10. Wolfinger and Rosenstone, *Who Votes?* 17–30.

11. Estimates of turnout derived from surveys are generally somewhat higher than those based on numbers of actual ballots cast, apparently for four main reasons. First, aggregate estimates of turnout are based on the proportion of the voting-age population casting ballots. Since this estimate includes people who are ineligible to vote, the aggregate underestimates turnout. Second, the aggregate estimate of turnout does not count spoiled ballots, again underestimating turnout. Third, estimates from surveys overestimate turnout because they tend to oversample among persons more likely to vote; rarely are dormitories, prisons, or rest homes included in sample survey designs. Fourth, response error — falsely claiming to have voted — can lead to inflated estimates in sample surveys. For a thorough discussion of the reasons for this phenomenon see Wolfinger and Rosenstone, *Who Votes?* Appendix A, 115–18.

12. This higher reported turnout among Californians may be accounted for by the facts that California candidate elections are highly competitive and that in 1972 several controversial and vigorously contested ballot propositions were on the ballot, with subjects including criminal penalties for possession of marijuana, anti-obscenity, the death penalty, property-tax reduction, and school busing.

13. Wolfinger and Rosenstone, *Who Votes?* 35–36.

14. Campbell, "Surge and Decline."

15. Wolfinger, Rosenstone, and McIntosh, "Presidential and Congressional Voters Compared."

16. Wolfinger and Rosenstone also found that turnout among the young varies with education. Turnout among uneducated youths is one-third of that among youths with a college degree. Students vote about 16 percent more than do their nonstudent counterparts. Analysis of turnout among the young reveals no evidence consistent with the theory that the low rate is a result of their not yet assuming adult social roles (Wolfinger and Rosenstone, *Who Votes?* 37–60).

17. Wolfinger, Rosenstone, and McIntosh, "Presidential and Congressional Voters Compared."

18. Campbell, "Surge and Decline."

19. Arsenau and Wolfinger, "Voting Behavior in Congressional Elections," 17.

20. Burnham, "The Changing Shape of the American Political Universe"; and Rusk, "Effect of the Australian Ballot Reform on Split Ticket Voting."

21. Lengle, *Representation and Presidential Primaries,* 29–52.

22. The qualified-majority requirements are as follows: Sierra Leone, 67 percent; Weimar Germany, 50 percent; Denmark, 40 percent for constitutional changes and 30 percent for ordinary laws; Scotland and Wales, 40 percent (Butler, "A Framework for U.K. Referendums," 8).

23. Of the 6,606,856 persons who voted on Proposition 13 in the 1978 primary election, 395,194 were ineligible to vote on party nominees because they declined to state their party. With these persons removed, the number who voted on Proposition 13 and for governor can be compared directly. By this measure, 355,597 more votes were cast for Proposition 13 than for governor.

24. Mueller, "Voting on the Propositions," 1201. Mueller defines controversial propositions as bonds, initiatives, and referendums. Noncontroversial propositions are those placed on the ballot by the state legislature. Mueller's abstention measure is also based upon total votes cast in the election.

25. In reviewing the rates of dropoff for different types of initiatives in Washington, Hugh A. Bone found that initiatives on public morals and personal life style had the lowest dropoff (11–12 percent), while initiatives whose content concerned state and local government had the highest dropoff (27 percent) ("The Initiative in Washington," 3).

26. La Palombara and Hagan, "Direct Legislation," 408–9.

27. Hugh A. Bone and Robert C. Benedict have studied dropoff in the state of Washington over a more extensive time frame than the twenty years examined here. Based on data from 1914 to 1973, they note that "the participation rates on all types of propositions have increased continuously since 1930," and they go on to conclude that "long term analysis shows virtually no association between degree of participation on the issues and the direction of the vote" ("Perspectives on Direct Legislation," 340, 345). John Mueller documented a similar long-term trend towards greater participation on noncontroversial propositions in California, but he did not speculate about the effects of greater participation (Mueller, "Voting on the Propositions," 1197–1213).

28. Clubb and Traugott, "National Patterns of Referenda Voting," 143.

29. For a discussion of the effects of ballot position in candidate elections see Mueller, "Choosing among 133 Candidates"; Taebel, "Effect of Ballot Position on Electoral Success"; and Walker, "Ballot Forms and Voter Fatigue."

30. Senate Subcommittee on the Constitution, *Voter Initiative Constitutional Amendment,* 50.

31. *New York Times,* 27 November 1978, A-18.

32. Hatfield, "Direct Democracy Now."

33. California Polls 6205, 9–16 October 1962, and 6206, 30 October–1 November 1962, The Field Institute, San Francisco, California.

34. In 1962 there were two rather controversial statewide propositions: Proposition 23, a reapportionment of the state senate; and Proposition 24, an initiative to define and limit the rights of subversives.

35. *Los Angeles Times* Poll 6, 6 June 1978.

36. Everson, "Initiatives and Voter Turnout: a Comparative State Analysis"; and idem, "Initiatives and Voter Turnout: The Case of 1978."

37. Reported in *Citizen Participation* 1 (September/October 1979): 14.

38. Everson, "Initiatives and Voter Turnout: A Comparative State Analysis," 6.

39. Everson, "Initiatives and Voter Turnout: The Case of 1978," 5-8.

40. Data on the 1978 election were compiled from Michael Barone, Grant Ujifusa, and Douglas Matthews, *The Almanac of American Politics 1980* (New York: E. P. Dutton, 1979); and "Surprises Occur in Governors Races," *State Government News* 21 (November 1978): 2.

CHAPTER 6

1. Pitkin, *The Concept of Representation,* 61, emphasis added. Besides descriptive representation, Pitkin reviews other more formalistic perspectives on representation. The authoritarian view, for instance, sees the representative as someone who has been authorized to act and the represented as obligated to accept the consequences of his decisions. Accountability theorists see the representative as someone who is held to account and must answer for his actions; the persons to whom he must eventually account are the represented. In both systems elections are the critical events.

2. Griffiths and Wollheim, "How Can One Person Represent Another?"

3. See Lee, *The Politics of Nonpartisanship,* 28-34; and Hawley, *Nonpartisan Elections,* 8-14.

4. In addition to Lee, *The Politics of Nonpartisanship,* and Hawley, *Nonpartisan Elections,* see Adrian, "Some General Characteristics of Nonpartisan Elections"; Rogers and Arman, "Nonpartisanship and Election to City Office"; and Salisbury and Black, "Class and Party in Partisan and Non-Partisan Elections."

5. Hawley, *Nonpartisan Elections,* 82, emphasis added.

6. Ibid., 84.

7. Davis, *Presidential Primaries.*

8. See Key, *American State Politics,* 134-45; Ranney and Epstein, "The Two Electorates"; Ranney, "Turnout and Representation in Presidential Primary Elections"; and Lengle, *Representation and Presidential Primaries.*

9. Lengle, *Representation and Presidential Primaries,* 94-112.

10. Ranney, "The Representativeness of Primary Electorates," 224.

11. Key, *American State Politics,* 153.

12. Hamilton, "Direct Legislation," 129.

13. Based on aggregate data since 1970, the average dropoff on propositions for Massachusetts is 17 percent. See chapter 5 for a more detailed analysis.

14. Regrettably, the Massachusetts Poll did not ascertain the education level of the respondents, thus making it impossible to explore the relationship of education to any other variables considered in later analysis of the Massachusetts Poll data. The best available measure of socioeconomic status in this poll is income, which clearly is not as informative as education would have been.

15. In chapter 5, I documented that these differential voting rates do not, however, occur equally on all types of ballot measures. With data from the 1968 Center for Political Studies National Election Study, Clubb and Traugott have shown that differences in dropoff rates among different educational, income, and racial groups tend to be minimal when overall voter interest in a proposition is relatively high. It is mainly when initiative and referendum contests lack widespread salience that voters in the lower socioeconomic status groups drop off at higher rates than their higher-status counterparts. Clubb and Traugott assume that low overall

dropoff and a close race indicate strong voter interest (Clubb and Traugott, "National Patterns of Referenda Voting").

16. See the series of front-page articles on statewide propositions appearing in the *Boston Globe* between 6 and 11 October 1976.

17. While the ratio of representation is a useful device for summarizing and comparing populations, as is done here, because the ratio is a function of both the percentage difference and the size of a group, a small change within a small category will present a higher score than would the same small change in a large category. To limit the effects of this problem, I have collapsed the categories of demographic variables when possible.

18. Verba and Nie, *Participation in America,* 96; and Dahl, *A Preface to Democratic Theory,* 112–14.

19. Clubb and Traugott, "National Patterns of Referenda Voting," 165.

20. Another way of comparing the level of participation in candidate and proposition contests is to draw a Lorenz curve for each population of voters. Economists and demographers who must often compare the distribution on a given variable across several populations frequently employ this device and its statistical measure, the Gini index. When compared with the perfect representational equality of those who voted for governor, the Gini index for Proposition 4 voters of 0.12 (the measure of the cumulative joint distribution of turnout and voting on the proposition) is a clear indication of a representational bias for those who voted on the proposition. The cumulative joint distribution of the population of Proposition 4 voters and the total sample of eligible voters shows an even greater departure from the line of equality, with a Gini index of 0.22. One of the best descriptions of Lorenz curves and the Gini index is found in David C. Leege and Wayne L. Francis, *Political Research — Design, Measurement, and Analysis* (New York: Basic Books, 1974), 274–78.

21. Walker, "Ballot Forms and Voter Fatigue," 436.

22. Proponents of initiatives are often unhappy with the titles assigned them (see Tallian, *Direct Democracy,* 87–88; California General Assembly, Committee on Elections and Reapportionment, *Public Hearings on Initiative Process,* 10 October 1972, 21–22; Hensler and Hensler, "Evaluating Nuclear Power," 191).

23. The outcomes for the California propositions were as follows:

Election	Proposition	Percentage Voting Yes
1972 General	2, Health science bond	60%
1974 General	4, University of California board of regents	55
1976 Primary	15, Nuclear power	33
1976 General	13, Greyhound racing	25
1976 General	14, Agricultural labor relations	38
1978 Primary	8, Behr tax initiative	47
1978 Primary	13, Property taxes	65
1978 General	5, Anti-smoking	46
1978 General	6, Homosexual teachers	42
1980 Primary	9, Jarvis income-tax initiative	39
1980 Primary	10, Uniform standard for rent control	35
1980 Primary	11, Oil surtax	44

CHAPTER 7

1. Campbell et al., *The American Voter* and more recently, Keith et al., The Myth of the Independent Voter.

2. Campbell, "A Classification of Presidential Elections"; Kessel, *The Goldwater Coalition;* Weisbord, *Campaigning for President;* and Natchez and Bupp, "Candidates, Issues and Voters."

3. Miller et al., "A Majority Party in Disarray." For a different interpretation of the same election see Popkin et al., "Comment: What Have You Done for Me Lately?" See also Pomper, *Voters' Choice,* 5-17, 151-54, 191-205.

4. See Campbell et al., *The American Voter;* Campbell, "Surge and Decline," 60-61; and Flanigan and Zingale, *Political Behavior of the American Electorate,* 18-27.

5. Two recent expressions of this view are found in Hatfield, "Direct Democracy Now"; and Tallian, *Direct Democracy.*

6. Key, *Public Opinion and American Democracy,* 47.

7. Pomper, "From Confusion to Clarity," 415; Campbell et al., *The American Voter,* 400.

8. Berelson, Lazarsfeld, and McPhee, *Voting,* 25.

9. California Poll 8206, 1-4 October 1982, The Field Institute, San Francisco, California.

10. Rothschild and Ray, "Involvement and Political Advertising Effect"; and Rothschild, "The Effects of Political Advertising on the Voting Behavior of a Low Involvement Electorate."

11. Campbell et al., *The American Voter,* 480.

12. Lazarsfeld, Berelson, and Gaudet, *The People's Choice,* 43.

13. Keith et al., *The Myth of the Independent Voter.*

14. Hamilton, "Direct Legislation," 133.

15. Senate Subcommittee on the Constitution, *Voter Initiative Constitutional Amendment,* 92, 113.

16. Key, *Public Opinion and American Democracy,* 85-89.

17. Jennings and Zeigler, "The Salience of American State Politics," 525.

18. Center for Political Studies, *American National Election Study,* 1948 (Ann Arbor: Inter-university Consortium for Political and Social Research, 1948) question 26. See also Campbell, Gurin, and Miller, "Political Issues and the Vote"; and Lane and Sears, *Public Opinion,* 57-58.

19. Converse et al., "Continuity and Change in American Politics," 1092.

20. Gallup Opinion Index, report 157, August 1978, 26-29. In 1979, during another gasoline shortage and after the decline in production in Iran, only 46 percent of respondents believed that the United States had to import oil from other countries (*San Francisco Chronicle,* 21 May 1979, 5).

21. Erskine, "The Polls: Textbook Knowledge."

22. Center for Political Studies, *American National Election Study,* 1952-82. In 1976, 58 percent correctly stated that after the election, the Democratic party held the majority in the House of Representatives (Center for Political Studies, *American National Election Study,* 1976). Even though Americans are surprisingly uninformed, they are better informed about politics than the citizens of England, Germany, and Italy (Almond and Verba, *The Civic Culture,* 96).

23. Center for Political Studies, *American National Election Study,* 1976.

24. Not all Americans view being informed about politics as necessary for participation. Herbert McClosky found that roughly half of the citizenry agreed with the statement, "People ought to be allowed to vote, even if they can't do so intelligently." Even more persons felt that issues and political arguments are beyond the understanding of most voters (McClosky, "Consensus and Ideology in American Politics"). Similarly, 49 percent of James Prothro and Charles Grigg's sample felt that information should not be a precondition for participation in a city referendum (Prothro and Grigg, "Fundamental Principles of Democracy," 283).

25. Lutrin, "The Public and Ecology," 356.

26. Wolfinger and Greenstein, "Repeal of Fair Housing in California." Over 99 percent of Californians reported that they knew Proposition 13 was on the ballot (California Poll 7806, 29-31 May 1978, The Field Institute, San Francisco, California).

27. Colorado Poll 795, 20-31 August 1980, Research Services, Denver, Colorado.

28. See Campbell et al., *The American Voter;* Lazarsfeld et al., *The People's Choice;* and Dixon, "Party Identification and the Party Vote," 707.

29. Survey of Attitudes on Nuclear Power, May–June 1976, Rand Corporation, Santa Monica, California.

30. On self-assessment items such as these, it is important to recognize the potential bias inflating the reported knowledge or information. Some respondents may report having heard of the legislative bills when in fact they have not. To ensure that the respondent feels comfortable about giving the accurate answer the questions should be worded as these are.

31. California Poll 7904, 12–19 November 1979, The Field Institute, San Francisco, California.

32. Wilson and Banfield, *City Politics,* 324.

33. Harris, *California Politics,* 116.

34. McHenry, "The Pattern of California Politics," 52.

35. California Poll 7904.

36. Mueller, "Voting on the Propositions," 1206.

37. There is reason to believe that the voter handbook figure is overreported, since 15 percent of the same sample indicated using the handbook for candidate contests and the handbook only contains information on ballot propositions (California Poll 8206, 1–4 October 1982).

38. California Poll 7207, 7–18 November 1972, The Field Institute, San Francisco, California.

39. States that do not have such a handbook or pamphlet are Arizona, California, Massachusetts, Montana, North Dakota, Oregon, Rhode Island, and Washington.

40. Balmer, *State Election Services in Oregon,* 41, 58; Eugene C. Lee, "California," in Butler and Ranney, *Referendums,* 112; and Mueller, "Voting on the Propositions," 1211–12.

41. Benedict, "Some Aspects of the Direct Legislation Process in Washington State," 126.

42. La Palombara, *The Initiative and Referendum in Oregon,* 119.

43. Lee, "California," 112.

44. Mueller, "Voting on the Propositions," 1211–12.

45. Balmer, *State Election Services in Oregon,* 41, 58.

46. Bone, *The Initiative and the Referendum,* 17.

47. La Palombara, *The Initiative and Referendum in Oregon,* 119–20.

48. Rudolf Flesch, *The Art of Readable Writing* (New York: Harper and Brothers Publishers, 1949); Colin Harrison, *Readability in the Classroom* (Cambridge: Cambridge University Press, 1980); George R. Klare, *The Measurement of Readability* (Ames: Iowa State University Press, 1963); idem, "Assessing Readability," *Reading Research Quarterly* 10, no. 1 (1974–75):62–102; Irving Lorge, "Predicting Readability," *Teachers College Record* 45 (March 1944): 404–19.

49. The readability levels of the four popular magazines are given below:

Magazine	Number of Words in Sample	Average Number of Words per Sentence	Readability		
			Fry	Dale-Chall	Flesch
Time, 11 August 1980	8,405	20.4	12.4	11.3	49.6
Newsweek, 22 June 1981	8,216	21.5	12.3	11.8	49.6
People, 22 June 1981	9,130	17.8	9.4	8.7	64.7
Reader's Digest, May 1981	11,466	15.5	10.1	9.7	61.8

Readability figures in the columns headed "Fry" and "Dale-Chall" represent readability grade levels. Those in the column headed "Flesch" represent readability scores on the Flesch readability index (0 = very difficult, 100 = very easy). For more information see Appendix D.

50. Common Cause of California and the People's Lobby, a group that advocates more widespread use of the initiative process, recognized the problems of the handbook some years ago and included in Proposition 9, the fair political practices act, a provision removing from

the attorney general the responsibility of writing the section analyzing ballot propositions and giving this responsibility to the legislative analyst. When the reform was instituted in the 1976 primary election, it was assumed that the text written by the legislative analyst would be less technical and complicated than had previously been the case. The expectations of the reformers were not fulfilled. The section of the handbook written by the legislative analyst is no less complex; in fact, the handbook prepared for the recent 1980 primary election was the most difficult to read of any published since 1974.

51. Converse, "The Nature of Belief Systems in Mass Publics," 206–61.

52. Achen found that part of the effect Converse cited for inconsistent opinions was the result of fuzzy questions (Achen, "Mass Political Attitudes and the Survey Response").

53. Quoted in Lee and Berg, *The Challenge of California*. 2 ed, 106.

54. See Converse and Markus, "Plus ça change. . . ."

55. Only 8 percent reported that they had seen or heard anything about Proposition 23, the state senate reapportionment (California Poll 6206, 30 October–1 November 1962, The Field Institute, San Francisco, California). This low level of awareness is surprising because most accounts of the 1962 election have argued that these two propositions were widely followed (see Anderson and Lee, "The 1962 Election in California").

56. Hensler and Hensler, "Evaluating Nuclear Power," 28–29.

57. Among the voters who indicated that they knew little or nothing about the proposition were: those who had not finished high school (30 percent); persons earning under five thousand dollars (26 percent); and nonwhites (21 percent) (Survey of Attitudes on Nuclear Power, May–June 1976, Rand Corporation, Santa Monica, California).

58. CBS News/*Los Angeles Times* Poll 6, 6 June 1978.

59. Of voters earning less than ten thousand dollars with less than a high school education, 22 percent reported paying a lot of attention to the news about the proposition. But of voters earning less than ten thousand dollars who had attended college, over 45 percent, or more than double the percentage in the lower education category, reported paying a lot of attention to news about the proposition.

60. Colorado Poll 803, 22–29 October 1980, Research Services, Denver, Colorado. The data for this poll unfortunately did not contain an education question.

61. Lockard, *The Politics of State and Local Government*, 251.

62. Sapolsky, "The Fluoridation Controversy," 244–45.

63. Anderson, "Voting and Misvoting," 13.

64. Mueller, "Voting on the Propositions," 1202–3.

65. Wolfinger and Greenstein, "Repeal of Fair Housing in California," 756–57.

66. Survey of Attitudes on Nuclear Power, May–June 1976, Rand Corporation, Santa Monica, California.

67. Groth and Schultz, *Voter Attitudes on the 1976 California Nuclear Initiative*, 9.

68. Forty-four percent of the voters who had an income of less than ten thousand dollars per year and who had not completed high school were confused on this proposition. Among voters of the same income category who had attended college, only 8 percent were confused. For all income categories, the better educated were consistently less likely to be confused.

69. Smith and Townsend, "Prop. 10: Its Defeat Hailed and Lamented," 1, 22.

70. *Los Angeles Times* Poll 30, 3 June 1980.

CHAPTER 8

1. Heard, *The Costs of Democracy*, 16.

2. Jacobson, "Impact of Broadcast Campaigning," 775.

3. Owens and Olson, "Campaign Spending and the Electoral Process in California, 1966–1974," 505.

4. See Mann and Wolfinger, "Candidates and Parties in Congressional Elections," 621–24.

5. Brestoff, "The California Initiative Process," 940–41; and Harris, *California Politics,* 116.

6. See Lee, "California," in Butler and Ranney *Referendums,* 105; and Berg, "The Initiative Process and Public Policy-Making in the States," 54–55.

7. For a discussion of the campaign for Proposition 20, the coastal zone initiative, see Scott, *Governing California's Coast,* 319–63; on the campaign for Proposition 9, the political reform initiative, see Smith, "Beating the Big Boys," 40–78. For a general treatment of precinct work see Wolfinger, "The Influence of Precinct Work on Voting Behavior."

8. The consumer price index (CPI) for California provides the best available measure of the rate of inflation, even though this measure is not totally applicable in determining the impact of inflation on campaign costs. For example, estimates of costs for television and radio advertising indicate that during the last five years, these costs have increased at a rate slightly less than the California CPI. On the other hand, costs for postage have increased faster than the California CPI. During the twenty years from 1958 to 1978, the California CPI increased by approximately 130 percent, while first-class postage rates increased by 275 percent and bulk rates increased by 320 percent. These consumer price indices are as follows:

Year	Consumer Price Index	Year	Consumer Price Index
1954	91.8	1970	135.0
1956	93.3	1972	144.7
1958	100.0	1974	168.6
1960	103.6	1976	197.8
1962	106.3	1978	228.9
1964	109.9	1979	253.7
1966	114.3	1980	293.1
1968	122.3	1982	348.2

9. Using 1978 as the baseline year, the expenditures for the 1956 Proposition 4 would be $11,968,270, as compared with the $7,111,924 spent on the 1978 Proposition 5 campaign.

10. The Survey of Attitudes on Nuclear Power conducted by the Rand Corporation revealed that only a little over one-third of the voters knew which side had spent more in the campaign on Proposition 15, the nuclear initiative (see table 8.7).

11. California Fair Political Practices Commission, *Campaign Contribution and Spending Report,* 289–98.

12. Baus and Ross, *Politics Battle Plan,* 251.

13. Wilson and Banfield, *City Politics,* 324.

14. Christenson, "The Power of the Press," 239.

15. Hamilton and Cohen, *Policy Making by Plebiscite,* 149–50.

16. Mueller, "Reason and Caprice," 157–85.

17. Gregg, *Newspaper Endorsements,* 23; and idem, *Editorial Endorsements,* 11.

18. Baker, "Reapportionment by Initiative in Oregon," 518.

19. Henderson and Rosenbaum, "Prospects for Consolidating Local Government," 695.

20. Baker, "Reapportionment by Initiative in Oregon," 518.

21. Sapolsky, "The Fluoridation Controversy," 245–46.

22. Hoffman and Ferguson, "Voting Behavior," 772.

23. Levin and Eden, "Political Strategy for the Alienated Voter," 50.

24. Levin, *The Alienated Voter,* 58.

25. In addition to Levin and Eden, "Political Strategy for the Alienated Voter," 50, see Nettler, "A Measure of Alienation"; Horton and Thompson, "Powerlessness and Political Negativism"; McDill and Ridley, "Status, Anomia, Political Alienation and Political Participation"; and Templeton, "Alienation and Political Participation."

26. Citrin et al., "Personal and Political Sources of Political Alienation," 2–3.

27. For example, see Boskoff and Zeigler, *Voting Patterns in a Local Election,* 17.

28. Senate Subcommittee on the Constitution, *Voter Initiative Constitutional Amendment,* 7.

29. Ibid., 190–92.

30. The alienated and distrustful were twice as likely to view propositions as making no difference in their control over government. (Twenty-three percent of the very trusting/nonalienated said propositions would make no difference, which was nearly half; 47 percent of the alienated/distrustful gave that response.)

31. Levin and Eden, "Political Strategy for the Alienated Voter," 50; Horton and Thompson, "Powerlessness and Political Negativism"; McDill and Ridley, "Status, Anomia, Political Alienation and Political Participation"; Nettler, "A Measure of Alienation"; Thompson and Horton, "Political Alienation as a Force in Political Action"; Coleman, *Community Conflict;* and Templeton, "Alienation and Political Participation."

32. Horton and Thompson, "Powerlessness and Political Negativism," 485.

33. Ibid., 489.

34. Wright, "Alienation and Political Negativism," 114–15, emphasis added.

35. Stone, "Local Referendums," 214.

36. Sapolsky, "The Fluoridation Controversy."

37. Boskoff and Zeigler, *Voting Patterns in a Local Election,* 17.

38. Stone, "Local Referendums," 216. Some studies contain no independent empirical validation of the alienation-negativism linkage. Of those with evidence, Nettler's 1959 study is among the weakest. His conclusions that among the alienated "there is a strong proclivity" for "voting against" are based on "37 known alienated individuals" (Nettler, "A Measure of Alienation," 670–77).

39. Clubb and Traugott, "National Patterns of Referenda Voting," 167; Shepard, "Participation in Local Policy Making"; Stone, "Local Referendums," 219–28; and Wright, "Alienation and Political Negativism, 125.

40. Mueller, "Reason and Caprice," 157.

Chapter 9

1. The focus of one of the key works in the voting behavior field was "how voters come to vote as they do" (see Berelson, Lazarsfeld, and McPhee, *Voting,* vii). The second key work in the field sought to "account for variation in whether a given individual voter is going to vote and which candidate he will choose" (see Campbell et al., *The American Voter,* 19).

2. In the CBS News election night coverage on November 7, 1978, Walter Cronkite and Leslie Stahl predicted that the California anti-homosexual initiative would be defeated. Cronkite then said, "In other words, that is a pro-homosexual rights vote." To which Stahl replied, "Correct" (tape provided by the Television News Archives, Vanderbilt University, Nashville, Tennessee).

3. For a discussion of the problem of nonattitude responses see Converse, "The Nature of Belief Systems in Mass Publics."

4. My analysis of changing patterns of voting intention is not a study of the changes experienced by any single individual or group of individuals but a comparison of representative samples of all voters taken at several points in time. Thus, being measured here are changes in voting intentions among the population of intended voters. To study change in individual voting intentions would require panel data, which unfortunately do not exist.

5. See Plaut, "Voting Behavior on a Fluoridation Referendum"; Bowman, Ippolito, and Levin, "Self Interest and Referendum Support"; and Wolfinger and Greenstein, "Repeal of Fair Housing in California."

6. Hamilton and Cohen, *Policy Making by Plebiscite,* 181.

7. Alford, "The Role of Social Class in American Voting Behavior," 184–85.

8. Blume, "Open Housing Referenda"; Hamilton, "Direct Legislation"; Hahn, "Northern

Referenda on Fair Housing"; and Wolfinger and Greenstein, "Repeal of Fair Housing in California."

9. Wilson and Banfield, *City Politics,* 76–77; Hamilton, "Political Ethos"; idem, "Direct Legislation," 130–31; and Wolfinger and Field, "Political Ethos and the Structure of City Government."

10. Dalton and Reich, "Florida Statewide Survey"; Florida State University Policy Science Program, Preliminary Reports, November 1978; and Dalton, "Direct Participation."

11. Some of the independent variables correlated highly with the vote on one particular proposition but not on others. For instance, being a public employee was related to voting on Proposition 13, the property-tax initiative, but not to voting on most other propositions for which I had data.

12. Voters are not different from decisionmakers in other contexts. For example, Herbert Simon has persuasively argued that administrative decision making is a matter of "satisficing," finding an alternative that is good enough, rather than maximizing, selecting the best alternative from all available options (Simon, *Administrative Behavior,* XXV).

13. Wolfinger and Greenstein, *Repeal of Fair Housing in California,* 766.

14. Ordinary least squares (o.l.s.) regression analysis with a dichotomous dependent variable may result in standard errors that are slightly erroneous. I am reporting the o.l.s. estimates rather than the logit estimates because they are more easily analyzed and explained.

CHAPTER 10

1. James Bryce saw the development of a constitutional initiative as one of the most problematic aspects of direct legislation. Continuously subjecting changes in the Constitution to a popular vote would mean the loss of one of the important characteristics of constitutions — permanence (see Bryce, *The American Commonwealth,* 1:454–55).

2. Two excellent discussions of this form of democracy can be found in Schumpeter, *Capitalism, Socialism, and Democracy;* and Dahl, A Preface to Democratic Theory, 4–33.

3. See Baker, "American Conceptions of Direct vis-à-vis Representative Governance," 16; Bone, *The Initiative and the Referendum,* 5; Key and Crouch, *The Initiative and Referendum in California,* 555; and Eugene C. Lee, "California," in Butler and Ranney, *Referendums,* 98.

4. The literature on state legislative responsiveness to constituency concerns is summarized by Fred R. Harris and Paul L. Hain: "Legislators do substantively represent dominant constituent opinion reasonably well" (Harris and Hain, *America's Legislative Process,* 139). See also Patterson, Hedlund, and Boynton, *Representatives and Represented,* 138–54.

5. For an excellent description of some of the inconsistencies in American public opinion see Ladd, "What the Voters Really Want," 40–44, 46, 48.

6. For a more complete discussion of the intensity problem see Kendall and Carey, "The 'Intensity' Problem and Democratic Theory."

7. Bell, "The Referendum," 19–20.

8. Butler and Kitzinger, *The 1975 Referendum,* 279–89.

9. See Nuechterlein, "The Demise of Canada's Confederation"; and Jones and Wilford, "Further Considerations on the Referendum."

10. Adrian and Press, *Governing Urban America,* 163.

11. Bryce, *The American Commonwealth,* 1:455.

12. James Madison, no. 10, in Fairfield, *The Federalist Papers,* 21.

13. For an analysis of the U.S. Senate open-meeting provisions see "Committees Opened 93% of 1975 Meetings"; see also Statler, "Let the Sunshine In?"; and Binderglass, "New Jersey's Open Meetings Act."

14. Boyle, *The Initiative and Referendum,* 19.

15. Wilcox, *Government by All the People,* 95–96.

16. Senator Pressler was a cosponsor of Senate Joint Resolution 33, "Joint Resolution Proposing an Amendment to the Constitution of the United States with Respect to the Proposal

and the Enactment of Laws by Popular Vote of the People of the United States," 96th Cong. 1979/80.

17. Senate Subcommittee on the Constitution, *Voter Initiative Constitutional Amendment*, 6–8, 90–102.

18. Austin Ranney, "The United States of America," in Butler and Ranney, *Referendums*, 85.

19. See La Palombara and Hagen, "Direct Legislation"; and Lee, "California," 97–120.

20. Ranney, "The United States of America," 84.

21. Bell, "The Referendum," 28.

Appendix D

1. Herbert Spencer, "Philosophy of Style," *Westminster Review* 58 (1852): 317–459.

2. Rudolf Flesch, *The Art of Readable Writing* (New York: Harper and Brothers Publishers, 1943).

3. William A. McCall and Lelah M. Crabb, *Standard Test Lessons in Reading* (New York: Bureau of Publications, Teachers College, Columbia University, 1925).

4. George R. Klare, "Assessing Readability," *Reading Research Quarterly* 10 (1974/75): 69.

5. For a treatment of the Dale-Chall formula, the Extended Fry graph, and readability assessment generally see Colin Harrison, *Readability in the Classroom* (Cambridge: Cambridge University Press, 1980).

6. Albert J. Harris and Milton D. Jacobson, *Basic Elementary Reading Vocabularies* (New York: Macmillan, 1972).

Bibliography

Achen, Christopher H. "Mass Political Attitudes and the Survey Response." *American Political Science Review* 69 (December 1975): 1218–31.

_____. "Measuring Representation: Perils of the Correlation Coefficient." *American Journal of Political Science* 21 (November 1977): 805–15.

Adrian, Charles R. "Some General Characteristics of Nonpartisan Elections." *American Political Science Review* 46 (1952): 766–76. Later revised and published in *Democracy in Urban America,* edited by Oliver P. Williams and Charles Press, 251–63. Chicago: Rand McNally, 1961.

_____. "A Typology for Nonpartisan Elections." *Western Political Quarterly* 12 (1959): 449–58.

Adrian, Charles R., and Press, Charles. *Governing Urban America.* 4th ed. New York: McGraw-Hill, 1972.

Aikin, Charles. "The Initiative, the Referendum, and Representative Government." Paper presented to the International Political Science Association, Jablonna Round Table Meeting, September 1966.

Alford, Robert R. "The Role of Social Class in American Voting Behavior." *Western Political Quarterly* 16 (March 1963): 180–95.

Allen, Ronald J. "The National Initiative Proposal: A Preliminary Analysis." *Nebraska Law Review* 58 (1979): 965–1052.

Almond, Gabriel A., and Verba, Sidney. *The Civic Culture.* Princeton: Princeton University Press, 1963.

Anderson, Dennis M. "Voting and Misvoting on the Ohio Election Day Registration Referendum." Paper presented to the Ohio Association of Economists and Political Scientists, Worthington, Ohio, 10 March 1979.

Anderson, Dewey. *California State Government.* Stanford: Stanford University Press, 1942.

Anderson, Jack. "Tax Revolt: The Opening of U.S.-Wide Movement." *Deseret News,* 13 June 1978, A3.

Anderson, Totten J., and Lee, Eugene C. "The 1962 Election in California." *Western Political Quarterly* 16 (June 1963): 396–420.

Arsenau, Robert B., and Wolfinger, Raymond E. "Voting Behavior in Congressional

Elections." Paper delivered at the annual meeting of the American Political Science Association, New Orleans, 2–5 September 1973.

Atkin, Charles K.; Bowen, Lawrence; Nayman, Oguz B.; and Sheinkopf, Kenneth G. "Quality versus Quantity in Televised Political Ads." *Public Opinion Quarterly* 37 (Summer 1973): 209–24.

Atkin, Charles, and Held, Gary. "Effects of Political Advertising." *Public Opinion Quarterly* 40 (Summer 1976): 216–28.

Baer, Michael A., and Jaros, Dean. "Participation as Instrument and Expression: Some Evidence from the States." *American Journal of Political Science* 18 (May 1974): 365–83.

Bain, Herbert M., and Hancock, Donald S. *Ballot Position and Voter's Choice.* Detroit: Wayne State University Press, 1957.

Baker, Gordon E. "American Conceptions of Direct vis-à-vis Representative Governance." *Claremont Journal of Public Affairs* 4 (Spring 1977): 5–18.

_____. "Judicial Review of Statewide Initiatives in California: Proposition 13 in Recent Historical Perspective." Paper presented at the annual meeting of the American Political Science Association, New York City, 31 August–3 September 1978.

_____. "Reapportionment by Initiative in Oregon." *Western Political Quarterly* 13 (June 1960): 508–19.

Ballew, Steven E. "The Constitutionality of Budgeting by Statewide Statutory Initiative in California." *Southern California Law Review* 51 (July 1978): 847–75.

Balmer, Donald G. *State Election Services in Oregon.* Princeton: Citizens' Research Foundation, 1972.

Barnett, James D. "Judicial Review of Exceptions from the Referendum." *California Law Review* 10 (July 1922): 371–83.

_____. *The Operation of the Initiative, Referendum and Recall in Oregon.* New York: Macmillan Co., 1915.

Baus, Herbert M., and Ross, William B. *Politics Battle Plan.* New York: Macmillan Co., 1968.

Beard, Charles A., and Schultz, Birl E. *Documents on the State-Wide Initiative, Referendum and Recall.* New York: Macmillan Co., 1912.

Becker, Ted, and Slaton, Christa. "Hawaii Televote: Measuring Public Opinion on Complex Policy Issues." Paper presented at the American Political Science Association meetings, Washington, D.C., 29 August 1980.

Beer, Samuel H. "In Search of a New Public Philosophy." In *The New American Political System,* edited by Anthony King, 5–44. Washington, D.C.: American Enterprise Institute, 1978.

Bell, Derrick A., Jr. "The Referendum: Democracy's Barrier to Racial Equality." *Washington Law Review* 54 (1978): 1–29.

Benedict, Robert C. "A Test of the Direct Legislation Process: The Presence of an Informed Voter?" *The Social Science Journal* 17 (October 1980): 21–39.

_____. "Some Aspects of the Direct Legislation Process in Washington State: Theory and Practice." Ph.D. diss., University of Washington, 1975.

Benedict, Robert; Bone, Hugh; Laveal, Willard; and Rice, Ross. "The Voters and Attitudes toward Nuclear Power: A Comparative Study of 'Nuclear Moratorium' Initiatives." 1979. Mimeo.

Bennett, Stephen E., and Klecka, William R. "Social Status and Political Participation: A Multivariate Analysis of Predictive Power." *Midwest Journal of Political Science* 14 (August 1970): 355–82.

Berelson, Bernard R. "Democratic Theory and Public Opinion." *Public Opinion Quarterly* 16 (Fall 1952): 313–30.

Berelson, Bernard R.; Lazarsfeld, Paul F.; and McPhee, William N. *Voting: A Study of Opinion Formation in a Presidential Campaign.* Chicago: University of Chicago Press, 1954.

Berg, Larry. "The Initiative Process and Public Policy-Making in the States: 1904–1976." Paper presented at the annual meeting of the American Political Science Association, New York City, 31 August–3 September 1978.

Bethell, Tom. "The Changing Fashions of Liberalism." *Public Opinion* 2 (January/February 1979): 41–46.

Bicker, William E. "The Vote on Proposition 2 – A Post-Election Study, November, 1972." University of California, Berkeley. Mimeo, 15 December 1972.

Binderglass, Richard J. "New Jersey's Open Meeting Act: Has Five Years Brought 'Sunshine' over the Garden State?" *Rutgers Law Journal* 12 (Spring 1981): 561–83.

Black, J. William. "Maine's Experience with the Initiative and Referendum." *Annals of the American Academy of Political and Social Science* 43 (September 1912): 159–78.

Blake, Robert R.; Mouton, Jane S.; and Hain, Jack D. "Social Forces in Petition Signing." *Southwestern Social Science Quarterly* 37 (March 1956): 385–90.

Blank, Robert H. "Socio-Economic Determinism of Voting Turnout: A Challenge." *Journal of Politics* 36 (August 1974): 731–52.

_____. "State Electoral Structure." *Journal of Politics* 35 (1973): 988–94.

Blume, Norman. "Open Housing Referenda." *Public Opinion Quarterly* 35 (Winter 1971/1972): 563–70.

Bognador, Vernor. "Referendums and Separatism." Paper presented at the Conference on Referendums, Ditchley Park, England, 26–28 October 1979.

Bolt, Ernest C., Jr. *Ballots before Bullets: The War Referendum Approach to Peace in America, 1914–1941.* Charlottesville: University Press of Virginia, 1977.

Bone, Hugh A. *The Initiative and the Referendum.* New York: National Municipal League, State Constitutional Studies Project, May 1975.

_____. "The Initiative in Washington: 1914–74." *Washington Public Policy Notes* 2 (October 1974).

_____. "Open Government by Initiative: Notes on Washington's Experience." *Policy Studies Journal* 2 (Summer 1974): 257–61.

_____. "Washington's Open Government: A Look at Initiative 276." *National Civic Review* 65 (October 1976): 437–45.

Bone, Hugh A., and Benedict, Robert C. "Perspectives on Direct Legislation: Washington State's Experience, 1914–1973." *Western Political Quarterly* 28 (June 1975): 330–52.

Boskoff, Alvin, and Zeigler, Harmon. *Voting Patterns in a Local Election.* New York: J. B. Lippincott Co., 1964.

Boss, Michael. "Revolution or Choice? The Political Economy of School Financial Referenda." *Western Political Quarterly* 29 (March 1976): 75–86.

Bourne, Jonathan, Jr. "Functions of the Initiative, Referendum and Recall."

Annals of the American Academy of Political and Social Science 43 (September 1912): 3-16.

Bowman, Lewis; Ippolito, Dennis; and Levin, Martin. "Self-Interest and Referendum Support: The Case of a Rapid Transit Vote in Atlanta." In *People and Politics in Urban Society,* edited by Harlan Hahn, 119-36. Beverly Hills: Sage Publications, 1972.

Boyle, James. *The Initiative and Referendum.* 2d ed. Columbus, Ohio: A. H. Smythe, 1912.

Boynton, G. R.; Patterson, Samuel C.; and Hedlund, Ronald D. "The Missing Links in Legislative Politics: Attentive Constituents." *Journal of Politics* 31 (August 1969): 700-721.

_____. "The Structure of Public Support for Legislative Institutions." *Midwest Journal of Political Science* 12 (May 1968): 163-80.

Brady, David W. *Congressional Voting in a Partisan Era.* Lawrence: University Press of Kansas, 1973.

Brestoff, Nick. "The California Initiative Process: A Suggestion for Reform." *Southern California Law Review* 48 (1975): 922-58.

Brody, Richard A. "North, South, East, and West, It's Prop. 13 We Love . . . : The Jarvis-Gann Initiative in the Counties of California." Stanford University, October 1978.

Bryce, James. *The American Commonwealth.* 2 vols. New York: Macmillan Co., 1889.

_____. *Modern Democracy.* 2 vols. New York: Macmillan Co., 1921.

Budgor, Joel; Capell, Elizabeth A.; Flanders, David A.; Polsby, Nelson W.; Westlye, Mark C.; and Zaller, John. "The 1896 Election and Congressional Modernization: An Appraisal of the Evidence." *Social Science History* 5 (February 1981): 53-90.

Buenker, John D. "The Progressive Era: A Search for a Synthesis." *Mid America* 51 (July 1969): 175-93.

Burdick, Eugene, and Brodbeck, Arthur J., eds. *American Voting Behavior.* Westport, Conn.: Greenwood Press, Publishers, 1959.

Burnham, Walter Dean. "The Changing Shape of the American Political Universe." *American Political Science Review* 59 (March 1965): 7-28.

Burns, Richard Dean, and Dixon, W. Addams. "Foreign Policy and the 'Democratic Myth': The Debate on the Ludlow Amendment." *Mid America* 47 (October 1965): 288-306.

Butler, David. "A Framework for U.K. Referendums." Paper presented at the Hansard Society Conference on Ground Rules for National Referendums in Great Britain, Nuffield College, Oxford, 3 July 1980.

Butler, David, and Kitzinger, Uwe. *The 1975 Referendum.* New York: St. Martin's Press, 1976.

Butler, David, and Ranney, Austin. *Referendums: A Comparative Study of Practice and Theory.* Washington, D.C.: American Enterprise Institute, 1978.

California Fair Political Practices Commission. *Campaign Contribution and Spending Report.* Sacramento, 1978.

_____. *Campaign Costs: How Much Have They Increased and Why? A Study of State Elections, 1958-1978.* Sacramento, 1980.

California General Assembly, Committee on Elections and Reapportionment. *Public Hearing on Initiative Process.* 10 October 1972.

California State Legislature. Assembly Interim Committee on Constitutional Amendments, *Background Study on the Initiative.* November 1965. Part II. 13 December 1965.

_____. *Hearings before the Full Committee,* 13-14 December 1965.

"California's Low-Income Housing Referendum: Equal Protection and the Problem of Economic Discrimination." *Columbia Journal of Law and Social Problems* 8 (1972): 135-55.

Campbell, Angus. "A Classification of Presidential Elections." In *Elections and the Political Order,* edited by Angus Campbell, Philip E. Converse, Warren E. Miller, and Donald E. Stokes, 63-77. New York: John Wiley and Sons, 1966.

_____. "Surge and Decline: A Study of Electoral Change." In *Elections and the Political Order,* edited by Angus Campbell, Philip E. Converse, Warren E. Miller, and Donald E. Stokes, 40-62. New York: John Wiley and Sons, 1966.

Campbell, Angus; Converse, Philip E.; Miller, Warren E.; and Stokes, Donald E. *The American Voter.* New York: John Wiley and Sons, 1960.

Campbell, Angus; Gurin, Gerald; and Miller, Warren E. "Political Issues and the Vote: November, 1952." *American Political Science Review* 47 (June 1953): 359-85.

Campbell, Bruce A. *The American Electorate: Attitudes and Action.* New York: Holt, Rinehart, and Winston, 1979.

Campbell, Donald. "Computational Criteria for Voting Systems." *British Journal of Political Science* 7 (1977): 85-98.

Carlsen, William. "Top Court OKs Prop 13 Tax Loophole." *San Francisco Chronicle,* 11 May 1982, 1.

Carrisoza, Phillip. "High Court Oks L.A. Transit Tax, Narrows Prop. 13." *Los Angeles Daily Journal,* 3 May 1982, 1, 13.

"Casino Petitions Voided: Backers Practiced Flagrant Fraud, Buchanan Says." *Rocky Mountain News,* 11 September 1982, 1.

Casstevens, Thomas W. "Reflections on the Initiative Process in California State Politics." *Public Affairs Report* 6 (February 1965).

Caster, Lauren J. "Referendum: The Appropriations Exception in Nebraska." *Nebraska Law Review* 54 (1975): 393-404.

Christenson, Reo M. "The Power of the Press: The Case of 'The Toledo Blade.'" *Midwest Journal of Political Science* 3 (August 1959): 227-40.

Citrin, Jack. "Comment: Political Issue and Trust in Government." *American Political Science Review* 68 (September 1974): 973-89.

Citrin, Jack; McClosky, Herbert; Shanks, J. Merrill; and Sniderman, Paul M. "Personal and Political Sources of Political Alienation." *British Journal of Political Science* 5 (1975): 1-31.

Claude, Richard. "Supreme Court Policy-Making and Electoral Reform." *Policy Studies Journal* 2 (Summer 1974): 261-66.

Clausen, Aage R. "Response Validity: Vote Report." *Public Opinion Quarterly* 32 (Winter 1968/69): 588-606.

Clubb, Jerome M., and Traugott, Michael W. "National Patterns of Referenda Voting: The 1968 Election." In *People and Politics in Urban Society,* edited by Harlan Hahn, 137-69. Beverly Hills: Sage Publications, 1972.

Coleman, James S. *Community Conflict.* New York: Free Press, 1957.

"Committees Opened 93% of 1975 Meetings." *Congressional Quarterly Weekly Report* 34 (24 January 1976): 152-55.

Commons, John Rogers. "Direct Legislation in Switzerland and America." *Arena* 22 (December 1899): 725-39.

_____. "Referendum and Initiatives in City Government." *Political Science Quarterly* 17 (December 1902): 609–30.

Commonwealth of Virginia, Division of Legislative Services. *Minutes of Joint Subcommittee Studying Adoption of Initiative and Referendum.* 19 October 1979.

"Conservative Cry: 'Our Time Has Come.'" *U.S. News & World Report,* 26 February 1979, 52.

"The Constitutionality of Municipal Advocacy in Statewide Referendum Campaigns." *Harvard Law Review* 93 (1980): 535–63.

Converse, Philip E. "Attitudes and Non-Attitudes: Continuation of a Dialogue." In *The Quantitative Analysis of Social Problems,* edited by Edward R. Tufte. Reading, Mass.: Addison-Wesley, 1970.

_____. "Information Flow and the Stability of Partisan Attitudes." *Public Opinion Quarterly* 26 (Winter 1962/63): 578–99.

_____. "The Nature of Belief Systems in Mass Publics." In *Ideology and Discontent,* edited by David E. Apter, 206–61. New York: Free Press, 1964.

Converse, Philip E., and Markus, Gregory B. "Plus ça change . . . : The New C.P.S. Election Study Panel." *American Political Science Review* 73 (March 1979): 32–49.

Converse, Philip E.; Miller, Warren E.; Rusk, Jerrold G.; and Wolfe, Arthur C. "Continuity and Change in American Politics: Parties and Issues in the 1968 Election." *American Political Science Review* 63 (December 1969): 1083–1105.

Conway, M. Margaret. "Voter Information Sources in a Nonpartisan Local Election." *Western Political Quarterly* 21 (March 1968): 69–78.

Cover, Albert. "The Constitutionality of Campaign Expenditure Ceilings." *Policy Studies Journal* 2 (Summer 1974): 267–73.

Crain, Robert L. "Fluoridation: The Diffusion of an Innovation among Cities." *Social Forces* 44 (June 1966): 467–76.

Crain, Robert L., and Rosenthal, Donald B. "Structure and Values in Local Political Systems: The Case of Fluoridation Decision." *Journal of Politics* 28 (February 1966): 169–95.

Crane, Wilder W., Jr. "Do Representatives Represent?" *Journal of Politics* 22 (May 1960): 295–99.

Crouch, Winston W. "The Constitutional Initiative in Operation." *American Political Science Review* 33 (August 1939): 634–45.

_____. *The Initiative and Referendum in California.* Los Angeles. Haynes Foundation, 1938.

_____. "Municipal Affairs: The Initiative and Referendum in Cities." *American Political Science Review* 37 (June 1945): 491–504.

Crozier, Brian. *The Minimum State: Beyond Party Politics.* London: Hamish Hamilton, 1979.

Curry, Bill. "Miami Area Voting on Near-Wipeout of Property Tax." *Washington Post,* 19 September 1979, A-3.

Cyr, A. Bruce. "The Calculus of Voting Reconsidered." *Public Opinion Quarterly* 39 (Spring 1975): 19–38.

_____. "Further Reflections on 'the Elitist Theory of Democracy.'" *American Political Science Review* 60 (June 1966): 296–97.

Dahl, Robert A. "On Removing Certain Impediments to Democracy in the United States." *Political Science Quarterly* 92 (Spring 1977): 1–20.

_____. *A Preface to Democratic Theory.* Chicago: University of Chicago Press, 1956.

Dahl, Robert A., and Tufte, Edward R. *Size and Democracy.* Stanford: Stanford University Press, 1973.

Dalton, Russell J. "Direct Participation: Constitutional Revision in Florida." Florida State University, September 1979.

Dalton, Russell J., and Reich, Anneliese. "Florida Statewide Survey." Policy Science Program, Florida State University.

Davis, James. *Presidential Primaries: Road to the White House.* New York: Thomas Y. Crowell Co., 1967.

Dawson, Paul A., and Zinser, James E. "Broadcast Expenditures and Electoral Outcomes in the 1970 Congressional Elections." *Public Opinion Quarterly* 35 (Fall 1971): 398–402.

_____. "Political Finance and Participation in Congressional Elections." *Annals of the American Academy of Political and Social Science* 425 (May 1976): 59–73.

DeBow, Ken. "Tilting at the Windmill of Special Interest Lobbying Power: The Case of California under Proposition Nine." Paper presented at the Western Political Science Association meetings, Portland, Oregon, 22–24 March 1979.

Dennis, Jack. "Support for the Institution of Elections by the Mass Public." *American Political Science Review* 64 (September 1970): 819–35.

DeWitt, Benjamin Parke. *The Progressive Movement.* New York: Macmillan Co., 1915.

Diamond, Roger J.; diDonato, Peter R.; Marley, Patrick J.; and Tubert, Patricia V. "California's Political Reform Act: Greater Access to the Initiative Process." *Southwestern University Law Review* 7 (Fall 1975): 553–61.

Dirck, Joe. "Bush Refuses to Concede Nomination to Reagan." *Columbus Citizen Journal,* 22 May 1980, 1.

Dixon, Warren. "Party Identification and the Party Vote: A Suggested Model." *Social Science Quarterly* 51 (December 1970): 706–14.

Dodd, W. F. "Some Considerations upon the State-Wide Initiative and Referendum." *Annals of the American Academy of Political and Social Science* 43 (September 1912): 203–15.

Downs, Anthony. *An Economic Theory of Democracy.* New York: Harper and Row, 1957.

Dreyer, Edward C. "Media Use and Electoral Choices: Some Political Consequences of Information Exposure." *Public Opinion Quarterly* 35 (Winter 1971/72): 544–53.

Dzublenski, Joe. "The Continuing Campaign to Inhibit the Initiative." *California Journal* 7 (August 1976): 280–81.

Eaton, Allen H. *The Oregon System: The Story of Direct Legislation in Oregon.* Chicago: A. C. McClurg and Co., 1912.

Eckhardt, K. W., and Hendershot, G. "Transformation of Alienation into Public Opinion." *Sociological Quarterly* 8 (Autumn 1967): 459–67.

Erikson, Robert S.; Luttbeg, Norman R.; and Holloway, William V. "Knowing One's District: How Legislators Predict Referendum Voting." *American Journal of Political Science* 19 (May 1975): 231–46.

Erskine, Hazel Gaudet. "The Polls: The Informed Public." *Public Opinion Quarterly* 26 (Winter 1962/63): 669–77.

_____. "The Polls: Textbook Knowledge." *Public Opinion Quarterly* 28 (Spring 1963): 139.

Eu, March Fong. "A History of the California Initiative Process." Sacramento: State of California, 1979. Photocopy.

Everson, David H. "Initiatives and Voter Turnout: The Case of 1978." Paper presented at the annual meeting of the Southwestern Political Science Association, Houston, Texas, 2-5 April 1980.

_____. "Initiatives and Voter Turnout: A Comparative State Analysis." Springfield: Illinois Legislative Studies Center, Sangamon State University, March 1980.

_____. "The Effects of Initiatives on Voter Turnout: A Comparative State Analysis." *Western Political Quarterly* 34 (September 1981): 415-25.

Ewing, Cortez A. M. "Primaries as Real Elections." *Southwestern Social Science Quarterly* 29 (March 1949): 294-95.

Fairfield, Roy P., ed. *The Federalist Papers.* 2d ed. Baltimore: Johns Hopkins University Press, 1981.

Fairlie, Henry. "The Unfiltered Voice: The Dangerous Revival of the Referendum." *New Republic,* 24 June 1978, 16-17.

Fairlie, John A. "The Referendum and Initiative in Michigan." *Annals of the American Academy of Political and Social Science* 43 (September 1912): 146-58.

Finifter, Ada W. "Dimensions of Political Alienation." *American Political Science Review* 64 (June 1970): 389-410.

Fiorina, Morris P. "The Decline of Collective Responsibility in American Politics." *Daedalus* 109 (Summer 1980): 25-45.

Fitzgerald, Maureen S. "Computer Democracy." *California Journal* 11 (June 1980): 1-15.

_____. "Initiative Fever: Many Try, but Few Reach the Ballot." *California Journal* 10 (December 1979): 433-34.

Flanigan, Michael. "The Initiative Process in Contemporary America: A Critical Review." Paper presented at the 1981 National Seminar, National Center for Initiative Review, Denver, Colorado, 6 November 1981.

Flanigan, William H. and Zingale, Nancy H. *Political Behavior of the American Electorate.* 4th ed. Boston: Allyn and Bacon, 1979.

Friedman, Gordon David. "Issues, Partisanship and Political Subcultures: A Study of Voting in Statewide Referenda in New Jersey, 1944-1966." Ph.D. diss., University of North Carolina, 1971.

Friedrich, Carl J. *Constitutional Government and Democracy: Theory and Practice in Europe and America.* 4th ed. Waltham, Mass.: Blaisdell Publishing Co., 1968.

Fromson, Jeffrey E. "Referendums and Judicial Intervention." *Ohio State Law Journal* 30 (1969): 189-201.

Galbreath, C. B. "Provisions for State-Wide Initiative and Referendum." *Annals of the American Academy of Political and Social Science* 43 (September 1912): 81-109.

Gallup, George, "National Initiative Favored." *San Francisco Chronicle,* 15 May 1978, 10.

Gamm, Larry. "Voter Education and Participation: Pennsylvania Local Referenda." *National Civic Review* 65 (February 1976): 75-82.

Gamson, William A. "The Fluoridation Dialogue: Is It an Ideological Conflict?" *Public Opinion Quarterly* 25 (Winter 1961/62): 526-37.

Gans, Curtis B. "Conservatism By Default." *Nation,* 14 October 1978, 372-74.

Gazey, Penelope J. "Direct Democracy—A Study of the American Referendum." *Parliamentary Affairs* 24 (Spring 1971): 123-39.

Gilbert, Charles E. "Some Aspects of Nonpartisan Elections in Large Cities." *Midwest Journal of Political Science* 6 (1962): 345-62.

Giles, Michael; Gatlin, Douglas; and Cataldo, Everett. "Parental Support for School Referenda." *Journal of Politics* 38 (1976): 442-51.

Ginsberg, Benjamin. "Elections and Public Policy." *American Political Science Review* 70 (March 1976): 41-50.

Glantz, Stanton A.; Abramowitz, Alan I.; and Burkhart, Michael P. "Election Outcomes: Whose Money Matters?" *Journal of Politics* 38 (1976): 1033-38.

Glaser, William A. "Television and Voting Turnout." *Public Opinion Quarterly* 29 (Spring 1965): 71-86.

Godwin, R. Kenneth, and Shepard, W. Bruce. "Political Processes and Public Expenditures: A Re-examination Based on Theories of Representative Government." *American Political Science Review* 70 (December 1976): 1127-36.

Goldberg, Arthur S. "Discerning A Causal Pattern among Data on Voting Behavior." *American Political Science Review* 60 (December 1966): 913-23.

_____. "Social Determinism and Rationality as Bases of Party Identification." *American Political Science Review* 63 (March 1969): 5-25.

Goodhart, Philip. *Referendum*. London: Tom Stacy, 1971.

Goodman, Jay S.; Arseneau, Robert; Cornwell, Elmer E., Jr.; and Swanson, Wayne R. "Public Responses to State Constitutional Revision." *American Journal of Political Science* 17 (June 1972): 571-96.

Goodman, Leo A. "Some Alternatives to Ecological Correlation." *American Journal of Sociology* 64 (May 1959): 610-25.

Graham, Virginia. *A Compilation of Statewide Initiative Proposals Appearing on Ballots through 1976*. Washington, D.C.: Congressional Research Service, Library of Congress, 1978.

Gray, Virginia. "A Note on Competition and Turnout in the American States." *Journal of Politics* 38 (1976): 153-58.

Greenberg, Donald S. "The Scope of the Initiative and Referendum in California." *California Law Review* 54 (1966): 1717-48.

Gregg, James E. *Editorial Endorsements: Influence in Ballot Measures*. Davis: University of California, Institute of Governmental Affairs, 1970.

_____. *Newspaper Endorsements and Local Elections in California*. Davis: University of California, Institute of Governmental Affairs, 1966.

Griffin, Kenyon N., and Horan, Michael J. "Merit Retention Elections: What Influences the Voters?" *Judicature* 64 (August 1979): 78-88.

Griffiths, A. Phillips, and Wollheim, Richard. "How Can One Person Represent Another?" *Aristotelian Society,* supp. vol. 34 (1960): 212.

Groth, Alexander J., and Schultz, Howard G. *Voter Attitudes on the 1976 California Nuclear Initiative*. Institute of Governmental Affairs Environmental Quality Series, no. 25. Davis: University of California, December 1976.

Gurr, Ted Robert. *Why Men Rebel*. Princeton: Princeton University Press, 1970.

Guthrie, George. "The Initiative, Referendum and Recall." *Annals of the American Academy of Political and Social Science* 43 (September 1912): 17-31.

Hager, Philip. "State High Court Oks County's Transit Tax." *Los Angeles Times,* 1 May 1982, IA-1.

Hahn, Gilbert, and Morton, Stephen C. "Initiative and Referendum – Do They Encourage or Impair Better State Government?" *Florida State University Law Review* 5 (1977): 925–50.

Hahn, Harlan. "Correlates of Public Sentiments about War: Local Referenda on the Vietnam Issue." *American Political Science Review* 64 (December 1970): 1186–99.

————. "Northern Referenda on Fair Housing: The Response of White Voters." *Western Political Quarterly* 21 (September 1968): 483–96.

Hahn, Harlan, and Almy, Timothy. "Ethnic Politics and Racial Issues: Voting in Los Angeles." *Western Political Quarterly* 24 (December 1971): 719–31.

Hall, John S., and Piele, Philip K. "Selected Determinants of Precinct Voting Decisions in School Budget Elections." *Western Political Quarterly* 29 (September 1976): 440–57.

Hamilton, Howard D. "Direct Legislation: Some Implications of Open Housing Referenda." *American Political Science Review* 64 (March 1970): 124–38.

————. "Political Ethos: The Evidence in Referenda Survey Data." *Ethnicity* 2 (1975): 81–98.

————. "Voting Behavior in Open Housing Referenda." *Social Science Quarterly* 51 (December 1970): 715–29.

Hamilton, Howard D., and Cohen, Sylvan H. *Policy Making by Plebiscite: School Referenda.* Lexington, Mass.: Lexington Books, 1974.

Harris, Fred R., and Hain, Paul L. *America's Legislative Process: Congress and the States.* Glenview, Ill.: Scott, Foresman and Co., 1983.

Harris, Joseph P. *California Politics.* 4th ed. San Francisco: Chandler Publishing Company, 1967.

Hatfield, Mark. "Direct Democracy Now." *Citizen Participation* 1 (November/December 1979): 5–6, 21.

Hawley, Willis D. *Nonpartisan Elections and the Case for Party Politics.* New York: John Wiley and Sons, 1973.

Hays, Samuel P. "The Politics of Reform in Municipal Government in the Progressive Era." *Pacific Northwest Quarterly* 55 (October 1964): 157–69.

Heard, Alexander. *The Costs of Democracy.* Chapel Hill: University of North Carolina Press, 1960.

Helson, Harry; Blake, Robert; and Mouton, Jane. "Petition-Signing as Adjustment to Situational and Personal Factors." *Journal of Social Psychology* 48 (1958): 3–10.

Henderson, Thomas A., and Rosenbaum, Walter A. "Prospects for Consolidating Local Government: The Role of Elites in Electoral Outcomes." *American Journal of Political Science* 17 (November 1973): 695–719.

Hennessy, Timothy M. "Problems in Concept Formation: The Ethos 'Theory' and the Comparative Study of Urban Politics." *Midwest Journal of Political Science* 14 (November 1970): 537–64.

Hensler, Deborah R., and Hensler, Carl. "Evaluating Nuclear Power: Voter Choice on the California Nuclear Initiative." Santa Monica, Calif.: Rand Corporation, 1979.

Hetrick, Carl C. "Policy Issues and the Electoral Process." *Western Political Quarterly* 25 (June 1972): 165–83.

Hichborn, Franklin. "Sources of Opposition to Direct Legislation in California." *The Commonwealth – Part II,* no. 25 (11 November 1931): 512–39.

Hicks, Robert E. "Influences on School Referenda in Ohio: Factors Affecting the Voting on Taxes and Bond Issues." *American Journal of Economics and Sociology* 31 (June 1972): 105–8.

Hoffman, Paul J., and Ferguson, Jenniellen W. "Voting Behavior: The Vote on the Francis Amendment in the 1962 California Election." *Western Political Quarterly* 17 (December 1964): 770–77.

Hofstadter, Richard. *The Age of Reform: From Bryan to F.D.R.* New York: Vintage Books, 1955.

Hollingsworth, Charles M. "The So-Called Progressive Movement: Its Real Nature, Causes and Significance." *Annals of the American Academy of Political and Social Science* 43 (September 1912): 32–48.

Horton, John E., and Thompson, Wayne E. "Powerlessness and Political Negativism: A Study of Defeated Local Referendums." *American Journal of Sociology* 67 (March 1962): 485–93.

Houghton, N. D. "Arizona's Experience with the Initiative and Referendum." *New Mexico Historical Review* 29 (July 1954): 183–209.

Hovland, Carl I., and Weiss, Walter. "The Influence of Source Credibility on Communication Effectiveness." *Public Opinion Quarterly* 15 (Winter 1951/52): 635–50.

Hyink, Bernard; Brown, Seyom; and Thacker, Ernest. *Politics and Government in California.* 9th ed. New York: Thomas Y. Crowell, 1975.

"Initiative Makes a Big Comeback as Groups Seek to Bypass the Legislature." *California Journal* 3 (August 1972): 229–33.

Ippolito, Dennis S., and Levin, Martin L. "Public-Regardingness, Race, and Social-Class: The Case of a Rapid Transit Referendum." *Social Science Quarterly* 51 (December 1970): 628–33.

"Is There a Parade?" *Nation,* 14 October 1978, 363–64.

Jacobson, Gary C. "The Effects of Campaign Spending in Congressional Elections." *American Political Science Review* 72 (June 1978): 469–92.

_____. "The Impact of Broadcast Campaigning on Electoral Outcomes." *Journal of Politics* 37 (August 1975): 769–93.

Jaffe, Alvin N. "The Constitutionality of Supermajority Voting Requirements: *Gordon v. Lance.*" *University of Illinois Law Forum,* 1971, 703–18.

Janowitz, Morris, and Miller, Warren E. "The Index of Political Predisposition in the 1948 Election." *Journal of Politics* 14 (November 1952): 710–27.

Jennings, M. Kent, and Zeigler, Harmon. "Class, Party, and Race in Four Types of Elections: The Case of Atlanta." *Journal of Politics* 28 (May 1966): 391–407.

_____. "The Salience of American State Politics." *American Political Science Review* 64 (June 1970): 523–35.

Johnson, Claudius. "The Initiative and Referendum in Washington." *Pacific Northwest Quarterly* 36 (January 1945): 29–62.

Johnson, Gerald W. "Research Note on Political Correlates of Voter Participation: A Deviant Case Analysis." *American Political Science Review* 65 (September 1971): 768–86.

Johnson, Lewis Jerome. "Direct Legislation as an Ally of Representative Government." In *The Initiative, Referendum and Recall,* edited by William Bennett Munro, 139–63. New York: D. Appleton and Co., 1912.

Jones, Barry, and Wilford, Rick. "Further Considerations on the Referendum: The

Evidence for the Welsh Vote on Devolution." *Political Studies* 30 (March 1982): 16-27.

Jones, Ruth S., and Jones, E. Terrence. "Issue Saliency, Opinion Holding, and Party Preference." *Western Political Quarterly* 24 (September 1971): 501-10.

Jordan, David James. "Constitution Constraints on Initiative and Referendum." *Vanderbilt Law Review* 32 (1979): 1143-66.

Katz, Elihu. "The Two-Step Flow of Communication: An Up-to-Date Report of an Hypothesis." *Public Opinion Quarterly* 21 (Spring 1957): 61-78.

Kaufman, Walter C., and Greer, Scott. "Voting in a Metropolitan Community: An Application of Social Area Analysis." *Social Forces* 38 (March 1960): 196-204.

Keefe, William J., and Ogul, Morris S. *The American Legislative Process: Congress and the States.* Englewood Cliffs: Prentice-Hall, 1964.

Keith, Bruce E.; Magleby, David B.; Nelson, Candice; Orr, Elizabeth; Westlye, Mark C.; and Wolfinger, Raymond E. *The Myth of the Independent Voter.* Washington, D.C.: American Enterprise Institute, forthcoming.

Kelley, Stanley, Jr. *Professional Public Relations and Political Power.* Baltimore: Johns Hopkins Press, 1956.

Kelley, Stanley, Jr.; Ayres, Richard E.; and Bowen, William G. "Registration and Voting: Putting First Things First." *American Political Science Review* 61 (June 1967): 359-79.

Kelley, Stanley, Jr., and Mirer, Thad W. "The Simple Act of Voting." *American Political Science Review* 68 (June 1974): 572-91.

Kemp, Jack. *An American Renaissance: A Strategy for the 1980s.* New York: Berkeley Publishing Corp., 1981.

Kendall, Willmoore, and Carey, George W. "The 'Intensity' Problem and Democratic Theory." *American Political Science Review* 62 (March 1968): 5-24.

Kessel, John H. *The Goldwater Coalition: Republican Strategies in 1964.* Indianapolis: Bobbs-Merrill Co., 1968.

Key, V. O., Jr. *American State Politics: An Introduction.* New York: Alfred A. Knopf, 1956.

———. "The Politically Relevant in Surveys." *Public Opinion Quarterly* 24 (Spring 1960): 54-61.

———. *Public Opinion and American Democracy.* New York: Alfred A. Knopf, 1965.

———. "Public Opinion and the Decay of Democracy." *Virginia Quarterly Review* 37 (Autumn 1961): 481-94.

———. *The Responsible Electorate.* New York: Vintage Books, 1966.

Key, V. O., Jr., and Crouch, Winston W. *The Initiative and Referendum in California.* Berkeley: University of California Press, 1939.

Key, V. O., Jr., and Munger, Frank. "Social Determinism and Electoral Decision: The Case of Indiana." In *American Voting Behavior,* edited by Eugene Burdick and Arthur Brodbeck. New York: Free Press, 1959.

Kilpatrick, James. "The Year of the Taxpayer." *San Francisco Chronicle,* 2 June 1978, 52.

Kim, Jae-on; Petrocik, John; and Enokson, Stephen. "Voter Turnout among the American States: Systemic and Individual Components." *American Political Science Review* 69 (March 1975): 107-24.

King, Anthony. *Britain Says Yes: The 1975 Referendum on the Common Market.* Washington, D.C.: American Enterprise Institute for Public Policy Research, 1977.

Kingdon, John W. "Opinion Leaders in the Electorate." *Public Opinion Quarterly* 34 (Summer 1970): 256–61.

Klapper, Joseph T. *The Effects of Mass Communications.* Glencoe, Ill.: Free Press, 1960.

Korda, Bob. "Masters of the 'Meta Message': Woodward and McDowell, Keepers of the Treasure Chest." *California Journal* 10 (May 1979): 159–61.

Kraft, Joseph. "Populist Hedonism." *Washington Post,* 11 June 1978, C7.

Kuttner, Robert. *Revolt of the Haves: Tax Rebellions and Hard Times.* New York: Simon and Schuster, 1980.

Lacy, Donald P., and Martin, Philip L. "The Extraordinary Majority: The Supreme Court's Retreat from Voting Equity." *California Western Law Review* 10 (1974): 551–89.

Ladd, Everett Carll, Jr. "What the Voters Really Want." *Fortune,* 18 December 1978, 40–48.

Lane, Robert E., and Sears, David O. *Public Opinion.* Englewood Cliffs: Prentice-Hall, 1964.

La Palombara, Joseph G. *The Initiative and Referendum in Oregon: 1938–1948.* Corvallis: Oregon State College Press, 1950.

La Palombara, Joseph, and Hagan, Charles. "Direct Legislation: An Appraisal and a Suggestion." *American Political Science Review* 45 (June 1951): 400–422.

LaPorte, Todd, and Metlay, Daniel. "They Watch and They Wonder: The Public's Attitudes toward Technology." Institute of Governmental Studies, Working Paper no. 6. University of California, Berkeley, February 1973.

Lazarsfeld, Paul; Berelson, Bernard; and Gaudet, Hazel. *The People's Choice: How the Voter Makes Up His Mind in a Presidential Campaign.* 3d ed. New York: Columbia University Press, 1968.

Lee, Eugene C. "The Initiative and Referendum: How California Has Fared." *National Civic Review* 68 (February 1979): 69–84.

———. *The Politics of Nonpartisanship.* Berkeley: University of California Press, 1960.

Lee, Eugene C., and Berg, Larry L. *The Challenge of California.* 2nd ed. Boston: Little, Brown, 1976.

Lengle, James I. *Representation and Presidential Primaries: The Democratic Party in the Post Reform Era.* Westport, Conn.: Greenwood Press, 1981.

Levin, Murray B. *The Alienated Voter: Politics in Boston.* New York: Holt, Rinehart, and Winston, 1960.

Levin, Murray B., and Eden, Murray. "Political Strategy for the Alienated Voter." *Public Opinion Quarterly* 26 (Spring 1962): 47–63.

Levy, Mickey. "Voting on California's Tax and Expenditures Limitations Initiative." *National Tax Journal* 28, no. 4 (December 1975).

Lewis, Anthony. "Fed Up." *San Francisco Chronicle,* 24 November 1978, 69.

"Limitations on Initiative and Referendum." *Stanford Law Review* 3 (April 1951): 497–509.

Lindenfeld, Frank. "Economic Interest and Political Involvement." *Public Opinion Quarterly* 28 (Spring 1964): 104–11.

Lindquist, John H. "Socioeconomic Status and Political Participation." *Western Political Quarterly* 11 (December 1964): 608–15.

Lineberry, Robert L., and Fowler, Edmund P. "Reformism and Public Policies in American Cities." *American Political Science Review* 61 (September 1967): 701–17.

Lipow, Arthur. "Plebiscitarian Politics and Progressivism: The Direct Democracy Movement." Paper prepared for the annual meeting, American Historical Association, December 1973.

Lippmann, Walter. *Public Opinion.* New York: Macmillan Co., 1949.

Lipset, Seymour Martin, and Raab, Earl. "The Message of Proposition 13." *Commentary,* September 1978, 42–46.

Lobingier, Charles Sumner. *The People's Law; or, Popular Participation in Law-Making.* New York: Macmillan Co., 1909.

Lockard, Duane. *The Politics of State and Local Governments.* 2d ed. Toronto: Collin-MacMillan Canada, 1969.

Lowell, Abbott Lawrence. "Referendum in Switzerland and America." *Atlantic Monthly* 73 (April 1894): 517–26.

_____. "Referendum in the United States." In *The Initiative, Referendum and Recall,* edited by William Bennett Munro, 126–38. New York: D. Appleton and Co., 1912.

Lutrin, Carl E. "The Public and Ecology: The Role of Initiatives in California's Environmental Politics." *Western Political Quarterly* 28 (June 1975): 352–72.

Lyndenberg, Steven D. *Bankrolling Ballots.* New York: Council on Economic Priorities, 1979.

Macaluso, Theodore F. "Parameters of 'Rational' Voting: Vote Switching in the 1968 Election." *Journal of Politics* 37 (February 1975): 202–35.

McClosky, Herbert. "Consensus and Ideology in American Politics." *American Political Science Review* 58 (June 1964): 365.

_____. "Political Participation." In *International Encyclopedia of the Social Sciences,* edited by David L. Sills, 252–65. New York: Macmillan Co., 1978.

McClosky, Herbert, and Dahlgren, Harold E. "Primary Group Influence on Party Loyalty." *American Political Science Review* 63 (September 1959): 757–76.

McClosky, Herbert; Hoffman, Paul J.; and O'Hara, Rosemary. "Issue Conflict and Consensus among Party Leaders and Followers." *American Political Science Review* 54 (June 1960): 406–27.

McCombs, Maxwell E., and Shaw, Donald L. "The Agenda-Setting Function of Mass Media." *Public Opinion Quarterly* 36 (Summer 1972): 176–87.

McDill, Edward L., and Ridley, Jeanne Clare. "Status, Anomia, Political Alienation, and Political Participation." *American Journal of Sociology* 68 (1962): 205–13.

McGrory, Mary. "California's Social Experiment." *Chicago Tribune,* 12 June 1978, sec. 4, 3.

McHenry, Dean E. "The Pattern of California Politics." *Western Political Quarterly* 1 (March 1948): 44–53.

Mann, Thomas E., and Wolfinger, Raymond E. "Candidates and Parties in Congressional Elections." *American Political Science Review* 74 (September 1980): 617–32.

Mansfield, Harvey C., Jr. "Hobbes and the Science of Indirect Government." *American Political Science Review* 65 (March 1971): 97–110.

Marando, Vincent L. "Voting in City-County Consolidation Referenda." *Western Political Quarterly* 26 (March 1973): 90–97.

Margolis, Michael. "From Confusion to Confusion: Issues and the American Voter (1956–1972)." *American Political Science Review* 71 (March 1977): 31–44.

Martin, Philip L. "The Supreme Court's Quest for Voter Equality in Bond Referenda." *Baylor Law Review* 28 (1976): 25–37.

Matthews, Jay. "Initiative Process Gains Popularity: 50 Ballot Measures Seen in 1982." *Washington Post,* 29 May 1982, A-11.

Mayhew, David. "A Note on Electoral Reform." *Policy Studies Journal,* Summer 1974, 299–302.

Meehl, Paul E. "The Selfish Voter Paradox and the Thrown-Away Vote Argument." *American Political Science Review* 71 (March 1977): 11–31.

Metz, A. Stafford. "An Analysis of Some Determinants of Attitude toward Fluoridation." *Social Forces* 44 (June 1966): 477–84.

Mikesell, John L., and Blair, John. "An Economic Theory of Referendum Voting: School Construction and Stock Adjustment." *Public Finance Quarterly* 2 (October 1974): 395–410.

Milbrath, Lester W., and Goel, M. L. *Political Participation.* 2d ed. Chicago: Rand McNally College Publishing Co., 1977.

Miller, Arthur H. "Political Issues and Trust in Government: 1964–1970." *American Political Science Review* 68 (September 1974): 951–73.

———. "Rejoinder: Political Issues and Trust in Government." *American Political Science Review* 68 (September 1974): 989–1002.

Miller, Arthur H.; Miller, Warren E.; Rainey, Alden S.; and Brown, Thad A. "A Majority Party in Disarray: Policy Polarization in the 1972 Election." *American Political Science Review* 70 (September 1976): 753–78.

Miller, Warren E., and Levitin, Teresa E. *Leadership and Change: The New Politics and the American Electorate.* Cambridge, Mass.: Winthrop Publishers, 1976.

Morgan, David; Kirkpatrick, Samuel; Fitzgerald, Michael; and Lyons, Williams. "Direct Democracy and Political Development: Longitudinal Referenda Voting Patterns in an American State." In *Impact of the Electoral Process,* edited by Louis Maisel and Joseph Cooper, 235–64. Beverly Hills: Sage Publications, 1977.

Mowlam, Marjorie. "Popular Access to the Decision-making Process in Switzerland: The Role of Direct Democracy." *Government and Opposition* 14 (Spring 1979): 180–97.

Mowry, George E. "The California Progressive and His Rationale: A Study in Middle Class Politics." *Mississippi Valley Historical Review* 36 (September 1949): 239–50.

———. *The California Progressives.* New York: New York Times Book Co., 1951.

———. *The Progressive Era, 1900–1920. The Reform Persuasion.* American Historical Association pamphlet 212. Washington, D.C.: 1958.

Mueller, John E. "Choosing among 133 Candidates." *Public Opinion Quarterly* 34 (Fall 1970): 395–402.

———. "The Politics of Fluoridation in Seven California Cities." *Western Political Quarterly* 19 (March 1966): 54–68.

———. "Reason and Caprice: Ballot Patterns in California." Ph.D. diss., University of California, Los Angeles, 1965.

———. "Voting on the Propositions: Ballot Patterns and Historical Trends in California." *American Political Science Review* 63 (December 1969): 1197–1213.

Munro, William B., ed. *The Initiative, Referendum and Recall.* New York: D. Appleton and Co., 1912.

Murasky, Donna. "*James* v. *Valtierra*: Housing Discrimination by Referendum?" *University of Chicago Law Review* 39 (1971): 115–42.

Natchez, Peter B., and Bupp, Irvin C. "Candidates, Issues, and Voters." In *Political*

Opinion and Behavior, edited by Edward C. Dreyer and Walter A. Rosenbaum, 427–50. 2d ed. Belmont: Wadsworth Publishing Co., 1970.

National Economic League. *The Initiative and Referendum.* Boston, 1912.

Nelson, Michael. "Power to the People—The Crusade for Direct Democracy." *Saturday Review,* 24 November 1979, 12–17.

Nettler, Gwynn. "A Measure of Alienation." *American Sociological Review* 22 (December 1957): 670–77.

New York Senate Research Service. *The Popular Interest versus the Public Interest . . . A Report on the Popular Initiative.* Albany, 1979.

Nicholson, Marlene Arnold. "Campaign Financing and Equal Protection." *Stanford Law Review* 26 (April 1974): 815–54.

Nie, Norman H.; Verba, Sidney; and Petrocik, John. *The Changing American Voter.* Cambridge: Harvard University Press, 1976.

Nimmo, Dan. *Political Communication and Public Opinion in America.* Santa Monica, Calif.: Goodyear Publishing Co., 1978.

_____. *The Political Persuaders: The Techniques of Modern Election Campaigns.* Englewood Cliffs: Prentice-Hall, 1970.

Noble, David W. "The Paradox of Progressive Thought." *American Quarterly* 5 (Fall 1953): 201–12.

Norton, James A. "Referenda Voting in a Metropolitan Area." *Western Political Quarterly* 16 (March 1963): 195–213.

Nuechterlein, Donald E. "The Demise of Canada's Confederation." *Political Science Quarterly* 96 (Summer 1981): 225–40.

Oberholtzer, Ellis Paxson. *The Referendum in America.* Philadelphia: University of Pennsylvania, 1893.

_____. *The Referendum, Initiative and Recall in America.* New York: Charles Scribner's Sons, 1911.

Orbell, John M. "An Information-Flow Theory of Community Influence." *Journal of Politics* 32 (1970): 322–38.

Oren, Craig N. "The Initiative and Referendum's Use in Zoning." *California Law Review* 64 (1976): 74–107.

Ostlund, Lyman E. "Interpersonal Communication Following McGovern's Eagleton Decision." *Public Opinion Quarterly* 37 (Winter 1973/74): 601–10.

Owens, John R., and Olson, Edward C. "Campaign Spending and the Electoral Process in California, 1966–1974." *Western Political Quarterly* 30 (December 1977): 493–513.

Page, Benjamin I., and Brody, Richard A. "Policy Voting and the Electoral Process: The Vietnam War Issue." *American Political Science Review* 66 (September 1972): 979–95.

Paris, Johnathan S. "The Proper Use of Referenda in Rezoning." *Stanford Law Review* 29 (April 1977): 819–51.

Pateman, Carole. *Participation and Democratic Theory.* Cambridge: Cambridge University Press, 1970.

Patterson, Samuel C.; Hedlund, Ronald D.; and Boynton, G. Robert. *Representatives and Represented: Bases of Public Support for the American Legislatures.* New York: John Wiley and Sons, 1975.

Patterson, Thomas E. *The Mass Media Election.* New York: Praeger Publishers, 1980.

Patterson, Thomas E., and McClure, Robert D. *Political Advertising: Voter Reaction to Televised Political Commercials.* Princeton: Citizens' Research Foundation, 1973.

————. "Television and the Less-Interested Voter: The Costs of an Informed Electorate." *Annals of the American Academy of Political and Social Science* 425 (May 1976): 88–97.

Penniman, Howard R., and Scammon, Richard M. "As the World Turns . . . Right?" *Public Opinion* 2 (June/July 1979): 41–44.

People's Lobby. *National Initiative and Vote of Confidence (Recall) — Tools for Self-Government.* Los Angeles: People's Lobby Press, 1974.

Phelps, Edith M., ed. *Selected Articles on the Initiative and Referendum.* Debaters Handbook Series. Minneapolis: H. W. Wilson Co., 1909.

Pillsbury, A. J. "The Initiative, Its Achievements and Abuses." *Commonwealth — Part II,* no. 25 (11 November 1931): 426–33.

————. "Prophecies of Good and Evil in Relation to Direct Legislation." *Commonwealth — Part II,* no. 25 (11 November 1931): 416–25.

Pitchell, Robert J. "The Electoral System and Voting Behavior: The Case of California's Cross-Filing." *Western Political Quarterly* 12 (June 1959): 459–85.

————. "The Influence of Professional Campaign Management Firms in Partisan Elections in California." *Western Political Quarterly* 11 (June 1958): 278–300.

Pitkin, Hanna F. *The Concept of Representation.* Berkeley and Los Angeles: University of California Press, 1972.

————. *Representation.* New York: Atherton Press, 1969.

Pitt, Leonard. *California Controversies.* Glenview, Ill.: Scott, Foresman and Co., 1968.

Plaut, Thomas F. A. "Analysis of Voting Behavior on a Fluoridation Referendum." *Public Opinion Quarterly* 23 (Summer 1959): 212–22.

Pollock, James K. *The Initiative and Referendum in Michigan.* Ann Arbor: University of Michigan Press, 1940.

Pomper, Gerald M. "Ethnic and Group Voting in Nonpartisan Municipal Elections." *Public Opinion Quarterly* 30 (Spring 1966): 79–97.

————. "From Confusion to Clarity: Issues and American Voters, 1956–1968." *American Political Science Review* 66 (June 1972): 415–29.

————. *Voters' Choice: Varieties of American Electoral Behavior.* New York: Dodd, Mead and Company, 1975.

Popkin, Samuel; Gorman, John W.; Phillips, Charles; and Smith, Jeffrey A. "Comment: What Have You Done for Me Lately? Toward an Investment Theory of Voting." *American Political Science Review* 70 (September 1970): 779–805.

Prewitt, Kenneth, and Nie, Norman. "Review Article: Election Studies of the Survey Research Center." *British Journal of Political Science* 1 (1971): 479–502.

Price, Charles M. "The Initiative: A Comparative State Analysis and Reassessment of a Western Phenomenon." *Western Political Quarterly* 28 (June 1975): 243–62.

————. "Seizing the Initiative: California's New Politics." *Citizen Participation* 3 (September/October 1981): 5, 19–20.

Prothro, James W., and Grigg, Charles M. "Fundamental Principles of Democracy: Bases of Agreement and Disagreement." *Journal of Politics* 22 (May 1960): 276–94.

Radabaugh, John Sheldon. "Tendencies of California Direct Legislation." *Southwestern Social Science Quarterly* 42 (June 1961): 66–78.

Radosevich, Ted C. "Electoral Analysis of the Clean Water Bond Law of 1974: Patterns of Support in a Continuing Environmental Issue." Institute of Governmental Studies, Working Paper no. 15. University of California, Berkeley, August 1975.

Rae, Douglas W. "Decision-Rules and Individual Values in Constitutional Choice." *American Political Science Review* 63 (March 1969): 40–56.

———. *The Political Consequences of Electoral Laws*. New Haven: Yale University Press, 1967.

———. "Political Democracy as a Property of Political Institutions." *American Political Science Review* 65 (March 1971): 111–20.

Ranney, Austin. *Curing the Mischiefs of Faction*. Berkeley and Los Angeles: University of California Press, 1975.

———. "The Representativeness of Primary Electorates." *Midwest Journal of Political Science* 12 (1968): 224–38.

———. "Turnout and Representation in Presidential Primary Elections." *American Political Science Review* 66 (March 1972): 21–38.

Ranney, Austin, and Epstein, Leon D. "The Two Electorates: Voters and Non-Voters in a Wisconsin Primary." *Journal of Politics* 28 (1966): 598–616.

Ranney, Austin, and Kendall, Willmoore. *Democracy and the American Party System*. New York: Harcourt Brace Jovanovich, 1956.

Rappard, William E. "The Initiative, Referendum and Recall in Switzerland." *Annals of the American Academy of Political and Social Science* 43 (September 1912): 110–45.

Ray, Michael L. "Marketing Communication and the Hierarchy of Effects." In *New Models for Mass Communication Research,* edited by Peter Clarke, 147–76. Beverly Hills: Sage Publications, 1978.

Redburn, Steve; Buss, Terry F.; Foster, Steven K.; and Binning, William C. "How Representative Are Mandated Citizen Participation Processes?" *Urban Affairs Quarterly* 15 (March 1980): 345–51.

Resch, Tracy. "The Application of the Equal Protection Clause to Referendum-Made-Law: *James* v. *Valtierra*." *University of Illinois Law Forum,* 1972, 408–28.

Reston, James. "Proposition 13, a Silly Answer to a Silly Question." *Salt Lake Tribune,* 11 June 1978, 16.

Ricci, David M. "Democracy Attenuated: Schumpeter, the Process, Theory, and American Democratic Thought." *Journal of Politics* 32 (May 1970): 239–67.

Riker, William H., and Ordeshook, Peter C. "A Theory of the Calculus of Voting." *American Political Science Review* 62 (March 1968): 25–42.

Robinson, John P. "Interpersonal Influence in Election Campaigns: Two Step-flow Hypotheses." *Public Opinion Quarterly* 40 (Fall 1976): 304–19.

Robinson, W. S. "Ecological Correlations and the Behavior of Individuals." *American Sociological Review* 15 (June 1960): 351–56.

Rogers, Chester B., and Arman, Harold D. "Nonpartisanship and Election to City Office." *Social Science Quarterly* 51 (March 1971): 941–45.

Rogin, Michael P., and Shover, John L. *Political Change in California: Critical Elections and Social Movements, 1890–1966*. Westport, Conn.: Greenwood Publishing Co., 1969.

Rose, Douglas D. "Comment: The American States' Impact on Voter Turnout." *American Political Science Review* 69 (March 1975): 124–37.

Rothschild, Michael L. "The Effects of Political Advertising on the Voting Behavior of a Low Involvement Electorate." Ph.D. diss., Stanford University, 1974.

Rothschild, Michael L., and Ray, Michael L. "Involvement and Political Advertising Effect: An Exploratory Experiment." *Communications Research* 1 (July 1974): 264–85.

Rusk, Jerald G. "The Effect of the Australian Ballot Reform on Split Ticket Voting: 1876–1908." *American Political Science Review* 64 (December 1970): 1220–38.

Sabato, Larry J. *The Rise of Political Consultants: New Ways of Winning Elections.* New York: Basic Books, 1981.

Salisbury, Robert H., and Black, Gordon. "Class and Party in Partisan and Non-Partisan Elections: The Case of Des Moines." *American Political Science Review* 57 (September 1963): 584–92.

Sapolsky, Harvey M. "The Fluoridation Controversy: An Alternative Explanation." *Public Opinion Quarterly* 33 (Summer 1969): 240–48.

Schattschneider, E. E. *Party Government.* New York: Holt, Rinehart and Winston, 1942.

_____. *The Semisovereign People.* Hinsdale, Ill.: Dryden Press, 1975.

Schorr, Daniel. "Proposition 13 in High Places." *San Francisco Examiner,* 28 June 1978, 37.

Schumpeter, Joseph A. *Capitalism, Socialism, and Democracy.* New York: Harper and Row, 1942.

Scott, Stanley. *Governing California's Coast.* Berkeley: Institute of Governmental Studies, 1975.

Seeley, James J. "The Public Referendum and Minority Group Legislation: Postscript to *Reitman* v. *Mulkey.*" *Cornell Law Review* 55 (July 1970): 881–910.

Seeman, Melvin. "On the Meaning of Alienation." *American Sociological Review* 24 (December 1959): 783–91.

Sethi, S. Prakish. *Advocacy Advertising and Large Corporations.* Lexington, Mass.: D. C. Heath and Co., 1977.

Shaffer, William R. "Partisan Loyalty and the Perceptions of Party, Candidates and Issues." *Western Political Quarterly* 25 (September 1972): 424–34.

Shapiro, Michael J. "Rational Political Man: A Synthesis of Economic and Social-Psychological Perspectives." *American Political Science Review* 63 (December 1969): 1106–19.

Sheleff, Leon Shasklosky, and Susser, Bernard. "The Referendum-Election: One Person, Several Votes." *Parliamentary Affairs* 28 (Summer 1975): 299–311.

Shepard, W. Bruce. "Participation in Local Policy Making: The Case of Referenda." *Social Science Quarterly* 56 (June 1975): 55–70.

_____. "Political Preferences, Participation, and Local Policy-Making: A Study of Referendum Voting Behavior in American Cities." Ph.D. diss., University of California, Riverside, 1972.

Sherrod, Drury R. "Selective Perception of Political Candidates." *Public Opinion Quarterly* 35 (Winter 1972): 554–62.

Shirley, Don. "Criticism for the Columbus Poll." *Washington Post,* 17 July 1979, B2.

Shively, W. Phillips. "'Ecological' Inference: The Use of Aggregate Data of Study Individuals." *American Political Science Review* 63 (December 1969): 1183–96.

Shockley, John S. "The Initiative Process As Issue Voting: An Exploratory Study

Based upon Money in the Nuclear Energy and Mandatory Deposit Campaigns in the 1976 Elections." Southern Illinois University. Mimeo.

Showell, Morris. "Political Independence in Washington State." *Public Opinion Quarterly* 16 (Fall 1952): 399–409.

Simon, Herbert. *Administrative Behavior.* 3d ed. New York: Free Press, 1976.

Slonim, Marc, and Lowe, James H. "Judicial Review of Laws Enacted by Popular Vote." *Washington Law Review* 55 (1979): 175–209.

Smith, J. Allan. *The Spirit of American Government.* New York: Macmillan Co., 1967.

Smith, Kenneth L. "Beating the Big Boys: Common Cause and the California Campaign for Political Reform." D.P.A. diss., University of Southern California, 1978.

Smith, Michael P., and Rose, Douglas. "Citizen Participation and Urban Water Uses." In *Delivery of Urban Services,* edited by Elinor Ostrom, 127–70. Urban Affairs Annual Reviews. Beverly Hills: Sage Publications, 1976.

Smith, Roger, and Townsend, Dorothy. "Prop. 10: Its Defeat Hailed and Lamented." *Los Angeles Times,* 5 June 1980.

Soule, John W., and Strand, Paul J. "Public Attitudes toward Homosexuality: The Proposition 6 Case in California." Paper presented at the Western Political Science Association meetings, Portland, Oregon, 22–24 March 1979.

Statler, Stuart M. "Let the Sunshine In?" *American Bar Association Journal* 67 (May 1981): 573–75.

Stewart, Robert G. "The Law of Initiative Referendum in Massachusetts." *New England Law Review* 12 (1977): 455–524.

Stone, Clarence N. "Local Referendums: An Alternative to the Alienated-Voter Model." *Public Opinion Quarterly* 29 (Summer 1965): 213–22.

Sturm, Albert L. "The Procedure of State Constitutional Change — With Special Emphasis on the South and Florida." *Florida State University Law Review* 5 (1977): 569–602.

Taebel, Delbert A. "The Effect of Ballot Position on Electoral Success." *American Journal of Political Science* 19 (August 1975): 519–26.

Tallian, Laura. *Direct Democracy: An Historical Analysis of the Initiative, Referendum, and Recall Process.* Los Angeles: People's Lobby Press, 1977.

Templeton, Fredric. "Alienation and Political Participation: Some Research Findings." *Public Opinion Quarterly* 30 (Summer 1966): 249–61.

Thelen, David P. "Social Tensions and the Origins of Progressivism." *Journal of American History* 56 (September 1969): 323–41.

Thomas, David Y. "The Initiative and Referendum in Arkansas Come of Age." *American Political Science Review* 27 (February 1933): 66–75.

Thomas, Norman C. "The Electorate and State Constitutional Revision: An Analysis of Four Michigan Referenda." *Midwest Journal of Political Science* 12 (February 1968): 115–29.

_____. "Voting Machines and Voter Participation in Four Michigan Constitutional Revision Referenda." *Western Political Quarterly* 21 (September 1968): 409–20.

Thompson, Wayne, and Horton, John E. "Political Alienation as a Force in Political Action." *Social Forces* 38 (March 1960): 190–95.

Traugott, Michael W., and Clubb, Jerome M. "'Surge and Decline' and the Referendum Electorate." Paper presented at the Conference on Voter Turnout, San Diego, California, 16–19 May 1979.

Traugott, Michael, and Katosh, Jack. "Response Validity in Surveys of Voting Behavior." *Public Opinion Quarterly* 43 (Fall 1979): 359–77.

Trautman, Philip A. "Initiative and Referendum in Washington: A Survey." *Washington Law Review* 49 (1973): 55–87.

Troldahl, Verling C., and Van Dam, Robert. "Face-to-Face Communication about Major Topics in the News." *Public Opinion Quarterly* 29 (Winter 1965–66): 626–34.

Tufte, Edward R. *Data Analysis for Politics and Policy*. Englewood Cliffs: Prentice-Hall, 1974.

———. "Electoral Reform: An Introduction." *Policy Studies Journal,* Summer 1974, 240–42.

Turner, Julius. "Primary Elections as the Safe Alternative to Party Competition in 'Safe' Districts." *Journal of Politics* 15 (May 1953): 197–210.

U.S. Congress, Senate, Committee on the Judiciary, Subcommittee on the Constitution. *Voter Initiative Constitutional Amendment: Hearings on Senate Resolution 67*. 95th Cong., 1st sess., December 1977.

Vander Zanden, James W. "Voting on Segregationist Referenda." *Public Opinion Quarterly* 25 (Spring 1961): 92–105.

Verba, Sidney, and Nie, Norman. *Participation in America*. New York: Harper and Row, 1972.

Waldron, Ellis, and Wilson, Paul B. "Mapping Montana Elections." *Montana Public Affairs Report* 28 (September 1979).

Walker, Jack L. "Ballot Forms and Voter Fatigue: An Analysis of the Office Block and Party Column Ballots." *Midwest Journal of Political Science* 10 (1966):448–63.

———. "A Critique of the Elitist Theory of Democracy." *American Political Science Review* 60 (June 1966): 285–95.

———. "The Diffusion of Innovations among the American States." *American Political Science Review* 63 (September 1969): 880–99.

Waltz, Jon. "Some Firsthand Observations on the Election of Judges." *Judicature* 64 (October 1979): 185–88.

Watson, Richard A., and Romani, John H. "Metropolitan Government for Metropolitan Cleveland: An Analysis of the Voting Record." *Midwest Journal of Political Science* 5 (1961): 265–390.

Weinstein, Michael A. "A Critique of Contemporary Democratic Theories." *Western Political Quarterly* 24 (March 1971): 41–45.

Weisberg, Herbert F., and Rusk, Jerrold G. "Dimensions of Candidate Evaluation." *American Political Science Review* 64 (December 1970): 1167–86.

Weisbord, Marvin R. *Campaigning for President*. New York: Washington Square Press, 1966.

Welch, W. P. "The Effectiveness of Expenditures in State Legislative Races." *American Politics Quarterly* 4 (July 1976): 333–66.

"Why the Shift to Conservatism?" *U.S. News & World Report,* 23 January 1978, 24–25.

Wicker, Tom. "A New Revolution." *New York Times,* 9 June 1978, A27.

Wiebe, Robert H. "Business Disunity and the Progressive Movement, 1901–1914." *Mississippi Valley Historical Review* 44 (March 1958): 664–85.

Wilcox, Allen R., and Weinberg, Leonard B. "Petition-Signing in the 1968 Election." *Western Political Quarterly* 24 (December 1971): 731–40.

Wilcox, Delos F. *Government by All the People; or, the Initiative, the Referendum and the Recall as Instruments of Democracy.* New York: Macmillan Co., 1912.

Will, George. "Californians Vote to Undo What Has Been Done." *Los Angeles Times,* 8 June 1978, B7.

Williams, Daniel C.; Weber, Stephen J.; Haaland, Gordon A.; Mueller, Ronald; and Craig, Robert. "Voter Decisionmaking in a Primary Election: An Evaluation of Three Models of Choice." *American Journal of Political Science* 20 (February 1976): 37–49.

Williams, Oliver P., and Adrian, Charles R. "The Insulation of Local Politics under the Nonpartisan Ballot." *American Political Science Review* 53 (1959): 1052–63.

Williams, R. J., and Greenaway, J. R. "The Referendum in British Politics: A Dissenting View." *Parliamentary Affairs* 28 (Summer 1975): 250–60.

Willis, Charles L. "Analysis of Voter Response to School Financial Proposals." *Public Opinion Quarterly* 31 (Winter 1967/68): 648–51.

Wilmar, Michael B. P. "Judicial Limitations on the Initiative and Referendum in California Municipalities." *Hastings Law Journal* 17 (May 1968): 805–15.

Wilson, James Q., and Banfield, Edward C. *City Politics.* Cambridge: Harvard University Press and MIT Press, 1963.

————. "Political Ethos Revisited." *American Political Science Review* 65 (December 1971): 1048–63.

————. "Public-Regardingness as a Value Premise in Voting Behavior." *American Political Science Review* 58 (December 1964): 876–88.

Wilson, Woodrow. "The Issues of Reform." In *The Initiative, Referendum and Recall,* edited by William Bennett Munro, 69–91. New York: D. Appleton and Co., 1912.

————. *The State: Elements of Historical and Practical Politics.* Boston: D. C. Heath and Co., 1897.

Winslow, C. I. "The Referendum in Maryland." *American Political Science Review* 27 (February 1933): 75–79.

Wolfinger, Raymond E. "The Influence of Precinct Work on Voting Behavior." *Public Opinion Quarterly* 22 (Fall 1963): 387–98.

Wolfinger, Raymond E., and Field, John Osgood. "Political Ethos and the Structure of City Government." *American Political Science Review* 60 (June 1966): 306–26.

Wolfinger, Raymond E., and Greenstein, Fred I. "Comparing Political Regions: The Case of California." *American Political Science Review* 63 (March 1969): 74–85.

————. "The Repeal of Fair Housing in California: An Analysis of Referendum Voting." *American Political Science Review* 62 (September 1968): 753–70.

Wolfinger, Raymond E., and Heifitz, Joan. "Safe Seats, Seniority, and Power in Congress." *American Political Science Review* 59 (June 1965): 337–49.

Wolfinger, Raymond E., and Rosenstone, Steven J. "The Effect of Registration Laws on Voter Turnout." *American Political Science Review* 72 (March 1978): 22–45.

————. *Who Votes?* New Haven: Yale University Press, 1980.

Wolfinger, Raymond E.; Rosenstone, Steven J.; and McIntosh, Richard A. "Presidential and Congressional Voters Compared." *American Politics Quarterly* 9 (April 1981): 245–56.

Wood, Tracy, and Hicks, Jerry. "Rent Initiative — What's in a Name?" *Los Angeles Times,* 26 December 1979, 1, 4, 5.

Wright, James D. "Alienation and Political Negativism: New Evidence from National Surveys." *Sociology and Social Research* 60 (January 1976): 111–34.

LEGAL CASES

Amador Valley Joint Union High School District v. *State Board of Equalization*, 583 P.2d 1281, 149 Cal. Rptr. 239 (1978).

Baker v. *Carr*, 369 U.S. 186 (1962).

Baker v. *Regional High School Dist. No. 5*, 476 Fed. Supp. 319 (1979).

Buckley v. *Valeo*, 424 U.S. 1 (1976).

Carmen v. *Alvord* 644 P.2d 192, 182 Cal. Rptr. 506 (1982).

Cipriano v. *City of Houma*, 395 U.S. 701 (1969).

Citizens Against Rent Control v. *City of Berkeley*, 454 U.S. 290 (1981).

Citizens for Community Action at the Local Level v. *Ghezzi*, 386 Fed. Supp. 1 (1974).

Citizens for Jobs and Energy v. *Fair Political Practices Commission*, 547 P.2d 1386, 129 Cal. Rptr. 106 (1976).

City of Eastlake v. *Forest City Enterprises, Inc.*, 426 U.S. 668 (1976).

City of Phoenix v. *Kolodziejski*, 399 U.S. 204 (1970).

Diamond v. *Bland*, 447 P.2d 733, 91 Cal. Rptr. 501 (1970).

Fair Political Practices Commission v. *Superior Court*, 599 P.2d 46, 157 Cal. Rptr. 855 (1979).

First National Bank of Boston v. *Bellotti*, 435 U.S. 765 (1978).

Gage v. *Jordan*, 23 Cal.2d 794, 147 P.2d 387 (1944).

Gordon v. *Lance*, 403 U.S. 1 (1971).

Hardie v. *Eu*, 556 P.2d, 301, 134 Cal. Rptr. 201 (1976).

Hunter v. *Erickson*, 393 U.S. 385 (1969).

James v. *Valtierra*, 402 U.S. 137 (1971).

Kramer v. *Union School District*, 395 U.S. 621 (1969).

Lance v. *Board of Education*, 153 W.Va. 559, 170 S.E.2d 783 (1969).

Lefkovits v. *State Board of Elections*, 400 Fed. Supp. 1005 (1975).

LoRisco v. *Schaffer*, 341 Fed. Supp. 743 (1972).

Los Angeles County Transportation Commission v. *Richmond*, 643 P.2d 941, 182 Cal. Rptr. 324 (1982).

Luther v. *Burden*, 42 U.S. 1 (1849).

McFadden v. *Jordan*, 32 Cal.2d 330 (1948).

Mihaly v. *Westbrook*, 403 U.S. 915 (1971).

Pacific States Telephone and Telegraph Company v. *Oregon*, 223 U.S. 118 (1912).

People v. *Ramos*, 30 Cal.3d. 553 (1980).

Perry v. *Jordan*, 34 Cal.2d 87, 207 P.2d 47 (1949).

Reitman v. *Mulkey*, 387 U.S. 369 (1967).

Reynolds v. *Sims*, 337 U.S. 533 (1964).

Rockwell v. *Superior Court of Ventura County*, 556 P.2d 1101, Sup. 134 Cal. Rptr. 650 (1976).

Rosebud Sioux Tribe v. *Kneip*, 430 U.S. 584 (1977).

Santa Barbara School District v. *Superior Court of Santa Barbara County*, 530 P.2d 605, 118 Sup. Cal. Rptr. 637 (1975).

Salyer Land Co. v. *Tulare Water District*, 410 U.S. 719 (1973).

Torres v. *Puerto Rico*, 442 U.S. 465 (1979).

Town of Lockport, New York v. *Citizens for Community Action at the Local Level*, 430 U.S. 266 (1976).

Weaver v. *Jordan*, 411 P.2d 289, 49 Cal. Rptr. 557 (1967).

Wesberry v. *Sanders*, 376 U.S. 1 (1964).

Index

263